Philip A. Kuhn

Rebellion and Its Enemies
in Late Imperial China

Militarization and Social Structure, 1796–1864

Harvard University Press
Cambridge, Massachusetts
London, England

TO DELIA AND FERDINAND KUHN

Harvard East Asian Series 49

The Council on East Asian Studies at Harvard University,
through the Fairbank Center for East Asian Research,
administers research projects designed to further scholarly understanding
of China, Japan, Korea, Vietnam, Inner Asia, and adjacent areas.

Preparation of this volume has been aided by a grant
from the Ford Foundation.

Library of Congress Catalog Card Number 80-80470

ISBN 0–674–74951–0 (cloth)
ISBN 0–674–74954–5 (paper)

PREFACE TO THE PAPERBACK EDITION

Since this book was written, so much work has been done on Chinese local politics that it is probably a mistake to reprint it without extensive revisions. Short of going through that, however, I can at least share with the reader some thoughts on how the book *might* have been revised, had I undertaken to do it. The two main points I have in mind are (1) the relationship of the militarization of the 1850's to social tensions of the 1820's and 1830's, and (2) the adequacy of my general analytic scheme in light of new knowledge about the northern sectarian tradition.

(1) *Dating the decline of Ch'ing local control.* This book makes the general assertion that, although the Ch'ing response to the White Lotus Rebellion of 1796–1804 revealed the weakness of its regular armies and precipitated local elite activism in militia defense, yet it was primarily the local militarization of the 1840's and 1850's that tipped the balance of power away from bureaucratically organized, centrally controlled imperial forces and toward personalistic, locally recruited irregular forces. From this realignment of military power I developed a picture of power-devolution in other spheres of administration, a devolution that influenced the pattern of local government into the twentieth century.[1]

The question of when that devolution began, and the relative importance of militarization in the process, is now complicated by James Polachek's important study of local elite activism during the 1820's.[2] What apparently happened was that the escalating rate of surtaxes in the grain tribute system generated resistance among groups of lower degree holders (*sheng-yuan/chien-sheng*) in certain areas of the lower Yangtze. By the late 1820's, these people were organizing local networks of collaboration, not only to resist extortionate taxation by the classic method of engrossment, or proxy remittance (*pao-lan*), but also to bring suit against local authorities through the channel of "capital appeals" (*ching-k'ung*). Local networks of this sort became objects of official repression, and the movement never

---

1. Later I followed up some of my own suggestions in Chapter VI about the effects of this nineteenth-century elite activism upon twentieth-century local government. See my "Local Self-Government under the Republic: Problems of Control, Autonomy, and Mobilization" in Frederic Wakeman, Jr., and Carolyn Grant, eds., *Conflict and Control in Late Imperial China* (Berkeley and Los Angeles: University of California Press, 1975), 257–298.

2. James Polachek, "Literati Groups and Literati Politics in Early Nineteenth Century China," Ph.D. dissertation (University of California, Berkeley, 1974).

got far off the ground.[3] It struck me, as I read further in this kind of material, that what Polachek has opened up may be the early stages of a process of local elite incursion into the *formal* structure of local fiscal management, a process that was illegal in the context of the 1820's but became not only legitimate but even encouraged in the context of the 1850's. What the state had considered an intolerable presumption by the local elite became, in the context of rebel-suppression, a necessary assumption of local authority. Militarization, then, instead of being the occasion for elite mobilization, was rather the occasion for legitimizing certain kinds of activity already in the early stages of development. The principal objection here would be that Polachek's cases all concern Kiangnan, whereas the militarization I describe in Chapter IV began in quite a different regional context. Yet I would be inclined at least to see the local activism precipitated by the grain tribute as symptomatic of an inclination and a capacity for broader involvement in local management. Of such involvement the lower elite had long been capable. Their managerial capacities became legitimate in the process of the Kiangnan elite's resistance to the Taipings a generation later.

(2) *Principles of local organization reconsidered.* Most of the documentation for this study comes from South and Central China. Were I to revise in the light of recent research, I would have to deal much more systematically with correlations between the leadership, scale, and format of local military groups, and with the regional provenance of the data. G. William Skinner's work on regional trading systems and urban hierarchies has suggested the possibility of a taxonomy of local social forms that varies in relation to a zonal pattern of economic organization, leading out from core to periphery in each "physiographic macroregion."[4] Some reasonable propositions, based on Skinner's model, would have to be tested with militarization data before this book could be properly brought up to date. To begin with, it would be important to define more precisely the social and economic characteristics of the border areas where militarization developed earliest, and to define the systematic features of the spread of militarization from such border areas to the core districts of regions.

Another, perhaps more important, improvement of this study would be a more methodical treatment of differences between North and South

3. A summary treatment of one such case is in my "Local Taxation and Finance in Republican China," *Select Papers from the Center for Far Eastern Studies,* no. 3, (University of Chicago, 1979). See the case of Yü Hsien-keng, 114 ff.

4. See Skinner's argument in *The City in Late Imperial China* (Stanford University Press, 1977); and our discussion of how this argument has been extended to a "zonal" system of analysis in the "Introduction" to *Select Papers* (Chicago), vii–ix.

China. In particular, I would correct some facile generalizations about the isomorphism between what I termed "orthodox and heterodox" modes of organization in local society.

I would certainly begin by re-examining the superficial identification of South Chinese secret-society networks (Triads) as essentially heterodox. Myron Cohen pointed out to me (in personal conversation) that the right way to characterize the Triads was as "illegal, but orthodox." Not only their mimicry of orthodox kinship forms, but also their acceptance of conventional (albeit restorationist) views of monarchy as an institution, suggest the appropriateness of including them in the orthodox world. Since this Mafia-like group was indeed orthodox in its views of kinship, of hierarchy, of kingship, and of history (all, one must admit, basic desiderata for a world-view), it is not surprising to see their forms of militarization as in certain ways similar to those of the gentry-led establishment. In this respect, as in others, they contrast with the sectarian tradition of the north.

Susan Naquin, in her now classic study of the 1813 Eight Trigrams revolt[5] and in a subsequent study of the 1774 Wang Lun uprising,[6] provides us with a picture of alternative modes of organization that must lead us to a higher-level generalization about how local militarization was related to its social matrix. Naquin properly criticizes my hypothesis (p. 165) that the "same kinds of linkages and the same levels of organization" would be found crossing the orthodox and heterodox subcultures.[7]

The world Naquin recreates exhibits alternative forms of organization, apparently characteristic of the sectarian tradition. First, the White Lotus congregations were clearly incongruent with settlement patterns. On the village level, devotees typically included but a fraction of village inhabitants, and congregations typically overspread village boundaries. On higher levels, the sects were not centered on commercial towns, nor was there a hierarchy of connections that reflected the market hierarchy. Instead, sects were composed of small, discrete congregations whose members might be drawn from several nearby villages. Loose connections with other congregations might result from the seemingly random travels of sect leaders.[8] Commonly, leaders were travelers by trade: healers, teachers of martial arts (various forms of "boxing," fencing, etc.) and of yogic

5. *Millenarian Rebellion in China: The Eight Trigrams Uprising of 1813* (New Haven: Yale University Press), 1976.

6. "Shantung Rebellion: The Wang Lun Uprising of 1774" (forthcoming, quoted with permission of the author).

7. *Millenarian Rebellion,* 324.

8. For instance, Naquin, "Shantung Rebellion," 65.

meditation. Many of their disciples had similar callings: one group, Naquin tells us, included a "travelling actress, hired laborer, cart-pusher, [and] sellers of fish, dried beancurd, and horses."[9]

Occupations of these sectarians suggest a mode of spatial coordination within rural society that was, in effect, a complementary ecology existing alongside that of the administrative-commercial system of "nested hierarchies." In this mode, people moved laterally among villages more than they did along the marketing routes leading into higher-level settlements. If such an alternative ecology could be shown to have existed it would help us understand the special characteristics of the heterodox-sectarian subculture and its contrasts with the subculture of orthodoxy. Finally, it may be possible to offer some informed speculations about how these two subcultures interacted to produce various forms of local militarization. For convenience, I shall refer to the kind of spatial coordination associated with orthodoxy as the "nested-concentric" mode, and that associated with heterodoxy as the "tinker-peddler" mode.

First, in the nested-concentric mode, movements and interconnections of people followed the roads and rivers from the villages to the market center to which they were oriented, and then to higher-level centers. Those best adapted to the ecology of this mode interacted with enduring institutions of exchange, learning, worship, and social control: the entrepôts of a hierarchic market network; the official system of education, bureaucratic recruitment, and Confucian worship; the temples of the Buddhist and folk-syncretic religions; and the law court and revenue offices of the county yamen. This mode was, so to speak, institutionally "heavy": the scheduled, the permanently housed, the deeply stratified. The peasant household was linked into this mode at least by its tax-obligations, and to whatever extent it was growing or processing goods for market.

Second, in the tinker-peddler mode, movement and interconnections of people followed routes *not* associated with those of the commercial-administrative hierarchy. The paths of a "healer" or boxing-master probably, like those of tinkers and peddlers, were from village to village, laterally among settlements rather than vertically through a marketing system. This mode of spatial coordination was institutionally "light": the sporadic, the unhoused, the shallowly stratified (actually, we do not know whether boxing-masters and healers worked their routes according to schedules, as tinkers and peddlers must have). Instead of lasting, large-scale networks, this mode required only loose articulation among local units. In the case of sectarians, only when an unusually charismatic,

9. Ibid., 66.

aggressive leader forged a temporary alliance of adherents in many communities did large-scale networks appear.

It would be unreasonable to suppose that the two modes of coordination I have just outlined existed as discrete systems. Instead, we can assume that most rural folk participated in aspects of both. To what degree? Accepting these modes in an ideal-typical sense, one might postulate correlations with processes of historical change: social disorder and administrative weakness might attenuate the forces that bound people into the nested-concentric mode, a process of community closure that would make the tinker-peddler mode relatively more powerful a form of coordination in rural areas.[10]

The relevance of all this to the problem of local militarization lies in the capacity of these two modes to merge under certain conditions. First, note the differing characteristics of the two modes with respect to militarization. The nested-concentric mode emphasizes ascriptive forms of participation, since it is by definition founded on institutions linked to settlement patterns. Such ascriptive forms would, in some communities, also involve kinship organizations. The point is that militarization could draw upon a conscription pool composed of all adult male inhabitants of a settlement and would unite the militia of settlements that were commercially or administratively related. By contrast, the tinker-peddler mode involved human networks that were not ascriptive but voluntary. People affected by the doctrines and techniques of traveling adepts were not bound by communal institutions of enduring identity and economic strength. Nor could their spatial networks achieve either the defensibility or the mobilizational power of settlement-based groups. The strategic-hamlet strategy was a logical weapon against sectarian military bands during the Chia-ch'ing period; the military capacities of the nested-concentric mode were turned against such bands with considerable effect (see Chapter II.A). Because they were voluntary, sects as such had the impetus of faith. But for the same reason, they were incapable of long-term or large-scale coordination and defense.

But what happened if the process of militarization brought the two modes together? Such an event did actually happen in the cases of the Nien and the Red Spears (and probably the Boxers as well). Here was a powerful combination. Elizabeth Perry's exploration of Huai-pei militariza-

10. I allude here to G. W. Skinner's suggestive article, "Chinese Peasants and the Closed Community: an Open and Shut Case," *Comparative Studies in Society and History*, 13.3, 270–281 (1971).

tion reveals just such a pattern of interaction.[11] This first came about through what might be termed the domestication of Nien violence during the 1850's. From their original form as militarized bandits or smugglers (my level two, or *ku*-type), the Nien movement formed links to settlements that were in the process of setting up defensive walls and militia. Nien (essentially, bandit) chieftains would ally with militia captains in such settlements, who would then serve as either active or passive components of the Nien organization. These militia captains (who often led lineage-based settlements) turned (in Perry's terms) from "protective" to "predatory" activities, or mixed the two in a "predatory-protective synthesis."[12] The Red Spears movement, which began in the same area in the 1920's, emerged from a less complicated, level-one type of militia organization under local elite leadership. Here, however, was an interesting variation: itinerant teachers of martial arts and of meditation-magic techniques (for becoming invulnerable) were actually patronized by elite settlement leadership and were invited to train village men in peasant-style military skills. The effect of all this was to give heterodoxy a solid base in the nested-concentric social order and to imbue nested-concentric militarization with a certain heterodox flavor.

It remains to be seen to what extent this "domestication" of the heterodox tradition served to weaken its millenarian message (as in the Nien case) or to give heterodoxy a loyalist orientation (as, perhaps, in the Boxer case). It may be that "domestication" had an inherently orthodox bias in the ritual-cosmological realm: the heterodoxy of the sectarian way of life may have been a logical corollary of their denial of the ritual side of territoriality. By basing itself on modes of spatial coordination that denied the primacy of the commercial-administrative hierarchy of settlements, the sectarian way of life necessarily denied the cosmological significance of that hierarchy as well.[13]

The foregoing discussion casts some doubts on one of the central analytic points of this book: that "ladders of militarization" assume roughly the same shape whether they are orthodox or heterodox in politics and cosmology.

11. Elizabeth Jean Perry, "From Rebels to Revolutionaries: Peasant Violence in Huai-pei, 1845–1945," Ph.D. dissertation (University of Michigan, 1978). Also see my own analysis of the Nien in John K. Fairbank, ed., *Cambridge History of China: Late Ch'ing, 1800–1911,* Vol. 10 (Cambridge, England: Cambridge University Press, 1978), 307–316.

12. Perry, "From Rebels to Revolutionaries," 188.

13. See Arthur Wolf's article on isomorphism between societal and cosmological hierarchies: "Gods, Ghosts, and Ancestors," in Wolf, ed., *Religion and Ritual in Chinese Society* (Stanford University Press, 1974), 131–182. On this question, I am indebted again to Myron Cohen for his stimulating insights.

This point must be modified in the light of what has been learned about the northern sectarians. The idea remains useful if one is considering *only* those forms of militarization that originate *within* the nested-concentric mode of coordination. These may, of course, vary considerably in political coloration, though it is doubtful that they do in religious orientation. Conversely, it may be found that patterns of militarization within the tinker-peddler mode will also vary in political alignment (though again, one would predict that religious or cosmological traits would be similar in their basic symbolic structure). In sum, the point about isomorphism may yet be useful within the limited universe of evidence in which it was conceived. The book's more general finding seems still to have some value: that in shaping the characteristics of militarization and conflict in recent Chinese history, social forms have taken primacy over political orientation.

P A K

Cambridge, Massachusetts

ACKNOWLEDGMENTS

It is a privilege to join that large and still growing fraternity of Modern China scholars who begin their acknowledgments with the name of John King Fairbank. His intellectual guidance and personal inspiration have sustained me at all stages of research and writing. I am also indebted to a number of other historians who have been kind enough to read and criticize the manuscript: Professors Albert Craig, Ho Ping-ti, Benjamin Schwartz, Frederic Wakeman, Mary C. Wright, and Yang Lien-sheng. Their advice has saved me from many blunders, though many doubtless remain because of my own ignorance or stubbornness. To Professor David Hamilton, whose interests parallel my own, I am grateful for many long conversations that invariably sent me back to the library doubting my own assumptions.

Professors Saeki Tomi and Suzuki Chūsei and Miss Takashima Eiko made my Fulbright year in Japan both instructive and pleasant. I owe thanks also to the Ford Foundation, whose Foreign Area Training Program financed the initial stages of research; and to the University of Chicago's Social Sciences Divisional Research Committee for aid in the final preparation of the manuscript. Sally C. and Anthony F. Kuhn have rendered moral and editorial support far beyond the call of familial duty.

P A K

Chicago November 1969

CONTENTS

I *Local Militia and the Traditional State*

A   The Boundaries of Modern History   1
B   The Historical Importance of State Militia Institutions   10

II *The Development of Ch'ing Militia Policy, 1796–1850*

A   Local Control Problems During the White Lotus
     Rebellion   37

B   Ch'ing Militia Policy on the Eve of the Taiping
     Rebellion   50

III *The Structure of Local Militarization in South and
     Central China*

A   Scales of Local Organization   64

B   Principles of Local Organization   76

C   The Relation of the T'uan to Bureaucratic Divisions   93

IV *The Rise of Rebellion and the Militarization of the
     Orthodox Elite*

A   From Local to Imperial Defense: Chiang Chung-yuan   105

B   Hu Lin-i Builds a "Personal Army"   117

C   Tseng Kuo-fan and the Hunan Army   135

D   Liu Yü-hsun and the Defense of Nanchang   152

V *Parallel Hierarchies of Militarization*

A　　Orthodox and Heterodox Hierarchies　　　　　165

B　　Interaction and Integration　　　　　　　　175

VI *Militia, the State, and Revolution*

A　　Socio-strategic Problems of the Taiping Rebellion　189

B　　The Breakdown of the Traditional State　　　211

Bibliography　　　　　　　　　　　　　　227

Glossary　　　　　　　　　　　　　　　241

Index　　　　　　　　　　　　　　　　247

FIGURES

1	Map of South and Central China	xiv
2	Structure of the Sheng-p'ing association	70
3	Map of the Sheng-p'ing association	74
4	Multiplex organization based on lineage links	82
5	T'uan-lien configurations in Lin-hsiang, Hunan	84
6	Leadership of five t'uan-lien bureaus in Nanchang	88
7	Sources of funds for the defense of Hsiang-hsiang	92
8	Parallel military hierarchies in South and Central China	166
9	Pre-existing relations among commanders and staff officers of the Hunan Army	184
10	Hunan topography seen in terms of elite connections	187
11	Taiping local government organization	191
12	Resistance to the Taipings in Huang-kang	197
13	Officially recognized *t'uan*-heads in the Chang-tien confederation	199
14	Rewards of rank for the defenders of P'ing-chiang	205
15	Rewards for t'uan-lien and rank purchase contributions in Fen-i district	206

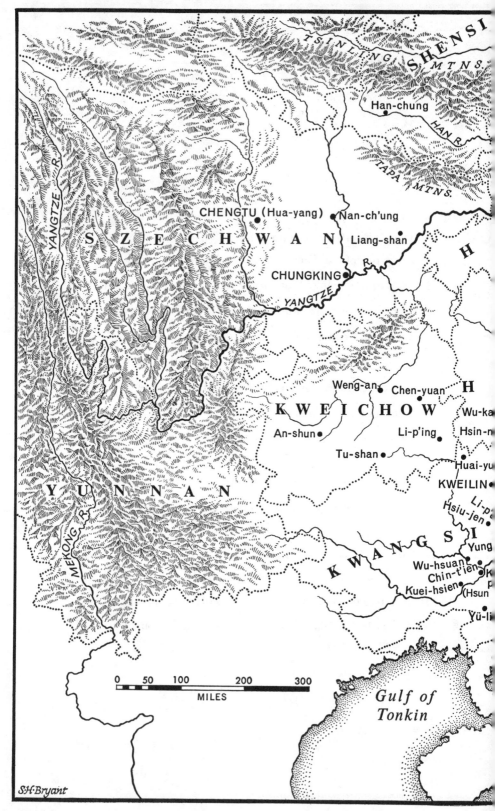

Figure 1.

SOUTH AND CENTRAL CHINA
about 1850

Showing places mentioned in the text

NOTE ON CONVENTIONS: Local gazetteers are referred to in the notes by place, date, and page references, for example, Nanchang 1870, 5:7–8. When an exact date within a Chinese lunar year is not ascertainable, both applicable Western years are cited, for example, Hsien-feng reign, fifth year, = 1855/1856. Transliterations of place-names follow the Wade-Giles system except for well-known "post office" spellings, for example, Nanking, Changsha.

I. LOCAL MILITIA AND
THE TRADITIONAL STATE

A. The Boundaries of Modern History

Perhaps the most vexing problem for the student of modern Chinese history is how to distinguish between the decline of the Ch'ing regime and the decline of traditional Chinese society as a whole. This problem cannot be dismissed as a mere juggling of abstractions, for it involves the most basic elements of our perception: our characterization of the period we are dealing with, and our identification of historical motive forces. Such an elementary question of definition has been forced upon us by the awkward confluence of events in the early nineteenth century, in which a dynasty already weak was confronted with a radically new challenge in the form of militant Western expansionism. Unless one supposes (and the case has yet to be made effectively) that quite independently of outside influences Chinese society was already on the brink of decisive changes by the late Ch'ing period, then one must assume it was the Western intrusion that transformed a dynastic decline of a largely traditional type into a social and intellectual revolution in which nearly the whole of the old culture was swept away.

At some point, then, the influence of outside factors—new techniques, new ideas, new patterns of social organization—must be assumed to have become a decisive force in the evolution in China's history; but at what point? More than one school of interpretation has been prepared to recognize the Opium War as the decisive moment and to treat the whole of the ensuing era as in one way or another the inevitable consequence of the opening of China by the West. Marx made the baldest statement of this case in 1853, when he predicted that, now that China was stripped of her protective isolation, "Dissolution must follow as surely as that of any mummy carefully preserved in a hermetically sealed coffin, whenever it is brought into contact with the open air."[1] In contrast to Marx himself, who had only a qualified sympathy for capitalism's Asian victims, Chinese Marxist historians have naturally seen things from the victims' point of view and have related the movement of modern history primarily to the struggle against imperialism. The beginning of this struggle, and hence the beginning of China's modern history, was the Opium War. But besides generating anti-imperialism, the Western intrusion also set in motion basic changes in the inner constitution of Chinese society. Out of the "semi-feudal, semi-colonial" postwar era grew the class struggles that were to carry China inevitably toward her present condition. A nagging doubt in this line of interpretation is the question of whether Western contact should be assigned the whole credit for setting off these internal changes. An intelligentsia eager to believe that China had within herself all the prerequisites for the transition to modernity—belonged, that is, to the universal current of world history and not to a unique stream of her own—can only with difficulty assign to outside influence a predominant role in the overthrow of "feudalism." Nevertheless, the primacy of the anti-imperialist theme and the need for neat periodization have required that the "opening of China" serve as the beginning of modern history, the point at which a traditional dynastic decline was transformed into the decline of traditional civilization.

There is no denying the need to round off our own periods of study at arbitrary and useful points, but the convenience of the year 1840 should not lead us to beg the question of when, purely on the merits of the case, the "modern" period should be considered to have begun. Without going into deeper discussions, for the moment let us say that "modern" here refers to that period in which the motion of history is governed primarily by forces exogenous to Chinese society and Chinese tradition. It is that period, in other words, when the "decline" we observe is no longer simply the waning of the Ch'ing dynasty and its attendant social evils, but a more profound process that is leading Chinese history irrevocably out of its old paths and producing basic changes in social and intellectual organization. Such

1. Dona Torr, ed., *Marx on China, 1853–1860: Articles from the New York Daily Tribune* (Bombay, 1952), 4.

a process differs from the dynastic cycle in that never again can Chinese state or society be reestablished on the old pattern.

Despite our best efforts to liberate ourselves from dynastic cycle historiography, certain of its assumptions seem to remain with us: particularly that which relates the long-term stability of Chinese political institutions to factors of continuity in local society. In this view, administrative entropy and dynastic succession neither sprang from the substructure of Chinese life nor permanently affected it. The rise and fall of regimes, the clash of cliques in high state affairs, were but surface waves on a deep pool of stability. Clearly, some interdynastic crisis periods have had greater, and others less, effect upon local society. At the time of the Manchu conquest at least, a key element of stability appears to have been the continued dominance of the traditional elite, that educated status group Westerners have customarily called "the gentry," which had largely monopolized China's intellectual and political life since the eleventh century. This elite provided the pool of talent and education from which the new regime could staff its bureaucracy. It assured the maintenance of those customary community services without which Chinese local government could not operate; and, through its devotion to the social status quo, it made possible the reestablishment of local order, without which a reliable registration and taxation system could not be built. On a national scale, it served as the vital link between the bureaucracy and the local communities, between the urban administrative centers and the rural hinterland. In sum, it was this elite which, by virtue of its undiminished community influence, its tradition of orthodox learning, and its ethic of administrative service, made possible the reintegration of the traditional state in a shape similar to that of its predecessor.

Here it may be useful to clarify the terms "gentry" and "elite" for purposes of the discussion that follows. On the question of where the boundary lines of "gentry" should be drawn, social historians have differed. To Chang Chung-li, the gentry comprises all holders of academic degrees, from the lowest (the *sheng-yuan,* or district scholar) to the highest (the *chin-shih,* or metropolitan graduate). Ho Ping-ti argues persuasively that *sheng-yuan* be excluded from the gentry, on the ground that their social status was in no sense comparable to that of higher degree holders. To my purposes neither of these views is entirely applicable: neither is quite successful in relating status to the context in which it is recognized, or power to the context in which

it is wielded. I shall therefore work toward a broad functional definition of an "elite" segmented according to its power and prestige on
various scales of organization. The group I shall call the "national
elite" had influence that transcended its regional origins, and connections that reached to the apex of national political life. The
"provincial elite" had close links to the former group, but its interests
and influence were more narrowly confined. The "local elite" by
contrast, lacked the social prestige and powerful connections of the
former two groups but might still wield considerable power in the
society of village and market town.

From the national and provincial elites—the "big gentry" (*ta-
shen*)—the *sheng-yuan* and *chien-sheng* seem clearly to be excluded.
From the standpoint of the avowed goals of the "gentry" life—service
as an official—neither *sheng-yuan* nor *chien-sheng* were seen as potential bureaucrats. Their lack of such established status placed them in
a distinctly lower category when seen from the perspective of the na-
tionwide official class. Yet such lower degree holders (and even some
wealthy and educated commoners) might easily dominate community
life in poor and backward rural areas. Thus I shall occasionally use
the borrowed tag "gentry" to refer to degree holders in general; but
my working analysis of the "elite" will distinguish the scales of organization at which such persons enjoyed status and wielded influence,
and will also recognize that, at the local level, commoners might exercise powers that were in some cases hardly distinguishable from those
of degree holders.[2]

The elite was able to dominate China's political life because of its
dual identity: as a stratum of community leadership and as a corps
of state bureaucrats. As Ch'ü T'ung-tsu and others have pointed out,
the elite must be understood as comprising two groups, the "scholar-
gentry" and the "official-gentry." Scholar-gentry were those holders of
academic degrees who held no official posts but lived in their home
communities, dominating local affairs by virtue of their status, wealth,
and connections; whereas official-gentry were holders of government

2. Probably the best brief summary of the role of the gentry in Chinese government is Ch'ü T'ung-tsu's study, *Local Government in China under the Ch'ing*
(Cambridge, Mass., 1962). 169–192. A general study of the position of the gentry
in the nineteenth century is Chang Chung-li, *The Chinese Gentry: Studies on
Their Role in Nineteenth-Century Chinese Society* (Seattle, 1955), and his companion work, *The Income of the Chinese Gentry* (Seattle, 1962). Ho Ping-ti's
analysis is presented in his *The Ladder of Success in Imperial China: Aspects of
Social Mobility, 1368–1911* (New York, 1962), 34–41.

office, always serving away from home. Though they exercised a broad, informal regulating influence on all aspects of community affairs, the scholar-gentry stood formally outside the state apparatus and were the objects of state control and regulation. Thus they can be seen, in one aspect, as the top stratum of local society, subject to the taxing and policing authority of the local bureaucracy. But the bureaucracy itself was drawn from degree-holding gentry; on the local level this meant that the upper layers of the scholar-gentry could consort with the district magistrate on terms of social equality and shared values; and on the national level, that the gentry as a whole— official and non-official—formed a broadly interactive status group, bound together by networks of informal connections, that was truly a governing elite. The interconnections between the two segments of the gentry meant that serious clashes of interest between bureaucrats and local communities could be resolved with a minimum of conflict; and that the bureaucratic system as a whole, socially and intellectually embedded in the elite, could ride out periods of storminess on the upper levels of state affairs.

The stability of China's political institutions, then, had deep roots in her social system; and it is this that leads us to doubt that the "modern" period of China's history can be demarcated by largely external events. To classify the whole of the post-Opium War period as part of China's "modern" history, however convenient as an administrative device, avoids the question of whether there was not, at some point during the mid or late nineteenth century, a stage at which the Chinese state could still have been rebuilt along traditional lines. Had Western expansionism for some reason stayed its hand in the 1860's let us say, was it not still possible that a new and vigorous native dynasty might at length have built a new regime on the old foundations? If, as we have just suggested, the stability of political institutions was closely related to the power and cohesion of the literate elite, then clearly the question to ask at this point is whether the traditional elite was, by the 1860's, still in a position to dominate national affairs to such an extent that any new regime must be founded upon its political philosophy and be responsive to its interests.

Looking back a hundred years, a number of ominous developments suggest that new forces were already at work to undermine traditional Chinese society; that China of the mid-Ch'ing period suffered from persistent and spreading maladies that went beyond mere dynastic decline and would inevitably condition her future. The phenomenal population rise (from 150 to 300 million during the eighteenth century); the inflation in prices (perhaps as much as 300 per cent over the same period); the increasing monetization of the economy and the aggravation of economic competition in rural society: all these factors suggest the need for a new historical formulation that will identify basic processes of change in pre-Opium War China and free us in some measure from our uneasy dependence upon the dynastic cycle.[3] We might then hypothesize that the West was impinging, not just upon a dynasty in decline, but upon a civilization in decline: a civilization that would soon have had to generate fresh forms of social and political organization from within itself. It hardly needs pointing out, however, that such a formulation is far from having been established; and our thinking on Ch'ing social history will have to take account of the abundant evidence of continuity in social institutions well into the nineteenth century. With respect to the power of the traditional elite, the evidence is particularly compelling.

Certainly any attempt to assess the condition of the late Ch'ing elite must take as a datum one of the nineteenth century's most remarkable features: the prolonged survival of the Chinese state, together with its ruling house, in the face of seemingly irresistible pressures within and without. The trouble brewing in Canton during the opening decades of the century, during which the economic forces behind the tea and opium trades were about to burst their institutional bonds, was but one of the many troubles gathering for the Chinese state. Competing for official attention was a potentially greater menace, the rise of internal rebellion. The White Lotus Rebellion, which erupted in 1796 and was suppressed only with much time and treasure, was but the first of a long train of disturbances that culminated in a complex of great revolts at mid-century. Chief among these, the Taiping Rebellion, grew out of the ethnic feuds, overpopulation, and misgovernment in China's southernmost provinces. Its leadership was a sect of pseudo-Christians, whose apocalyptic vision of a heavenly kingdom on earth was born of the sufferings of the immigrant Hakka people of Kwangtung and Kwangsi. Hung Hsiu-ch'üan, prophet and

3. For an interesting review of these factors, see Kitamura Hirotada, "Shin-dai no jidaiteki ichi: Chūgoku kindaishi e no tembō," Shisō, no. 292:47–57 (1948). See also Ho Ping-ti, "The Significance of the Ch'ing Period in Chinese History," Journal of Asian Studies, 26.2:189–195 (February 1967); and his Studies on the Population of China, 1368–1953 (Cambridge, Mass., 1959), 270. Materials on the Ch'ing inflation may be found in Nan-k'ai ta-hsueh li-shih-hsi, Ch'ing shih-lu ching-chi tzu-liao chi-yao (Peking, 1959), 410–433.

Heavenly King, was a man transformed by illness, inspired by Christian missionary tracts, and convinced that the alien Manchus were devils who must die if China were to live. After the initial rising in 1850, the Taipings fought northward toward the Yangtze valley and then eastward toward the walled city of Nanking, where in 1853 they established their Heavenly Capital with claim to legitimate dominion over the empire. Their adherents grew to over two million, their armies occupied scores of cities, their flotillas thronged the inland waterways.[4]

The defeat of this antagonist, whose imperial pretensions were as dangerous to the dynasty as its fanatical armies, was well beyond the resources of the regular Ch'ing military forces; these, enfeebled by opium and corrupt leadership, had declined in competence and morale even below the point they had reached at the time of the White Lotus revolt. The court turned in desperation to the elite in the provinces. Led by Tseng Kuo-fan, a Hunanese scholar who had served in the metropolitan administration and had wide influence in his home area, the elite marshaled its resources to raise new armies; it was these armies, commanded mostly by holders of civil degrees, that with great effort destroyed the Taipings and burned their capital. The Heavenly Kingdom, crushed in 1864, vanished almost without trace. The new armies then turned against another rebellion, that of the Nien in the north central provinces, and destroyed that as well.

Thus the Chinese state, along with its Manchu overlords, was enabled to survive because significant segments of the elite identified the dynasty's interests with their own and took the lead in suppressing the dynasty's domestic enemies. The fact that the dynasty was thereby enabled to outlive its mid-century crisis by nearly fifty years points unmistakably to the toughness and resiliency of the Chinese social and political orders and, further, to the persisting power and cohesion of the elite. The victory of the elite, as we know, was achieved at the price of diminishing the powers of the central government. But this victory can also be seen as an indication that the foundations upon which the traditional state rested were yet firm; and that the specifically "modern" factors that were to shake these foundations in

4. A comprehensive bibliography of primary and secondary sources is Teng Ssu-yü's *The Historiography of the Taiping Rebellion* (Cambridge, Mass., 1962). The foremost history in English is Franz Michael's *The Taiping Rebellion: History and Documents,* vol. I: *History* (Seattle, 1966). See my review of this book in *Journal of the American Oriental Society,* 87.3:321–324 (1967).

later decades had yet to work a decisive change in the direction of Chinese history. The ability of the elite to triumph over such formidable challenges suggests that we can reasonably seek the beginnings of the old order's decline (as distinct from the decline of the dynasty) no earlier than 1864, the year the Taiping Rebellion was destroyed.

If we consider that the viability of the old order persisted at least as late as 1864, and attribute that viability in large measure to the undiminished power of the elite to hold state and society together, then it is reasonable to suppose that the ensuing decline was due to certain new and fatal maladies within the elite itself. Certain institutions and certain qualities that had made possible the victory of 1864 were weakened or destroyed in the decades that followed, leading to the destruction not only of the ruling dynasty but of the traditional state system. We shall consider this problem further in Chapter VI of this study.

The relationship between the elite and the bureaucratic state is most effectively studied in terms of those concrete institutional forms that comprised its day-to-day reality: the ways in which common interests and reciprocal expectations were worked out in practice. Just as a religion must be studied by looking beyond general statements of belief to the actual rites and sacraments of the cult, so too, the connections between the local elite and the state apparatus can be understood through the various practical mechanisms by which they were activated, not merely by general statements about shared values. It should be remembered, for instance, that although the elite owed its ascendency to factors not specifically related to state patronage—the power and prestige of learning, leisure, and wealth—yet the state added to these a long list of specific legal powers and immunities, such as virtual exemption from corporal punishment, exemption from labor service, the privilege (for those with high academic degrees) of visiting the local magistrate on terms of social equality, and many others. Even more important, the state offered that most precious commodity in old China, an official career: the surest road to fame and fortune, and the ultimate guarantor of one's local position. For their part, the lower strata of the scholar-gentry committed themselves to the constant grind of the examination system, which not only served to qualify them for official appointment, but was in fact required for maintaining their formal status. Besides being the primary mechanism by which the state drew talent into its service, the examination system served the local elite as a focus of year-to-year efforts, a recurrent reaffirmation of the goal of state service, a reassertion of the essential practical values of the orthodox literary heritage.

Such were some ways in which the relationship between elite and state was expressed in institutional form in normal times. I intend here, however, to examine the mechanisms whereby the interests of the elite were linked to those of the imperial state under the unusual circumstances of the nineteenth century, in a context of the increasing militarization of Chinese society. The new armies—both orthodox and heterodox—that arose in mid-century were but the most visible component of a process that had been at work since the White Lotus Rebellion two generations earlier. This was a period of increasing population pressure upon the land; desperation gave place to lawlessness, and in certain areas a bankrupt peasantry provided a growing source of recruits for bandit and rebel gangs. Communal feuding, particularly in the ethnically heterogeneous border regions of the south, took on new ferocity as competition for land gained momentum. By the 1830's the effects of the opium traffic had begun to complicate these problems, both by disrupting the normal monetary balance in rural China and by spawning congeries of outlaw groups to distribute and protect the hugely profitable drug. As local security decreased, rural communities took steps to protect themselves by erecting walls and raising militia. These trends were the early stages of a larger process of militarization that has lasted into the present century. The militarization that emerged first in the border regions in the early decades of the nineteenth century spread into the river valleys by the 1850's, involving ever larger numbers of men in military activity and ultimately breeding new forms of military organization.

Local militarization posed acute problems for the imperial state; for if irregular military force could not be regularized and brought under control, if the widespread militarization of local communities could not be brought into a predictable relationship to the state, then the security of the state itself might soon be shaken. It was military force by which the Manchus had conquered China, and even after two centuries of cultural assimilation, military force still provided the ultimate guarantee of the dynasty's dominance over the state apparatus, just as it had always guaranteed the dominance of the state apparatus over local society. The formal structure of Ch'ing armies suggests the extraordinary caution with which the court viewed even its own military instruments. The Eight Banners could of course be expected to render the most undeviating loyalty to the throne; descendents of the original Manchu conquerors and their Chinese allies, they had been brought under the close political control of the royal family. But in addition to these strategically placed troops, the court had to depend, for internal control as well as external campaigning, on the Army of the Green Standard (*lü-ying*): a larger force, ethnically Chinese, that was carefully dispersed in small garrisons throughout the provinces. The command structure of these garrisons was intermeshed with the civil bureaucracy at certain points, in such a way as to create a series of checks and balances among the contingents in each area. Its chief officers were carefully rotated so that none could establish personal loyalties among his subordinates; and finally, these troops could be brought together in large bodies only under high commanders specially deputed from the capital, to meet the needs of the moment.[5] With such meticulous security arrangements in its own military forces, the court was naturally alarmed by the widespread development of irregular military units in the countryside, even when such units were commanded by orthodox elite.

As we shall discover, though, local militarization did not mean anarchy. Although the military monopoly of the state was decisively broken by the events of the nineteenth century, the forms of local militarization tended to crystallize along axes of existing political and social organization. I shall attempt to describe these forms and to relate them to the long-term political destiny of the Chinese state: to the reasons that underlay the victory of 1864 and the irretrievable decline thereafter.

B. The Historical Importance of State Militia Institutions

Lei Hai-tsung and the "A-military Culture"

It was on the eve of the Marco Polo Bridge incident that the historian Lei Hai-tsung (1902–1962) completed the major portion of his study, *Chinese Culture and the Chinese Military*. In the late 1930's, when China was living under the shadow of foreign conquest, it would have been surprising had historical inquiry been untouched

5. Lo Erh-kang, *Lü-ying ping-chih* (Chungking, 1945), 12–17.

by national feeling. For Lei Hai-tsung, the central question to which all other questions had to be related was: what are the historical roots of China's weakness?[6]

It was Lei's conviction that China's weakness was not a product of the disasters that had befallen her in the modern period but stemmed from inbred defects of character and organization that could be traced to late antiquity. Specifically at fault was China's "a-military culture" (*wu-ping ti wen-hua*), which had resulted from the divorcement of the bulk of her male populace from national military service after the fall of the Ch'in empire in 206 B.C. In the slaughter of the late third century the Chinese people had lost all taste for soldiering, and Chinese institutional structure reflected this aversion throughout the imperial era and beyond. The Ch'in army was the last to have been broadly conscripted, integrally bound to the fate of its nation and thus activated by patriotic fervor. Soon after the founding of the Han empire, military service became the lot of prisoners or hired paupers; and thereafter it remained either a mercenary or a hereditary occupation, in either case quite divorced from the concerns of the civilian populace. The culture that resulted was passive, stagnant, and parochial, weak in resistance to external enemies and weak in loyalty to domestic regimes.[7]

However bleak her past and present, China's future might be bright. Lei's was a mind that expanded naturally over large themes of cultural evolution and sought to relate the anti-Japanese war to broad patterns of Chinese history. It was China's unique destiny to persevere as a civilization long after other ancient civilizations had perished; and this perseverence involved not fossilization but a series of rebirths. The first cycle of Chinese history ended with the decline and destruction of China's ancient civilization during the inundation of the north by barbarian tribes during the fourth century A.D. The second cycle began, in Lei's calculation, with the battle of the Fei River in 383, in which the remnants of the Chin dynasty, now relocated in the Yangtze valley, held the barbarians at bay and assured the survival of a Chinese regime in the south. It was the existence of the newly opened and increasingly rich and vigorous south that made possible the rebirth of Chinese civilization two centuries later in a new imperial age. Writing while the fight against the Japanese

6. Lei Hai-tsung, *Chung-kuo wen-hua yü Chung-kuo ti ping* (Changsha, 1940).
7. Lei, *Chung-kuo wen-hua*, 22–44, 125–126, 216–218.

was raging, Lei likened the national struggle in his own time to the battle of the Fei River and suggested that it marked the beginning of a third cycle, in which a new China would arise from the physical and social rubble of the war. This renaissance, like the earlier one, was assured by the abiding vigor of the Chinese people, guaranteed still by the vigor of the south, and strengthened this time by a new infusion of national consciousness. The war was thus a necessary purgative for Chinese society, ridding it of old ills and liberating the still vital energies of the nation.[8]

There is a certain inconsistency between Lei's dark view of old China as passive and stagnant, enervated by a persisting, radical distinction between military and civilian roles, and his faith in the undiminished vigor and martial quality of the Chinese people, which was only now being brought forth by the struggle for national survival. Was a society that had been so completely dominated by a "purely civil ethos" (ch'un-ts'ui wen-te), a genuinely "a-military culture," capable of responding to the challenges now before it? Conceivably the needs of his argument and his vision of a new and more martial China led Lei to overstate somewhat the civil-military separation in traditional Chinese society. Though traditional China lacked both the national conscription of the legalist Ch'in state and the universal conscription of the modern nation, can it be said to have embodied an absolute distinction between soldier and civilian? Lack of national conscription can be seen as one element in a general pattern of particularism: the traditional state ruled an empire that was neither technologically nor socially capable of national consciousness of the modern type. Yet national military service is not the only way in which civilians could assume military roles. Significantly, Lei bases his theory of the "a-military culture" primarily on the patterns of military-civil separation that emerged during the Former Han dynasty and devotes relatively little attention to the remainder of the imperial era, from Han onwards, which he sees as simply the repetition of a pattern, the confirmation and solidification of the "a-military culture."[9] However, the record suggests that, during the post-Han epoch, the civil-military distinction was not always as sharp as Lei's argument requires; that a number of historical circumstances did generate institutions in which military and civilian roles were not clearly separable; and further, that the Chinese state recurrently

8. Lei, Chung-kuo wen-hua, 206–222.
9. Lei, Chung-kuo wen-hua, 125–126.

fostered institutions of this sort to meet its own administrative needs. It will be our purpose here to demonstrate that, by the nineteenth century, the idea of state militia had had a long history in China, and that this history had conferred upon it a considerable respectability and a certain accumulation of administrative precedent.

"Militia" and "Militarization"

It will be useful to examine first the terms "militia" and "militarization," because they will form the background of much of the discussion that follows. "Militia" we shall take to embrace those institutions in which the civil and military roles of the participants are in a substantial degree interconnected.[10] In historical writing, "militia" has covered institutions of a broad range of types; this is quite understandable, for the word has never had any theoretical precision. The imprecision of its use indeed suggests the numerous ways civil and military roles can be linked in practice. In greater detail, certain general characteristics of militia overspread the range of its concrete historical forms:

Economic. The militiaman's relation to his regular occupation is not wholly severed. He remains a part of the economy of his home community.

Administrative and Social. The militiaman remains, in some significant ways beyond his economic role, connected to his home community, and to the social and administrative agencies of civilian life. His formal legal identity is not defined wholly by his membership in a military organization.

Psychological. Service in a militia organization does not require conformity to a purely military set of values. The goals and stock responses of civilian life are not abandoned.

In terms of the roles played by their participants, then, militia institutions are neither purely military nor purely civil but embody elements of both. Indeed, the concepts "civil" and "military" assume something of a dipolar, ideal-typical character with respect to militia institutions, which stand somewhere between the two.

10. The *Shorter Oxford English Dictionary* (1955) defines "civil" as "pertaining to the *ordinary* life and affairs of a citizen, as distinguished from *military, ecclesiastical,* etc." (p. 317). The reader should keep in mind throughout this discussion the parallels that may be drawn between military and ecclesiastical roles, in their relation to and interaction with civil roles.

This dipolarity of civil and military indicates the need for "militarization" as a companion concept to "militia." Militarization can be seen as both a process and a range of types. It is a process in which men are separated from the institutions of civil life. It is also the range of institutional types representing the many possible degrees of separation. Thus the term "level of militarization" expresses the degree to which a given institution departs from the civil pole and approaches the military. In economic terms, militarization normally involves some separation from productive pursuits. The more a man is specialized and proficient in arms, the more training is needed and the less time and energy remain for normal economic activity. In a settled, agricultural society, greater separation comes with greater mobility. If military activity removes a farmer from his fields during the crucial periods of the crop season, the separation is virtually complete.

Clearly the mechanics of the militarization process differ markedly in different social contexts. The modern citizen army may require that its members be separated physically from their communities for a period of years and attain a degree of expertise comparable to that of a fully professional soldier. Yet there are special administrative provisions that preserve the ties of such troops to their home communities, such as rules whereby a man's job, and even his seniority rights, must be kept open to await his return. Such factors clearly place members of a citizen army on a lower level of militarization than members of a standing, professional army, though their modes of life while in service may be outwardly indistinguishable. To take another case, factors of mobility and expertise are probably of less significance in a stockbreeding, nomadic society than in a settled agricultural one. A society in which the skills of war (such as horseback riding) are at the same time the skills of everyday life, and in which a significant proportion of property is ambulatory, is one in which the distinction between civilian and soldier is least distinct.

In the above discussion, the starting point for the elaboration of the concepts of "militia" and "militarization" is the combination of roles played by the participants, rather than any specific form of state organization or any particular administrative structure or political coloration. This approach is particularly suited to a study in which the role of the state is, so to speak, not defined in advance. It assumes that, in addition to state militia, there are militia institutions and modes of militarization that are not products of state activity and whose relations with the state may be ambiguous or openly antagonistic. On the other side of the coin, the state is inevitably involved with such groups: if it does not absorb or make allies of them, it has either to control or destroy them. For the moment, however, it is particularly state militia systems that we are to examine.

The Fu-ping Militia System

With the resurgence of the centralized empire in the late sixth and early seventh centuries arose a type of state militia called *fu-ping*, which became the best known and most widely idealized militia system in the history of Chinese military administration.[11] A brief discussion of the development of this system will be useful for an understanding of some of the administrative and social problems we shall observe in the militia institutions of later periods.

The term *fu* meant originally a regional military headquarters, with a complement of soldiers permanently attached to it. During the chaotic period following the fall of the Han dynasty, the commanders of such regional military organizations had held civil power as well as military, being invested concurrently with a civil official title. Attached to such a headquarters were hereditarily indentured soldiers who were not listed in the regular civil registers and whose social status was distinctly lower than that of the general populace. Such troops were the official counterparts of the private military retainers (*pu-ch'ü* and *chia-ping*), common in China since the late second century, who were indentured to powerful local families. Both the soldiers of the *fu* and the private retainers constituted, with their families, a species of permanent military serfdom.[12]

During the Northern Wei dynasty, founded in the late fourth century by a confederation of the nomadic Hsien-pi tribes known as T'o-pa, the northern frontiers were guarded by six marches (*chen*) in which tribal leaders served as generals and held authority in both military and civil affairs. The soldiery of the marches was permanent

11. The most detailed monograph on *fu-ping* is Ku Chi-kuang, *Fu-ping chih-tu k'ao-shih* (Shanghai, 1962). Other important studies drawn upon for this account are Ch'en Yin-k'o, *Sui-T'ang chih-tu yuan-yuan lueh-lun kao* (Peking, 1963), 124–140; T'ang Ch'ang-ju, *Wei-Chin Nan-pei-ch'ao shih lun-ts'ung* (Peking, 1955), 193–288; Ts'en Chung-mien, *Fu-ping chih-tu yen-chiu* (Shanghai, 1957). See also Étienne Balazs, *LeTraité economique du "Souei-Chou"* (Leiden, 1953), esp. 241-275.
12. Ku, *Fu-ping*, 5–10, 81–86. T'ang, *Lun-ts'ung*, 250.

and hereditary; it was originally drawn from prominent Hsien-pi families, whose service as tribal fighters was considered a customary right. These troops were participating in an older tribal tradition, in which military units were coterminous with the tribes themselves and soldiers were bound to their commanders by blood relations and common surnames.[13] This tradition was soon menaced, however, by the rapid acculturation of the Hsien-pi people to Chinese ways. The military contingents of the marches soon found themselves discriminated against by the aristocrats and bureaucrats at court: separated physically and culturally from the more sinicized political center, they were denied equal access to official preferment and social prestige. The designation of the soldiery as *fu*-households (*fu-hu*) in the Chinese manner formalized the situation in which military service at the frontiers was being transformed from a hereditary privilege to a hereditary serfdom. In 523 the simmering grievances of the marches erupted in a major rebellion, which signaled the fall of the Northern Wei. Out of the military turmoil arose two competing warlord groups which split north China between them. That dominated by the military figure Yü-wen T'ai, who himself sprang from the society of the marches, founded the short-lived Western Wei kingdom and in the process of consolidating its control, created new forms of military organization.

Yü-wen T'ai's New Policies. Like his rivals in the Eastern Wei state, Yü-wen T'ai sought to garner the military power of the marches for himself and with it to establish a strong, centralized regime. First he attempted to resuscitate elements of the Hsien-pi military tradition that had been eroded by nearly two centuries of sinicization. He ordered all those on the military rolls to assume Hsien-pi surnames or to resume former ones, the troops of each basic unit to share the surname of their commander.[14] This renascent tribalism was apparently designed to strengthen the internal coherence of military units, to restore the prestige of military service, and at the same time to satisfy those elements of the Hsien-pi community who felt themselves threatened by the sinicization process. This component of the early *fu-ping* system was evidently supposed to give the idea of the "military household" (*chün-hu*) a positive value by linking it to

13. Wang Yü-ch'üan, *Ming-tai ti chün-t'un* (Peking, 1965), 14–15.
14. Ku, *Fu-ping*, 34ff.

the old value system of nomadic society, thus offsetting the opprobrium attached to such status by the Chinese. But far from intending a genuine return to older forms, Yü-wen T'ai's new policies were really an effort to centralize military power in the hands of the court, through a pyramidal command structure headed by six "pillars of the state" (*chu-kuo*), powerful members of Yü-wen's own military clique. The various regional headquarters (*fu*) of this command hierarchy drew their troops from a network of special military administrative communities, which were composed of families inscribed on military rolls and hereditarily obliged to furnish men for military service. This early version of the *fu-ping* system, it should be understood, was not founded to provide a locally oriented and locally controlled soldiery, but rather to provide the local basis for a centrally controlled force that would be responsive to the military needs of the court. The tendency toward centralization increased substantially under the Western Wei's successor state, the Northern Chou, which was also controlled by the Yü-wen house.[15]

The military systems of the Western Wei and Northern Chou represented not merely a centralization but also an expansion of the military establishment. In 543 there were absorbed into the new command structure the existing local retainers (*hsiang-ping*) of independent military strongmen. Such contingents, some undoubtedly of the *pu-ch'ü* type, were henceforth inscribed on the military registers and at least partly controlled by the central military command. These units were not based in walled strongholds (*ch'eng* or *fang*) like the regular military families, but lived in the countryside and were closely linked to the rural economy. Their administrative absorption into the *fu-ping* system had the effect of supplementing the regular troops, which were mostly cavalry and largely non-Han in ethnic composition, with Han infantry based on a farming economy. This division between urban and rural based military communities persisted into the late sixth century; by Sui times, there was an administrative distinction between two types of military communities: those based in walled compounds (*chün-fang*) and their rural counterparts (*hsiang-t'uan*), each *fang* or *t'uan* having a headman (*chu*). These communities were the sources from which the military headquarters (*fu*) on various levels of the centralized hierarchy drew their troops.[16]

15. Ku, *Fu-ping*, 52–53, 136.
16. T'ang, *Lun-ts'ung*, 275–279; Ku, *Fu-ping*, 27–34.

The *fu-ping* system, as it came to maturity in the late sixth and early seventh centuries under the Sui and T'ang, incorporated certain of the important features of the Western Wei and Northern Chou systems. First, it was centrally controlled: locally based contingents served turns in guard units at the capital and could be dispatched on expeditions by the central military command. Second, it maintained the administrative distinction between hereditary military communities and the operational military units into which they fed. The innovations of the Sui and T'ang, however, were highly significant and gave the system a fresh and distinctive character. In the year 590 the throne decreed that thenceforth all military families be settled on the land and made administratively subject to the civil magistrates. The consequent dispersion of military communities is suggested by the fact that after 636 the walled military communities (*fang*) seem to have disappeared, and their rural counterparts (*t'uan*) to have succeeded to their functions.[17] These developments must be seen in the contexts of greater internal stability, which made walled compounds in the interior less important; a determined effort to settle the people on the land and increase production; and the end of the period in which the distinction between Han and their non-Han conquerors played a determining role in military organization.

It should not be inferred that the linking of military families to the civilian economy and to the regular civilian administration meant that all civilians thenceforth shared military duties equally. Service in the *fu-ping* during T'ang times was based largely on a property qualification: militiamen were supposed to be selected triennially from among wealthy farming families; once chosen, they were inscribed on the service rolls until age sixty. There were marked variations among different regions with respect to the incidence of service, some areas having no military obligations at all.[18]

The families of those selected for militia service were administratively subject to civil authority in their civilian roles, but also to military authority through the approximately 600 regional military headquarters (in T'ang times called *che-ch'ung-fu,* the term *che-ch'ung* being part of the title of the headquarters commander, *che-ch'ung tu-wei*). Thus there remained a certain formal difference, in administrative terms, between families subject to military service and

17. Ku, *Fu-ping*, 101–102; *T'ang, Lun-ts'ung*, 279.
18. Ku, *Fu-ping*, 183–192, 153–158; Ts'en, *Fu-ping*, 57–62.

families who were not. The distinctive element of the T'ang system was that militiamen were expected to provide their own rations out of the production on their allotted lands, instead of being subject to the regular taxes. Inasmuch as members of their families did not share such tax exemption, the financial burden on militia households was particularly heavy. At any rate, the linking of military service to agricultural production was the condition under which the state was able to shift the financial burden of troop support directly onto the shoulders of the peasants themselves.[19]

An administrative characteristic of the *fu-ping* system that has some theoretical importance for militia systems in general was the distinction between tactical and administration units. A tactical unit (made up of troops actually in service) exists for purely military purposes; it governs militiamen only in their military role. An administration unit, by contrast, is a local control grouping, of which the most important function is to serve as a registration pool from which militiamen are drawn into tactical units, and to which they return when their tour of service is over.[20] In the case of the *fu-ping* system, the administration units encompassed those farming families that were regularly obliged to provide males for military service. Under the Sui, as we have seen, the administration units controlled self-contained communities, the hereditarily obligated families of the *fang* and *t'uan*. The basic administration unit of the T'ang *fu-ping* system was called a *ti-t'uan*: the term referred to a land area and to the population within it. The populace of the *ti-t'uan* would be listed in two registers: a regular civilian register held by the local magistrate; and a military register, listing those males liable for service, held by the *che-ch'ung-fu*, the lowest-level military headquarters. *Ti-t'uan* (*ti* meaning locality) were to be distinguished from *chün-t'uan* (*chün* meaning military), which was the military unit drawn from the *ti-t'uan*, consisting of militiamen actually in service. When in service the militiaman came under the authority of the *che-ch'ung-fu*, and through it was controlled by the guard army to which he was attached. Thus the *ti-t'uan*, as an administration unit, can be considered as the land and population area within which the *che-*

19. Ku, *Fu-ping*, 204–207.
20. The distinction between tactical and administration units was pointed out by Charles Hucker in the case of the Ming military system: "The Governmental Organization of the Ming Dynasty," *Harvard Journal of Asiatic Studies*, 21:56 (1958). His terminology is appropriate also for the analysis of the *fu-ping* system.

ch'ung-fu could call up militiamen for service. In some respects the *ti-t'uan* was considered analogous to the *chou*, the basic civil unit, though in areas of heavy military liability there might be more than one *ti-t'uan* in a single *chou*.[21] The chief militia officer, the *che-ch'ung tu-wei*, must in most respects be considered as merely the head of the administration unit, the *ti-t'uan*; as a military figure his powers were extremely limited; his rank with respect to the central military bureaucracy was very low, and on the local level he could conduct no military operations without express orders from the capital.[22]

The division within the *fu-ping* system between widely dispersed administration units and centrally controlled tactical commands was highly important in the history of Chinese government because it influenced the development of military systems through the Ming and Ch'ing periods. In T'ang times, it made possible the integration of military forces with the civilian economy; even in later times when this integration was either unsuccessful or wholly abandoned, the regional dispersion of garrisons simplified the problem of troop support. Politically the system was designed to strip local commanders of initiative and independence while making high military officers in the capital dependent on distant and widely scattered contingents of troops, which were brought together in large formations only under carefully routinized procedures and at the behest of the top organs of government.

Elements of Militia Organization in Other State Institutions

Besides the *fu-ping*, a number of other Chinese military systems can be classed as militia, or else exhibit some elements that resemble or are derived from militia. In the following brief discussion, we shall try to avoid being distracted by formal differences among these institutions and will instead look for elements of kinship and similarity that may lead to a broad assessment of the state's historical involvement with militia.

Military Agricultural Colonies. A variety of militia with a history stretching through the whole imperial era was the military agricul-

---

21. Ku, *Fu-ping*, 137–139, 153. It is not entirely clear whether *chün-t'uan* referred to the formal military unit (*t'uan*), of which there were from four to six per *fu* or to the entire military component of the *che-ch'ung-fu*.
22. Ku, *Fu-ping*, 158–164.

tural colony (*t'un-t'ien*).[23] Such colonies were first proposed during the Former Han dynasty as a means of solving the logistic problems of remote border garrisons set up for defense against Inner Asian peoples. In the second century B.C. the minister Ch'ao Ts'o persuaded the throne that the practice of sending yearly troop replacements to such border posts and supporting them over long distances was both exhausting to the troops and expensive to the state, and that instead there be established permanent colonies that could be self-supporting and self-defending. The colonists might be criminals under sentence or ordinary subjects drafted for the purpose. More influential was the expedient of the general Chao Ch'ung-kuo, who in 61 B.C. recommended that regular soldiers be settled on border lands under the command of military officers, and each man assigned a fixed acreage to cultivate.[24]

After the Han, agricultural colonies remained a part of Chinese military administration, unchanged in basic principle, until the second great period of alien conquest (from the eleventh through the fourteenth centuries). Originally an instrument for defending border regions, they were now set up throughout the heartland of the empire and served less for external defense than for internal repression, as alien ruling groups sought to garrison the interior provinces of China and thus control the Han majority. But the recovery of the empire by the native Ming did not bring about a reversal of this fundamental trend in military administration; and the system of the early Ming represented the high point of development of the military agricultural colony. The huge hereditary garrison network that spread over the empire in Ming times was designed to be substantially self-supporting, with each administrative contingent assigned lands to farm, and a certain portion of regular troops kept constantly busy on them. The proportion of those assigned to farming was greater in the interior than in frontier provinces. The division of labor on

23. See the useful historical survey of *t'un-t'ien* in Wang Yü-ch'üan, *Ming-tai ti chün-t'un*, 11–26. An informative summary of the evolution of local military systems may be found in I-yang 1874, 11:2b–4.

24. Sun Chin-ming, *Chung-kuo ping-chih shih* (Hong Kong, 1959), 44–47. Yang Lien-sheng has suggested that such land assignments may have been the prototype of the land allotment system of the Northern dynasties and of the "equal field system." "Notes on the Economic History of the Chin Dynasty," *Studies in Chinese Institutional History* (Cambridge, Mass., 1961), 138–139. A Sung dynasty type of military agricultural colony, the "archery militia," is described in Ogasawara Seiji, "Sō-dai kyūsenshū no seikaku to kōzo" in Tōkyō Kyōiku Daigaku, *Tōyōshigaku ronshū* 3:81–94 (1954).

these military lands tended to increase, however, so that by the mid-fifteenth century it was no longer a case of soldiers supporting themselves by farming. The fact that this system in its original form lasted only about sixty years after the Ming conquest suggests that the administrative difficulties involved in the large-scale merging of military and economic activities could only be mastered, as in the case of the *fu-ping* system, in a period of exceptionally effective government; and, in any event, not for long. In Ch'ing times, military agricultural colonies were employed for certain special purposes in border areas, in minority tribal regions, and on land assigned to grain transport detachments, but never played a major role in troop support.[25]

Militia as a Form of Labor Service: the Min-chuang. Organized on the same basis as forced labor, the Ming system known as "civilian stalwarts" (*min-chuang*) relied upon local conscription to meet local military needs. As its regular garrisons decayed, the Ming state had frequent recourse to recruitment from civilian households. It was not until the mid-fifteenth century, however, that there emerged a regular system of militia conscription. Once a voluntary service paid for by tax remission, the "civilian stalwarts" became a form of compulsory labor service by the end of the fifteenth century. As prescribed in 1494, a district would draft a force of from 500 to more than 1,600 men, depending upon its total population. The drafting process was made part of the regular tax and labor assessment apparatus: the *li-chia*, or tithing system, whereby the population was grouped into units of 110 households, the ten richest to be responsible for tax registration and collection. The *li* also served as the administration unit for the militia, with the burden falling upon the rich households. Twice monthly in spring, summer, and autumn, and thrice monthly in winter, the militia gathered and drilled in a central place. They were the military arm of district-level government and responded to the magistrate's summons in emergencies. But the system had not been in operation for many years before it underwent a fundamental change: as it was found to be inconvenient for militiamen to travel long distances to the district seat, and distasteful for the sons of the rich to serve in person, hiring soon took the place

25. Wang Yü-ch'üan, *Ming-tai ti chün-t'un*, 39–55. Charles Hucker, "The Governmental Organization of the Ming Dynasty," *Harvard Journal of Asiatic Studies*, 21: 57 (1958). Local gazetteers contain much information on the history of *t'un-t'ien*, e.g., Wu-ling 1863 23:18–21b; Yu-hsien 1871 20:4b.

of conscription. Unemployed men from the city and suburbs were paid to serve as substitutes and soon became a permanent force, paid from the proceeds of an additional tax levied through the *li-chia* system. Thus the "civilian stalwarts" lost its militia character and at length degenerated into a corps of yamen attendants, in which form it survived into Ch'ing times. As its usefulness declined and its expenses rose, its numbers were periodically reduced. The fate of the "civilian stalwarts" illustrates the tendency of a system of conscript militia (like labor service in general) to decline into a system of taxation and paid service, when there is no compelling ideological pressure in the other direction.[26]

Hereditary Garrison Systems of the Ming and Ch'ing. The late dynasties displayed a system in which there was a formal separation between civilian and military households, with certain portions of the populace hereditarily obligated for military service. This separation relieved most people of military responsibilities, except for local institutions such as the "civilian stalwarts" discussed above. Nevertheless, the hereditary garrison systems themselves exhibited certain remnant characteristics of militia institutions. First, like the *fu-ping* system, there was a separation between administration and tactical units. Both the garrisons (*wei-so*) of the Ming and the Army of the Green Standard of the Ch'ing were widely dispersed in small communities, from which troops were brought together in large formations only under the command of high officers specially appointed by the throne as the occasion required. Second, during the early Ming period, there was a determined effort to make the military forces economically self-sufficient through a widespread system of military agricultural colonies, described above. Although the Army of the Green Standard was a direct successor of the Ming garrison system in basic organizational pattern, there was no sustained attempt to link it directly to agriculture; nevertheless, the inadequacy of their stipends commonly forced the soldiers to seek an unauthorized livelihood in their local communities.[27]

In one sense it may be said that the Ming and Ch'ing systems embodied a thorough separation between soldier and civilian, in that

26. Liang Fang-chung, "Ming-tai ti min-ping," *Chung-kuo she-hui ching-chi-shih chi-k'an*, 5.2; 201–234 (1937).

27. The basic work on the *Lü-ying* is Lo Erh-kang's *Lü-ying ping-chih* (Chungking, 1945).

most of the people (those on the civil registers) were exempt from state military service. The Ch'ing rulers, particularly, were convinced of the futility of trying to mix military and civilian roles. The Yung-cheng Emperor cited Confucius' dictum, "To lead an uninstructed people to war is to throw them away." If the people were busy farming, where would they find time for military instruction? If they were sent off to fight in emergencies, how could they farm efficiently? He scorned accounts of the supposed merging of civil and military administration during the Chou period as legends too remote to be authenticated and praised the basic efficiency of the system whereby "the people support the soldiers and the soldiers protect the people."[28]

Yet, seen in another way, the hereditary garrison systems unmistakably embodied certain of the characteristics of a militia, quite apart from their economic functions during the Ming, particularly the fastening of permament military obligation upon certain communities and the management of such communities as administration units separate from the major tactical commands. Thus in a certain sense even the Army of the Green Standard can be regarded as a recognizable, though greatly mutated, descendent of militia institutions.

Militia as a Component of Local Control: Pao-chia. It is suggestive of the far-reaching influence of military institutions upon Chinese society that the structure of local administration bore a close historical relationship to forms of military organization. We refer here to organs of local government such as pao-chia and *li-chia* that grouped civilians into hierarchically arranged decimal units for purposes of police control or tax collection. A brief examination of the pao-chia system, an administrative device of multiple functions and complex history, will help fill in the background to our discussion of local militarization.

The pao-chia system dates from Wang An-shih's reform movement of the late eleventh century. As originally conceived, it had two functions, which were separate in practice but related in history and theory: as an administrative base for militia conscription, and as a

28. Lo Erh-kang, *Lü-ying*, 211, quoting *Yung-cheng tung-hua-lu* (Tung-hua records, Yung-cheng reign), *chüan* 7 (1729). The passage appears in Analects, XIII, xxx. See James Legge, *The Chinese Classics*, I (Hong Kong, 3rd ed., 1960), 275.

surveillance and mutual responsibility organization. As first propounded in 1071, the regulations called for the registration of ten households as a group called a *pao*, fifty households (or five *pao*) as a "large *pao*" (*ta-pao*) and ten large *pao* as a "head-*pao*" (*tu-pao*). Each level had a headman selected from among the local inhabitants. The able-bodied males of the *pao* were registered as local militia and permitted to keep certain types of weapons; and, under the headmen of their respective administration units, were required to protect their neighborhoods from bandits. The second function, even more important in the light of the system's later development, was to control local society through registration, mutual surveillance, and group responsibility. Any failure to report illegal behavior or suspicious persons meant group punishment for *pao* members.[29]

Problems of border defense and rising military expenses soon led the court to use the newly instituted pao-chia system as a method of troop conscription. The military horizons of pao-chia were expanded from the defense of local communities to the defense of larger areas. Able-bodied males received military training and served turns of duty alongside regular troops. The *pao* thus became administration units for a state militia system and remained so for more than a decade.[30] After the collapse of Wang An-shih's reform movement the pao-chia system continued to play a part in local government, but the trend was increasingly towards its demilitarization.

By Ch'ing times, the police and registration functions of pao-chia were clearly dominant. Save for a brief period in 1644, pao-chia came within the purview of the Board of Revenue rather than the Board of War. In the early Ch'ing reigns, it was assiduously promoted by the throne as a local security measure. Its organizational divisions varied somewhat in different times and places, but a typical pattern called for the grouping of ten households as a *p'ai*, ten *p'ai* as a *chia*, and ten *chia* as a *pao*. Each household was to list its members on a door placard. As a special effort to strengthen surveillance and reporting, headmen were relieved of the responsibility for apprehending criminals, thus furthering the trend toward demilitarization. During the eighteenth century, repeated efforts were made to include

29. Li Tao, *Hsu tzu-chih t'ung-chien ch'ang-pien* (Taipei, Shih-chieh shu-chü reprint, 1961), 218:6–7b. The exact meaning of the term *chia* in *pao-chia* remains obscure.

30. Ikeda Makoto, "Hokōhō no seiritsu to sono tenkai," *Tōyōshi kenkyū*, 12.6: 20–22 (1954).

all sections of the populace in the system, including the local gentry, who were to be registered along with commoners. The headmen of the various decimal units, however, were to be commoners: a feature of the system that was evidently designed to provide a counterweight to the gentry's already weighty influence in their local communities. Thus the post of pao-chia headman was an unwelcome one, with little prestige and much responsibility; the government's concern was to make such men compliant and reliable instruments of the local bureaucracy. After 1740, pao-chia gradually became associated with the court's efforts to obtain reliable census data, but in the minds of local bureaucrats its security functions remained paramount.[31]

The nineteenth-century writer Kung Tzu-chen argued that the term pao-chia ought not to be used for a local organization primarily designed for enforcing mutual responsibility. Pao-chia, he wrote, was a term invented by Wang An-shih and used to designate an administrative base for militia conscription. Such an absurd system had been seen neither before nor since, and the term therefore belonged on the historical scrapheap. A system of mutual responsibility, like that of the Ch'ing period, bore a closer resemblance to the "mutual security" (*hsiang-pao*) system described in the *Rites of Chou* and was something entirely different from pao-chia.[32] Kung's contention seems to have little merit, for one of the passages in the *Rites of Chou* that describes *hsiang-pao* also makes it clear that such mutual responsibility groups were at the same time to serve as administration units for some sort of local militia.[33] The ambiguity of the term *pao* (protect, but also guarantee) is suggestive of the ambiguity of systems of this sort, in which external defense and internal police functions are closely related.

Further, there is ample reason to believe that the term pao-chia was not entirely misused in referring to the Ch'ing system; although its overt military functions had been abandoned since Sung times, cer-

31. Hsiao Kung-ch'üan, *Rural China: Imperial Control in the Nineteenth Century* (Seattle, 1960), 43–83. Ho Ping-ti, *Studies on the Population of China, 1368–1953* (Cambridge, Mass., 1959), 36–55. Wada Sei, *Shina chihō jichi hattatsu shi* (Tokyo, 1939), 145–165. A comprehensive history of *pao-chia* and related institutions is Wen Chün-t'ien's *Chung-kuo pao-chia chih-tu* (Shanghai, 1936).

32. Kung Tzu-chen, "Pao-chia cheng-ming" in *Kung Tzu-chen ch'üan-chi*, I (Shanghai, 1959), 96–97. *Hsiang-pao* was also a term used in the mutual responsibility–collective punishment system devised by Shang Yang for the state of Ch'in. Wen Chün-t'ien, 85.

33. *Chou-li* (*Ssu-pu ts'ung-k'an* ed.), 3:33b; Sun I-jang, *Chou-li cheng-i* (*Ssu-pu pei-yao* ed.), 22:11ab.

tain aspects of its military character remained. A system of numerically uniform groups arranged in a pyramidal command relationship not only resembles the structure of a military organization, but in fact may have been anciently part of a military organization. The *Rites of Chou*, a classical text much in the minds of Wang An-shih's reform group, purports to describe the bureaucracy of the early Chou dynasty, though the work itself is of comparatively late authorship and no doubt contains much that is merely utopian. Despite its dubious factuality, however, its influence has been enormous. With respect to militia organization, its main interest is in its depiction of a society in which units of civil and military administration are entirely congruent. Lower-level civil groupings are simultaneously administration units for the state military system. Military units on each level consist of the drafted males from the corresponding civil units, the number of soldiers in each contingent corresponding exactly to the number of households in its civil counterpart. Civil officers from the top of the system to the bottom serve as military commanders in time of war.[34] The high degree of regimentation implied by this model of combined civil-military management was clearly present in the Ch'ing pao-chia system, at least in the most optimistic expectations of its sponsors.

Quite apart from its historical and theoretical connections with military forms, and to some extent a confirmation of them, was the ability of the *pao* to resume its function as an administration unit for militia. Kung Tzu-chen's distaste for local militarization was not shared by all officials. The late-seventeenth-century magistrate Huang Liu-hung, for instance, saw pao-chia as a good base upon which to build a large force of local militia under the direct supervision of the district government. The trouble with Wang An-shih's system, thought Huang, was not the militarization of village manpower, but the use of that manpower beyond the confines of its home areas; and to use the pao-chia as a militia base for purely local police and defense was indeed in the true tradition of Chou government. With a conscripted militia under his command, the magistrate could properly exercise his responsibilities for local order, which he could not with only the rabble of yamen underlings assigned him by statute. Huang figured that by drafting one able-bodied male from each

---

34. *Chou-li* (*Ssu-pu ts'ung-k'an* ed.), 7:1b–2. Tu Yu, *T'ung-tien* (Commercial Press ed.), 28:163. A system based on the same principle was reportedly devised by Kuan Chung for the state of Ch'i. See the chart in Wen Chün-t'ien, 83.

household (save households of gentry, government employees, widows and orphans, paupers and invalids) an average district could raise a militia of 6,150 men. Those selected were to be inscribed on a special register, separate from the regular pao-chia registers that listed the entire populace.

On an appointed day, the entire militia was to pass in review before the magistrate, who would personally supervise the checking of names against the registers. The contingent of each *pao,* drawn up behind its special flag, was then to kneel while the magistrate's edict was read: "If bandits are seen, you must apprehend them. If an alarm is sounded, you must hasten to aid those in danger. If you are summoned, you must obediently and promptly assemble. If you gain merit you will be speedily rewarded; and if demerit, speedily punished. The leaders of squads and the headmen of the *pao* and the *hsiang* (rural subdistricts) are commanding and instructing you with the authority of the magistrate, and you must follow them obediently. The court has its statutes, the officials have their penal codes. When mustered, comport yourselves as eager and brave militia; when dispersed, as filial subjects. Thus may your native areas be eternally protected, and peace extend to ten thousand generations." Each year in the ninth month there was to be a great parade, in which the whole militia displayed its skill in marching and countermarching, regulated by flag-waving, horn-blowing, and cannon fire. The five *pao-chang,* one for each rural *hsiang* and one for the city and suburbs, kowtowed before the magistrate's pavilion, where they were invested with the ranks of center, left, right, front, and rear general. Other pao-chia officers were also given military ranks, and the militia of each *hsiang* was designated an army. In the ensuing maneuvers, an unseen enemy was repelled, pursued, and surrounded, and afterwards all the troops were feasted with meat and wine.[35]

The Idea of Militia in Chinese History

Having delineated briefly some of the historical forms of state militia in Chinese society, it remains to summarize the major ideal and institutional sources that lay behind the idea of militia as it existed by late Ch'ing times.

35. Huang Liu-hung, *Fu-hui ch'üan-shu* (1694), 21:1–32b. Huang, whose dates are unknown, was from Hsin-ch'ang, Kiangsi, and is said to have served as a magistrate in Shantung around 1670. Wang Chih, *Ch'ung-te-t'ang kao* (preface 1759), 4:3–5.

The Influence of Non-Chinese Peoples from Inner Asia. One characteristic of stockbreeding, nomadic, or semi-nomadic society, considered from the standpoint of military organization, is that a high level of militarization is relatively compatible with the requirements of production. The skills of war, most obviously horseback riding, are at the same time the skills of everyday life. Also, the mobility that goes with militarization does not disrupt the production process as seriously as it can in an agricutural society. We have seen in the early stages of the *fu-ping* system, during the Western Wei and Northern Chou periods, the positive value placed on an entire community's serving constantly and traditionally as a source of military manpower. Such a conception underlay the effort of Yü-wen T'ai to reinvigorate tribal values among the Hsien-pi people and even to extend such values to elements of the Han population. A short-lived adaptation of this system to agricultural society during the early decades of the T'ang was made possible by the continuing prestige attached to such service by prominent families, some of whom were themselves not far removed from nomadic cultural traditions.[36]

In a later age, the extension of the *t'un-t'ien* system to the interior provinces received some impetus from the military traditions of the alien Liao, Chin, and Yuan ruling groups. The military systems of the Ming and Ch'ing dynasties, with their networks of hereditary garrisons in interior China, their division between administration and tactical units, and (in early Ming times) the reliance on *t'un-t'ien,* can in certain respects be traced to the military systems of China's Inner Asian conquerors.[37] Indeed, if one wants to trace the connection between militia and nomadism back into the shadows of prehistory, one can speculate that the Chou conquerors at the end of the second millenium B.C. embodied in their feudal system (praised in legend for its union between soldier and civilian) the half-remembered military forms of a mobile, tribal society.[38]

Chinese Utopianism: the Idealization of Feudal Institutions. Even more than that of most cultures, Chinese political theory has been

36. Much of the *fu-ping* officer corps was in fact drawn from families descended from former nomads. See Edwin Pulleyblank, *The Background of the Rebellion of An Lu-shan* (London, 1955), 63. Ku, *Fu-ping,* 92–93.

37. Wang Yü-ch'üan, *Ming-tai ti chün-t'un,* 14–16. See Ts'en Chung-mien's comparison of the military systems of various tribal societies, *Fu-ping,* 63–68.

38. See Wolfram Eberhard's argument to this effect in his *Conquerors and Rulers: Social Forces in Medieval China* (Leiden, 1952), 5–9.

nostalgic for lost virtue: in particular the virtue of the "Three Ages" (*san-tai*), the dynasties of Hsia, Shang, and Chou, the first of which is entirely legendary, the second (until the advent of modern archaeology) nearly so, and the third only semi-historical. The feudal system of the early Chou, especially, has been idealized as the fount of Chinese political wisdom. In addition to their general contributions to the Chinese political ethos, the institutions of Chou have been the source of various utopian conceptions, of which some have supported radical reform programs and others have survived fragmentarily in the slogan reserve of political discourse. Two of these utopian concepts in particular have been influential in the development of militia institutions: the ideal of the "well-field" community (eight families whose fields were arranged in a pattern resembling the ideograph for "well") as presented in the *Mencius*; and the merging of civil and military roles on all levels of society, as described in the *Rites of Chou* and *Kuan-tzu*.

The admirable qualities of the eight-family group that was supposedly the basic unit of Chou society were self-sufficiency, voluntarism, and community harmony. The well-field dream dwelt in that corner of the Confucian mind which had never accepted imperial big government with its rewards and punishments, its legions of clerks and bureaucrats, and its centrally controlled armies. The well-field group was bound together in its economic life by a common obligation to provide their feudal lord with one ninth of their produce; this commonality of interests was supposedly paralleled by community effort in other aspects of rural life, including local security. The self-sufficient community was, at the same time, self-defending. Mencius described such a community as "befriending each other in their leaving and entering, and aiding each other in defending and keeping watch (*shou-wang hsiang-chu*)."[39] In the real world, where rural communities were not necessarily as harmonious as those in the well-field vision, it was harder to mobilize community effort for local defense. In such circumstances the Mencian utopia played a prominent part in the efforts of local defense leaders to rally support, and by Ch'ing times "aiding each other in defending and keeping watch" had become a cliche in the vocabulary of the local elite.[40]

Another fragment of the feudal tradition that became a cliche in

39. Chiao Hsun, *Meng-tzu cheng-i* (Peking, 1958), 212.
40. For instance, Po-po 1832, 7:5b; Hsiang-hsiang 1874, 5:7; Hsu Nai-chao, *Hsiang-shou chi-yao* (1849), 3:7b.

later times was of rather different character. The phrase "entrusting military functions to the peasants" (*yü-ping yü-nung*, sometimes *yü-ping yü-min*, "civilians" being substituted for "peasants") is drawn from that aspect of the utopian tradition that sought the just ordering of society on the basis of an elaborate and symmetrical bureaucracy. In contrast to the Mencian picture of community self-defense, *yü-ping yü-nung* must be seen as an instrument of state power; the very wording suggests affirmative action by the state. Of particular importance to such a system was the congruence of civil and military administration units, the officers on each level of government being at the same time military commanders and the peasantry providing troops as the occasion required. This extension of military organization to the whole of society has been discussed above in connection with the pao-chia system. Though it is almost certain that the verbal roots of the expression *yü-ping yü-nung* lie in the *Kuan-tzu*, a compendium of ancient literature dating in part from the third century B.C., it was not until Sung times that the phrase itself became a stock nostrum of Chinese political theory.[41]

The original context of this kind of thinking in antiquity, namely the attempt to build up state power through efficient techniques of government, might lead us to see *yü-ping yü-nung* as a typical legalist slogan. It is certainly quite different in its origins and connotations from the local voluntarism in the Mencian well-field image. Yet by the time of the late dynasties the phrase had acquired overtones of distaste for large standing armies, and of that ideal union of civil and military capacities that was part of the ancient Confucian ideal of personal excellence. The ambiguity and broad suggestiveness of *yü-ping yü-nung* should be kept in mind; local militia institutions lay in that shadowy territory where state power interacted with local society and where ambiguous meanings had an indispensable role to play.

It appears that the utopian component of the militia tradition did not achieve real prominence until Sung times; though it conditioned the Chinese historical view of the *fu-ping* system, for instance, it was

---

41. A late T'ang discussion of the *fu-ping* system does not mention *yü-ping yü-nung*; see the excerpt from *Yeh-hou chia-chuan* in Wang Ying-lin's *Yü-hai* (1806 ed.) 318:18–24. However, Ou-yang Hsiu's *Hsin T'ang-shu* (K'ai-ming ed., 3751) does use the phrase with reference to *fu-ping*, though in slightly modified form. For the roots of the expression, see *Kuan-tzu* (Wan-yu wen-k'u ed.) vol. I, pp. 103, 109; *Kuan-tzu chi-chiao*, Kuo Mo-jo, *et al.*, eds. (Peking, 1956) 330.

not a major factor in the development of the *fu-ping* system itself.[42] During the late dynasties, however, it grew considerably in currency; and it may be suggested as an hypothesis that it was one of a number of utopian concepts that were increasingly attractive in theory as they became decreasingly attainable in practice.

Militia and Local Society

The organization of historical research would be much simpler if the ordering of society were as neat as the charts in a magistrate's yamen, for prescriptive codes and procedures are more accessible than the information about how society really works. Nothing can illustrate the gap between the normative and the descriptive more clearly than the quasi-military codes of the pao-chia system: the layered decimal units of organization were not a reflection of any existing numerical divisions in Chinese society but were superimposed upon that society in an effort to fragment and control it. Beneath the lattice of normative, positive government lay what we may call, for the moment, the "natural" configurations of Chinese society. In these natural configurations, just as in the mechanisms of state control, there existed a potential and an impetus toward militarization. Let us now introduce, briefly, the problem of local militarization that was not the result of government initiative and pose in preliminary form the question of how such local militarization was to be brought into a stable relationship with the state.

Violence was a stream that ran through China's rural landscape in certain well-defined beds: diked and controlled in the best of times, but at other times breaking forth to inundate local society. Militarization that grew from the needs of the natural units of local organization was of course more in evidence during times of major social breakdown but also existed in attenuated form during periods of relative stability. The forms assumed by such militarization were various, as were the social units upon which they were based: lineage and village, bandit gang and secret society, all served as bases for local militarization as their circumstances required. Three widely

---

42. Though Yü-wen T'ai did invest *fu-ping* with an element of utopian symbolism, it was the symbolism of the "six armies" of the Chou state, rather than that of the interchangeability of civil and military roles. See Ch'en Yin-k'o, *Sui T'ang chih-tu yuan-yuan lueh-lun kao* (Peking, 1954), 126–127.

separated examples will illustrate the variety of forms such militarization might take.

The Origins of Pao-chia. If we look behind the state-managed pao-
chia system of the eleventh century, we find that Wang An-shih's
legislation was in fact derived from observation of local practice. An
investigation of village conditions near Kaifeng revealed that the
peasants had traditionally coped with banditry on their own initiative "by grouping rural households far and near into *pao* and *chia*
(*t'uan-wei pao-chia*)." These multivillage leagues, presumably organized by the rural elite, had cooperated in defense and police work.
By the mid-eleventh century this system had fallen into disuse, and
local disorder had increased apace. It was the memory of this local
system that served as the seed for the state system known as pao-
chia.[43]

A Local Crop-Watching Corps. The late Ming playwright, Ch'i
Piao-chia (1602–1645), who made a name for himself as a reforming
official, described a method of protecting local grain supplies in time
of famine that was probably based upon observation of community
practice in his home district of Shaohsing, Chekiang. Community
solidarity in time of famine was a matter of life and death, not only
for those who needed relief, but also for those who still possessed
some grain. Ch'i's formula linked famine relief to militia protection:
the ideal of mutual aid (*shou-wang hsiang-chu*) required that those
without food be succored, and that they in return serve as guards
for those who had grain or other property to protect. Households
who had received relief grain would select able-bodied males as local
militia. This was the method of uniting for defense (*t'uan-chieh fang-
hu chih fa*). The diligence and obedience of the militiamen were not
left to chance but were to be a condition for the continuance of
grain relief. Such a system would have the advantage of providing
for defense against bandits from outside the village at the same time
as it would neutralize class antagonisms inside the village. This

43. Li Tao, ed., *Hsü tzu-chih t'ung-chien ch'ang-pien,* 218:7. Wada Sei, *Shina
chihō jichi hattatsu shi,* 33. It still remains a mystery exactly what *chia* meant
in Wang An-shih's day. His own system did not include any unit called *chia*.
It is possible, though not at this point provable, that *chia* carried an ancient
meaning of armor, or armored soldiery; thus *pao-chia* would mean "the soldiery
of the pao."

purely nonofficial effort, based on local initiative and management, existed alongside the pao-chia system, with which it had no administrative connection.[44]

The Origins of the Red Spears. Unlike the two examples considered above, which were firmly within the boundaries of orthodoxy, the Red Spears Society (Hung-ch'iang Hui) illustrates how readily local militarization could form links with China's heterodox subcultures. The Red Spears arose amid the intolerable conditions of rural life in North China during the early decades of the twentieth century. The society took the form of a large federation of village militia organizations, which could trace their spiritual inspiration to the heterodox White Lotus sect. In 1915 rural Honan was scourged by an outlaw known as Lao-yang-jen and his band of several tens of thousands. But government troops sent to suppress him worked even greater atrocities, and the destitute farmers rose to defend themselves. Virtually helpless against the rifles of their persecutors, the ragged local defense units turned to the magical charms and incantations that were the stock in trade of the White Lotus Society and of its descendents, the Boxers. Believing themselves invulnerable, the militiamen formed a surprisingly potent local force. Portions of these village defense units became detached from their home bases and were brought together into larger groups, which played a significant role in the civil warfare of the 1920's.

It appears that the Red Spears were similar in their origins and development to White Lotus affiliates who had preceded them, particularly the Nien rebels of the mid-nineteenth century and the Boxers. In other words, they were the kind of local grouping that would have been recognized as dangerous by administrators of the old regime: besides their heterodox religion and their unauthorized militia, they tended to become involved with resistance to oppressive taxes and to various other injustices. Though their heterodoxy was somewhat less obtrusive in the ideologically confused world of the twentieth century than it would have been in the nineteenth, the Red Spears were seen by the Communist party during the 1920's as a way into the rural politics of Honan and Shantung and a likely base for revolutionary organization. Their "superstitious dogmas" notwithstanding, the Red Spears might still become "the armed force

44. Ch'i Piao-chia, *Ch'i Piao-chia chi* (Peking, 1960), 122–126.

of the peasant associations." The party did succeed to some extent in infiltrating them.[45]

The two basic types of militia institutions in Chinese society— those born of state prescription and those born of the needs of natural social units—would seem to exemplify that fundamental division between state and society suggested by the theory of Oriental Society, a remarkable extension into modern scholarship of Marx's untutored early views of Asia. According to this theory and its derivatives, a powerful despotic state seeks to impose its own forms of organization upon the natural units of rural society in order to control and tax them. The natural units themselves—scattered, self-contained, and isolated villages—have their own indigenous forms of organization, which remain largely impervious to change from without. The natural antagonism between state and local interests is damped down only by the state's overwhelming despotic authority.[46]

Indeed, there is much in our sources to support the theoretical distinction between natural and state-imposed institutions in local society. But it is not necessary to proceed to the conclusion that the two sprang from different social or historical sources; nor is it necessary to accept the idea that state and society were, by virtue of this distinction, placed in a situation of never-ending conflict that required purely despotic resolution. In the sphere of local militarization, as in other aspects of Chinese public life, the key institutions were those through which the interests of state and society were

---

45. "Resolutions on the Red Spears Movement" in C. Martin Wilbur and Julie Lien-ying How, eds., *Documents on Communism, Nationalism, and Soviet Advisers in China, 1918–1927* (New York, 1956), 303–305. On the origins and development of the Red Spears, see Suemitsu Takayoshi, *Shina no himitsu kessha to jizen kessha* (Dairen, 1939), 113–144; also Naganō Akira, *Shina-hei, tohi, kōsōkai* (Tokyo, 1938), 366–374.

46. The most elaborate theoretical treatise of this school is Karl Wittfogels's *Oriental Despotism: A Comparative Study of Total Power* (New Haven, 1957). On the origins of this line of interpretation in early Marxism, see Hélène Carrère d'Encausse and Stuart Schram, *Le Marxisme et l'Asie, 1853–1964* (Paris, 1965), 12–16, 140–143. In Japan the theory of Oriental Society (with respect to China, at least) has been very influential and has given rise to a number of variants. On this subject see the critical review by Hatada Takashi, "Chūgoku ni okeru senseishugi to 'sonraku kyōdōtai riron'," *Chūgoku kenkyū*, 13:2–12 (1950). Japanese sinology remains a prime subject for research. It may turn out that the long survival of primitive Marxist interpretations such as that of Oriental Society is related to the freeze put on the development of Japanese Marxism by militarism in the 1930's, which inhibited the development of unilinear theories like those advanced in China by Kuo Mo-jo and others.

mediated. One such institution was the *t'uan-lien* (grouping and drilling) system, which played a central part in local militarization during the late Ch'ing period, the development of which we shall explore.

II. THE DEVELOPMENT OF CH'ING MILITIA POLICY, 1796–1850

A. Local Control Problems during the White Lotus Rebellion

As the eighteenth century drew to a close, the Ch'ing government could fairly claim to have solved its military problems in Inner Asia. It had crushed its dogged enemies, the Zunghar Mongols. It oversaw Tibet's politics and protected her boundaries. Gurkha invasions of Tibet in 1788–1791 were met by an expeditionary force of 13,000, which, though it did not conquer the Gurkhas, did strengthen the Ch'ing grip on Tibet herself. These military glories in Central Asia were achieved, moreover, without seriously burdening China's economy.[1] As if all this pride and power were but a dazzling facade for inner decay, the last years of the Ch'ien-lung reign saw the outbreak of an internal rebellion that was to strain the financial and military resources of the dynasty for a decade. The White Lotus Rebellion (1796–1805) uncovered startling weaknesses in the apparently powerful Ch'ing military system. Officials charged with suppressing it were shocked by the lack of discipline and martial vigor among garrison forces. "The evils are beyond description . . . the generals know nothing of warfare, and the troops care nothing for the generals."[2]

Though it may be appropriate to view the 1790's as a watershed in the fortunes of the Ch'ing dynasty, this abrupt decline of military power is only intelligible seen in relation to the nature of the chal-

1. Suzuki Chūsei, *Shin-chō chūkishi kenkyū* (Tokyo, 1952), 1–11. Also see his *Chibetto o meguru Chū-In kankeishi* (Tokyo, 1962), 103–114.
2. Suzuki, *Shin-chō*, 160.

lenge. It is possible that even in its prime the Ch'ing military system might have been unable to meet the strenuous demands imposed upon it after the Ch'ien-lung reign. Superior foreign arms and widespread rural revolt, the nemeses of late Ch'ing rulers, posed problems that the regular military forces were neither technologically nor structurally equipped to handle. Campaigning in Central Asia was a different matter from coping with widespread social disintegration in rural China. At their lowest level of organization, the principal garrison forces, the Army of the Green Standard, were stationed mostly in district or prefectural cities.[3] Their power could not penetrate China's village substructure, where rebellion rose and flourished. Such garrisons were adequate in times of relative stability, but perhaps not in times of major social disruption.

The Origins and Character of the White Lotus Rebellion

The White Lotus Rebellion marked the re-emergence of a secret society that had led the anti-Mongol revolt of the late fourteenth century, a revolt which culminated in the founding of the Ming dynasty. The society itself, originally an ascetic salvationist sect of Amidist Buddhism, dates probably from the fifth century. By Yuan times it had absorbed the dualistic and potentially revolutionary doctrines and iconology of the Maitreya (*mi-le*) cult and of the Sect of Brightness (*ming-chiao*), a Chinese variety of Manichaeism. It soon became a center of anti-Mongol agitation and assumed the leadership of peasant revolts in North and Central China. The messianic fervor of the society and its sympathizers was instrumental in carrying to power Chu Yuan-chang, founder of the Ming; who, though probably a member himself, now proscribed the sect along with other heterodox groups. The White Lotus went underground again, discarded overt political slogans, and persisted as a village cult that promised personal salvation and the healing of disease. Despite determined persecution in Ming and Ch'ing times, the society survived and, by the mid-eighteenth century, again entered an activist phase. Uprisings in 1775 in Shantung and Honan revived the movement's chiliastic and overtly political character. Sect leaders now proclaimed the incarnation of the Buddha Maitreya and the emergence of a legitimate Ming claimant. Uprisings in early 1796 by the oppressed farmers

3. Lo Erh-kang, *Lü-ying ping-chih,* 90–153, 160–166.

of western Hupeh began a rebellion that was to last ten years and cost the Ch'ing great effort to suppress.[4]

Under decentralized White Lotus leadership, the rebellion thrived in the mountainous watershed between the Yellow and Yangtze rivers, where the Tsinling and Tapa ranges divide North China from South. Here the boundaries of Shensi, Szechwan, and Hupeh meet to form a border area, a sanctuary for rebels and a barrier to government troops. Despite their unkindly terrain, these mountains had received a large population influx during the mid-Ch'ing period. The government had sponsored migration into the Szechwan basin beginning in the late seventeenth century in order to repopulate devastated land; as the lowlands grew crowded, newcomers began to spill over into the northeastern mountains and to settle in higher, less fertile places. By 1729 the court was determined to stem the flood of immigrants but did not succeed in doing so. During the Ch'ien-lung period the migration continued, as increasing numbers of peasants fled starvation after bad harvests in neighboring provinces. A similar process was taking place in the Han-chung region of Shensi.[5]

In the mountains of the three-province border area, economic hardships were compounded with social and cultural dislocation. An investigator in the early Chia-ch'ing period found that the mountain population was composed largely of immigrants, with social and regional layers superimposed confusedly. Half were settlers from Hunan and Hupeh; another 30 or 40 percent from Kwangtung, Anhwei, and Kiangsi. The new communities, unruly and disorganized, had but weak kinship bonds and scanty education. There was much moving about, as settlers scratched a bare living from unfruitful soil, and some were known to have several abodes in the course of a year as they pursued the growing season up the mountainsides. Traditional control mechanisms like pao-chia, which could only be imposed on a settled population, were thus virtually useless, save within market towns and cities. Disorder was aggravated by the existence of a growing pool of outlaws, who lived in the deep forests and were entirely cut off from normal society. Observable in official documents

---

4. The most complete account of the rebellion and its historical context is Suzuki, *Shin-chō;* for the earlier history of the White Lotus Society, see Wu Han, *Chu Yuan-chang chuan* (Peking, 1949), 16–23.

5. Suzuki, *Shin-chō,* 70; Ho Ping-ti, *Studies on the Population of China, 1368–1953,* 139–143; for a vivid recent description of this depressed region see Graham Peck, *Two Kinds of Time* (Boston 1950), chap. 9.

as early as 1745, these *kuo-lu* bandits (the origin and meaning of the name are unclear) included military deserters, salt-smugglers, counterfeiters, and other petty fugitives and were natural sources of White Lotus recruits.[6]

The White Lotus, however, also found recruits in more fortunate circles; their organization reached into the lower levels of local government itself. "In the villages," wrote one observer, "the village heads and the chiefs of the settlers are White Lotus members, as are the yamen underlings and clerks in the cities. So the people who are supposed to ferret out the sect are in fact members of it." Furthermore, the White Lotus had become to some degree a cross-class movement. It included not only the dispossessed, but also property owners whose adherence to the sect stemmed less from economic distress than from conversion to White Lotus soteriology and anti-Manchuism. Its infiltration of local government and its extension across class lines meant that it could not be readily suppressed by regular agencies of local control.[7]

Military institutions seemed as useless as civil. The tactics of the White Lotus were those of a rebel group with ramified connections in the local community: guerrilla warfare by small, highly mobile bands, supplied and informed by the surrounding populace. The Ch'ing battalions, heavily armed, slow, and lacking local support, spent great effort for small success. Plaints of Ch'ing officials during the White Lotus campaigns provide a classic picture of the guerrilla problem: "The rebels are usually sated, while our troops are starving; the rebels have leisure while our troops labor away their fighting strength . . . when we do gain a victory, those whom we kill are perhaps a few hundred of the rebel rearguard, or the old, weak, and sick who cannot march." The pursuing regulars seldom made contact with the rebel main force. Further, popular rebellion was simply beyond the reach of standard military force: "The rebels are all our own subjects. They are not like some external tribe . . . that can be demarcated by a territorial boundary and identified by its distinctive clothing and language." Thus there was no distinguishing the rebels from the human stream in which they swam. "When they congregate and oppose the government, they are rebels; when they disperse and

6. Yen Ju-i, *San-sheng pien-fang pei-lan* (1830), 12:21–21b, 25; Suzuki, *Shin-chō*, 83.

7. Yen, *San-sheng*, 12:43.

depart, they are civilians once more."[8] The helplessness of the troops was reflected in their brutality toward the civilian population (Ch'ing troops became known by the bloody epithet "red lotus society"), which of course only fueled the rebellion. Reports of Ch'ing commanders were filled with inflated rebel casualty reports and perplexity at the ineffectiveness of military suppression. In 1796 the Hukuang governor-general, Pi Yuan, memorialized that government troops had killed tens of thousands, but that the rebellion was growing ever graver.[9] It was the conviction that regular military formations were not in themselves capable of putting down the rebellion that drove officials to seek auxiliary methods.

The Emergence of Local Defense and Control Systems

In view of the unchanging geographic verities of the region, it is not surprising that officials in the Hupeh-Shensi-Szechwan border area could look back to an administrative tradition that had grown up in this troubled area in Ming times. About 1634 the rebel-fighter (later martyr) Lu Hsiang-sheng (1600–1639) had instituted there a local defense and control system that was partly derived from his experiences fighting rebels in southern Hopeh several years earlier. Lu found that rebellion was nourished by refugeeism and by links between rebels and populace. In response he had stout walls (*chai*) built around selected villages, within which would be gathered the grain supplies of the surrounding countryside. At the approach of rebels the people from nearby villages would be brought within the walls. Around the fortified villages the people would be organized into groups (*t'uan*), each of which would bear the name of the fort to which it was attached. Those villages to be gathered into the P'ing-an *chai*, for instance, would be known collectively as the P'ing-an *t'uan*. Each group would be supervised by a group head (*t'uan-chang*), a local notable selected by the inhabitants. Under each group-head was appointed a drilling-head (*lien-chang*) to train and command a self-defense militia. This system, designed to deprive the rebels of food and recruits, Lu called "clearing the countryside" (*ch'ing-yeh*). Under its full title, "strengthening the   walls and clearing

8. Kung Ching-han, *Tan-ching-chai ch'üan-chi, wen-ch'ao, wai-p'ien* (1826), 1:5–6, 13.

9. Wei Yuan, *Sheng-wu chi* (Ku-wei-t'ang ed., 1842), 9:2b. Yen, *San-sheng*, 4:27.

the countryside" (*chien-pi ch'ing-yeh*), this strategic hamlet approach to rebel control became a standard administrative technique.[10] The term *t'uan-lien* in its modern meaning is first seen in connection with Lu Hsiang-sheng's system.[11]

Within a year after the rebellion's outbreak, officials in the affected area began to work out their own versions of local defense. In 1797 Fang Chi (1765?–1815?) took over the magistracy of Liang-shan, Szechwan, and found the district in imminent danger of being over-run by a number of White Lotus bands. From accounts of local history he learned that in earlier times the people had often taken refuge from invading armies in strongholds called *wu*. Fang was from Anhwei and, unacquainted with local terminology, "wondered about these accounts, thinking that a *wu* was nothing but a hidden nook in the mountains, hardly enough to defend one against bandits. I asked around town and finally someone said, 'a *wu* is the term for an ancient stronghold (*chai*), now in ruins.' That was all I could find out. Then someone told me, 'It is said that there is a place called Niu-t'ou *chai* five miles from town. Why not climb up there and have a look at

10. Lu Hsiang-sheng, *Lu Chung-su-kung chi* (1875), *nien-p'u*, 5b–8b; 2:19–22b, 38–41. See Hibino Takeo's important article, "Gōson bōei to kempeki shōya," *Tōhō gakuhō*, 22:141–155 (Kyoto, 1953). References to Lu's techniques in late Ch'ing writings suggest a direct line of administrative succession between him and nineteenth-century *t'uan-lien* practitioners. Ho Ch'ang-ling, ed., *Huang-ch'ao ching-shih wen-pien* (1886) 82:12; Hu Lin-i, *Hu Wen-chung-kung i-chi* (1875), 55:4. The term *chien-pi ch'ing-yeh* is seen as early as the *Chin-shu* (K'ai-ming ed., 104:1355.4), though it is not known whether it meant a comprehensive system of local control at that time.

11. The term originated during the late seventh century in reference to a state militia system designed for border defense. Under the T'ang system, militia and their families were grouped in special administrative areas under the command of a *t'uan-lien* commissioner (*t'uan-lien-shih*), who, like the powerful military governors (*chieh-tu-shih*) wielded both civil and military authority. Robert des Rotours, *Traité des fonctionnaires et traité de l'armée, traduits de la Nouvelle histoire des T'ang* (Leyden, 1948), 717.

In another border region, the mountainous minority tribal areas of Kwangsi, the term *t'uan-lien* was applied to voluntary, state-sanctioned, but unsubsidized village defense militia during the early Ch'ien-lung reign. Yang Hsi-fu (1701–1768), Kwangsi governor, wrote that the practice was very old and of undeterminable origin. *Huang-ch'ao ching-shih wen-pien* (1886), 88:23–23b. Certain of the institutions that Yang characterized as *t'uan-lien*, such as the *lang-ping*, had apparently originated as state-managed military agricultural colonies. Ku Yen-wu, *T'ien-hsia chün-kuo li-ping shu*, in *Ssu-k'u shan-pen ts'ung-shu*, *ch'u-pien*, ts'e 30, p. 4. The first systematic study of *t'uan-lien* is Franz Michael's "Military Organization and Power Structure of China during the Taiping Rebellion," *Pacific Historical Review*, 18.4, 469–483 (1949).

it?' " Fang did and was delighted to find a small plateau some 360 paces in circumference, set apart from the surrounding forest by steep cliffs, and partially fortified. The stronghold had evidently been erected in Sung times and parts were indeed in ruins but could be filled in with piles of stone. Upon his return Fang ordered that all such strongholds be reported to him and that they be repaired and provisioned with food and weapons. There was much popular skepticism; people objected that most strongholds had no water supplies. Fang replied that long sieges were most unlikely; such a fort could hold a three-day supply of water, and the rebels were unlikely to stay that long, since they were constantly pursued by government troops. Some remained doubtful, so Fang reinforced his defense plan by personally visiting all the strongholds and flogging anyone unwilling to follow orders.

As it turned out, the strongholds of Liang-shan were able to protect not only the country people of the district but a large number of refugees who came streaming in as the rebels approached. The rebels arrived only to find the people fled to the strongholds with their food supplies, and the passes all guarded by a force of local braves (*hsiang-yung*) recruited under official auspices. Following Liang-shan's example, more than 200 forts were built in nearby districts. It appears that although Fang Chi's local defense system was originally based upon available strongholds in the mountains, it was eventually extended to include fortification of villages in the farming areas; it thereby became applicable to areas in which there were no ready-made refuges.[12]

Fang Chi's strategic hamlet strategy was integrally linked to a system of local control and registration, just as Lu Hsiang-sheng's had been. Unlike Lu's system, however, Fang's was based on pre-existing pao-chia divisions. "The area controlled by a *pao-cheng* (that is, the geographical area of a *pao*) is to be taken as a *t'uan*." However, *t'uan* and *pao* had separate leadership and separate registers. The *t'uan*, supervised by one or two *t'uan*-heads, kept a register of able-bodied males aged ten to fifty from which the militia was to be selected. Militiamen drafted from this registration pool were listed in still another register. Thus the *t'uan* in Fang's system was primarily an administration unit for militia conscription. It also had

12. Liang-shan 1867, 6:4–8; for a biography of Fang Chi, see Ch'ien I-chi, ed., *Pei-chuan chi* (1893), 87:13.

surveillance and police functions paralleling those of pao-chia: strangers were "not permitted to enter and reside in the *t'uan*." Inasmuch as pao-chia was, in practice, commonly based on the natural village rather than upon the stipulated decimal divisions, the *t'uan* may probably be understood as a village unit. The *t'uan* were linked to fortified settlements by being grouped into "large *t'uan*" (*ta-t'uan*) each of which comprised up to ten-odd "small *t'uan*" (*hsiao-t'uan*). Each large *t'uan*, headed by a *t'uan* chief (*t'uan-tsung*) was charged with the defense of a fortified settlement. Thus Fang sought to make up for the inadequacy of government military power by providing security for his own people and cutting off their contacts with the rebels by means of a militarized local control system. Fang's was only one of several local control and defense systems launched in the border area during 1797.[13]

On a higher level, the Ch'ing generals Ming-liang and Te-leng-t'ai suggested that the court endorse *chien-pi ch'ing-yeh* and *t'uan-lien* as a general practice. In October 1797 they wrote in a joint memorial that the regular troops were only capable of defending walled administrative cities, while the rebels continued to get food, weapons, and manpower in the market towns and villages. In the valleys, towns and villages could be protected by walls (*pao*) and in the mountains by ramparts (*chai*). Each fortified settlement and its militia could be managed jointly by officials and local gentry and elders. With rebels walled out, and people and food walled in, the regulars would have little trouble defeating starved and isolated White Lotus bands. In 1798 a similar suggestion came from the general Le-pao, who had observed Fang Chi's system in operation. But the court, still hopeful of a standard military solution and wary of the disruptive side effects of such a drastic program, was lukewarm toward such proposals.[14]

The fact that t'uan-lien and *chien-pi ch'ing-yeh* arose in a number of places throughout the White Lotus area in 1797, in slightly variant forms, suggests that they were already well-established elements of the border region's administrative tradition. But these official projects may also be seen as an effort to systematize and control village defense

13. Tseng Tzu-po, magistrate of Nan-ch'ung, Szechwan, was another influential practitioner of *chien-pi ch'ing-yeh*. Some of his regulations are identical to Fang's, but it is not certain which came first. Yen, *San-sheng*, 13:47–52; Szechwan 1816, 116:24b. Fang's regulations are in Yen, *San-sheng*, 13:40b–47b.

14. Hua-sha-na, ed., *Te Chuang-kuo-kung nien-p'u* (1857) 7:38–40. Liang-shan 1867, 6:4–8. *Ch'ing shih-lu, Chia-ch'ing*, 23:3–6.

enterprises already being undertaken by the local elite. Ming-liang and Te-leng-t'ai had cited evidence to show that militia in reliable hands could be a major agency of rebel suppression. One illustrative case was that of Liang Yu-ku, formerly a magistrate in Kwangsi, who had retired to his native district (Hsiang-yang, Hupeh). Liang and his son, a local *t'ung-sheng,* had supervised the building of an earth-wall around the little ferry crossing of Ch'eng-shao-tu and had gathered the surrounding populace inside. A military *sheng-yuan,* Ts'ai Yun-sheng, had in the previous year recruited a band of mer-cenaries (*yung*), which now formed the core of the Ch'eng-shao-tu defense militia. The Liang-Ts'ai enterprise had kept the area free from White Lotus influence, and the court rewarded these local leaders with official ranks.[15] Clearly the prestige, connections, and talents of the local gentry were indispensable to rebel suppression. Despite increasing economic problems and incidence of rebellion, the traditionally dominant elite was still well entrenched in rural China. It was on this foundation that the Ch'ing bureaucrats strove to build their fortress.

After 1797 the *chien-pi ch'ing-yeh* and t'uan-lien strategy was fostered and developed by civil officials predisposed toward it by an inbred distaste for the regular military, until eventually it was taken up by the court and made into a major weapon in the Ch'ing armory. Its most influential practitioner and popularizer was Kung Ching-han (1747–1802), a Fukienese from an eminent official family that had a history of involvement with local militia.[16] Quite apart from the logistic and tactical difficulties of guerrilla warfare, Kung believed the very nature of popular rebellion made regular troops ineffective. The rebels' intricate connections with local communities gave them an advantage impossible to meet with force of arms alone. Population movement compounded the problem: so low had Ch'ing military prestige fallen that whole towns were vacated at the approach of rebels, and wandering bands of refugees were easy prey to White Lotus recruitment. Nor were city fortifications alone a realistic solu-tion. "A *chou* or *hsien* city with its surrounding villages is like a tree

15. Hua-sha-na, ed., *Te Chuang-kuo-kung nien-p'u,* 7:21b–22b, 39b.
16. Kung's essays were cited by the court in later years as official models for rebel-suppression. *Ch'ing shih-lu,* Hsien-feng, 33:15–15b, 34:27. Biographies of Kung are in *Ch'ing-shih lieh-chuan* (Taipei, 1962), 74:25–30; and *Ch'ing-shih* (Taipei, 1961), 5115. Kung's essays on rebel-suppression are in *Tan-ching-chai ch'üan-chi,* 1:1–31.

with its branches and leaves. If the branches and leaves are injured, then the trunk has no defense." It was not just the cities themselves, but the economic and administrative links between city and country-side that had to be defended.[17]

Kung insisted that village fortification be closely supervised by officials: provincial authorities were to appoint eighth or ninth rank functionaries (tso-tsa) to assist magistrates in carrying out chien-pi ch'ing-yeh. Within three months of the plan's inception, when all regulations were drawn up and all new officials appointed, the work of building walls and moving people could begin. Scattered house-holds had to be moved into fortified villages. Expenses of fortification and moving were to be borne by officials, and labor supplied by the people. Grain supplies were to be moved inside stockades and stored in public granaries. If there were rich households with large stocks of grain, "who have difficulty moving it all," the magistrate was to pro-vide funds to buy it: clearly a way of dealing with hoarders. Before moving the people into the forts, the magistrate was to conduct a rigorous pao-chia registration in order to root out White Lotus cells. He was then to choose the leaders of the strongholds from among "gentry or elders," and give them brevet rank. These leaders would then choose a number of deputies "to register and inspect the people, supervise public works, manage money and grain supplies, inspect those leaving and entering, train militiamen, and prepare for de-fense."

To avoid infiltration by rebels, the militia was not to be formed until police registration was complete. Each village was to have a cadre from the regular forces to assist in grouping and training the able-bodied males. The militia was to remain strictly non-professional and defensive, with no more than half its force permitted to leave the stockade to aid nearby villages under attack. Though Kung con-sidered this non-professional militia the cornerstone of his local con-trol system, the regular troops had a role to play. He expected that, once the White Lotus bands were cut off from sources of grain and recruits, they would be easy prey to pursuing Ch'ing battalions; but effective local control was a precondition to victory in the field.

Despite Kung's emphasis on local action, he by no means envisaged a devolution of military power and initiative into the hands of local leaders. The mercenaries (hsiang-yung) he regarded with suspicion

17. Tan-ching-chai, 1:9b, 13.

partly because they were effectively outside regular channels of official control. The militia of the fortified villages, however, were to be under constant control and scrutiny by officials. The heads of the fortified settlements themselves (*chai-chang* and *pao-chang*) were in effect civil officers tied to the regular civil hierarchy by brevet ranks, with duties and responsibilities that encompassed both civil and military affairs. Kung's system thus represented not a devolution of power but a reliance upon civil officials in preference to military and a tying of local defense to the network of bureaucratic accountability.[18]

Another prominent local control expert was Yen Ju-i (1759–1826), a Hunanese with close links to the nascent "statecraft" school of practical scholarship then emerging from the academies of Changsha. Yen began his career campaigning against rebellious Miao tribesmen in the mountainous border region of western Hunan. The policy developed by officials in that area (particularly the magistrate Fu Nai, 1758–1811) relied heavily on military agricultural colonies (*t'un-t'ien*) into which local Han peasants were gathered as a permanent militia to blockade the Miao in their mountain strongholds. Colonies were also set up in "pacified" Miao areas to forestall future disturbances. Yen's experience in Miao areas directly influenced his anti-White Lotus strategy, which was based on the premise that suppression "must jointly emphasize arms and food." Yen proposed that landless peasants and surrendered rebels be grouped into military agricultural colonies, where secure livelihood and military discipline would "transform rebels into loyal subjects" (*hua-tao wei-min*). He found, however, that such colonies were hard to establish in the White Lotus area, and in practice his methods more closely resembled *chien-pi ch'ing-yeh*. Walled villages were units of both mutual responsibility and local defense under the supervision of civil authorities.[19]

Like Kung Ching-han, Yen emphasized police work and effective civil government over conventional military campaigning. His pre-

18. *Tan-ching-chai*, 1:8–9.

19. Yen, *San-sheng*, 12:33, 37b, 41; *Ch'ing-shih*, 4503. Various biographies of Yen are in *Ch'ing-shih lieh-chuan*, 75:45; *Ch'ing-shih*, 4502; Yen Ju-i, *Lo-yuan wen-ch'ao* (preface, 1844), 1:1; Wei Yuan, *Ku-wei-t'ang wai-chi* (1878) 4:9b. Yen's *San-sheng* is the major contemporary geographical work on the White Lotus area. On Fu Nai's anti-Miao policies, see *Huang-ch'ao ching-shih wen-pien* (1886) 88:2b–3; *Miao-chiang t'un-fang shih-lu* (mimeographed ed., Yangchow, 1961) 1:18b–19; Ma Shao-ch'iao, *Ch'ing-tai Miao-min ch'i-i* (Wuhan, 1956), 44–51. Certain of Fu's military techniques later influenced Tseng Kuo-fan: *Tseng Wen-cheng-kung ch'üan-chi* (1876): *Tsou-kao*, 1:56b.

scriptions included, on the one hand, the strengthening of civil authority in rebellious areas by breaking up large districts into smaller ones and by reviving vestigial local police contingents such as the "civilian stalwarts." On the other hand, the promotion of local militia and pao-chia would enable civil authorities to instill a measure of military discipline into the population itself; this was Yen's alternative to disrupting rural society by the intrusion of military force from the outside. Here Yen's debt to the concept of military agricultural colonies is most apparent. A military officer, he suggested, controlled only the few thousand men in his command. But if the civil official gained the people's confidence then "the several tens or several hundreds of thousands of civilians he controls" would be "like soldiers under his parental authority."[20]

Yen's experience in the control of border areas found useful application along the seacoast, a special type of border area. As an adviser to Na-yen-ch'eng (1764–1833), who was transferred from the White Lotus campaigns to the Liang-kuang governor-generalship in 1804, Yen turned his attention to controlling coastal pirates. Pirates, like the White Lotus rebels, called for inner control as much as for outer defense because they, too, depended on links with the populace. T'uan-lien along the coast was accordingly designed as a militarized version of pao-chia. The same decimal units into which the people were divided by pao-chia registration were the bases of militia conscription. Pao-chia officers were placed in command of low-level militia units, as a complement to gentry leadership on higher levels. T'uan-lien, in Yen's prescription, meant not only militia, but rather the whole process of preparing the community to bear arms. Indeed, t'uan-lien sometimes referred only to the preliminary registration and police work: "Once t'uan-lien has been successfully carried out, then military functions can be vested in civilians (*yü-ping yü-min*)." Preparation for defense was an occasion for tightening the screws of local control. Overtly there is a "spirit of defending against external enemies"; covertly there is a "nipping of disloyalty in the bud."[21]

20. *Huang-ch'ao ching-shih wen-pien* (1886) 82:17b.

21. Yen, "Yen-hai t'uan-lien shuo" in *Huang-ch'ao ching-shih wen-pien* (1886) 83:31–33. Na-yen-ch'eng, *Na Wen-i-kung tsou-i* (1834) 11:41. See Na-yen-ch'eng's biography in Arthur W. Hummel, ed., *Eminent Chinese of the Ch'ing Period* (Washington, 1943), 584–587. His *Tsou-i* (11:40–48b) contain documents on his t'uan-lien policy in Liang-kwang. His transfer to Liang-kwang may be seen as one transmission line of t'uan-lien terminology and administrative technique from the White Lotus area to South China.

Thus for Yen, as for Kung Ching-han, local defense was never simply a matter of keeping armed rebels out. Rather, it consisted of establishing clear dividing lines in rural society. These dividing lines (physically, walls and stockades; organizationally, t'uan-lien and pao-chia) enabled officials not only to separate rebels from their sustenance but also to organize and control the "good" villagers in such a way as to prevent their becoming rebels themselves. T'uan-lien was not merely a local defense militia; it existed as much for internal control as for external defense and formed an integral part of a larger administrative system. During the Chia-ch'ing reign, it was hardly a breach of the military monopoly of the state. On the contrary, "t'uan-lien" to Chia-ch'ing officials often meant precisely the opposite: a way to bring spontaneous local militarization into a comprehensive, bureaucratized control apparatus under state supervision.

By 1805 the White Lotus Rebellion was crushed: though it had brought the eighteenth century's golden age to a sudden and violent end, it had never generated the kind of political leadership or the breadth of support that could seriously threaten the dynasty's existence. It so damaged the government's prestige and depleted its treasury, however, that it can fairly be inscribed in that long roll of popular uprisings that, over the course of a century, brought the dynasty to ruin.

Apart from the internal weakness of the rebel organization, the factors that contributed to the Ch'ing victory were several. Added to the local control and defense systems described above were a vigorous, if temporary, revival of the regular forces after the accession of the new emperor in 1799; and the hiring of local mercenaries (*hsiang-yung*) from among the landless and unemployed to supplement the regular troops. These mercenaries were of various types: some were hired by local elite (like Ts'ai Yun-sheng) and were used entirely for local defense. More highly militarized were those units—sometimes several thousands strong—hired by magistrates and prefects (like Fang Chi) to protect their jurisdictions. Though the latter type was numerous in the rebellion's early years, the expense of keeping them proved too great for most local administrators to sustain; beginning in 1798, many were disbanded and returned to their home villages to serve as local defense militia.

More highly militarized still were the mercenaries recruited to accompany the regular government forces on campaign. They were still called *hsiang-yung* (literally, local braves), but their connections with their home communities were decisively broken. Though more effective fighters than the government battalions, these mercenaries were an expensive and dangerous expedient. Some were of outlaw origin themselves and proved impossible to discipline; their loyalty could be secured only with lavish bonuses, which the hard-pressed regime could ill afford. Local administrators like Kung Ching-han and Yen Ju-i harbored deep suspicions of them; as Yen put it, such men "became accustomed to killing and burning" and were hard to reintegrate into civil life. After the rebellion was crushed, some 10,000 of them were brought into the regular Green Standard battalions, because a mass demobilization was considered too dangerous. But the government's fears about these troops were fully justified when a series of mutinies arose among them in 1806 and 1807.[22]

Despite its grave effects upon the dynasty's prestige and finances, the White Lotus Rebellion had little immediate effect upon its military institutions. Though the Banners and Green Standard were seen to be weak and corrupt, they continued for nearly half a century to serve as the empire's regular armies. The experience with mercenaries was disquieting to both the central and provincial bureaucracies, and the hiring of such units never became a part of official policy. Nevertheless, one significant strand of policy did emerge from the White Lotus experience: the highly bureaucratized local defense and control systems devised by such men as Fang Chi, Yen Ju-i, and Kung Ching-han were preserved in the storehouse of administrative precedent and played a prominent role in official thinking at the time of the Taiping Rebellion half a century later.

B. Ch'ing Militia Policy on the Eve of the Taiping Rebellion

By the late eighteenth century Ch'ing society was entering a phase of extreme instability. Of this fact the White Lotus Rebellion had been an unmistakable indication, though its limited area and uncertain message had served effectively to soften its impact on official thinking. Nevertheless, the basic realities of the new age had not

22. Suzuki, *Shin-chō*, 189–196, 214–217. Yen Ju-i, *San-sheng*, 12:24. A notable example of the kind of mercenary force that became attached to the government battalions is the private army of Lo Szu-chü (1764?–1840), an ex-bandit who became one of the most dogged antagonists of the White Lotus. Lo was ultimately brought into the regular military hierarchy. *Ch'ing-shih*, 4427–4429; *Ch'ing-shih lieh-chuan*, 39:21; Lo Erh-kang, *Hsiang-chün hsin-chih*, (Changsha, 1939) 148–149.

escaped the more sharp-eyed of the elite. The staggering rise of China's population, the attendant rise in commodity prices, the virtual exhaustion of the supply of new land, the ruin of small-holders by fragmentation of inheritance and their descent into debt and tenancy: all are themes visible in official and unofficial writings of the eighteenth century. Hung Liang-chi, whose hardheaded, pessimistic social analyses do indeed have a Malthusian tone, warned that one of the inevitable results of these trends was the creation of a growing mass of people who could find no place in the existing economic and social system. These rejected groups had to seek subsistence outside it in outlawry of various types and to seek social attachments in heterodox forms: the local gang, the secret-society brotherhood, the roving banditti.[23]

Though such situations had existed before in periods of administrative decline, it may well be asked whether the scale of late Ch'ing social problems did not spell disaster of a new sort for traditional Chinese society as a whole. The population explosion alone might lead to this conclusion, quite apart from such exogenous factors as the increasing monetization of China's economy by the inflow of foreign silver. If it was true that the level of crowding, of economic insecurity and rural disorder was something unique in China's history, then it may be that only a new approach to problems of local control and military security could avert the complete dissolution of the traditional order. The eruption in the White Lotus area had posed the problem in miniature. It was not simply that local government was growing corrupt and decrepit. Rather, traditional mechanisms of civil and military control were now incapable of dealing with a huge rural population in which traditional social relationships were rent by an increasingly desperate economic competition. Though the state itself was constitutionally unable to respond creatively to the problems of the new age, a number of scholars and officials were convinced that changes were needed.

The Ch'ing Military and Rebellion: Two Views

Ho Ch'ang-ling, a leader of the "statecraft school" of practical scholarship, was himself an official of long experience. Together with

23. Chapter 1 of Suzuki Chūsei's *Shin-chō* is a brilliant and concise treatment of the social problems of the eighteenth century. See also Ho Ping-ti, *Studies on the Population of China, 1368–1953*, 270–275, on population problems as they appeared to scholars of the period.

such men as T'ao Chu and Lin Tse-hsu, he belonged to that coterie of vigorous and conscientious administrators who shored up the sagging imperial structure at a time when the bureaucracy as a whole was deeply demoralized. Ho had ample experience of social disintegration in Kweichow, one of the empire's most unruly provinces, where he served as governor from 1836 to 1845. His view of the military system there was anything but reassuring. Its contribution to the task of bandit suppression had been minimal. Those granted imperial audience for bandit suppression included ten times as many civilians as military. Expenditures for military salaries were ten times those for civil, and military personnel were a hundred times more numerous; yet the military insisted on passing off responsibility for internal order onto civilian officials, saying that suppressing bandits (*tao*) was not their job. Inasmuch as any internal uprising could be labeled with the character *tao*, it is clear that there were few responsibilities the military could not effectively disclaim.

Ho's strictures amounted to an admission that the internal garrison system could not deal with the kind of local disorder out of which larger rebellion grew. The kind of local heterodox militarization represented by secret-society gangs, border-region bandits, or illegal salt or opium conveyors, was effectively outside the jurisdiction of the regular military, which could only be brought into play when rebellion had already grown to proportions that menaced the empire as a whole. Ho was aware that the high and increasing incidence of outlawry could only lead to more serious trouble and was not content to see it continue. He proposed, therefore, that the regular garrisons should establish additional contingents, amounting to between 5 and 10 percent of their total strength, which would have the special responsibility of catching bandits. They would have none of those miscellaneous duties, such as guarding prisoners, escorting shipments of tax silver, and the like, that burdened the regular troops. More unorthodox still, the special contingents should be hired from the underworld itself: men already committed to a violent mode of life, who would be familiar with bandit ways and bandit whereabouts. There is no indication that this proposal was ever put into effect officially, but it suggests the extent to which existing military institutions had become irrelevant to the task of maintaining order and the status quo in rural China.[24]

24. Ho Ch'ang-ling, "Chin-sheng hsia-yu ko-ying she pu-tao ping-ting-i" in Lo Ju-huai, ed., *Hu-nan wen-cheng* (1871), 14:8–11.

Tso Tsung-t'ang, another Hunanese scholar intimately connected to the statecraft school (later an eminent military leader and statesman), was deeply disturbed by the way China's military system had functioned in the Opium War. The problem went beyond incompetence: at fault was the practice whereby garrisons of the interior provinces were transferred on an ad hoc basis to meet threats along the coast. The garrison forces, he wrote, which were distributed in a network of small contingents throughout the provinces, had the mission of bolstering state authority and damping down rebellion. If they were transferred out to meet emergencies elsewhere, dangerous gaps would appear in the net of local control. It had been just such a gap (caused when Green Standard battalions were transferred out of Hupeh to suppress a Miao rebellion in the Hunan-Kweichow border area) that had made possible the uprising of the White Lotus Society in 1796. Now, fifty years later, the menace of a major new rebellion was still inchoate and undiscernable; yet the time might come when the removal of a local garrison would release explosive social forces with unspeakable results.

What Tso was saying, in effect, was that the internal garrison system was no longer capable of being mobilized as an expeditionary force, because rural society was now too unstable. It could barely keep the lid on the pot by staying in its prescribed locales and attending solely to the task of internal control. "If there is not a thorough reform in the near future," he wrote in 1840, "I fear that the situation may deteriorate beyond repair."

Tso thought the only solution was provincial self-sufficiency. He went on to advocate a vigorous program of military strengthening against the British, including the recruitment of naval mercenaries from among the fishing population, the training of elite contingents (*ch'in-ping*) by provincial officials, the building of forts, and the founding of new shipyards and munitions factories. These measures would presumably enable the coastal provinces to deal with the barbarians on their own without denuding the interior provinces of their garrison forces.[25]

Seen from the standpoint of the court in Peking, the military emergency could be dealt with in several ways, none wholly satisfactory. One possibility was a large expansion of the regular military system, which the now impoverished treasury could not afford; an-

---

25. Tso Tsung-t'ang, *Tso Wen-hsiang-kung ch'üan-chi* (reprint of the 1892 ed., Taipei, 1964), *shu-tu*, 1:10b–11b.

other was the ad hoc recruitment of mercenaries to meet particular emergencies, an expedient the court did adopt, though this was regarded as highly dangerous in view of the disruption that always attended their demobilization. A third possibility was to form a militia system on the local level, a policy question much discussed during the desperate decade of the 1840's and one that was complicated by the violent popular response to the British presence in the coastal provinces.

Militia and the Barbarian Problem

The tide of local militarization that swept the Canton area during the Opium War was not generated by officialdom but was a challenge to which officialdom had to respond. For the remainder of the decade, official views of local militia were in large measure conditioned by the experience of the famous incident of May 1841 in which gentry-led militia near Canton trapped a small British force in the countryside north of the walled city just as a truce was being arranged. The appearance of some 7,500 armed peasants on the hills around the village of San-yuan-li opened a chaotic skirmish in which the British lost one man killed and fifteen wounded. The peasant militia (which shortly grew to as many as 20,000 from 100 or more villages) had beaten back the intruders; thus they had demonstrated the power of an aroused and righteous people to cope with vicious barbarians whom the regular government dared not confront. If the San-yuan-li incident outraged the British, it terrified the Chinese officials, who feared, not unjustifiedly, that the xenophobic fervor of the populace would provoke the barbarians to renewed violence. A deputation consisting of the Canton prefect and two local magistrates hurried to the scene and persuaded the elite leaders to disperse. The militia faded back to their villages and the British were enabled to extricate their beleaguered companies.[26]

Prior to San-yuan-li, Canton officialdom had encouraged gentry-sponsored militia organizations in the Canton area; but now, a new set of considerations came to the fore. The superiority of British arms was bringing provincial officials to understand that the future

26. The definitive account of San-yuan-li and its context is Frederic Wakeman's *Strangers at the Gate: Social Disorder in South China, 1839–1861* (Berkeley, 1966), to which I am indebted for this episode. See also Suzuki Chūsei, "Shimmatsu jōgai undō no kigen," *Shigaku zasshi*, 62.10:1–28 (1953).

of the empire—to say nothing of their own careers—depended on their ability to "manage" (appease) the barbarians and avoid military defeats.

Ch'i-ying, the Manchu noble who was to become the star barbarian-manager of his day, had ample opportunity to observe the military power of the British as they pressed their attack up the Yangtze in 1842. By the time he assumed the Liang-kiang governor-generalship, he was convinced of the need to avoid further hostilities and wary of militia that might provoke them. In March 1843, he denounced a proposal by Li Hsiang-fen, acting director-general of grain transport, that t'uan-lien be set up along both banks of the Yangtze, from I-cheng eastward to Yangchow, to man artillery against the British. He stated that in principle it was a fine idea to "entrust military functions to civilians," but that it would be unwise as practical policy. Yamen clerks were sure to get involved and cause turmoil. Honest people had regular occupations and no time for military drill, whereas vicious types would flock to join. These vicious types would simply gorge themselves at the expense of the rich, practice boxing and fencing, and stir up trouble. "If in addition you put them in charge of cannon, the evils will be even more unspeakable" (that is, they would involve local officials in anti-British incidents). Though officials might appoint *t'uan* heads to control them, yet it was well known that only riffraff were willing to assume such duties (just as no respectable person would care to become a pao-chia headman). "If there is one such no-good, that is enough to cause trouble; if you gather innumerable no-goods, and depute power to them, and distribute them all over the riverbanks and seacoast, they would not only be useless for defense, but also be disturbing to the localities." When the situation required, respectable local leadership (gentry) would come to the fore and provide for local defense, as had the righteous people of Kwangtung in the recent past.[27]

It is significant that, to Ch'i-ying, "t'uan-lien" obviously meant a bureaucratically organized, pao-chia-based system of local militarization, rather than a spontaneous, unofficial, gentry-led system. Ch'i-ying presumed that officials could handle and restrain gentry leadership, just as Canton officials had restrained the gentry at San-yuan-li. But to make local militia a large-scale government-sponsored project was to traffic with the dark and dangerous forces lurking in

27. *Ch'ou-pan i-wu shih-mo* (Peking, 1930), Tao-kuang, 65:49–50.

rural society, with unpredictable consequences for both the rural status quo and the conduct of barbarian management. Once the gentry had come forward, the official might even enlist their services in avoiding anti-foreign incidents.[28]

Only a month after Ch'i-ying's memorial disparaging t'uan-lien, there was pressure brought upon the court to institute t'uan-lien throughout the empire. A provincial censor, T'ien Jun, asked the court's sanction for local militia forces "in order to prevent disasters in the wake [of the Opium War] and to save military expenses." This, however, was to be militia of a different sort. First, T'ien Jun had in mind precisely the kind of local power vacuum that had worried Tso Tsung-t'ang. The English barbarians had just been pacified and, in preparing for future emergencies, internal security had to be strengthened. It was far safer to have constant t'uan-lien in the countryside than to recruit and transfer regular troops on an ad hoc basis. Second, this t'uan-lien was to be entirely in the hands of gentry. Gentry leaders would be allowed to raise funds through a special tax on land, and no monies were to pass through official hands. "Talented men of good reputation" were to be chosen as troop leaders.[29] T'ien Jun's initiative probably represented a move by local elite to get the ear of the court over the heads of cautious local administrators.

Initially, the court's reaction was favorable. But first the throne referred the proposal to a number of civil and military officials in coastal provinces and solicited their reactions. By late July 1843, enough adverse response had come back to convince the court to drop the idea. A barrage of memorials made it clear that high provincial officials had no use for irregular local militarization, fearing that it would be as disruptive to rural society as it would be useless for serious fighting. Though most of the overt concern was over the prospect of internal disorder, it is probable that the barbarian problem lurked in the background. Coastal officials could not afford to let the delicate machinery of barbarian management slip out of their hands. For the next several years their fearfulness was echoed by the court, which not only refrained from endorsing local

28. This was suggested by Ch'i-ying a few years later as governor-general of Liang-kuang; *Ch'ing shih-lu*, Tao-kuang, 442:25b.

29. *Ch'ing shih-lu*, Tao-kuang, 390:30–31b; *Ch'ou-pan i-wu shih-mo*, Tao-kuang, 67:10. On Tien Jun see Lin-t'ung 1890, 3:2.

militia but encouraged officials to restrain them and especially to keep them from attacking foreigners who turned up in the interior.[30]

The militia problem took on a new twist during the controversy over whether the British were to be allowed inside the walled city of Canton: a right (so they thought) conceded them by treaty but which the Chinese were determined to withhold. Governor-general Ch'i-ying, pressed between the demands of the British and the xenophobia of the Cantonese, wavered and temporized. Unofficial village militia units—carrying on the San-yuan-li tradition—repeatedly attacked stray Britishers in the countryside near Canton; the British in turn demanded that Ch'i-ying control the populace and punish the offenders. In 1848, as the situation gradually slipped out of control, the court removed Ch'i-ying from his post and decided to try another barbarian-manager. Ch'i-ying's successor, Hsu Kuang-chin, now assumed the delicate task of cementing relations with the aroused elite of the Canton area, while at the same time dissuading the British from opening a full-scale attack to gain entry to the city. The key was to encourage the gentry-led militia movement enough to persuade the British that the fanatical populace could not be controlled, without actually precipitating a British attack. At length he succeeded: gambling on British restraint, he announced (falsely) that he had been forbidden by the throne to open the city. The British, under instructions from London, did not press the issue to war.[31]

Nevertheless, despite Hsu Kuang-chin's momentary triumph, the net effect of the experience of the 1840's was to reinforce the suspicion held by both the metropolitan and provincial bureaucracies toward irregular military forces. Even after 1850, when rebellion became the state's most fearful preoccupation, this cautious view persisted (see Chapter IV.D.); and only overwhelming events could bring about any change in it.

An Official Model of Local Militarization

The violence of the Cantonese militia movement must indeed have left scars upon the official mind, because from that context emerged

---

30. *Ch'ing shih-lu*, Tao-kuang, 393:21; 394:36b–37; *Ch'ou-pan i-wu shih-mo*, Tao-kuang, 67:10; 68:33; 77:39b.

31. See the excellent account by Wakeman, *Strangers at the Gate*, 71–105.

a model of local militarization that was to be the most influential of its day, one firmly founded in official control and bureaucratic organization. Hsu Nai-chao (d. 1860?) was Kwangtung director of studies when he published his miscellany *Min-kuo-chai ch'i-chung* (Seven titles from the Min-kuo studio) in 1849. This disaster manual included the *Wu-pei chi-yao* (Essentials of military preparedness), plus a work on famine relief, two works on flood control, and finally two famous treatises on troop training and military organization by the Ming general, Ch'i Chi-kuang. The *Wu-pei chi-yao*, a broad gleaning of wisdom on local defense drawn mostly from Ming and Ch'ing authors, is divided into two parts: one on city defense (*Ch'eng-shou chi-yao*) and another on village defense (*Hsiang-shou chi-yao*).[32] The *Hsiang-shou chi-yao* is a uniquely useful document because of its high official backing and wide influence. In 1850 Hsu Kuang-chin distributed the collection to local officials in Kwangtung and Kwangsi. Three years later it was officially commended by the throne and distributed throughout the provinces, and evidence of its use is found in local sources.[33] Its authoritative sponsorship makes it the nearest thing we have to an official model of local militarization on the eve of the Taiping Rebellion.

Official thinking on t'uan-lien, as reflected in Hsu's compendium, stressed bureaucratic authority, in which leadership elements were interchangeable at the will of civil officials (who were of course interchangeable themselves) and were bound into a skein of formal regulations. The local magistrate was to be the unquestioned head of the local militia. Not only was he to appoint and dismiss the leaders of local units, he was also to be the commander of the district militia in times of emergency. His relationship to t'uan-lien leaders was in some respects similar to his relationship to pao-chia headmen: the functionaries of both systems held their posts at the magistrate's pleasure and were considered parts of the official system of subdistrict

32. Hsu, from Hangchow, was one of five eminent brothers, including Hsu Nai-chi, famous for his role in the great opium debates of the 1830's; and Hsu Nai-p'u, a widely respected official and author of a work on techniques of local administration, *Huan-hai chih-nan* (A guidebook for officialdom; 1859). Hsu Nai-chao served briefly as governor of Kiangsu in 1853. Thereafter, in alternating phases of favor and disgrace he served in various other posts in the Yangtze area until his death in 1860. Hangchow 1898, 126:36b.

33. *Ch'ing shih-lu*, Hsien-feng, 20:17; Liu Chin-tsao, ed., *Ch'ing-ch'ao hsu wen-hsien t'ung-k'ao* (Shanghai, 1936), 9620; Kiukiang 1874, 24:5b.

administration.[34] The magistrate's control over militia was bolstered by his possession of accurate, up-to-date registers. Fang Chi's system of dual registers, one for the pool of draftable males and another for those actually drawn into service, was given prominent place in the official model. Fang's reliance upon the administrative base of pao-chia gave official t'uan-lien a distinctly bureaucratic flavor.[35]

Along with bureaucratic control went a low level of militarization. In the official view, the primary meaning of *t'uan* was not a unit of militia, but the administration unit from which the militia was conscripted and through which it was controlled. Tied to the *t'uan* of their own village areas, t'uan-lien militiamen were notably immobile and non-professional. Hiring gangs of outside toughs to serve as militia was expressly forbidden: "When selecting militiamen, use men from their own *t'uan* [to defend their own *t'uan* areas]." Such militiamen were strictly for village defense, and no more than half of such a contingent might leave to aid nearby settlements under attack.[36]

For all its bureaucratic rigor, the official t'uan-lien model embodied certain important ambiguities. The nature of these ambiguities can best be appreciated by examining more closely the relationship between pao-chia and t'uan-lien, a relationship central to the official theory of local militarization. It will be remembered that Yen Ju-i had used lower-level pao-chia functionaries as t'uan-lien leaders; and that other officials of the Chia-ch'ing period (like Fang Chi) had used pao-chia's administrative base to delimit *t'uan* areas. Ch'i-ying, no doubt drawing upon the precedents of the White Lotus period, understood t'uan-lien to mean a bureaucratically organized local militia system closely related to pao-chia. Were the two systems simply aspects of one another?

On the contrary, it appears that Hsu Nai-chao was at pains to distinguish t'uan-lien and pao-chia from one another. Both, he thought, were absolutely essential to village defense, but each had its own function to perform. Pao-chia, he wrote, "emphasizes division": it "divided"

34. Hsu, *Hsiang-shou*, 1:2, 3:7. In some t'uan-lien regulations, t'uan-lien leaders were to be given special wooden seals of authority (*ch'o-chi*) of a type commonly distributed to pao-chia headmen. Huang En-t'ung, *Yueh-tung sheng-li hsin-tsuan* (1846), 5:38a-b.

35. Hsu, *Hsiang-shou*, 3:1b–2.

36. Hsu, *Hsiang-shou*, 3:1–3.

the populace by superimposing artificial decimal divisions upon it. It "divided" natural loyalties by mutual surveillance and group liability. Once pao-chia was in force, one could "divide the good from the bad." But defense was more than a matter of police control. A community compartmented and controlled by pao-chia was not necessarily capable of defending itself, for "local defense requires uniting power and firming the popular will." T'uan-lien "emphasizes unity." The mobilization of a community to defend against outside enemies required a unifying of public sentiment.[37]

Here was the essence of the control–defense duality. If one were to put it in the vocabulary of the modern political purge, it would involve a sequence of unity–struggle–unity. Purge must precede unity, for it was to be unity on the terms of the established order, not unity of some undetermined quality. The arming of a militia and the solidification of the village could take place only after the security system had done its work. Only after a community was well sorted out could the authorities "entrust military functions to civilians." This was one of the curious and characteristic ambiguities of official militia theory: nothing could be more legalistic and coercive than pao-chia in its approved version; nothing could be more spontaneous and voluntaristic than the ideal picture of t'uan-lien, Yet, if local militarization were to occur within the perimeters of the established order, both were needed.

Much of this theoretical complexity arose from the fact that local defense inevitably brought out the contradiction between class divisions and community solidarity. A rural settlement, whose very existence was defined and perpetuated by kinship bonds and economic interdependence, had a natural interest in community defense. But such a settlement was invariably stratified in some degree, with some richer and some poorer; commonly with some landlords and some tenants. How was the community to be welded into a self-defending unit when some of its inhabitants had virtually nothing to defend in the way of property and harbored more deep-seated hostility toward landlords and usurers of their own settlement than toward secret-society or bandit intruders? The pao-chia system was an official effort to ensure that the villagers formed no links with heterodox groups, sheltered no suspicious outsiders. But an effective local defense effort

37. Hsu, *Hsiang-shou*, 1:1, 1:9.

required something more positive: a genuine reinforcing of kinship bonds and community feeling.

Consequently the official model was suffused with utopianism, designed precisely to further community solidarity and achieve the "unifying" effect of t'uan-lien. Hsu cited the Ming official Lü K'un (1526–1618), an influential political theorist, who considered local militia the highest manifestation of social harmony. The way to save the community was to "bring the people's hearts together." Lü pointed out that, whereas local bureaucrats were invariably outsiders and would soon be posted elsewhere, "we local people of the villages and 'well-fields' who have our graves, our relatives, our houses and our fields here," have an abiding natural interest in local defense. Even the poor had an interest in defending their villages, he wrote, for bandits made no social distinctions among their victims and all would suffer. In Lü's exhortations are echoes of the Confucian utopia, in which social antagonisms are submerged by common dangers, and compulsion overshadowed by voluntarism.[38]

Another important difference between t'uan-lien and pao-chia was the role of the scholar-gentry. As Hsiao Kung-ch'üan has pointed out, the degree-holding elite were not supposed to assume posts in the pao-chia system, partly because pao-chia was to act as a counterweight to their dominant local influence.[39] Despite rare exceptions,[40] it was generally true that pao-chia posts were assigned to commoners. With t'uan-lien, however, the situation was quite different: the cooperation of the elite was essential, and the leadership of t'uan-lien, at least on upper levels, was officially considered a gentry function.[41] The fact that t'uan-lien, in contrast to pao-chia, recognized and relied upon gentry leadership suggests the underlying weakness of bureaucratic authority in village China and the comparative strength of other forms of social organization. While pao-chia might be made to work to some extent in good times, it was not equal to the demands of bad times. Its bureaucratic, formalistic lines of authority were too weak to con-

38. Hsu, *Hsiang-shou*, 5:1b. For a similar effort to interest the poor in local defense, see Changsha 1871, 15:18.

39. Hsiao Kung-ch'üan, *Rural China: Imperial Control in the Nineteenth Century* (Seattle, 1960), 68.

40. Hsu, *Hsiang-shou*, 2:2. The process by which the elite became increasingly involved in pao-chia management during the late nineteenth century is discussed in Chapter IV.B.

41. Hsu, *Hsiang-shou*, 1:2, 1:4.

tain severe social and military crises. By contrast the natural ascendancy of the elite in their communities (only partly dependent on their formal state-sanctioned privileges) could survive many a shock. Thus, for all its bureaucratic structure, t'uan-lien drew upon non-bureaucratic sources of local power that pao-chia specifically shunned.

For all its utopian embellishments, and its mitigation of bureaucratic by personalistic authority, the official view of t'uan-lien was unshakable in its insistence on a low level of militarization and ultimate official control. This view represented a selective approach to the records of the White Lotus period, a clear sympathy with civil bureaucrats such as Kung Ching-han and Yen Ju-i, and a distaste for irregular mercenary troops, the *hsiang-yung*. Indeed, the *hsiang-yung* never found a respectable place in the official model, because of their unruly record and their perilous implications. Nor was the importance of the gentry ever to overshadow the supremacy of the regular bureaucrats. Like many other gentry enterprises, local defense was seen as simply one of those necessary tasks that the bureaucracy could not perform itself. One interesting rationalization of the t'uan-lien system was "official supervision and gentry management" (*kuan-tu shen-pan*), which left the gentry an ambiguous but definitely subordinate role to fill.[42]

Most important of all, however, was the clear implication that t'uan-lien was really a peripheral branch of the state bureaucracy itself. The investing of elite leaders with brevet ranks, the insistence on accurate registration, and the constant linking of militarization to the methods and administrative format of pao-chia, all point to this conclusion. Lying in the background of this conception was the long historical tradition of state involvement in militia management. From this tradition grew the idea that the mobilization of the populace for militia service was one of the state's proper functions. The use of the *t'uan* as an instrument of militia conscription and local control was plainly an outgrowth of the *t'uan's* historical origins as an administration unit in a state-controlled military system. To most of its early proponents, t'uan-lien seemed not a concession to newly arisen local interests, but a way of tightening the official grip on rural areas by reasserting the

42. Pa-ling 1891, 19:17. This formula calls to mind the similar phraseology *kuan-tu shang-pan* (official supervision and merchant management) used in the operation of the salt monopoly and later borrowed for use in early industrial enterprise.

state's traditional concern with compulsory, bureaucratically organized systems of conscription and control. It was not the savage patriotism of San-yuan-li, but the stern bureaucratic ethos of state militia that dominated the official model of local militarization.

III. THE STRUCTURE OF LOCAL MILITARIZATION IN SOUTH AND CENTRAL CHINA

A. Scales of Local Organization

The t'uan-lien system, as it emerged in the mid-nineteenth century, was a confluence of two historic streams: one, the administrative tradition of border-area officials, transmitted from Lu Hsiang-sheng through Fang Chi, Kung Ching-han, Yen Ju-i, and others, who sought to strengthen bureaucratic control over the countryside; and the other, the spontaneous militarization of the local elite who sought to protect their communities, their property, and their way of life. These two streams were, we may surmise, never wholly unconnected. Administrative codes influenced the structure and terminology of gentry defense enterprises but were themselves drawn partly from observation of local practice. After the White Lotus Rebellion the term t'uan-lien came increasingly into local use to refer to the gentry's own village defense organizations. But t'uan-lien had also become, by the end of the Chia-ch'ing reign, a marginal but clearly identifiable part of the Ch'ing state machine, complete with a body of administrative precedent. Thus by the time the mid-century crisis broke upon Chinese society, t'uan-lien had already assumed its characteristic ambiguous nature: it was hedged about with official codes, yet tied to the shifting, uncodable requirements of local practice. It is now the practice of local militarization that we must examine.

Our discussion in this part, and the next, will principally concern those forms of militarization undertaken by the orthodox elite. The militarization of heterodox groups will not be taken up in detail until

Chapter V. We shall adopt this approach in full knowledge that orthodox and heterodox militarization took place side by side and in close interaction with one another. Both socially and chronologically, they were part of the same process of community disintegration. But there is some justification for treating the orthodox side first, and in greater detail: the activities of the elite are incomparably better documented. In local gazetteers, official documents, and the collected works of individuals, we have a very full picture of how the elite rallied its forces against rebellion. Quite apart from the fact that they (temporarily, at least) won the battle, the literate elite naturally dominated the written record. Their adversaries, less literate and much less fortunate, left behind them a very sparse documentation: even the literate leadership and bureaucracy of the Taiping Kingdom left relatively few written records, because their gentry conquerors made sure that most of their documentary remains perished with them. The result of this disparity is that we can perceive, in the militarization of the orthodox elite, patterns of organization that are not immediately apparent in the scattered evidence from the other side. It is possible that patterns derived from the study of orthodox groups will make the patterns of heterodox militarization more discernable and will in the end make evident a general pattern of local militarization that covers both sides.

Simplex and Multiplex Scales of Village Militarization

The more one looks into the organization of Chinese society, the less one is impressed with the image of "mutually isolated," "self-sufficient" villages from which the various Oriental Society analyses begin.[1] In all spheres of life, militarization included, Chinese communities were bound together in networks of relationship that stretched from village to neighboring village, to market town, to district seat, and beyond. These relationships assumed certain conventional forms that differed greatly in nomenclature between one region and another but which were in many respects standard in both scale and function.

The basic unit of local military organization was the single village, the smallest defensible entity in the Chinese countryside. Chinese villages exhibit wide differences in size and density, not only through

1. As an example, see Sanō Manabu's *Shin-chō shakai shi,* I (Tokyo, 1947), 92. Actually Sanō's analysis is more complicated than his premises would seem to dictate.

gross interregional variation, but also within a single area, depending on those social and economic factors that govern village life: the fertility of the soil, the size and wealth of kinship groups, the nearness and convenience of transport. One can give but a general estimate of their size as varying between several hundred and several thousand persons.[2] It was a village's good fortune were it compact and well situated for defense, and the enclosure of such villages by walls was a common event during the chaotic nineteenth century. Though a brick or masonry wall was normally seen surrounding an administrative city, the walling of villages and market towns varied with the political stability of the times. Village defenses might be variously constructed, depending on local wealth and resources: stone ramparts in the hills, walls of tamped earth or brick in the flatland. In wide areas of the south, villages were nearly all walled by the mid-1850's.[3] The building of earth walls around villages provided the physical basis for the Nien Rebellion in the north central provinces during the 1850's and 60's.[4]

Not every village was physically defensible, nor did every village have the two other requisites for defense: effective leadership and surplus wealth. It was the village with these assets that gave rise to the smallest nucleus of local militarization: the simplex *t'uan,* or local defense association, sometimes known in official parlance as a "small *t'uan,*" (*hsiao-t'uan*). Through this body the local leadership raised and disbursed funds, recruited militia, and managed various other aspects of community defense. Leaders on this level were often lower degree holders—*sheng-yuan* or *chien-sheng*[5]—or those degree aspirants,

2. Hsiao Kung-ch'üan presents a large body of information on village size for the nineteenth century, but much of it remains to be systematized. *Rural China,* 12–20, 560–565.

3. Yü-lin 1894, 18:28. The terminology of walls was far from standardized and showed much ambiguity and overlapping of usage. One writer notes that "a *pao* [generally a type of earthwall] is really the same as a *ch'eng* [the wall of an administrative city]. With respect to a district seat, the term is *ch'eng*; with respect to villages and market towns, the term is *pao.*" Hsueh Ch'uan-yuan, *Fang-hai pei-lan* (1810), 9:3. Other terms for defensive walls were *chai* (rampart—the ideograph suggests a wooden stockade, but in practice stone seems to have been the rule); *yü* (an earthwall); *wei* (small defensive enclosures in general); and these do not exhaust the list of local variants. The name of the defensive wall was commonly part of the name of the settlement itself, e.g., Chang-chia-wei. On walled settlements see also Kuei-hsien 1894, 1:5b–6b.

4. See Chiang Siang-tse, *The Nien Rebellion* (Seattle, 1954), 32–44.

5. For a detailed description of academic degrees and the steps by which they were attained, consult Chang Chung-li, *The Chinese Gentry.*

the *t'ung-sheng*. Such leaders might also be holders of purchased brevet rank. But the leadership of simplex t'uan was by no means confined to men with formal degree status, and we can find in the record many examples of commoners who, by virtue of their wealth and community influence, were functionally indistinguishable from titled scholars in community defense. Considerations of this sort lead one to doubt the utility of an overly formal definition of elite status in rural China.[6]

Though the simplex *t'uan* was commonly based upon a single village, it sometimes came about that such a village served as an organizational nucleus for a small cluster of neighboring settlements. A village with the leadership and resources to fortify itself might provide a haven for the populace of its less fortunate neighbors; a few small and weak communities might thereby be able to pool their manpower for a defense militia. In P'an-yü and Nan-hai districts near Canton, for example, it is fairly certain that the simplex unit (known locally as *hsiang*) was frequently a small cluster of settlements rather than a single village.[7] Configurations differed greatly from region to region, depending on population density, communications, and kinship patterns; but the basic pattern of the simplex *t'uan* must be generally conceived as being defined by the single village.

Nevertheless, the requirements of local defense inevitably brought forth larger scales of organization. To overwhelm the defenses of an isolated village was a relatively simple business; but it was riskier to penetrate a confederation of fortified settlements where one's flanks and rear were constantly exposed to attack. Though the militia of a simplex *t'uan* posed no great threat of numbers, a confederation could concentrate men from an area of many square miles and thus

6. Maurice Freedman has made a convincing case for the definition of the local elite by functional as well as by formal criteria. *Lineage Organization in Southeastern China* (London, 1958), 53–55. There is ample evidence that in simplex-level militarization commoners often had leadership roles indistinguishable from those of lower degree holders. See for instance *Wu-yang t'uan-lien chi-shih* in Wu-yang 1888, supplement, chüan 2. Further illustration of commoners' roles in local militarization is shown in Figure 13.

7. It seems unlikely that *hsiang* can be equated in all cases with "village," as Frederic Wakeman suggests in *Strangers at the Gate,* 39. A list of donors to the Sheng-p'ing she (see Figure 2) shows that most *hsiang* contained several lineages; in Ta-lang hsiang, for instance, there were at least four lineages surnamed Hsieh, at least one Liu, at least two Kuo, and at least one Huang. In an area where single-lineage villages were the rule, this is a clear indication that more than one settlement was involved.

change the balance of forces very quickly. For these reasons the confederation of up to a score or more villages—sometimes called a
"large *t'uan*"—was a natural and virtually universal form of local
defense in rural China. Such a multi-village confederation I shall
call a "multiplex *t'uan*."

The head bureau (*tsung-chü*) of a multiplex *t'uan*, often located
at a standard market town, was commonly headed by at least one
member of the gentry. A bureau was fortunate if one of its leaders
belonged to the gentry's upper strata; the prestige of the provincial
graduate (*chü-jen*) or metropolitan graduate (*chin-shih*) could overspread a wide area and could serve as a link between rural society and
officialdom. It should be mentioned that the term *tsung-chü* was not
connected with militarization alone but had the more general significance of any office set up for a specific local project, usually
involving fund raising (such as dike maintenance or famine relief),
staffed by gentry under official patronage.[8]

There existed such wide variations in the number of villages compos-
ing multiplex confederations that only the most general figures can be
offered here. Te-leng-t'ai, describing the situation in White Lotus areas
during the Chia-ch'ing reign, found that a single confederation might
have as few as ten or more villages, or as many as several tens. An
account of conditions in the Huai-pei area during the 1850's states
that a *t'uan-chang* (leader of a simplex *t'uan*) would control his own
village, plus at most three or four nearby settlements, whereas a *t'uan-
tsung* (leader of a multiplex *t'uan*) might control several tens of
villages. Sometimes multiplex confederations may have arisen among
pre-existing groups of simplex *t'uan*, but more often militarization
seems to have resulted entirely from the initiative of leaders on the
multiplex scale, the individual villages themselves having neither
the resources nor the leadership to form their own bureaus. In such
cases the simplex *t'uan* can hardly be said to have existed as an
organized entity, and the term *t'uan* itself came to refer principally
to organizations on the multiplex scale.[9]

In the standard treatises and regulations on t'uan-lien, much

8. For a case in which a *tsung-chü* was established for dike maintenance, see
Lin Tse-hsu, *Lin Wen-chung-kung ch'üan-chi* (Taipei reprint, 1963), *Hu-kuang
tsou-kao*, 1:11–12, 2:1–3b. For a case involving famine relief, see Lin-hsiang 1872,
4:21a-b. The social composition of multiplex bureaus is well illustrated by Nanchang 1870, chüan 28; Huang-kang 1882, 24:28 (see Figure 13).

9. *Shan-tung chün-hsing chi-lueh* (Anonymous; Shanghai ed. of the Kuang-hsü
period) 22:1–2, 7a-b; Lin-hsiang 1872, 8:3b–4b, 8; Ch'ang-ning 1880, 5:23b.

attention was devoted to the mechanics of concentrating forces from a multiplex confederation at any given point within the area. In the regulations for Ho-hsien, Kwangsi, which were evidently derived from observation of local practice, militiamen were to be brought together by signal gongs. The threatened village would beat a gong continuously. All villages hearing continuous ringing would send militia in that direction while themselves beating gongs in series of five strokes. Villages hearing a five-stroke sound would dispatch militia toward it while beating their own gongs in series of three, and so on. Occasionally gunfire was used for signaling in like manner. This type of concentration was purely temporary, however; the characteristically defensive nature of the multiplex *t'uan* was safeguarded by dividing the militia of each village into two squads (*pan*), only one of which was to leave for the relief of nearby villages under attack.[10]

The Extended-Multiplex T'uan

Like simplex *t'uan*, multiplex *t'uan* were capable of confederating for common purposes. The resulting scale of organization might comprise a dozen or more multiplex and a hundred or more simplex units. A structure on this scale—which I shall call extended-multiplex —involved functions different from those of its multiplex components. The head bureau of an extended-multiplex *t'uan* could, of course, mobilize manpower and funds from a vast area. More important, its broad financial base enabled it to recruit and maintain an armed force on a higher level of militarization: men detached from their communities, who served for pay and were tending toward a professional mode of military life. Of this extended-multiplex type there are a number of outstanding examples, the most famous of which is the Sheng-p'ing association in the P'an-yü and Nan-hai districts near Canton, organized against the British during the 1840's. As Figure 2 shows, the structure of this organization involved the superposition of a directorate onto a group of twelve multiplex units, the largest of which was itself a confederation of at least 13 simplex units.[11] To

10. Hsu, *Hsiang-shou*, 4:4b–6.

11. The information upon which Figure 2 is based consists of a list of donors to the Sheng-p'ing bureau, grouped by *she* and *hsiang*, and augmented by information from the schools and markets sections of the P'an-yü gazetteer. The donor list is imperfect, because not all *hsiang* actually made money contributions. We know from other evidence, for example, that certain of the *she* listed here contained a larger number of *hsiang* than actually appear in the donor list. Because

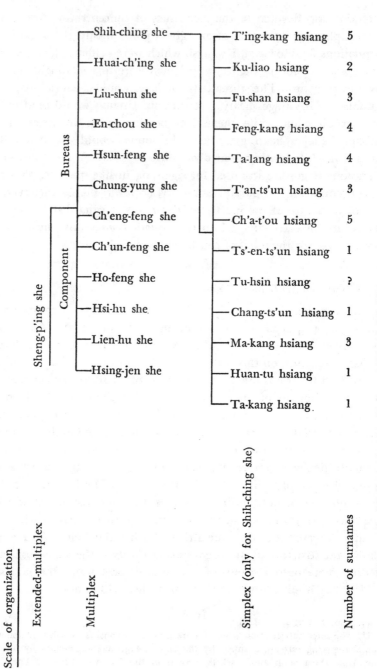

Figure 2. Structure of the Sheng-p'ing association.

Scale of organization				
Extended-multiplex	Multiplex		Simplex (only for Shih-ching she)	Number of surnames

Sheng-p'ing she

Component

Bureaus

- Shih-ching she
  - T'ing-kang hsiang — 5
  - Ku-liao hsiang — 2
  - Fu-shan hsiang — 3
  - Feng-kang hsiang — 4
  - Ta-lang hsiang — 4
  - T'an-ts'un hsiang — 3
  - Ch'a-t'ou hsiang — 5
  - Ts'-en-ts'un hsiang — 1
  - Tu-hsin hsiang — ?
  - Chang-ts'un hsiang — 1
  - Ma-kang hsiang — 3
  - Huan-tu hsiang — 1
  - Ta-kang hsiang — 1
- Huai-ch'ing she
- Liu-shun she
- En-chou she
- Hsun-feng she
- Chung-yung she
- Ch'eng-feng she
- Ch'un-feng she
- Ho-feng she
- Hsi-hu she
- Lien-hu she
- Hsing-jen she

Sources: *San-yuan-li shih-liao,* 141-151; P'an-yü 1871, 16:36b-52.

understand how this association was founded, we must return to the San-yuan-li incident and examine it from a different angle.

The presence of British troops in the countryside north of Canton during May 1841 had aroused the fury of the populace, but to transmute this fury into effective action required the organizing capacities of the gentry. On May 25, a gentry conference near the village of San-yuan-li resolved to resist the British with arms and set about raising militia from a wide area. When the incident actually took place on the last three days of the month, the British faced an angry crowd that swelled to perhaps 20,000 militiamen, drawn from an area of a hundred-odd villages that overspread portions of two districts.[12]

How was the mobilization at San-yuan-li accomplished with such extraordinary speed? How did the original gentry organizers know whom to talk to and where to seek help? It is not surprising to find that the area of response had already been delimited by long-standing patterns of gentry cooperation within very loosely articulated multiplex groups known as *she* (associations), which were generally centered in market towns. So customary was their functioning, and so informal their internal bonds, that they do not receive, as organizations, any formal treatment in local gazetteers. Nonetheless, their traces are unmistakable in the *she* schools (*she-hsueh*), which were founded in market towns by public subscription. Though there is much negative evidence that the *she* were not, as formal structures, engaged in militia coordination before the San-yuan-li incident, it is certain that they served as bases for multiplex defense organizations thereafter.[13]

The role of the *she* came into the open in the events that followed the incident. During the summer of 1841, just after San-yuan-li, gentry of the market town Shih-ching (about four miles northwest of San-yuan-li), led by the *chü-jen* Li Fang, petitioned the governor-

there is no way of being certain of the number of *hsiang* in any given *she*, I have refrained in the chart from indicating the number of *hsiang* and gave the *hsiang* list in the Shih-ching *she* (which seems relatively complete) only as an illustration. Further, there were various collaborators in the Sheng-ping association that for simplicity's sake I have not listed here, for example, temples, and merchant groups in the market towns. Thus the chart in Figure 2 should be regarded as merely a fair approximation.

12. Kuang-tung sheng wen-shih yen-chiu-kuan, ed., *San-yuan-li jen-min k'ang-Ying tou-cheng shih-liao* (1964 Daian reprint of the 1959 Canton edition), 6. Wakeman, *Strangers at the Gate*, 19, 38.

13. Neither Liang T'ing-tung nor Lin Fu-hsiang, both active in organizing militia during the Opium War, mentions the role of the *she* in the San-yuan-li mobilization. *San-yuan-li shih-liao*, 57, 63.

general to be permitted to construct a Sheng-p'ing She-hsueh (School of the Approaching-peace Association) to serve as a headquarters for raising funds and organizing militia on a regular basis—to solidify and routinize the local militarization that had occurred in late May. A well-ordered militia was even more important after the British had left, because added to the foreign menace was the widespread social dislocation and banditry stirred up by the war.[14] The resulting organization was in fact a coordinating bureau for twelve or thirteen multiplex *she* in surrounding market towns, which in turn coordinated a total of more than eighty *hsiang* (villages, or village clusters).[15] Though most of the *she* beneath it were already sponsoring association schools (*she-hsueh*), it is clear that the Sheng-p'ing She-hsueh was constructed specifically as a militia headquarters, borrowing only the customary and well-respected format of the *she-hsueh* for new purposes. Structurally, what had happened was the superposition of an added layer atop twelve multiplex organizations (the *she*), to accomplish tasks that were beyond the capacities of the multiplex *she* themselves: the mobilization of large numbers of men and the raising of large sums of money. The Sheng-p'ing association was sometimes referred to as a *tsung-she* (head *she*) to signify its higher organizational scale.[16]

Though the Sheng-p'ing *she-hsueh* (the "school" itself) was new in 1841, we have fragmentary evidence of the existence of the Sheng-p'ing association as early as 1825.[17] Though its purposes are obscure, inasmuch as no school was then associated with it, it is likely that this extended-multiplex association was useful in certain ways to the gentry of the area, perhaps in such spheres of traditional gentry concern as flood control or famine relief. In any event, the speed and efficiency of the San-yuan-li mobilization now becomes understandable: the interpersonal format—personal acquaintance and a history of customary cooperation among the gentry of a certain area—was already available on the basis of pre-existing multiplex and extended-multiplex associations, the *she*. These associations were now converted to the purposes of local militarization. It is noteworthy that although the term t'uan-lien was used frequently in contemporary references to the Sheng-p'ing association, the term *t'uan* (denoting a unit of local

14. Wakeman, *Strangers at the Gate*, 62. *San-yuan-li shih-liao*, 133–136.
15. P'an-yü 1871, 16:51.
16. *San-yuan-li shih-liao*, 156.
17. *San-yuan-li shih-liao*, 133.

organization) was replaced by the local variant *she*. Differences in terminology frequently overlay similar organizational forms, a topic that will be discussed at greater length in Chapter III.B.

In view of the informal nature of gentry cooperation, it is not surprising that the functions of the extended-multiplex bureau were not primarily those of command. Given the immediate menace to the area of the *she* and the common hatred of the British, the Sheng-p'ing bureau was able to coordinate the activities and concentrate the forces of a large area. Yet the real usefulness of the extended-multiplex bureau lay in its ability to perform certain functions that its constituent units could not perform for themselves: particularly the raising of large amounts of money and the hiring of a force of mercenaries on a level of militarization higher than that of the ordinary village militia. It was in this pooling of resources, more than in its power to command the movements of units below it, that the extended-multiplex bureau was most significant in nineteenth-century local organization.

To manage the tasks of funding and recruitment, the Sheng-p'ing association set up two separate offices. The first was the so-called *she-hsueh,* located within the town of Shih-ching; the second was a "public office" (*kung-so*) in the nearby market town of Chiang-ts'un, supervised by a local *chin-shih.* As the gentry managers reported to Governor-general Ch'i-kung by January 1843, the Chiang-ts'un office was purposely located in a relatively poor but densely populated area near the boundary of neighboring Hua-hsien; whereas the *she-hsueh* was in the rich mercantile center of Shih-ching. Therefore the Chiang-ts'un office had been highly successful in recruiting mercenaries, and the *she-hsueh* in raising money. Taken together, the two offices had raised 20,000 taels in subscriptions, of which 11,000 had actually been received. More than 10,000 mercenaries had actually been hired (mostly by the Chiang-ts'un office). Lower-scale *she,* of course, continued to organize militia on a lower level of militarization, and Ch'i learned that there were several tens of thousands of such men on hand in the villages.[18]

It would be too much to say that the Sheng-p'ing association "set a pattern for all later militia,"[19] unless one were referring particularly to the Canton area; here the Sheng-p'ing example did indeed inspire various other groups on the extended-multiplex scale, most famous

18. *San-yuan-li shih-liao,* 134. Wakeman, *Strangers at the Gate,* 62–63.
19. Wakeman, *Strangers at the Gate,* 63.

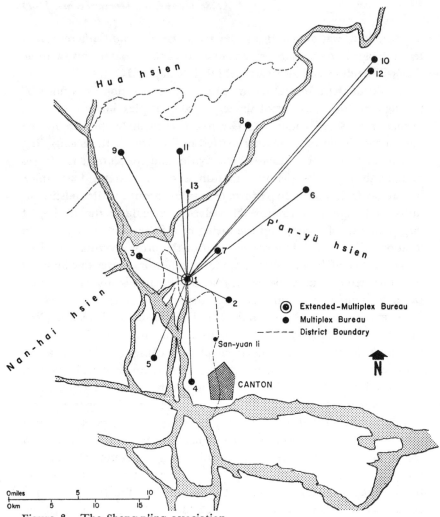

Figure 3. The Sheng-p'ing association.

Bureau	Settlement
1. Sheng-p'ing she	Shih-ching-hsu
2. Huai-ch'ing she	Fo-ling-shih
3. Liu-shun she	Lao-ya-kang
4. En-chou she	Ao-k'ou
5. Hsun-feng she	Hsun-feng-hsu
6. Chung-yung she	Chen-lung-hsu
7. Ch'eng-feng she	Ch'iao-t'ou-shih
8. Ch'un-feng she	Jen-ho-hsu
9. Ho-feng she	Shih-lung-hsu
10. Hsi-hu she	Hsi-hu-shih
11. Lien-hu she	Ch'ang-ling
12. Hsing-jen she	Chung-lo-t'an-hsu
13. Sheng-p'ing kung-so	Chiang-ts'un-hsu

Sources: San-yuan-li shih-liao, 141-151 and map; P'an-yü 1871, 16:51a-b; Nan-hai 1882, 4:16b; Nan-hai 1910, 6:31.

of which was the Tung-p'ing association, founded in 1843.[20] But similar organizations arose spontaneously throughout south and central China during the 1850's; evidently the extended-multiplex scale grew naturally from the needs of the times and from pre-existing patterns of local organization. In Yü-lin, Kwangsi, for instance, incessant social strife led the local elite to pool their resources in huge militia organizations. Militia work had begun as early as 1846; but it was then primarily on the simplex scale. Villages "imitated the method of *chien-pi ch'ing-yeh*" by constructing stout walls, mostly of tamped earth, which were high enough to hide a man standing and were guarded with whatever firearms were available. As the fury of rebellion increased, some areas came under repeated attack by several bandit groups in a single day;[21] "one from the east, one from the west, they pillaged and departed." Gentry defense efforts were spurred in 1851 when an army of God-worshipers (Pai-Shang-ti Hui) under Ling Shih-pa besieged the walled city of Yü-lin for forty days.[22]

In the face of this unending crisis, the scale of local militarization began to grow. By 1854, the scattered walled communities were linked by nine huge *t'uan,* several of which comprised over a hundred villages. The most prominent, the I-hsin (of one mind) *t'uan,* extended 20 miles in both length and breadth and contained ten multiplex units within it. This celebrated organization played a major part in the local wars of the 1850's; we lack precise information on the size of its funds and the numbers of its troops, but we do know that on many occasions it was able to muster forces of 2,000 or more *yung* to participate in lengthy campaigns against local rebels.[23] In Yü-lin the inflation of the scale of local defense efforts gave rise to an inflation of standard terminology, with organizations on the extended-multiplex level given the name "large *t'uan,*" and the multiplex units below them "small *t'uan.*" The commanders of the "small *t'uan,*" however, retained the usual title of *t'uan-tsung.* The name for simplex *t'uan*—defense forces of the hundreds of walled villages—is not recorded.

We find extended-multiplex units in other areas besides the Liang-kwang provinces: Nanchang district in Kiangsi had at least two such

20. See *San-yuan-li shih-liao,* 151–157, for documents on the Tung-p'ing association.

21. Yü-lin 1894, 18:20. Information on t'uan-lien in Yü-lin is found throughout chüan 18 of this gazetteer.

22. Chien Yu-wen, *T'ai-p'ing t'ien-kuo ch'üan-shih,* I (Hong Kong, 1962), 209–211. Yü-lin 1894, 18:4b–10.

23. For instance, Yü-lin 1894, 18:31b.

confederations, the most prominent of which was known as the "five bureaus" (*wu-chü*), headed by the influential *chü-jen* Liu Yü-hsun. Like the Sheng-p'ing association, Liu's group established a special headquarters in the countryside for recruiting mercenaries and with the rich resources of the Nanchang area built a genuinely professional fighting force, commanded by Liu himself and supported by assiduous fund-raising by allied multiplex bureaus in the surrounding market towns.[24]

Like everything else in traditional China, the character of local defense was much subject to interregional variation; hence generalizations about the number of simplex units involved in multiplex and extended multiplex confederations are inevitably unsatisfactory. Generally speaking, however, the sizes of these confederations were limited by intractable realities of communications and economics. An extended-multiplex confederation could not be so large in area as to make it excessively inconvenient for its leadership to keep in contact with its constituent parts. Nor could it be so small as to be unable to muster significant amounts of money and manpower. Presumably a rich region like Nanchang could support an extended-multiplex unit in a relatively small land area, whereas one in a comparatively poor region (such as Yü-lin) might have to reach further for its support.

B. Principles of Local Organization

The mind in search of order would like to believe that the end product of research into Chinese society in its various aspects—kinship, economics, cultural life, and militarization—will be a model that reveals levels of operation common to all these forms of social activity. Such a comprehensive description would exhibit natural scales of coordination into which all social activities were grouped. We are at the moment closest to such a description in the sphere of trade and marketing; William Skinner's depiction of the regularities of market structure suggests the kinds of regularities that may be sought in other spheres of life.[25]

As we have seen in the case of the *she* in the Canton area, it is clear that the search for the governing principles of local militarization

24. Nanchang 1870, 28. See the extended discussion of this case in Chapter IV.D below. See also Kiukiang 1874, 24:21.
25. G. William Skinner, "Marketing and Social Structure in Rural China," *Journal of Asian Studies* 24:3–43, 195–228, 363–399 (1965).

must range beyond the particular requirements of local defense and must relate militarization to other modes of social activity and organization. Here we shall be particularly concerned with those of kinship, economics, bureaucratic divisions, and ideology that influenced in one way or another the form and function of local militarization.

Lineage as a Defining and Interconnecting Principle

Questions of lineage organization are particularly important when we are considering the character of the lowest, or simplex scale of local defense, for the relationship between lineage and village was a close one in rural China. Maurice Freedman has pointed out that the frequency of single-lineage settlements in sub-Yangtze China, and particularly in the far southeast, was not simply a matter of these areas having been particularly immune from invasion and hence relatively stable in residential patterns; congruency between residential and kinship units was in fact a result of a tendency toward homogeneity within each settlement, "a desire to form a single lineage in one village territory."[26] It is apparent that in cases of single-lineage settlements, village leadership and its interests were identical to lineage leadership and its interests. Even when more than one lineage inhabited a given settlement, it appears that village leadership became simply a consortium of lineage leaders.[27]

In the south and southeast, where lineages were strongest and also most closely linked to residential patterns, lineage is particularly vital to a discussion of militarization. This is because of the melancholy tradition of interlineage vendettas (*hsieh-tou*) that marked southern society during the Ch'ing period and even thereafter. These ruinous fights, sometimes over vital economic rights, but as often over seemingly trivial points of honor, involved the mobilization of both manpower and funds within lineage boundaries, and the organization of intervillage warfare by lineage leadership.

The economic base for militarization was, except in the case of the poorest villages, built into the lineage organization in the form of a certain amount of common property, the income from which was avail-

---

26. Maurice Freedman, *Chinese Lineage and Society* (London, 1966), 8. I am deeply indebted to Mr. Freedman's work, both in the above cited monograph and in his earlier *Lineage Organization in Southeastern China* (London, 1965).

27. Freedman, *Chinese Lineage and Society*, 89–90. Sanō, *Shin-chō shakai shi*, II, 19.

able for the support of corporate activities. The corporate survival of a local lineage depended upon the continuation of ancestral sacrifices —identifying and reinforcing the bonds of common agnatic descent by which the lineage was defined—which entailed a certain amount of expense. The social and economic position of the lineage was promoted or maintained by schooling, another corporate effort requiring surplus wealth. Ritual sacrifices and education were thus the two principal activities supported by income from lineage-owned lands; but the lineage as property owner could also turn its resources to the support of local defense. Items such as lineage support of families of fallen militiamen, rewards to wounded fighters, and presumably fortification of villages, were met in part out of commonly owned land income. When such resources were insufficient, lineage leadership sometimes levied special taxes upon their kinsmen specifically for military use.[28]

The importance of interlineage feuding in Chinese military development is a subject that needs more exploration. It is apparent that the southern countryside, by virtue of its continuous state of militarization, was a spawning ground for both military leadership and military technique. The river valleys of eastern Kwangtung, particularly in the area of Ch'ao-chou (present Ch'ao-an) and Chia-ying (present Mei-hsien), which were notorious for their tradition of fierce lineage feuding, furnished recruits for both orthodox and heterodox forces in the civil wars of the mid-nineteenth century. The hot-blooded "Ch'ao-yung" detachments that stiffened Ch'ing armies in the early years of the anti-Taiping struggle were as unruly and contumacious as they were aggressive in battle; and proved thereby a headache to their government masters and a plague to the populace.[29] On the other side, it is worth remembering that among early adherents of the Taiping cause were numerous gangs of Kwangtung outlaws who had migrated westward to Kwangsi, among whom were men nurtured in lineage feuding. It was apparent to Ch'ing commanders that the tightness of Taiping defenses at the siege of Yung-an (1851) was in part the work of leaders from the Ch'ao-chou–Chia-ying area whose knowl-

28. Freedman, *Lineage Organization*, 107–110.
29. Wang K'ai-yün, *Hsiang-chün chih* (1909) 2:1. Chien Yu-wen, *Ch'üan-shih*, I, 370. Tseng Kuo-fan, *Tseng Wen-cheng-kung ch'üan-chi, shu-cha*, 2:3. Yao Ying's letters to Wu-lan-t'ai contain various references to Ch'ao-chou mercenaries. *T'ai-p'ing t'ien-kuo*, 8:692–694, 700–701.

edge of siege defense techniques had grown from experience in feuds among walled villages in their home districts.[30]

Lineage organization and local defense had a complex interacting relationship: if lineage served as an organizational base for militarization, it is also true that militarization could serve to reinforce traditional bonds of kinship solidarity. The cross-class nature of large lineages commonly meant that kinsmen faced each other across wide gulfs of social and economic inequality. This inequality often took the form of a landlord-tenant relationship, in which kinship bonds were made to serve the stability of the tenancy system and sometimes (one supposes) to soften the rigor of economic exploitation. In this context, lineage militarization had a key function in providing a center of organization alternative to groups—such as secret societies— that sought to mobilize the peasantry against their landlord exploiters. Once intralineage aggressions were diverted outwards against neighboring lineages, there arose a special sort of class warfare in which rich lineages oppressed poor. From interlineage conflict might result a state of permanent economic exploitation fastened upon poorer lineages by their larger and richer neighbors.[31] Here was plainly a kind of interlineage imperialism, whereby class differences within a powerful, highly stratified lineage were diluted and attenuated by the benefits stemming from the collective exploitation of a poor lineage nearby; just as class conflict within developed, capitalist nations was muted by nationalism, expansionism, and the economic subjugation of weaker societies.[32]

30. Chiang Chung-yuan, *Chiang Chung-lieh-kung i-chi, hsing-chuang*, 7a-b. From this area sprang such prominent Taiping leaders as Lai Han-ying and Lo Ta-kang. See Lo Erh-kang, *T'ai-ping t'ien-kuo shih-kao* (Peking, 1955) 287, 290.

31. Freedman, *Lineage Organization*, 111–112; *Chinese Lineage and Society*, 162.

32. Frederic Wakeman has argued, not to my entire satisfaction, that the anti-British movement around Canton in the 1840's produced a basic change in South China, in which "by 1845, society began to polarize into wealthy and poor." He contends that the unity of highly stratified lineages, hitherto maintained by traditional kinship bonds, was weakened by the accession of the rich and prestigious to undisputed control of lineage properties. This new turn of events is attributed to the militia movement of the 1840's, in which (1) poor militiamen from different areas were brought together and thus suddenly realized their common class identity and (2) gentry gained new dominance over lineage organizations because of their leadership of local militarization and the consequent need that a rich and respectable front be presented to local bureaucrats. (*Strangers at the Gate*, 115–116). To show a basic change taking place in the 1840's, Wakeman would have had to show not only elite dominance of lineage organization and wealth after that time, but the lack of such dominance before.

The importance of the local lineage as a base for rural militarization was by no means limited to those areas in Kwangtung and Fukien where lineage feuds were most prevalent. The same factors associated with lineage that made possible a sustained pitch of military activity in these areas were available also in other areas; and though neither lineage feuding nor single-lineage settlement was as common in the central Yangtze provinces, yet lineage resources and organizational principles could be turned to the purpose of militarization in emergencies. The evidence is unmistakable that this is in fact what happened: the rise of rebellion in the 1850's brought lineage into play on the lower levels of militarization in Central China just as chronic interlineage conflict had in the case of South China. In Hsiang-hsiang, Hunan, for instance, a determined effort by officials to base militia on the pao-chia system was not sufficient to displace the lineage as the primary unit of militarization. Not only did powerful lineages take the lead in mobilizing local forces, but the patterns of militia finance were in part based on commonly owned land specially set aside to produce income for t'uan-lien expenses, in obvious imitation of the common pattern of lineage sacrifice and school lands.[33] In Nanchang district, Kiangsi, the beginnings of local militarization in 1852 depended wholly on the resources and leadership of two important lineages, the Liu of Tzu-ch'i and the Wan of Ho-ch'i, which boasted extensive land holdings, numerous degree holders, and intricate connections with the bureaucracy.[34]

Having considered lineage as an organizing principle on the simplex scale of local militarization (which to anyone familiar with Chinese social organization must seem like merely an elaboration of what one might expect) we must now proceed to a discussion of lineage as an organizing principle on the multiplex scale. Just as there seems to have been a natural tendency toward lineage homogeneity within the single settlement, there was also a tendency of rich, successful lineages to subdivide and form branch lineages in new settlements. In Maurice Freedman's description, "a local lineage may be grouped with other local lineages on the basis that the ancestors of these lineages are all descended agnatically from a common ancestor, the whole unit in turn being focussed on an ancestral hall or other piece of property." This

33. Hsiang-hsiang 1874, 5:15b–16.
34. Extensive information on lineage and militarization in Nanchang is in Nanchang 1870, chüan 28, 35, and 36. The Nanchang case is examined in detail in Chapter IV.D below.

"whole unit" Freedman calls a "higher-order lineage."[35] Each new branch of such a grouping possessed the essential physical attributes of a viable local lineage—the ancestral hall and the wealth to support it—while remaining aware of its ancestry in common both with collateral branches and with members of the senior settlement. The ancestral hall of the senior settlement would remain in operation, though often on a less lavish scale than those of its offshoots. Thus the higher-order lineage, overspreading a number of village settlements, formed a natural unit of intervillage cooperation, one which could easily be turned to the purposes of multiplex local organization.

The multiplex t'uan-lien group organized by the Ssu lineage of Chien-ch'ang, Kiangsi (the present Yung-hsiu), will illustrate how a higher-order lineage served as the base for a defensive confederation. About 14 miles south of the district seat lay a mountainous area called Feng-lin-ling, within which was a local subdivision known as Shou-an *hsiang*. In this *hsiang* the Ssu were an especially large and prosperous lineage, a force in local society since Sung times. They had been deeply involved in local defense work at the time of the Revolt of the Three Feudatories in the late seventeenth century and were again leaders in defense against the Taipings. As a local chronicler put it, "Since the beginning of the rebellion, there were many communities that dared not organize t'uan-lien [thinking they could remain uninvolved], but were destroyed nonetheless; our lineage reckoned that it was better to militarize and stand a chance of survival."[36]

The Ssu were divided into at least six branches, which lived in separate, neighboring settlements and formed a self-contained residential cluster. The fact that this was a genuine higher-order lineage with strong internal ties, preserved by a consciousness of common ancestry and probably maintaining a common ancestral hall, can be inferred from the pattern of generational names shared by all the settlements in the complex (Figure 4). Shared ideographic elements in the given name were the rule for siblings or cousins in the same generation and are a sign that the lineage retained a consciousness of its corporate existence. The militarization of this higher-order lineage began about 1853, and throughout the crisis of the 1850's its militia were engaged constantly in local defense.

Though we may accept the case of the Ssu higher-order lineage as, so to speak, a pure form (a multiplex unit in which the internal bonds

35. Freedman, *Chinese Lineage and Society*, 20–21.
36. Chien-ch'ang 1871, 5:27a-b.

Figure 4. Multiplex t'uan-lien based on lineage links: numbers of Ssu 司 militiamen killed in action during the Taiping Rebellion, according to generational name component and native settlement.

Generational name component		Settlement name					
		Ku-ts'un	Hsi-yuan	Sha-lung	Kuo-p'o	Ku-p'o	Tung-t'ang
I	一	1	1	–	–	–	–
Chung	中	4	3	–	–	–	–
I	以	11	5	–	2	–	–
Ying	應	3	3	4	–	2	–
Chin	金	1	1	–	–	–	–
Li	立	1	–	–	–	–	–
Hsi	細	1	–	–	–	–	–
Hsi	熙	–	–	2	–	–	1
Chü	居	–	–	1	–	–	–
Ch'ao	朝	–	–	–	–	1	1

Source: Chien-ch'ang 1871, 5:27b-28.

were furnished entirely by kinship) this form seems to have been rather an exception on the multiplex scale. Most multiplex units about which we have full information have more than one surname in their leadership bureaus. This is not surprising when we consider that many simplex bureaus, too, had more than one lineage represented in the leadership group. In the case of multi-lineage simplex bureaus, it is plain that the governing factor was a small multi-lineage settlement, closely bound together in its residence pattern and economic interests and thus possessed of a common interest in community defense. The situation is less clear, however, in the case of multi-lineage bureaus at the multiplex scale of organization. What factors enabled local militarization to transcend the narrow interests of local lineages and individual communities?

The Market Community as an Organizing Principle

The great merit of William Skinner's study of Chinese markets is that it relates such complex matters as social stratification and informal rural organization to the ambits of movement described by people in their everyday lives.[37] The fact that an ordinary peasant was phys-

37. "Marketing and Social Structure in Rural China," *Journal of Asian Studies*, 24:3-43, 195-228, 363-399, (1964-65).

ically present in his standard market town more than a thousand times in the course of his life, rubbing shoulders there with his counterparts from other households in the market community, means that his circle of personal acquaintance was, for all practical purposes, coterminous with the market area itself. Similarly, for the elite, the market community defined the area within which they carried on their crucial functions of mediation and organization. The market town was where they met the community at large and carried on their varied activities of informal social control. Besides bringing people together in their economic lives, the market town served also as a center of community activity in most other spheres of rural life, such as religion, recreation, and marriage-arrangement. In view of the central role of the market town and the defining functions of the marketing community, it is logical that these units should have been important factors in local militarization.

T'uan-lien configurations in Lin-hsiang, Hunan (Figure 5), reveal a complex pattern in which the forms of militarization were closely associated with market structure but not wholly determined by it. Towns like T'ao-lin, which contained markets of standard or higher status (designated *shih* or *chen*) served as loci for extended-multiplex bureaus.[38] Surrounding them were multiplex *t'uan*, some centered on market communities too small to have the *shih* or *chen* designation, and some on substantial villages. The place of the simplex scale of militarization in Lin-hsiang is obscure; evidently it was organizationally too weak to have left any traces in the historical record. Although only field work would enable us to delineate precisely the trade interrelationships of rural Lin-hsiang, our data leave very little doubt that the market community played an important part in defining the boundaries of local defense associations. It was at the trading centers that the elite was able to identify itself with the interests of the rural communities; and it was the market community that enabled local society to transcend the narrow interests of village and lineage. In other areas, too, we find abundant evidence of the relevance of market structure to local militarization.[39]

38. I use here Skinner's classification scheme for market scale. See "Marketing and Social Structure." The base map for Figure 4 contains some imperfections; a few of the multiplex *t'uan* bureaus listed in Lin-hsiang 1872, 8:3b–4b, are not locatable on it. In view of its completeness elsewhere, these defects can be considered marginal.

39. For instance, Nanchang 1870, 1:28–31, 28:1–13.

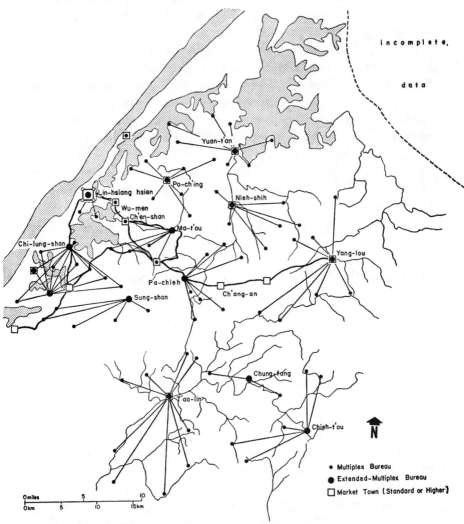

Figure 5. T'uan-lien configurations in Lin-hsiang, Hunan.

Nevertheless it is apparent that a number of t'uan-lien associations were not simply aspects of the marketing community but were structured according to other criteria. For instance, the important market town of Ch'ang-an (which later became the district seat) contained no head bureau, as did several nearby towns of lesser commercial importance. The head bureau at Ma-t'ou actually included two fair-sized market towns within its circle of influence, and the bureau at Chi-lung-shan included one. Ma-t'ou presents a particularly interesting case in the light of evidence dating from 1862, when an effort was made to build up the district's system of charitable relief granaries (*i-ts'ang*). The raising of grain contributions to the granaries was handled by "wealthy families" operating through what are described as "head bureaus" (*tsung-chü*), which were in most cases the same head bureaus that were managing t'uan-lien work. In the case of grain contributions, however, collection was always done at substantial market towns, no doubt because of the convenience of commercial facilities and transport. In the Ma-t'ou area, the community grain-collection effort reverted to the market town of Ch'en-shan, the commercial center to which the town of Ma-t'ou was oriented. Thus the head bureau is listed, for purposes of grain collection, as being at Ch'en-shan rather than at Ma-t'ou. The key fact, however, is that Ma-t'ou contributed the lion's share of the grain: twice as much as the next largest contributor and more than a third of the total amount collected by the head bureau. The commercial facilities of the large market town may have been useful for transactions of this sort, but Ma-t'ou had the wealth. This economic dominance of the marketing community is unquestionably of prime importance in understanding why the lineages centered around Ma-t'ou had been able to take control of local militarization.[40]

40. Lin-hsiang 1872, 4:21a-b. The earliest efforts at extended-multiplex organization were those of Ch'eng Ch'i-i, a *sheng-yuan*, who in 1852 "united eight *t'uan*" and established a head bureau at a place called Chi-lung-shan. The difficulty is that there appear to have been rival head bureaus, or at least two different head bureaus, in the case of the Chi-lung-shan confederation. Another *sheng-yuan*, Wu Chih-chün, is also said to have been "chosen as director of the head bureau" of the eight-*t'uan* Chi-lung-shan grouping in the same year. Circumstantial evidence suggests that Wu's bureau was at the boat-landing—a minor commercial center—called Cha-pu. Cha-pu, like Ma-t'ou, excelled all others in its confederation when relief granaries were established a decade later. This rich bureau seems in the end to have had preponderant influence, for its leader was credited with the most outstanding contribution to the defense of the district. Both bureau-heads were killed in action in 1855. Lin-hsiang 1872, 11:13–15; 4:18b–19.

With the example of Ma-t'ou as a beginning, one can offer some hypotheses as to why militarization did not always adhere to the boundaries of the marketing community and why the head bureau was not always located in a market town. The practical necessities of militia work imposed certain peculiar organizational requirements. First, t'uan-lien in its characteristically low level of militarization required that sizable numbers of village men be available for training in spare hours and for defense of their home communities in the event of attack. Therefore the organizational centers of militia work had obviously to be close to the particular population that was to be defended, and from which militiamen were to be drawn. But which settlements were to house the head bureaus of multiplex or extended-multiplex t'uan? Though it is certainly true that market towns were customary and convenient meeting places for the elite that organized such bureaus, the elite in any marketing community were particularly interested, not necessarily in protecting a commercial center miles away but in protecting their own lands and lineages. Thus a rural lineage that had the manpower, money, and influence to organize militia would certainly begin near its own homes and lands. If the elite of that lineage were at the same time in a position of leadership throughout the surrounding area, it would be quite natural for the office of its own militia association to become at the same time the head bureau of a multiplex or extended-multiplex t'uan. In troubled times, the rural elite was likely to stick close to its sources of funds and manpower; thus a standard or even a minor market center might assume a greater importance in military affairs than it had in commercial. In Nanchang, for instance, the head bureau of t'uan-lien in the area called Chung-chou was not established in any of the rich market towns in the vicinity but in a rural area near Tzu-ch'i, the home of Liu Yü-hsun's rich and populous lineage.[41] Thus the localism inherent in low-level militarization was one factor that tended in some instances to draw leadership bureaus away from central market places. The very lineage that was likely to provide the leadership for a t'uan-lien confederation was the lineage that was able to afford protection for its own home settlement.

Sometimes the connection between market centers and t'uan-lien bureaus depended, not so much upon the influence of the commercial structure over other spheres of activity as upon underlying political factors that governed both commerce and militarization: where a par-

---

41. Nanchang 1870, 28:2.

ticular lineage had a controlling interest in a market, it might also become the controlling element in a t'uan-lien confederation based on that market. Lineages of the Chung surname had founded the market at Lo-kang, near Canton, in the fifteenth century. When local defense was organized in 1847, it was three villages of the Chung surname that founded the Ch'ang-p'ing *she-hsueh* as headquarters of an extended-multiplex *t'uan* embracing more than a hundred communities.[42]

The Financial Basis of Local Militarization

Unlike the pao-chia system, which ideally could be run with minimal expense, local militarization required money: not only for hardware such as weapons and fortifications but also for the support of men temporarily separated from their normal sustenance. A protracted crisis, in which men were needed for service often and for long periods required substantial expenditure; and to maintain a force of out-and-out mercenaries required even more. The sustained financial needs of local militarization during the rebellion bred new forms of funding, which in turn had decisive impact upon forms of local organization.

Private wealth played a vital role in militia finance particularly in the early stages of militarization. The leader of a simplex *t'uan* might indeed stand out in his community by virtue of his personal wealth, but at higher scales of organization personal wealth was of even greater importance. Men defending their own village could subsist on their own resources but required more support as their ambit of movement widened. Whatever fund-raising methods might be devised once a multiplex confederation was formed, the initial impetus had to come from men whose personal investment was substantial enough to inspire confidence in the venture's success as well as to justify their own leadership position. Leadership of voluntary associations in Chinese society involves a heavy personal commitment and particularly a financial commitment.[43] Consequently it is not surprising to find signs of

42. P'an-yü 1871, 16:50b, 18:12b.
43. William Skinner writes, of community associations among the Chinese in Thailand, "The responsibility of the officers of an association for its budget is clear-cut: they must either secure the necessary donations to balance it or make up the difference from their own pockets. Any project planned by the officers of an association . . . is primarily their own responsibility. They make the first contribution and generally the largest." *Leadership and Power in the Chinese Community of Thailand* (Ithaca, 1958), 122–23.

considerable wealth among leaders of multiplex and extended-multiplex bureaus. In Nanchang (see Figure 6), unmistakable evidence of personal wealth is the large number of men in head bureaus who purchased official ranks and titles. Though prices were reduced steadily

Figure 6. Leadership of five t'uan-lien bureaus in Nanchang district, Kiangsi, about 1853.

Status	Chung-chou	Nan-chou	Wan-she	Pao-an	Ting-an	Total
Regular gentry						
Chü-jen	2	1	–	2	3	
Kung-sheng	–	2	–	2	–	
Sheng-yuan	1	2	2	6	2	25
Purchased status						
Kung-sheng	1	–	–	–	–	
Chien-sheng	1	–	–	–	1	
Official ranks						
and titles	1	9	5	2	–	20

Source: Nanchang 1870, 28:1b-6.

during the latter half of the nineteenth century, some of these ranks and titles were still quite expensive. The high proportion of men with purchased status in some bureaus suggests that many of these market-town t'uan-lien associations drew upon merchant as well as gentry talent.[44] The dominant role of the wealthy in supporting and controlling community defense was given a cooperative coloration in such conventional phrases as "the rich contribute wealth, the poor contribute strength."[45]

44. Hsu Ta-ling, Ch'ing-tai chüan-na chih-tu (Peking, 1950) is a comprehensive account of the purchase system. For the various categories of rank-purchase, see pp. 80–96. Prices for different ranks at various periods appear after p. 111. There is always the question, of course, whether wealth was the precondition of militia management or the result of it. In any given case, both might be true. At any rate, there is abundant evidence of the importance of personal wealth in the formation of both simplex and multiplex t'uan. For instance, Huang Chin-ch'i, of Huang-chou, Hupeh, a holder of lower ninth brevet rank, "contributed family wealth" and "became a leader of t'uan-lien." Huang-chou 1884, 22:35. In Lin-hsiang, two chien-sheng and a t'ung-sheng, all of the Yü lineage, "contributed funds to muster a large number of local men and defend their area as a t'uan." Lin-hsiang 1872, 11:13. Lo Ch'ing-chang, who held the purchased rank of district director of studies, paid large sums of his own fortune to build a militia force in Kuei-hsien: "He liberally rewarded and feasted the men and gained their loyalty." Kuei-hsien 1894, 4:14. Liang Lien-fu, "Ch'ien-chai chien-wen sui-pi" in Chin-tai-shih tzu-liao, no. 1:4 (1955).

45. Hua-jung 1882, 6:9b.

Another traditional factor that should not be overlooked is the role of lineage wealth drawn from commonly held lands. We have already noted that such resources were important in small-scale lineage feuding, but their infrequent mention during the later stages of militarization suggests that their relative importance waned as the scale and ferocity of fighting increased. Nevertheless, even late in the Hsien-feng reign there is evidence of lands being set aside, in the typical manner of lineage management, particularly for the support of militia. Evidently this traditional funding method remained important to village-level organizations in some areas.[46]

But during the crisis decades emerged new forms of local funding to feed the rapidly growing appetite of militarization. In the 1850's much of the available private wealth was diverted into the rank-sale system, whereby funds were collected for the use of both the central government and the new armies that were being formed by the provincial elite (this subject will be further discussed in Chapter VI.A). This made it all the more necessary for local t'uan-lien associations to find reliable and adequate sources of support elsewhere. Because personal wealth and traditional lineage-owned resources were relatively inexpansible, the leaders of local defense associations turned to richer and deeper veins of support: nothing less than the whole agricultural and mercantile wealth of the community.

To exploit agricultural production a number of methods were employed, the most common of which involved assessment of special taxes, computed either on land acreage (*an-mou*) or on harvests (*an-liang*). These requisitions, sometimes known as contributions (*chüan*) had received imperial sanction at least as early as 1856. In areas of heavy tenancy, such taxes amounted to an assessment on rent levied on landlords and passed on in turn to tenants. Rates and methods varied widely, even within a single district. The significant feature of virtually all these taxing arrangements, however, was that they were carried out by the t'uan-lien associations themselves and managed by gentry rather than by yamen clerks and runners. The fact that funds were managed by "upright gentry" and kept out of the clutches of yamen underlings was continually cited as a guarantee of honest dealing, because it was an accepted element of local mythology that corruption was an evil visited by the official system upon local society and could not originate within the gentry itself. There was very little

46. Hsiang-hsiang 1874, 5:28.

a magistrate could do to check on receipts and disbursements by influential gentry operating through t'uan-lien bureaus, and the private taxing power of these bureaus gathered both strength and immunity as time went on. Sometimes the gentry of a district would arrange to pool a certain proportion of these special taxes to hire a band of mercenaries at the district seat, but by and large the taxing authority of individual t'uan bureaus remained a buttress of localism and a counterweight to the power of the rank-sale system to attract local resources.[47]

The situation in Kweichow illustrates the various forms assumed by these new taxes in the agricultural sector. Kweichow, a chronic deficit area, had traditionally met military expenses by funds transferred from neighboring provinces. With the outbreak of rebellion, however, these extraprovincial sources quickly dried up. The deficit was now filled by the expanded sale of ranks, by the newly instituted likin trade tax, and by various new agricultural taxes. By 1861, ad hoc official levies on land were regularized by acting governor Han Ch'ao into a tax known as li-ku, a direct supplement to regular tax levies, assessed on acreage. Evidently this innovation was so disruptive to rural society that Han's successor, Chang Liang-chi, was forced to turn taxing authority over to the gentry. The tax, now known as i-ku, was managed by gentry bureaus (shen-chü, almost certainly the same bureaus that were managing t'uan-lien) and was shared between local defense associations and the provincial government. The i-ku tax was evidently but little subject to official regulation; its stated rates varied from one tenth to one twentieth of grain yields, but in view of the fact that it nourished both local and provincial coffers, the actual rates may well have been higher. The misery of the peasantry was compounded by a special household tax (hu-chüan), which seems to have been levied from time to time by local officials as the need arose.[48]

The taxing authority of the t'uan-lien bureaus would not have been nearly so important in China's modern history had it not been that the raising of taxes for local militarization proceeded side by side with

47. Hsiang-hsiang 1874, 5:12; Huang-ch'ao cheng-tien lei-tsuan, (1903) 338:8b; Hsu Nai-chao, Hsiang-shou chi-yao, 8:2b; Sasaki Masaya, "Juntoku-ken kyōshin to tōkai jūrokusa," Kindai Chūgoku kenkyū, 3:206. Ning-hsiang 1867, 42:80b.

48. Ling T'i-an, Hsien-T'ung Kuei-chou chün-shih shih (1932) 1:46–47b. Wada Sei, Shina chihō jichi hattatsushi, 275.

the involvement of the gentry in the regular taxing process. As we shall discover in the next chapter, when we deal with the relationship between t'uan-lien associations and bureaucratic administrative divisions, this involvement was closely related to unauthorized forms of tax farming, such as the practice known as *pao-lan,* whereby gentry supposedly forced their services as tax collectors upon local communities. The power to tax the community for t'uan-lien expenses, which many a magistrate was compelled to authorize during the mid-century decades, now lent legitimacy to the gentry's infiltration of the taxing process as a whole. It was undoubtedly the tendency for t'uan-lien bureaus to become involved in the regular tax-collection process, sometimes entirely supplanting the official taxing machinery, that led high provincial officials like Hu Lin-i and Tseng Kuo-fan to oppose the granting of any direct taxing power to such bureaus.[49]

Besides agriculture, trade became a lucrative source of local funds. The mercantile tax known as likin, instituted first in Yangchow in 1853 and quickly adopted throughout the provinces to defray military expenses, inevitably played a role in the financing of t'uan-lien associations.[50] The administration of likin, like the administration of many other local enterprises, required talent and resources that the normal machinery of district government was unable to muster; the result was reliance on gentry-staffed bureaus (*chü*) to carry out chores of day-to-day collection and accounting. During the early years of likin (throughout most of the 1850's), before the tax was effectively integrated into provincial and national finance, the collection bureaus were sometimes the same bureaus that ran local defense associations. The process by which likin was wrested from the t'uan-lien bureaus and furnished with its own administrative system forms part of the still inadequately explored financial history of the mid-nineteenth century. Already by 1859, however, there is evidence that likin was playing a diminishing role in the financing of strictly local militarization,

49. Lu Tao-ch'ang, *Wei-hsiang yao-lueh* (1885) 2:3b.
50. The origins and operation of likin have been intensively studied. Consult Lo Yü-tung, *Chung-kuo li-chin shih (Shanghai,* 1936), and Edward Beal, *The Origin of Likin, 1853–1864* (Cambridge, Mass., 1958). The need for ad hoc financing of military campaigns had led to earlier proposals to tax merchants; for instance, Chou T'ien-chueh, a high military commissioner in Kwangsi, had suggested about 1851 that special taxes be levied on pawnshops, variety shops, traveling merchants, oil pressers, and other small businesses. Hsu Nai-chao, *Hsiang-shou chi-yao,* 8:3.

giving way to a gentry-dominated tax system based primarily on agricultural production. The defense of Hsiang-hsiang against Shih Ta-k'ai's attack in 1859, for instance, relied only peripherally on likin revenues and predominantly on "contributions," actually special taxes raised district-wide by gentry on the basis of rent incomes (see Figure 7).

Figure 7. Funds for the defense of Hsiang-hsiang, Hunan, 1859 (figures rounded off to whole taels).

Source	Amount
"Contributions" (chüan) raised district-wide	103,395
Likin	3,000
Special "contributions" raised by magistrate	1,000
Funds raised and spent directly by individual t'uan	10,273
Total	117,668

Source: Hsiang-hsiang 1874, 5:22b-26b.

The independence of individual t'uan-lien bureaus with respect to fund raising gave rise to serious problems. Seen from the viewpoint of the district bureaucracy, the diversity between the resources of rich and poor areas could lead to dangerous weak points in a district's defenses. Consequently officials became involved in efforts to centralize and standardize the financial activities of the t'uan-lien bureaus. P'ing-chiang, a strategically located district in the northeast corner of Hunan, exhibited in the early 1850's a highly fragmented defense system, in which were wide variations in wealth within multiplex t'uan themselves, so tightly was finance controlled by individual lineages. The situation was made worse by the unevenness of the military burden born by different regions within the district. Finally in 1858 or 1859, as part of a general effort to extend official control over local militarization, officials established four "united head bureaus" (lien tsung-chü), one for each hsiang, and granted them broad taxing authority. We do not know how (or whether) a working relationship was established between these new bureaus and the old multiplex t'uan; but the effort may be taken as symptomatic of official concern over the anarchic tendencies of t'uan-lien funding.[51]

51. P'ing-chiang 1875, 36:6b–11b.

C. The Relation of the T'uan to Bureaucratic Divisions

We must now reopen the question of the relationship between local militarization and official, bureaucratic systems like pao-chia and *li-chia*, the local security and tax-collection networks. In my discussion of the theoretical basis of t'uan-lien (Chapter II.B) I pointed out the polarity between bureaucratic and non-bureaucratic principles of organization in Chinese official thinking and suggested that the *t'uan*, even as envisioned by its official patrons, drew upon non-bureaucratic sources of authority that pao-chia specifically avoided, particularly the natural ascendency of the local elite in their home communities. But now that we have explored briefly the question of inherent scales of organization in rural China, it is time to consider the relationship between t'uan-lien and bureaucratic divisions in a fresh light. Local militarization tended naturally to crystallize on certain scales of organization; pao-chia and *li-chia*, too, had their ascending scales of integration. However much we should like to maintain the ideal distinction between natural and administrative modes of organization, the evidence insists that the two modes were not wholly distinct in practice.

First, there is the question of where official systems such as pao-chia came from. Did they represent simply the musings of desk-bound bureaucrats who sought to impose upon local society neat, symmetrical patterns of control? That such was not the case has already been seen in the origins of the pao-chia system in Sung times: The official system was derived from observation of local practice. The fact that local practice does not naturally involve decimal divisions is not at issue: officials simply sought to bureaucratize and standardize scales of rural organization already in existence. What we have in pao-chia is an abstraction and simplification of simplex (single-village) and multiplex (multivillage) scales of natural rural cooperation. The existence of such scales of organization preceded the official effort to standardize and bureaucratize them and to use them for its own purposes. Chinese bureaucrats were not, in fact, cut off from the realities of rural social life, free to devise ideal tables of organization in isolation from real problems of government. Socially, many could themselves look back a generation or two to rural origins; by virtue of the considerable social mobility built into the system, China's bureaucracy was recurrently immersed (over a span of several generations) in the life of the countryside. Further, the ideals of empirical scholarship that infused the Chinese elite at various periods, particularly during the Ch'ing, saved the bureaucracy from a sterile and self-sustaining utopianism. An unavoidable awareness of what was actually going on in rural society, coupled with an active empirical interest in such matters, insured that the drawing up of official regulations was constantly influenced by natural forms of local organization.

T'uan-lien and Pao-chia Reconsidered

Analyses of the pao-chia system that stress its fragmenting effect upon local society (such as that of Hsiao Kung-ch'üan) are correct up to a point: certainly the state was concerned to make pao-chia headmen instruments of its own police authority rather than mere tools of local interests and hence sought to have them preside over artificial, rather than indigenous, units of social organization. But this is only part of the story. One of the recurring administrative dilemmas of the Ch'ing system (one common to most political systems) was how to reconcile security with efficiency. We ourselves are constantly putting up with inefficiencies of all sorts for the sake of our own overriding security principle: the dispersion and balancing of power. The Ch'ing state faced the security problem from a different standpoint; being neither technologically nor ideologically equipped to exercise a thoroughgoing despotism, it fragmented and duplicated administrative authority throughout the bureaucracy in such a way that there could be only one ultimate center of power: the throne. It could be argued that the regime's requirements of internal security sometimes brought the administrative system to the brink of impotence. At any rate, the local magistrate had to live with the multifarious security provisions of that system and still produce results: for it was results—effective tax collection, the maintenance of order—that governed his career (leaving out of account such mitigating factors as bribery, connections, customary presents, and the like). A magistrate could not justify disorder in his district by pleading that the pao-chia system, as officially prescribed, insured that the headmen would be men of no consequence and hence incapable of exerting any influence; or that the very artificiality of the decimal principles on which pao-chia was organized made it a weak and ineffective unit of local coordination. Because results were what counted, tampering with the system (or allowing it to conform itself to existing social topography) was the path of least resistance. Thus we find frequent evidence that the tasks of these bureaucratic decimal systems were relegated to the natural units on the corresponding scale of organization; that in times of crisis, bureaucrats could not but place responsibility for police control and even tax collection upon those agencies in the countryside capable of exerting real power or at least permit such agencies to absorb the functions of the pao-chia and li-chia systems.

Of the absorption by natural units of the functions of administration units there are examples scattered plentifully throughout the record. When in 1846/1847 the Canton authorities ordered the implementation of pao-chia (one of many periodic attempts to revive the system) a number of communities around the market town of Lo-kang responded by establishing a *she-hsueh:* "The Ch'ang-p'ing she-hsueh was built jointly by the four *yueh,* Ching-tzu, Ch'ing-tzu, Kang-yuan, and T'ang-t'ou. There was established a *she*-headman and a deputy; a *yueh*-headman [for each *yueh*] and a *hsiang*-headman [for each *hsiang*]. The various headmen strictly proclaimed the rules and regulations, in order to eliminate the sources of banditry. In emergencies, there were consultations at the *she-hsueh.*"[52] Now the *yueh* in this area was a small, non-official multiplex grouping that served various purposes of intervillage and interlineage cooperation, but particularly local defense.[53] Though it may at some time have been connected with the *hsiang-yueh* lecture system (an officially promoted but locally run indoctrination program) it seems not to have been so at this time. We have already identified the *hsiang* around Canton as either a single village or a small cluster of closely related settlements. The *she* in this case was like the other *she* we have observed in Cantonese market towns: a gentry-dominated multiplex association that served a variety of community purposes, including local defense. Thus the wholly natural three-level regional association, built up of *hsiang, yueh,* and *she,* was simply furnished with headmen and called pao-chia. Another example of this kind is the system adopted in Ho-hsien, Kwangsi, in which the standard decimal divisions were entirely disregarded and the basic mutual responsibility unit made congruent with the natural village.[54] On occasion, the *li-chia* tax collecting system was similarly altered to conform to natural village units.[55]

The plentitude of such cases forces us to consider whether the nat-

52. P'an-yü 1871, 16:50.
53. Freedman, *Chinese Lineage and Society,* 82–89.
54. Hsu Nai-chao, *Hsiang-shou chi-yao,* 1:2b–3.
55. Hsiao, *Rural China,* 523.

ural and administrative units were not simply aspects of the same thing: the potentialities, and the needs, for various scales of organization inherent in China's rural society. It was not that natural units were somehow masquerading as administrative units or falsely claiming their functions but rather that the close historical connections of the two modes of coordination, and rural society's built-in scales of organization, made natural and administrative units in certain cases interchangeable.

Let us consider in greater detail the relationship between the *t'uan*, as a natural unit of coordination based on gentry leadership, and the administrative substructure of rural government. It will be recalled that despite the solidly civilian character and function of pao-chia by Ch'ing times, at least one official still saw its capacities for militarization: Huang Liu-hung's militia system was a recrudescence of an administrative practice that had not been generally used since the eleventh century and a suggestion of pao-chia's shadowy antecedants in ancient Chinese feudal society.

Huang Liu-hung did not include the *t'uan* in his militia system; either it was not known to him or else its non-bureaucratic nature did not appeal to him. There is, however, reliable evidence that in at least one area the *t'uan* had become a recognized unit of local militarization, under gentry leadership, by the late sixteenth century. The 1574 edition of the Wu-hsi, Kiangsu, gazetteer describes a *t'uan-pao* system that had grown up during the period of Japanese invasions. This was a time when the regular *min-chuang* militia was in disrepair, and rural areas had to shift for themselves. Every household with at least three able-bodied males would provide one militiaman; ten militiamen would form a *chia* and five *chia* a *pao*. These tactical units were evidently led by the headmen of the standard *pao* and *chia* registration units. In their military role, however, these headmen were to obey the orders of the *t'uan-chang*, a figure whose area of command was based entirely on natural factors. The *t'uan* were to be roughly based on the natural divisions known as *hsiang* (here a large subdistrict grouping comprising scores or hundreds of villages) but might be further adapted to local topography, strategic requirements, and residence patterns. These natural divisions bore no direct relation to decimal registration systems and contained unequal numbers of *pao* within them. The *t'uan-chang* himself was to be a man of "extraordinary talent and bravery," who was to be "put forward by the masses" —obviously a member of the local elite. Though the system is also described in later gazetteers, it is clear that it had died out by Ch'ing times. An 1813 gazetteer considered it too dangerous to employ, despite the inability of local garrisons to furnish adequate local security.[56]

This system is similar to Huang Liu-hung's save for its recognition of the *t'uan*, as an elite-led unit, placed over the *pao*. The *pao* was considered adequate to its task (police surveillance) on a civilian basis; but militarization was thought to require the kind of leadership that could be drawn only from the natural units of coordination. Thus the administrative units of *pao-chia* were integrated into what was essentially a natural unit of local action: a fact that suggests that the *pao* itself may already have had close links to natural units—most probably the villages—in its normal operation.

T'uan-lien and the Li-chia System

The *li-chia* tax collection and registration system was of course also organized on simplex and higher scales; and not surprisingly, we find that the *t'uan* was capable of intruding into this realm, too. A most interesting example comes from Lin-hsiang, where we have already observed the scales assumed by local defense associations. The Lin-hsiang gazetteer says of the *li-chia* system, "Under the reigning dynasty the district was divided into ten *li*, each of which was in turn divided into *A* and *B* [*shang, hsia*]; *A* and *B* each had five *chia*, thus making a total of 100 *chia*." Three-level systems of this sort were fairly common, though of course nomenclature varied widely.[57] But the account continues: "In the 20th year of Tao-kuang [1840/1841], the 100 *chia* were reorganized into 99 *t'uan*, and *t'uan*-registers were then compiled."[58]

Of the reasons for this reorganization we are told nothing. An abundance of circumstantial evidence, however, leads to only one conclusion: that tax collection in Lin-hsiang was being transferred from the regular bureaucratic *li-chia* apparatus to the natural, gentry-dominated units represented by the *t'uan*. The ingrained malpractice of *pao-lan* (engrossment), a form of unauthorized tax-farming in which local elite assumed the prerogative of collecting the taxes of commoners for commission, can be found throughout the Ch'ing period.[59] It

---

56. Wu-hsi 1574, 9:2b–3; 1751, 5:5, 10:23. Wu-hsi Chin-kuei 1813, 6:33.
57. Hsiao, *Rural China*, 530–536.
58. Lin-hsiang 1872, 3:6b.
59. Hsiao, *Rural China*, 132–139, has an excellent description of *pao-lan*.

seems to have been particularly rampant, however, during the troubled nineteenth century and was related to the general administrative and financial crisis of the times. Just across the eastern borders of Lin-hsiang in the district of Ch'ung-yang, Hupeh, occurred a case of *pao-lan* that was partly responsible for a sizable local rebellion in January 1842.

Ch'ung-yang had for years been ravaged by taxing rackets, in which revenue clerks extorted excessive levies under the rubric of "meltage fees," a customary surcharge susceptible to flagrant abuse. By 1841 this oppression had touched off two tax-resistance riots in the countryside. To such an intolerable situation the elite of the community had inevitably to respond. A clique of lower gentrymen, headed by a man named Chung Jen-chieh, brought the whole matter into magistrate's court, where there ensued a running legal battle. Chung Jen-chieh, a wealthy *sheng-yuan* with widespread influence among the lower gentry, had some years earlier run afoul of officialdom through improper conduct in a lawsuit, had been stripped of his title and been banished from the district. Now illegally returned, he had emerged as the leader of resistance to the Ch'ung-yang yamen clerks.

The clerks now struck back by accusing Chung's clique of *pao-lan* —of collecting and transmitting taxes for commission—and of extorting legal fees from taxpaying households. There seems little doubt that Chung and his sympathizers had somehow become involved in the taxing procedure, an illegal practice that obviously threatened the clerks' own illegal practices. Finally the case reached the provincial yamen at Wuchang where it was decided by having everyone involved —clerks and *sheng-yuan* alike—dismissed from the district rolls.

This even-handed settlement settled nothing, and violence followed. A complicated train of events ended with Chung, at the head of a large mob, breaking into the district city in pursuit of his enemies. The magistrate, along with numerous clerks, was killed. Now that rebellion was irreversible, Chung threw open granaries and prison, mobilized peasants from all parts of the district into a ragged army, and marched forth, styling himself "marshall," to conquer the neighboring district city of T'ung-ch'eng.

By this rebellion, the first serious threat to China's heartland since the Chia-ch'ing reign, the court was panicked. The Opium War was just entering a critical stage, and the mid-Yangtze garrisons were depleted. But the rebels were ill organized and ill equipped. By mid-March their lines had been broken and their leaders captured.[60]

60. Wei Yuan, *Ku-wei-t'ang wai-chi* (1878) 4:34–36. *Ch'ing shih-lu,* Tao-kuang,

To understand these complex events it is necessary to dig beneath the official explanations, which leaned heavily on Chung's *pao-lan* activities, his supposedly rebellious and ambitious nature, and the villainy of the "riffraff" (*p'i-kun*) who flocked to his banners. An objective contemporary account points out that the increasing role of the gentry in tax collection, in Ch'ung-yang and elsewhere in central China, was closely related to the worsening financial situation in the countryside, which was inflamed by the drastic increase in the price of silver.[61] With local society in a state of near bankruptcy, preyed upon all the while by corrupt yamen underlings, *pao-lan* of the sort that emerged in Ch'ung-yang can be seen as but one aspect of gentry intervention in the taxing process: as one of a number of ways in which community leaders sought to interpose themselves between the village and the district seat. Excessive taxes could drive small, weak households to seek the protection of large, influential ones, because by allowing the elite to pay their taxes for them, they could avoid many of the illegal surcharges.[62] Thus *pao-lan* had a dual significance: it was, to be sure, a profit-making enterprise of the gentry. But it was also a way in which lineage and community interests could be protected from rampant official extortion. Chung Jen-chieh himself had a wide reputation as "a wealthy man of virtuous conduct";[63] and the fact that he enjoyed considerable popular support (which emerges unmistakably from both Wei Yuan's account and the *Shih-lu*) suggests that his *pao-lan* enterprise was probably a response to his community's desperate need for protection of this sort.

Looking back now at Lin-hsiang, it is apparent that the reorganization of the tax collection system in 1840/41 cannot have been unrelated to what was going on just across the district border in Ch'ung-yang. The turmoil in Ch'ung-yang was the occasion for gentry militarization in several nearby districts, including, along with Lin-hsiang, those of P'ing-chiang and Liu-yang.[64] The admission of the *t'uan*, as a gentry-dominated association, into the taxing apparatus was almost certainly a move by local officials to stave off trouble by legitimizing the considerable local taxing powers the gentry were already assuming. By

---

364:12b–13b; 365:2–3; 366:22–25b; 367:4b–5, 13a-b; 371:39a-b. See Chung Jen-chieh's "confession" in *Chin-tai-shih tzu-liao*, no. 1:2–4 (1963). See also an account in Hsiao, *Rural China*, 135–136.

61. Wei Yuan, *Wai-chi*, 4:35b.

62. Hsiao, *Rural China*, 134.

63. Hu Lin-i, *I-chi*, 52:18.

64. P'ing-chiang 1875, 37:6. Chiang Chung-yuan, *Chiang Chung-lieh-kung i-chi, hsing-chuang*, 13b.

admitting natural local units into the system, the magistrate could forestall the kind of "tax-refusal" (k'ang-liang) that was plaguing officials throughout the central provinces and at the same time make it more likely that regular quotas would be met. This was a way of turning pao-lan to advantage by acquiescing in the inevitable. Because the t'uan were already beginning to levy taxes on local communities to meet the expenses of militarization, it was but one step further to give the t'uan the legitimate taxing functions formerly resident in the li and chia units.[65] At first the outer format of li-chia was maintained by placing the t'uan formally under the li in place of the old chia divisions; but once the needs of militarization came to the fore, the old li-chia structure was completely dissolved, and the t'uan regrouped themselves in patterns that were not consistent with the boundaries of the li units.[66]

The relationship between t'uan-lien and administrative rural subdivisions had two aspects: first, the interchangeability of natural and administrative units at the same scale of organization; second, the development of natural units that were not at all congruent with existing administrative subdivisions. In cases where administrative units such as the pao, li, or chia had already conformed themselves in some measure to the contours of local society, interchangeability was a practical possibility. In many other instances, however, the very weakness and unimportance of the pao-chia registration system had made such an adjustment unnecessary.

The decline of pao-chia registration in parts of China during the nineteenth century was a common theme of contemporary documents. A local source from the lower Yangtze region noted that since the Ch'ien-lung reign, pao-chia had been "sometimes in force, and sometimes not" and had been on balance largely a dead letter.[67] Material from Ho-hsien, Kwangsi, reveals that by the nineteenth century pao-chia had fallen into complete disorder; door placards were filled in with no regard for accuracy; the posts of pao and chia headmen were

65. One essayist recommended that officials entrust tax-collection to t'uan leaders and thereby stave off local disorder. Wang Ying-fu, "T'uan-lien lun, hsia" in Sheng K'ang, ed., Huang-ch'ao ching-shih-wen hsu-pien (1897), 81:10b–11. Tseng Kuo-fan, in a memorial of 1854, noted that in some areas pao-chia, too, had adapted itself to the prevailing trend and was serving as a format for tax-collection. Tseng Wen-cheng-kung ch'üan-chi (1876), tsou-kao, 2:30–31.

66. Compare the list of li and t'uan, Lin-hsiang 1872, 3:7–8b, with the list of multiplex t'uan, 8:3b–4b.

67. Chu-chi 1908, 15:5b.

so undesirable that names were simply written down "emptily" on the registers, the persons involved being either non-existent or not really serving in those capacities.[68] The outbreak of the Taiping Rebellion stimulated official efforts to rebuild pao-chia; in a number of provinces, new pao-chia regulations were promulgated in response to orders from the throne, an action that suggests total breakdown.[69] The ineffectiveness of its registration procedures, to say nothing of its ineffectiveness as a police organ, meant that in most areas pao-chia could not reliably serve as a registration base for militia conscription as some of its official theorists hoped it could.

It is not surprising, then, to find that the irrelevance of pao-chia to real local problems, coupled with the pressing needs of militarization, resulted in a non-congruence between *t'uan* boundaries and standard administrative boundaries. The extended multiplex *t'uan* in Yü-lin, Kwangsi, seem to have been organized with scant regard for local administrative divisions.[70] In other districts, natural and administrative divisions were jumbled together in t'uan-lien organization in a way that suggests an absence of any general organizing principle.[71] But perhaps the most revealing indicator of the dominance of natural over administrative organization was the extent to which multiplex and extended multiplex *t'uan* were organized without respect even to district boundaries. Although official models of t'uan-lien varied in many small details, they invariably placed the magistrate at the head of militia forces within his district. Whatever might be conceded to local initiative and unique local conditions, the principle of bureaucratic supervision at district level was not to be sacrificed. We find, however, that the requirements of strategy, the bonds of kinship and of customary association, were frequently more important demarcators of local defense associations than were district boundaries;[72] and any

68. *Hsiang-shou chi-yao*, 1:2b–3.
69. *Ch'ing Shih-lu*, Hsien-feng, 22:17b; 29:1b; 33:29b; 34:16; 36:4b; 37:8b; 38:11. See also Yeh P'ei-sun, "Ch'ih-hsing pao-chia" in Hsu Tung, ed., *Pao-chia shu* (1848), 2:1–8, for an indication of the difficulties pao-chia was encountering even during the Ch'ien-lung reign.
70. Yü-lin 1894, 3:1–19b.
71. P'ing-chiang 1875, 36:7–9.
72. The famous Sheng-p'ing association near Canton included communities from the two districts of P'an-yü and Nan-hai. In Nanchang, a wealthy *chien-sheng* founded a t'uan-lien bureau that mobilized the resources of more than 120 villages; this confederation was linked by kinship ties that overspread the boundary between Nanchang and Chin-hsien districts. Chang Yueh-ling, a *sheng-yuan* of P'ing-chiang, Hunan, assisted Chiang Chung-yuan in suppressing the Cheng-i t'ang

multiplex *t'uan* that overspread district boundaries were effectively beyond the supervisory reach of district-level bureaucrats.

The ultimate importance of real power factors in determining *t'uan* boundaries is underscored by the extreme flexibility of official thinking on this subject. As the prefect K'uei-lien saw it, any pre-existing rural division could be used as a base for militarization: "either a *tu* [a unit of the *li-chia* system], or a *ts'un* [probably also referring to the *li-chia* division], a *chia* [of the pao-chia system] or a *hsiang* [a suburban administrative division] or a lineage" could be used, according to local conditions; "the important thing is the effective uniting of power (*sheng-shih lien-lo*)."[73]

The Nature of the T'uan

Perhaps we have now reached a point where we can attempt to solve one of our basic problems of definition. It will be remembered that in the official model of t'uan-lien, the *t'uan* was a registration and conscription unit from which militia were to be drafted. In terms of military organization, it was an administrative rather than a tactical unit. In Lu Hsiang-sheng's prescription, the *t'uan* was a kind of local control grouping linked to a fortified stronghold. To Fang Chi and Yen Ju-i, the *t'uan* was closely associated with the *pao* and duplicated certain of the *pao*'s police and surveillance functions. To all these officials, the *t'uan* was primarily a format for official supervision of local defense and police. Yet most of its proponents recognized the indispensable role of the gentry as *t'uan* headmen, which suggests that the essentially natural derivation of the *t'uan* was never far from their thoughts.

We have found that the *t'uan* was indeed a natural unit of coordination, dominated by gentry, and capable of various scales of organization. It was closely associated with such collectivities as lineage and marketing community but rested also on the personal wealth and influence of individual members of the elite. Its scales of organization paralleled those of bureaucratic divisions such as pao-chia and *li-chia*, leading in some cases to confusion and integration of administrative and natural units of coordination. Certain questions remain unanswered, however. Was the *t'uan* concerned only with local defense, or

---

in neighboring Liu-yang and later was assigned by Chiang "to supervise t'uan-lien in P'ing-chiang and Liu-yang." Nanchang 1870, 28:8–9. P'ing-chiang 1875, 37:7.

73. K'uei-lien, "Yü t'uan-lien shih" in Ko Shih-chün, ed., *Huang-ch'ao ching-shih-wen hsu-pien* (1898 ed.) 81:8.

did it embody other community concerns as well? Was it a local unit seen only in times of crisis, or was it a perpetual feature of local organization?

I have already described how the Sheng-p'ing association north of Canton was an outgrowth of pre-existing patterns of gentry cooperation and acquaintanceship based on the "association" (*she*), which existed on both multiplex and extended-multiplex scales of organization. Although these associations entered a spectacular phase of activity during the Opium War, the fact is that they were already in existence, albeit loosely articulated, before that time. In many cases the principal evidence of their existence was the *she-hsueh* or association school, which drew in the resources of a multiplex-scale area for the purpose of education. The *she-hsueh*, however, clearly served a broader purpose: as a center for consultation among the elite on various questions of common concern. When a local emergency arose in the case of rebellion or invasion, the *she-hsueh* served as natural centers for the management of local militarization. An association (such as the Sheng-p'ing itself) that had not had a school attached to it before, now undertook to build one as a center for managing militia affairs.

Although t'uan-lien was a term frequently used in connection with the Sheng-p'ing militia, the association itself was called *she* rather than *t'uan*. This is one of the numerous cases of varying terminology that confuse our study of local institutions; what the people of the Canton area called *she* was usually called *t'uan* in other areas. The multiplex *t'uan*, like the *she*, was a unit of intervillage cooperation that was not merely a local defense organization, but had ties to many other aspects of community interest.

An example in Yü-lin will illustrate the generalized character of the *t'uan* as a gentry-led community institution. Liang Hsien-lin, a *chü-jen*, had returned home after serving in minor educational posts and was teaching in a local academy when the city came under siege by the God-worshiper Ling Shih-pa in 1852. Once the siege was broken, Liang joined two gentry associates to found a multiplex *t'uan* southwest of the city, evidently near his home area. During the next several years, this *t'uan* was active in raising funds and mobilizing militia for local defense in an area seething with rebellion and banditry. By the end of the Hsien-feng reign the region was in sad decline; local schools were nearly abandoned, evidently for lack of both leadership and resources. In 1860 Liang "established, within the *t'uan*, a literary society to conduct yearly examinations and to build up the scholars' morale," a society that remained in existence at least until the last decade of the century. Here was a case in which *t'uan* resources and existing patterns of *t'uan* leadership were turned to the service of customary gentry interests, specifically the furtherance of local education.[74]

Similar cases abound. Near Canton three *hsiang* had formed a multiplex association with headquarters in the market town of Lung-chüan-hsü which managed t'uan-lien during the Red Turban revolt of 1854. Afterwards the leadership of this association received permission from provincial authorities to use "leftover *t'uan* resources" to build a local academy. In P'ing-chiang, Hunan, during the T'ung-chih period, "surplus" t'uan-lien funds were used to found a *t'uan she-hsueh* with operating expenses to be supplied by the rents from specially allocated lands. In Yü-lin, the resources of the I-hsin *t'uan* were used to found a temple.[75] I have already pointed out the close connection in Lin-hsiang between local defense associations and the collection of relief grain, in which the *t'uan* had become a multi-purpose organization for carrying out gentry functions, including even tax collection.

It appears therefore that although the *t'uan* as such was a local defense association, it did on occasion grow out of customary gentry groupings such as the *she* and could subsequently take on additional functions commonly associated with multi-community gentry groupings. It can thus be seen as but one expression of customary patterns of gentry association on the multiplex or extended-multiplex scale: an expression that became widespread during the mid-nineteenth century when effective local management of funds and manpower required something more dependable than customary, informal gentry interaction. This form of organization, a gentry creation for local militarization and control during a time of administrative weakness, was legitimized by a long administrative tradition in which the *t'uan* formed part of a respectable, officially prescribed system of local control. At a time when the basic premises of state power were at issue, this sort of legitimation had a key role to play in binding the elite to the traditional state system. The *t'uan* retained an important place in local administration in the last decades of the nineteenth century, and even in the Republican period influenced the development of rural institutions (see Chapter VI.B).

74. Yü-lin 1894, 15:22b–23.
75. P'an-yü 1871, 16:47; P'ing-chiang 1875, 26:7; Yü-lin 1894, 7:10.

IV. THE RISE OF REBELLION AND THE MILITARIZATION OF THE ORTHODOX ELITE

A. From Local to Imperial Defense: Chiang Chung-yuan

As the social crisis of mid-century propelled China toward civil war, the pace of local militarization quickened. As economic crises and exploitation drove the poor outside the established order, as scarcity sharpened the conflict among ethnic and linguistic groups, both heterodox and orthodox leadership became increasingly concerned with military organization. On the heterodox side, this meant not only the arming and organization of local secret-society chapters, and the proliferation of roving bands of freebooters, but also the amalgamation of embattled and alienated groups into a messianic religious movement. On the orthodox side, it meant not only the proliferation of community-based t'uan-lien associations, but also the emergence of higher-level military forms.

In times of crisis, the first response of the Ch'ing military leadership was to hire paid fighters, or *yung*, to supplement the regular forces, whose numbers were fixed by statute. Broadly speaking, the term *yung* was used to denote any irregular forces of a loyalist character. Thus the militia of a t'uan-lien association were sometimes described as *t'uan-yung* (*yung* from the *t'uan*). But generally *yung* referred to forces on a higher level of militarization: men who were entirely detached from their communities and who depended for their sustenance upon pay or loot. Some such units were recruited directly by government officials, such as the notorious *yung* from Ch'ao-chou. Others originated as bandit gangs and attached themselves to government forces in hopes of more regular and more abundant rewards. The practice of hiring *yung* in times of crisis meant that a large Ch'ing army of the nineteenth century was actually a motley assortment of *yung* units attached to an equally motley assortment of regular battalions transferred from various provincial garrisons.[1]

From the standpoint of the political future of the empire, however, the most important type of *yung* force was that recruited by members of the civil gentry. It was the emergence of such forces at the time of the Taiping Rebellion, and their capacity to coalesce into larger units, that enabled the orthodox elite to meet the challenge of revolt then and for some fifty years thereafter. As we shall have occasion to point out in a later chapter, the tendency of this type of militarization to conform itself to pre-existing lines of affiliation within the elite was a key factor in the ability of traditional society to survive its mid-century crisis. In raising purely local forms of militarization to a new level, leadership came from the provincial and national elites; and especially from a remarkable constellation of Hunan gentry, whose fortunes and personal interconnections were to shape the fortunes of the empire over the next generation.

The Hsin-ning Revolts

Just west of the valley of the Hsiang River in southwestern Hunan rise the mountains of the Hunan-Kwangsi border, an area of increasing inter-ethnic strife, poverty, and secret-society activism during the late Tao-kuang reign. Misery and disorder were compounded by the fact that the Hsiang valley had become one of the routes by which the opium traffic spread northward into the Yangtze provinces. In 1836 the districts of Hsin-ning and Wu-kang were embroiled in a revolt led by a Yao tribesman named Lan Cheng-tsun. Lan, holder of a purchased *chien-sheng* degree, evidently had been persecuted by wealthy landowners of his own minority group and ultimately driven outside the law. He had then risen to leadership of a secret group known as the Black Lotus Society (Ch'ing-lien Chiao), a cult imported some years earlier from Szechwan, clearly a White Lotus affiliate. Though Lan's uprising was snuffed out in an unsuccessful attack on the city of Wu-

---

1. *Hsiang Jung Tsou-kao* in Hsiang Ta, et al., eds., *T'ai-p'ing t'ien-kuo*, (Shanghai, 1954), 7:132, lists the *yung* contingents attached to the "Great Camp of Kiangnan" in 1853.

kang, it succeeded in polarizing society in the border region and in spreading heterodox influence among the Han peasantry.[2]

The hill country now entered a period of drought; as if bent on self-destruction, the Ch'ing bureaucracy compounded local distress with its own corruption. Magistrate Li Po of Hsin-ning district, apparently in connivance with local rice merchants, manipulated the official granary system to drive up rice prices. Upon the hungry peasantry the yamen runners practiced their usual extortion and were particularly merciless to the relatives of a certain Lei Tsai-hao.[3] Lei, like Lan Cheng-tsun, was a tribesman of the Yao minority. Unfortunately for his persecutors, he was also a secret-society organizer, leader of a group called the Cudgel Society (Pang-pang hui). The Cudgel Society was a curious conglomerate that embodied elements of both the White Lotus and Triad traditions. It included some of Lan Cheng-tsun's former followers, who carried on the White Lotus cult with its vegetarian practices and Buddhist ritual. But it also contained a certain number of Triad cadres (*t'ieh-pan*), of whom some were ethnically Han. By virtue of its Triad components, the Cudgel Society was able to reach beyond the environs of Hsin-ning and form connections with a Han rebel, Li Shih-te, head of a Triad chapter across the border in Kwangsi. It also absorbed various bandit groups with no sectarian character. Clearly two fateful processes were at work: the sectarian movement was becoming enmeshed in the mechanisms of ethnic rebellion; and the ethnic movement itself was successfully reaching out for connections with the rebellious Han peasantry. In this sense it can be seen that the turmoil in Hsin-ning was an important precursor of later and greater events.[4]

2. On Lan Cheng-tsun and his background see Chiang Shih-yen, ed., "Ya-p'ien chan-cheng ch'ien-hou Hsin-ning, Wu-kang nung-min ch'i-i ti pu-fen tzu-liao" in *Hu-nan li-shih tzu-liao*, no. 1, 49–65 (1958). This rich source material must be studied in the context of a general inquiry into minority groups of that area, a prime subject for future research. See also Hunan 1958, I, 10. This gazetteer is a new, vernacular edition, which draws upon a variety of local sources, including both earlier gazetteers and oral tradition, and attempts to present rebel movements in a sympathetic light. On White Lotus affiliates in this region, see Ling T'i-an, *Hsien-T'ung Kuei-chou chün-shih shih* (1932) 1:77b–79.

3. Hu Lin-i, *I-chi*, 52:9a-b.

4. Hunan 1958, I, 15; Hsin-ning 1893, 16:6. Lo Erh-kang has pointed out the natural confusion among Ch'ing officials as to the affiliation of secret-society groups in this area and concludes from various evidence that many of the groups thought to be "vegetarian sects" were in fact Triads. *T'ai-p'ing T'ien-kuo shih chi-tsai ting-miu chi* (Peking, 1955), 74–76. The composition of the Cudgel Society suggests that the situation was more complicated than Lo supposes. This was an

In the summer of 1847, Lei Tsai-hao began to mobilize his followers for revolt. But by this time the elite of Hsin-ning had begun to rally its own forces. Chiang Chung-yuan (1812–1854), a *chü-jen,* had returned to his home in 1844 after passing several years in Peking. In Peking he had studied under his fellow provincial Tseng Kuo-fan and had prepared successfully for the special examination known as *ta-t'iao,* whereby scholars who had failed the regular metropolitan examination three times could qualify for direct official appointment. Chiang was made an expectant district director of studies.[5]

When Chiang reached Hsin-ning in 1844 he sensed imminent disaster and immediately set about mobilizing his lineage for defense. He was concerned, among other things, to keep poorer kinsmen out of Lei Tsai-hao's organization, which was actively recruiting in the villages. Therefore he "secretly organized them along military lines" and as an ideological complement "lectured them on principles of kinship loyalty and generational obedience." The elite of other lineages were doing likewise, most notably an energetic young military *sheng-yuan* named Teng Shu-k'un.[6]

By the autumn of 1847, news of Lei's impending revolt leaked out, and Chiang Chung-yuan gained the initiative. After mounting a propaganda campaign to turn Lei's followers against him, Chiang led a force of 2,000 militiamen, raised from his own and allied lineages, and dislodged Lei from his home base at Huang-pei-t'ung. During the remaining autumn months the campaign flowed back and forth in the border mountains and ended in Lei's betrayal by his own lieutenants. By early December it was all over, with Li Shih-te a suicide and Lei captured and executed. But of the rebel rank and file many escaped,

---

area where the two great heterodox traditions, White Lotus and Triad, were contiguous. Their interaction awaits further research.

5. Chiang Chung-yuan, *Chiang Chung-lieh-kung i-chi, hsing-chuang,* 1–2. The statement in Hummel, *Eminent Chinese,* 136, that Tseng Kuo-fan was Chiang's "friend" should probably be corrected to "teacher." Chiang was in too junior a status to figure among Tseng's circle of friends and is not mentioned as such in Tseng's letters. Instead he is probably one of "last year's students" (*men-sheng*) mentioned in Tseng's account of the 1844 *ta-t'iao* examination (letter of June 27, 1844; *Tseng Wen-cheng-kung chia-shu* [Taipei, 1957], 76.) See also Ho I-k'un, *Tseng Kuo-fan p'ing-chuan* (1937), 57–60.

6. Huang P'eng-nien, *Chiang Chung-lieh-kung mu-piao,* printed as a supplement to Chiang, *I-chi,* appendix, 6a-b. See also the biographical article by Teng Ssu-yü in Hummel, *Eminent Chinese,* 136–137; and Lo Erh-kang, *Hsiang-chün hsin-chih* (Changsha, 1939), 67–68. See the list of martyred *t'uan* leaders in Hsin-ning 1893, chüan 6.

among them an experienced cadre named Li Yuan-fa, who was soon to take up the flag of revolt.

From the Hsin-ning side, the fight had been waged largely by Chiang Chung-yuan's militiamen. Though provincial officials had been prepared to transfer large forces into Hsin-ning, Chiang had successfully induced them not to do so, on the sound premise that such "guest soldiers" would be more trouble than they were worth. During the campaign against Lei, brief official mentions of "able-bodied males" (*chuang-ting*) led by gentry were the only hints to the court that rebel suppression was being carried on by anyone save regular troops.[7] Nor is there any indication that either the court or provincial officials were prepared to follow up the implications of Chiang's success. Nobody was prepared to suggest that the elite be entrusted with military responsibilities of a higher order or that local militia like that of Hsin-ning be entrusted with any tasks beyond the policing of local village society.

For his part in the affair, Chiang was quickly rewarded with an acting magistracy in Chekiang, where he proceeded in 1849. This did not mean, however, that his Hsin-ning militia organization was disbanded. Despite Chiang's personal leadership role, the militia was the instrument of a lineage elite, not an individual. Though the militiamen returned to their homes, the organization persisted in attenuated form, under the leadership of Chiang's brothers and cousins, and played a role in the next crisis, which was not long in coming.[8]

By the winter of 1849 flood had succeeded drought, and famine began to grip Hsin-ning. Li Yuan-fa, an erstwhile servant in the district schools office, had been a cadre (*t'ieh-pan*) in Lei Tsai-hao's Cudgel Society, and it was he who now assumed the leadership of the Hsin-ning Triads. With a ragged band of 300 he broke into the city to rescue two of his followers who had been imprisoned. At this time the magistrate, Li Po, had been lucky enough to be temporarily detached for service at the provincial examinations, and his replacement, Wan Ting-en, had little knowledge of affairs in the district, having arrived only a month before. Now he was left alone in his yamen, his attendants and guards all fled, to face the invaders alone. Surrounded as he was by armed Triads, Wan was still able to summon a certain

7. *Ch'ing shih-lu*, Tao-kuang, 448:15–16, 27b; 449:14b–15, 27. See also Hsieh Hsing-yao, *T'ai-p'ing t'ien-kuo ch'ien-hou Kuang-hsi ti fan-Ch'ing yün-tung* (Peking, 1950), 3.

8. Hunan 1885, 89:2b. Huang P'eng-nien, 6b.

dignity and assured them that he would attend to their grievances. He was shouted down from a dozen quarters: why had no relief grain been distributed? Wan replied that funds had not in fact arrived, but that he was aware of their sufferings and would undertake to raise relief locally. Then someone cried out that the suppression of rebels in the past several years had been accompanied by indiscriminate slaughter and that the people were determined to have revenge on those responsible. Wan assured them that if such frightful things had indeed taken place the people should report them through channels and he would bring them justice.

Their anger somewhat released, the ragged group began to jostle toward the exit, reluctant to push the matter any further. But as Wan began to walk away, a drunken man lurched forward, sword in hand, and cut him down with a single stroke. As there was no reversing the course of events, Li and his followers opened the granaries and the prison and set about fortifying the city as best they could. We have no way of knowing whether the murder of Wan Ting-en was in fact a planned action, undertaken by one of Li's cadres to commit a reluctant peasantry to revolt, or whether it was really unforeseen. At any rate, Li found himself at the head of a rebellion that was to spread considerably farther than that of his late predecessor.[9]

While the rebels were taking over the city two local gentrymen, the *kung-sheng* Liu Ch'ang-yu (who was to become a leading general and provincial official) and his relative, the *sheng-yuan* Liu K'un-i (later an eminent statesman of the late nineteenth century) fled to the prefectural seat to plead for help. After alerting the regular garrisons, the prefect summoned Magistrate Li Po to return and work with the militia in Hsin-ning as he had done so effectively two years earlier. It was the local t'uan-lien militia that now became Li Yuan-fa's chief antagonist. Chiang Chung-yuan's brother, Chung-chi, mobilized once more the force that had opposed Lei Tsai-hao two years earlier. Together with militia commanded by Teng Shu-k'un, Chiang Chung-yuan's old collaborator, these gentry-led irregulars besieged Hsin-ning for twenty days; finally a large contingent of regular troops arrived

9. There are a number of accounts of the Li Yuan-fa uprising, which differ in some details. *Ling-hsiao i-shih sui-pi*, quoted in Hsieh Hsing-yao, 3–4; Hsin-ning 1893, 16:9a-b; Li Yuan-fa's deposition, printed in *Chin-tai-shih tzu-liao*, no. 1:6–9 (1963); legend has it that prior to his revolt Li Yuan-fa had been in contact with Hung Hsiu-ch'üan and his God Worshiping Society in Kwangsi, but the details are not believable. See Hunan 1958, 16.

but hung prudently in the background and never approached the city walls. Finally, their food reserves exhausted, Li Yuan-fa and his men broke out of the east gate of the city ("taking advantage of rain and darkness" as the local chronicler put it) and disappeared toward the border mountains. The regular troops then entered the city, and after an orgy of looting and slaughter the governor reported to Peking that they had retaken the city and killed Li Yuan-fa along with innumerable "rebels."[10]

Their return to Hsin-ning effectively blocked by government troops and gentry militia, the rebels moved southwest into Kwangsi in the spring of 1850. Roaming widely through the Hunan-Kwangsi border region, pursued constantly by government troops, Li's band gathered adherents from the poor peasants and minority tribes until it numbered several thousand. Through the early spring months of 1850 it struggled westward toward the point where the provinces of Hunan, Kwangsi, and Kweichow meet, and even penetrated Kweichow's southeastern border districts.[11]

Gentry resistance to Li Yuan-fa in Hsin-ning was at the outset a replica of the resistance to Lei Tsai-hao two years earlier. In the forefront were the militia led by the elite of the Chiang and Teng lineages. Teng Shu-k'un and Chiang's younger brother, Chung-chi, were joined by Liu Ch'ang-yu, a *kung-sheng* from a merchant family, Teng Hsin-k'o, a military *sheng-yuan*, and Ni Ch'ang-kao, holder of lower ninth purchased rank. The total gentry-led forces probably did not exceed the former level of about 2,000 men, with several hundred under each leader.[12] But the scale of operations was quite different this time. Lei Tsai-hao had sought sanctuary on the rugged Hsin-ning border, and gentry militia had largely confined their campaigning to the periphery of the district. Li Yuan-fa was either more desperate or more ambitious, so convinced of the nearness of major rebellion that he decided to sweep widely across the impoverished hill country and draw after him the dispossessed of many districts. In all he fought through no fewer than thirteen districts, mostly in northern Kwangsi.

To Li Yuan-fa's expansion of the struggle the Hsin-ning elite responded in kind. When Li set out into Kwangsi, Chiang Chung-chi

10. Hsin-ning 1893, 16:10; *Ling-hsiao i-shih sui-pi*, quoted in Hsieh Hsing-yao, 4. *Ch'ing Shih-lu*, Tao-Kuang, 475:15a-b; This report was not believed at court, however.

11. Hsieh Hsing-yao, 4–5; Hsin-ning 1893, 16:9–11; Hu Lin-i, *I-chi*, 52:19.

12. Hsin-ning 1893, 10a-b.

and Liu Ch'ang-yu marshalled their forces and set out after him, closely followed by Teng Shu-k'un and Ni Ch'ang-kao. What had begun as an effort to defend the status quo in their home district became a more ambitious effort to combat rebellion far beyond the district boundaries. It was bitter cold in the mountains and the militiamen, ill equipped for extended campaigning, suffered greatly. Somewhere in the mountains near Huai-yuan (now San-chiang) some 130 kilometers from Hsin-ning, Teng and Ni lost their way in the driving snow and were ambushed by Li's rebels. Teng and more than forty of his militiamen perished. Whether Chiang and his allies continued their pursuit at this point we do not know. Li, however, was constantly harried by government forces under Hsiang Jung, newly appointed provincial commander-in-chief of Hunan,[13] and was unable to settle in one place long enough to rally his forces. After campaigning fruitlessly southeastward as far as Hsiu-jen he led his decimated troop northward again to the familiar hills of Hsin-ning, hoping perhaps to disband and escape. But in May, government troops and militia surrounded him and slaughtered his remnant forces. Li himself was captured and sent to Peking for decapitation.

While Li Yuan-fa's rebellion raged, Chiang Chung-yuan was in distant Chekiang serving as a district magistrate. By the spring of 1850 his service in bandit suppression and flood relief had won him wide respect among senior officials. When the Hsien-feng Emperor succeeded to the throne in March and called for recommendations of talented men, Chiang's name was put up by his former teacher, Tseng Kuo-fan, then serving as junior vice president of the Board of Rites. Chiang was summoned to imperial audience, but the governor of Chekiang, Wu Wen-jung, asked that he be temporarily retained in Chekiang to supervise dike repair. Just as the work was finished, Chiang received formal notice from home that his father had died. This news made credible a horrifying rumor that reached him about the same time, to the effect that his whole family had been wiped out by Li Yuan-fa. Chiang fell seriously ill, to recover only when a letter arrived assuring him that his family was unscathed by the rebellion. But because of his father's death (evidently of natural causes) Chiang resigned his duties and set out for home to observe the customary mourning period.[14]

13. This represents Hsiang Jung's entrance into the fight against the southern rebellions. *Ch'ing shih-lu*, Hsien-feng, 3:15. He later became the principal government commander against the Taipings, whom he fought until his death in 1856.
14. Chiang, *I-chi, hsing-chuang*, 3b–4.

Chiang Chung-yuan and the Taiping Rebellion

As 1850 waned, the situation in South China was undergoing fateful changes. The God-worshiping Society (Pai Shang-ti hui) had gathered a formidable congregation of the dispossessed and desperate of central Kwangsi; had added to them bands of pirates and Triads from neighboring Kwangtung; had indoctrinated them all in a new politico-religious faith; and after defending themselves successfully against local government forces, proclaimed, on January 11, 1851, the advent of the Heavenly Kingdom of Great Peace (*T'ai-p'ing t'ien-kuo*). From their original base at Chin-t'ien, the Taipings fought their way to the walled city of Yung-an (now Meng-shan), which they occupied from September 1851 until April 1852 and where they undertook in earnest the formal organization of their civil and military institutions. Meantime, the government sought to rally its resources and contain the rebellion; in April 1851 the Grand Secretary Sai-shang-a was sent to Kwangsi as Imperial Commissioner; he was assisted by Wu-lan-t'ai, the deputy lieutenant-general of the Canton banner garrison, and by Hsiang Jung, who had been transferred to Kwangsi as provincial commander-in-chief. These men commanded a mixed force consisting of regular provincial troops and mercenaries hired for the occasion.

Sai-shang-a's appointment came in April; about this time Tso Tsung-chih (a brother of Tso Tsung-t'ang), who was serving as a Secretary of the Grand Secretariat, suggested that Sai ought to include on his staff the able *chü-jen* from Hsin-ning, Chiang Chung-yuan. Tso was from Hsiang-yin, Hunan, and if he was not personally acquainted with Chiang, he undoubtedly knew of him through Tseng Kuo-fan; at any rate, the Hunanese group at the capital seems to have been well aware of top Hunanese talent in its various locations throughout the empire. Accordingly Grand Secretary Ch'i Chün-tsao recommended Chiang to Sai-shang-a, and Chiang was duly summoned to the latter's staff in Kwangsi.[15]

In July Chiang arrived at Sai-shang-a's headquarters in Kweilin, where he was introduced to Wu-lan-t'ai, an able and dedicated Manchu

15. Chiang, *I-chi, hsing-chuang*, 4b. Some months earlier Chiang had considered joining the anti-Taiping campaign in some way, perhaps with a force of *yung*. He had been restrained by Tseng Kuo-fan, however, who forbade him to undertake any such duties while formally in mourning. Tseng now considered Chiang's service under Sai-shang-a morally acceptable as long as he restricted himself to staff work and steadfastly refused all ranks and honors. Tseng, *Ch'üan-chi, shu-cha*, 1:28b–29b; 36–37.

officer. Wu-lan-t'ai took Chiang under his wing, and the two men found themselves in close sympathy. Once he was aware of the military exploits of the Chiangs of Hsin-ning, Wu-lan-t'ai urged Chiang to recruit a detachment of Hsin-ning men for service against the Taipings. Chiang wrote home to his brother, Chung-shu, who then hired 500 men and marched into Kwangsi. Chung-shu was soon rendered *hors de combat* by dysentery, and the Hsin-ning *yung* marched to battle under Chiang Chung-yuan's command.

The first test of the Ch'u-yung or Hunan braves, as they were now called, was at the siege of Yung-an in late 1851. A few engagements dispelled the scorn of the government troops on the scene, who had derided their short stature and ragged appearance. Before long, however, Chiang found himself caught in a dispute between his friend and patron, Wu-lan-t'ai, and Hsiang Jung, provincial commander-in-chief. Wu was as blunt in his personal dealings as he was courageous at the front and was in constant friction with Hsiang, whom he considered both cowardly and incompetent. When Hsiang proposed using the "ancient method" of allowing the besieged rebels an escape route and then attacking them in passage, Wu-lan-t'ai pointed out that since the rebels numbered less than 10,000, and the government had several times that many, a properly conducted siege could end only with the rebels' starvation and defeat. Chiang agreed but found himself helpless in this dispute between his two superiors; he abruptly withdrew his men and returned to Hsin-ning. The Taipings did, in early April 1852, break out of Yung-an, aided no doubt by Hsiang's "ancient method," and surged northward toward Kweilin, the provincial capital. The march to Kweilin brought the Taipings over a key watershed: out of rivers draining toward the south coast and into rivers draining toward the Yangtze. Thus the siege of Yung-an may be seen in retrospect as a turning point in the struggle: the last chance for the Ch'ing to wipe out the Taipings before they emerged into the fertile recruiting ground of the central provinces.[16]

The Taipings reached the walls of Kweilin within a fortnight after leaving Yung-an and immediately laid siege to the city, a disaster that sent waves of shock throughout the Ch'ing establishment. For Chiang Chung-yuan it was the signal to emerge once more from Hsin-ning. Without official urging, he and Liu Ch'ang-yu raised funds to hire 1,000 men, and within a month were on the road to Kweilin. Before

16. Chiang, *I-chi, hsing-chuang*, 3b–7b.

he arrived he heard the news that Wu-lan-t'ai had died of wounds received at the siege. Much affected, he vowed revenge.[17] As events turned out, his second entry into Kwangsi was a decisive march onto the stage of national events; he and his force of Ch'u-yung were now committed to the anti-Taiping struggle.

Unsuccessful in their siege of Kweilin, the Taipings moved on to Ch'üan-chou (present Ch'üan-hsien); the city was taken and its populace slaughtered.[18] The Hsiang river now lay open before them: a highway into Hunan, leading to Changsha, Wuchang, and the rich Yangtze provinces. Their baggage and a substantial part of their forces were now loaded aboard boats and floated downriver toward the Hunan border. Chiang had pursued the Taipings from Kweilin to Ch'üan-chou. Finding them in control there, he hastened ahead to cut off their northward progress. Setting up an ambush on the west bank of the river, just short of the Hunan border at the ferry-crossing known as Shuai-i-tu, Chiang waited in concealment for the Taiping boats to appear.

On June 10, when the Taipings reached Chiang's barricade, their trapped fleet was bombarded at point-blank range and largely destroyed. The exact size of Taiping losses cannot be determined, but in view of the fact that over 300 boats were captured, in addition to those destroyed, the defeat must have been very damaging. In this holocaust died Feng Yun-shan, a founder of the Taiping movement and its ablest political leader, already wounded seriously at Ch'üan-chou. Unfortunately for the loyalist side, however, the east bank of the Hsiang had been left undefended, as the Ch'ing general, Ho-ch'un, had thought it prudent to ignore Chiang's pleas for concerted action. A large part of the Taiping force was thereby enabled to scramble to the eastern shore and escape into Hunan. Though the Taipings' line of march had been altered and their plans to move northward delayed, the defeat had not been decisive, and in southern Hunan their forces were to be greatly augmented.[19]

From Shuai-i-tu the path of the Ch'u-yung led northward to the

17. Chiang, *I-chi, hsing-chuang,* 5b–6; Kuo T'ing-i, *T'ai-p'ing t'ien-kuo shih-shih jih-chih* (Taipei, 1963), 151–179. Hu Lin-i. *Hu Wen-chung-kung i-chi* (1875), 54: 9a-b.

18. For the curious details of this battle see Chien Yu-wen, *Ch'üan-shih,* I, 383–387.

19. Chien, *Ch'üan-shih,* I, 387–389. Sai-shang-a's official report on the battle was almost entirely fanciful and failed even to mention Chiang and the Ch'u-yung. *Chiao-p'ing Yueh-fei fang-lueh* (1872), 13:7a-b.

defense of Changsha and thence into the large-scale campaigns of the Yangtze valley; but these events will be discussed in connection with Tseng Kuo-fan and the founding of the Hunan Army. Leaving Chiang with his bloody but inconclusive victory, we can look back and trace the evolution of the Ch'u-yung to a response by the elite of local lineages to strictly local problems. Lei Tsai-hao's rebellion, a small-scale affair largely on the periphery of Hsin-ning, had spurred a group of young gentry to recruit militiamen from among their own kinsmen: a measure which must be seen as a means for strengthening the internal cohesion of highly stratified lineages as well as for physical defense. The militia organizations of Chiang Chung-yuan and Teng Shu-k'un were nuclei of community organization that provided alternatives to secret-society groups recruiting in the villages. The leadership of these organizations was not formed on genealogical principles, but rather consisted of degree holders of military age: in 1847, Chiang Chung-yuan was 35, Teng Shu-k'un and Liu Ch'ang-yu both 29, and Liu K'un-i only 17.[20] Chiang Chung-yuan, as a member of the upper gentry, assumed leadership of the group as a whole, and it was his connections with the larger official world that were to make possible the involvement of Hsin-ning militia in larger events.

The rebellion of Li Yuan-fa, which affected no fewer than 13 districts in three provinces, represented a crucial intermediate step in Hsin-ning militarization. Li's decision to mobilize support in wide areas of the Kwangsi hill country, to catalyze rebellion of a larger order, had the effect of drawing his gentry opponents into wider campaigning. The militiamen who pursued Li into Kwangsi were forced to make commitments of a higher order; their support required, on the part of their leaders, a larger commitment of wealth. Thus by the time of Chiang Chung-yuan's involvement with the Taiping Rebellion, there already existed in Hsin-ning a body of men and a cadre of leaders able to separate themselves from family and community for periods of extended campaigning beyond the district borders.

The record is quite clear, though, that Chiang Chung-yuan owed his position on Sai-shang-a's staff to his connections as a degree holder and his record as a civil official and not to his record as a troop leader. He was known primarily as a successful student of Tseng Kuo-fan's, and an able magistrate. He proceeded to Kwangsi as a highly recommended staff adviser, not as a military leader. His career after 1852

20. See the biographies in Hummel, *Eminent Chinese*; on Teng Shu-k'un see Li Huan, ed., *Kuo-ch'ao ch'i-hsien lei-cheng, ch'u-pien*, 374:50a-b.

must, then, be seen as a product of two distinct aspects of his gentry status: his leadership of his own lineage and of the Hsin-ning elite and his connections with the broader elites of province and capital.

Chiang Chung-yuan's motives in becoming involved in the anti-Taiping campaign provide an enlightening illustration of how local gentry viewed their various community and regional responsibilities. There seems little question that his initial concern, in the case of Lei Tsai-hao's rebellion, was the safety of his home, his lineage, and his native district. Nor is it surprising that his brother pursued Li Yuan-fa far into Kwangsi, for he anticipated that as long as Li was at large he posed a particular threat to his home area; and as we have seen, Li did at length return to the Hsin-ning border. Even after 1850, when Chiang had already raised his force to a higher stage of militarization, the safety of Hsin-ning remained a primary concern for him. His move ahead of the Taipings to Shuai-i-tu, he wrote, aimed "to prevent their taking the land route westward to Hsin-ning" as well as to block the water route northward. After the success of his ambuscade, he had "thought that our Hunan might perhaps be successfully defended," but the subsequent entry of the Taipings into Tao-chou and other southern Hunan districts, virtually unopposed by Ch'ing commanders, dashed his hopes. No doubt the violently heterodox character of the Taipings made them a feared and hated opponent; but Chiang clearly had a predominantly local perspective, leading outward from his home district, to his home province, and only thence to affairs of the empire as a whole.[21]

B. Hu Lin-i Builds a "Personal Army"

Militarization was indeed a disease of border regions. Mountainous Kweichow, where Hu Lin-i served as a prefect during the years 1847–1854, was a border region that offered some of the most baffling challenges to bureaucracy that could be found anywhere in the empire. Added to the difficult terrain and poor communications were endemic feuding between Han and Miao; an active network of secret society groups, primarily in the White Lotus tradition; and an irrational tangle of administrative boundaries and consequent irregularities in tax procedures.[22]

21. Chiang, *I-chi*, 1:8.

22. On the confused administrative history of central Kweichow see Hu Lin-i's analysis in *I-chi*, 52:7b–14b. Documents from Hu's career in Kweichow comprise chüan 52–58 of this collection.

A *chin-shih* of 1836, from I-yang, Hunan, Hu began his career as a Hanlin academician (in which he was two years senior to Tseng Kuo-fan) and state historiographer. Called home from Peking by his father's death in 1841/42, he lived in retirement for several years; then, having bought himself the substantive rank of prefect, he took up his first post at An-shun, Kweichow, in 1847. Transferred eastward to Chen-yuan prefecture in 1850 and thence to Li-p'ing in 1851, he plunged into the manifold troubles of the Kweichow-Hunan-Kwangsi border area.

Problems of Local Control in Kweichow

In Chen-yuan, rebellion took the form of Miao uprisings; in Li-p'ing, of secret-society bandits. Taken together, Hu's experiences in these two prefectures formed the basis for his strategy of local control. The prevailing lack of physical security had led the people in these areas, both Han and Miao, to fortify their villages, which then became bases for community feuding and refuges for outlaws. Outside the administrative cities, the countryside was hostile or indifferent to the bureaucracy. In one of his pao-chia registration drives, Hu found in one village that only three out of 58 households were not implicated in banditry or rebellion. In other villages, loyal households were only 70 or 80 percent. This scarcity of loyal subjects undoubtedly reflected the uneven balance of military power, which in that region leaned against the government. Rebel intelligence about government troop movements was quick and reliable. Hu found to his dismay that "as soon as the official sets forth, the rebels flee. As soon as he has returned, the rebels congregate again." This "sudden gathering and sudden stopping" made the situation hard to control with standard military means. The natural difficulty of the mountain terrain strengthened the independence of the fortified villages and precluded moving large masses of troops against them. The official was thus in a difficult position. He could ignore the chaos around him and gloss it over with false reports (as Hu accused his predecessor of doing); he could bring regular garrison troops into the hills to attack stubborn strongholds; or he could devise more effective measures than either of these.[23]

To import troops was not, in Hu's opinion, a sound solution. For one thing, troops could not "separate the loyal from the disloyal," and

23. Hu, *I-chi*, 52:15, 53:11b.

Hu was repelled by the prospect of indiscriminate slaughter. Hu's strictures against the regulars are reminiscent of Kung Ching-han's (which Hu, like everyone else, had read) but went further. The Green Standard forces were wholly unsuited to the complicated job of rebel-suppression: "The rebels travel like rats and the soldiers travel like cows. You cannot use cows to catch rats." The rebels' guerrilla tactics were predictably effective in the hilly border region: "When the soldiers are few, the rebels will fight them; when the soldiers are many, the rebels will flee." Furthermore, the Green Standards were both troublesome and expensive. In addition to their statutory allowances for food and transport expenses, they constantly made extra demands on the local bureaucracy. In 1850, when 3,000 troops were stationed in Li-p'ing for three months, they had to be supplied 60,000 or 70,000 laborers (maintained at local expense) to move their baggage. There were constant requisitions beyond authorized amounts, and the officers "lost no opportunity to cause trouble." The local people, both Han and Miao, bitterly resented them, and it was commonly said, "the arrival of soldiers is worse than the arrival of bandits." And for all this, the troops were militarily useless. They would not dig fortifications and could only defend spots made impregnable by accident of nature.[24]

Having ruled out military suppression by outside forces, Hu sought to understand the roots of conflict in local society and then to combat rebellion with local resources. Hu's analysis of the mechanics of rebellion began with a clear-eyed criticism of his own colleagues, the local bureaucracy. The immediate cause of rebellion was, he thought, corruption among officials and not merely among those traditional scapegoats, the clerks and yamen runners. In recent years, corruption had often led "bad elements among the people" (*yu-min*) to organize local revolt. Thus it had been with the rebellions of Lei Tsai-hao and Li Yuan-fa in Hsin-ning and of the God Worshipers in Chin-t'ien. With official extortion as a "pretext," secret-society organizers were able to "rouse and incite the peasantry." The causal sequence was clear: the catalyst was corruption. A pre-condition was the presence of "bad elements," that is, an indigenous heterodox leadership already inclined toward rebellion but needing a popular issue around which to mobilize support. Once in possession of such an issue, the local rebel leader-

24. Hu, *I-chi*, 52:15, 19; 55:10b; Li-p'ing 1892, 5, *shang*:64–65b. The troops were regularly given extra pay while on campaign, but the amounts were still insufficient. For categories of pay see Lo Erh-kang, *Lü-ying ping-chih*, 269–297.

ship went to work on the peasantry with propaganda and organization, and a rebellion was begun.[25]

Hu's analysis of social disorder is noteworthy for its honesty and perspicuity, but also for its one-sidedness. To trace disasters to moral causes was a standard Confucian practice. Such long-term trends as population expansion, though they might be contributing factors, were not considered decisive. Granted, officials like Li Po in Hsin-ning can be singled out unmistakably as the proximate cause of rebellion. Yet one cannot help wondering if the general corruption among local officials in the nineteenth century so far exceeded that of earlier periods as to constitute, by itself, a decisive factor in social history. Presumably a society in which population is not pressing heavily upon resources can absorb more corruption than a society living on the margin of subsistence. Corruption should perhaps be viewed as a kind of natural disaster: even a slight alteration for the worse, in a community without substantial reserves, can push the peasantry over the line from marginal subsistence to marginal starvation.

As Hu saw it, then, there were several groups involved in traditional rural politics: the first, the peasantry, was normally passive, but its energies were the basic power of rebellion. The second, the "bad elements," or indigenous heterodox leadership, represented for Hu a constant malaise in the body politic that lay hidden until inflamed by misgovernment. But the official was not simply competing with heterodox leaders for the loyalty of the peasants, because there was a third and pivotal group, the local literati. This group comprised degree holders, as well as that *demi-monde* of partly educated but unsuccessful degree candidates out of which emerged men like Hung Hsiu-ch'üan, founder of the Taiping movement.

To preempt the services of this pivotal local group was the key to Hu's local control strategy, for the dangers in not doing so were all too apparent. Hu quoted the Sung official Fu Pi (d. 1085): "When desperate characters study and attend examinations but find no hope of success, they often grow disgruntled, develop rebellious ideas, and secretly conspire with one another. These types are scattered among the people and can really cause disasters. Thus it is important to gain their confidence and thereby bridle them." "These types," of course, had great potential; they were the handle by which the power of the people could be wielded. They were men of talent and must be

25. Hu, *I-chi*, 53:9.

obtained by him who is to rule rural China. As the Ming rebel-fighter, Hsu K'uei (*chin-shih* 1508) had written, "What place has no talented men? And what talented men cannot be used?" But if officials do not use them, "then the bold ones will think of rebellion, and the timid will be scattered before the wind." The key to using such men was to attach them in some way to the state system; this was after all one of the premises behind the examination system and the sale of ranks and degrees. By lavishing brevet ranks and titles upon the local elite and making them responsible for local order, they could be made enthusiastic supporters of the status quo. After all, wrote Hu, civil and military officials were used to having honors bestowed upon them and regarded them as natural perquisites. But the rustic literati were less spoiled. For them, "obtaining brevet ranks and official titles is like ascending to heaven."[26]

Hu's basic prescription for local order was to build a combined pao-chia and t'uan-lien system with the help of the local elite. The magistrate was to select two or three loyal and able gentry to "go into the countryside" carrying blank registers. Upon reaching a village they would search out the local leadership—"the upright, the talented, the wealthy and the titled"—and entrust them with the responsibility for both local order and local defense, inscribing their names in the registers. These local leaders were in turn to compile registers of all persons in their areas, making special note of those who were potential troublemakers, and bring one copy to the magistrate's yamen. Because the object was to induce the local elite to identify itself with the interests of officialdom, the magistrate was to go to extraordinary lengths to gain their confidence, even inviting those who were literate and presentable to a special banquet (the especially rough and coarse ones could be allowed to stand around the sides of the room), and in general "not pettily abiding by the usual official proprieties." These were courtesies customarily reserved for the upper gentry, who alone were considered the magistrate's social equals.[27]

The essence of Hu's method was to rely entirely upon real power factors in the countryside. In uniting pao-chia and t'uan-lien into a single system and entrusting both to the care of the local elite, Hu was acknowledging that police and defense were inseparable and could only be accomplished by those already in substantial control of local affairs. Therefore all was to be based upon natural units. The *t'uan*

26. Hu, *I-chi*, 54:3b; 55:8b.
27. Hu, *I-chi*, 57:15b–16b.

(and its police aspect, the *pao*) was to be a natural multiplex grouping of walled villages over a distance of five or ten miles. By placing the local elite in charge of pao-chia registration and police control, Hu was contravening one of the central principles of the Ch'ing pao-chia system, namely, the exclusion of the gentry from pao-chia and the placing of police responsibility in the hands of subservient nonentities. The devolution of pao-chia into the hands of the elite, and the ensuing consolidation of the elite's local governing powers, were important outgrowths of the mid-century crisis, a subject that will be explored further in Chapter VI.

The Militarization of Civil Authority:
The Personal Army (Ch'in-ping)

Such were the outlines of Hu Lin-i's local control system; but the momentum of dynastic decline had long since made Hu aware that local control was not enough. As early as 1844/45 he was arguing that high provincial officials must provide themselves with a personal contingent of troops (*ch'in-ping*), a kind of elite guard whose dependence upon their commander transcended normal bureaucratic lines of authority. Such a unit was to be selected from the cream of the regular detachments serving under governors and governors-general. Hu cited the precedent of the "wine-carriers army" (*pei-wei chün*) of the Sung generals Han Shih-chung (d. 1151) and Yueh Fei (1103–1141), whose armies included an elite contingent of personal troops (those who carried the wine-jars were closest to the general's person; thus *pei-wei* acquired the meaning of personal military retainers).[28]

Civil officials under the Ch'ing held an anomalous position in military affairs. On the upper levels of provincial administration, governors-general and governors had ultimate responsibility for both civil and military affairs within their jurisdictions. Besides supervising the provincial commander-in-chief (*t'i-tu*) the governor-general had a contingent of garrison troops directly responsible to him. Governors in some provinces held concurrently the office of *t'i-tu*. The military position of the governors-general was reflected in their epistolary title, *chih-chün* (regulator of military affairs) and since 1692 both governors and governors-general had held concurrent titles in the Board of War.[29]

---

28. Hu, *I-chi*, 52:2.

29. *Ta-Ch'ing hui-tien shih-li* (Kuang-hsu ed.) 23:10. On the distribution of *lü-ying* forces within the provincial bureaucracy, see Lo Erh-kang, *Lü-ying ping-chih*, 154–158.

Nevertheless, these high provincial figures were in a poor position to fulfill their heavy military responsibilities. Transfers from post to post insured that they were always in charge of unfamiliar bodies of troops, whose officers were strangers to them, and with whose training and selection they had had nothing to do. The hiring and firing of subordinate officers had to be arranged through the Board of War. In short, the whole weight of the system tended to keep the provincial official well apart from the intimate management of the troops he was charged with commanding in time of military emergency. The lines of authority were kept as bureaucratic as possible, stressing interchangeability of personnel and impersonality of command links. Furthermore, the provincial garrisons were seriously weakened by poor training and corrupt administration, ingrained faults that the civil administrator had little opportunity to remedy during his short incumbency.[30]

On the lower levels of administration, the discrepancy between responsibilities and powers in military affairs was even wider. Unlike the governors-general and governors, prefects and magistrates did not hold military appointments along with civil. During the Ming period, when the "civilian stalwarts" (*min-chuang*) system had been working, magistrates had indeed possessed something resembling a military force, and one treatise on the old *min-chuang* system even compared the magistrate's position to that of the local official in the *Kuan-tzu's* ideal prescriptions, who combined the functions of civil and military government.[31] But another account, describing the situation in the Ch'ing, noted that "military affairs are not the business of a district magistrate."[32]

But the nature of a magistrate's or prefect's duties inevitably involved him in military affairs. Like most officials in Ch'ing local administration, his responsibilities were general rather than specific, and territorial rather than functionally specialized. Because an official was held accountable for all events within his jurisdiction, he was frequently called upon to perform military duties, such as suppressing uprisings in cooperation with garrison troops, or defending his walled city, duties which his lack of military authority rendered him unable to perform properly. The few ill-trained police underlings at his disposal were barely adequate to catch petty thieves. It could be said that, although the local official's accountability embodied no clear

30. Lo, *Lü-ying*, 183.
31. T'ai-ho 1878, 9:2.
32. Nanchang 1849, 3 (*ping-fang*):1.

distinction between military and civil affairs, his powers were predominantly civil. Therefore it is not surprising that prefects and magistrates frequently resorted to "hiring braves" during the nineteenth century, when the rebellious condition of the countryside placed unusually grave military tasks in their hands. At the very least, their personal safety demanded it.

The disparity between the military powers and the military responsibilities of lower civil officials was naturally much on the minds of local bureaucrats. Shen Pao-chen, one of the ablest provincial officials of the age, considered the division between civil and military authority at prefectural and district levels to be one of the main weaknesses of Ch'ing administration. He insisted that, as long as civil officials had the responsibility to defend their cities, they ought to be given the means to do so. He therefore advocated that local contingents from the regular Green Standard forces be placed directly under the command of prefects and magistrates.[33]

By 1850, Hu's plans for a force of ch'in-ping had progressed beyond the stage of theory. While serving in Chen-yuan prefecture, he was called to neighboring Li-p'ing to aid in defending the provincial borders against Li Yuan-fa. It seems likely that he was already in command of a personal military force, a force that was augmented in 1851 when the Taiping danger became apparent.[34] It was in 1851 that Hu acquired the services of Han Ch'ao, an official "well versed in the writings of Ch'i, the Junior Guardian (Ch'i Chi-kuang)." Han, then in his fifties, had been rewarded with the rank of second-class assistant department magistrate in return for his advice on the defense of Tientsin in 1842. Later, while serving as magistrate of Tu-shan in Kweichow, he had recruited a small force of yung to fight local bandits and had thereby come to Hu's attention. Hu was greatly impressed with his expertise in both local control and military administration and invited him to Li-p'ing as his chief staff officer.[35]

Ch'i Chi-kuang (1528–1587), whose writings Han Ch'ao had studied so assiduously, was a Ming military theorist much in the minds of

---

33. Shen, Tsou-ch'ing pien-ping fen-li chün-hsien che (unpublished draft of a memorial of 1854; a copy of this draft is in the possession of Mr. David Pong, who is now engaged in a major study of Shen's career. I am much indebted to Mr. Pong for this reference).

34. Hu, I-chi, hsing-chuang, 3.

35. Han Ch'ao (1799/1800–1878/79) was from Ch'ang-li, Chihli. See Hu, I-chi, 54:8–11; Ch'ing-shih, 4808–4809; Chu K'ung-chang, Chung-hsing chiang-shuai pieh-chuan (1897), 29 shang:9–13. Han later served as acting governor of Kweichow.

nineteenth-century officials. He had been in the forefront of defense against the "Japanese pirates," the scourge of the coastal provinces during the sixteenth century. His influence upon nineteenth-century thinkers was certainly due in part to parallel historic circumstances: Ch'i, a regular military officer, had found the hereditary troops of the Ming garrisons ineffective against the Japanese pirates, much as Ch'ing officials found the hereditary Green Standard and Banner forces useless against foreign and domestic enemies. Ch'i therefore recruited troops himself and formed them into a strong, well-disciplined force loyal to himself, which was called the Ch'i-chia-chün (Ch'i's personal army). Ch'i's alternative to the huge, cumbersome, and ill-trained Ming units was a small but highly efficient force, which was constantly being tested and weeded out to reduce expenses.

Ch'i has been influential primarily as an expert on training and organization rather than as a tactician (Tseng Kuo-fan once had occasion to point out that Ch'i's own accomplishments in actual campaigning were rather commonplace).[36] His methods, as outlined in his treatises *A True Record of Troop Training* and *A New Manual of Effectiveness,* were widely admired for their attention to organizational detail and strict discipline. But equally important to his Ch'ing disciples was the personal mode of command embodied in his organizational precepts. This principle was precisely the opposite of that which governed the Ch'ing military: where the Ch'ing system avoided close and lasting contact between commanders and their troops, Ch'i's system fostered such contact. Where the Ch'ing system stressed the interchangeability of personnel, Ch'i's system stressed durable personal loyalties. The officers of each echelon chose their own subordinates and thus reinforced their formal authority with personal obligation.[37]

Ch'i's military classics were particularly appealing to bureaucrats who felt themselves entangled in static tables of organization and equipment. The glaring deficiencies of the regular Ch'ing military forces, as they rapidly became apparent in the dynasty's time of troubles, were not so much inadequacy of numbers, as abysmal quality and discipline, both of which were direct outgrowths of the cumber-

36. Tseng Kuo-fan, *Tseng Wen-cheng-kung ch'üan-chi, p'i-tu,* 2:15b.
37. Ch'i Chi-kuang, *Chi-hsiao hsin-shu* (reprinted and annotated in Hsu Nai-chao, *Min-kuo-chai ch'i-chung*) 1:5–6. Li Tsu-t'ao, "Tu Ch'i Wu-i Chi-hsiao hsin-shu Lien-ping shih-chi yu shu," *Mai-t'ang wen-lueh* (1865) 3:1b–2. See Ch'i's chronological biography, *Ch'i Shao-pao nien-p'u,* by Ch'i Tso-kuo (1847). For a modern biography, consult Hsieh Ch'eng-jen and Chu K'o, *Ch'i Chi-kuang* (Shanghai, 1961).

some and rigid bureaucratic methods by which the regular forces—both Manchu and Han—were governed. The fixed manpower quotas for each garrison, coupled with corruption, lax inspection and long periods of idleness, had produced a force that was indeed too large, in the sense that the costs of maintaining and deploying it far outweighed the results obtained. In terms of cost effectiveness, it was an immense liability to a government that was pressed for funds. Thus the Ch'ing military establishment lent momentum to the downward spiral of dynastic decline: the worse the troops, the longer it took them to quell an uprising; the longer it took them, the greater the cost; the more impoverished the government, the lower the quality of imperial administration and the greater the frequency of revolt. Though this is of course, a much oversimplified view of the matter, military thinkers of the time were increasingly aware of the need to break this cycle from the standpoint of cost effectiveness, and it was for this reason that they turned to Ch'i's methods of rigorous selection and inspection to produce small but highly efficient elite contingents.[38]

For all these reasons, Ch'i Chi-kuang's military thought was much in evidence among officials of the mid-nineteenth century, as they searched desperately for a way to reverse the rapid decline of China's military power. Tso Tsung-t'ang urged that Ch'i's methods be employed to build up *yung* forces along the coast during the Opium War. Though many thousands of *yung* had been hired, Tso found no evidence that they were being effectively organized and trained. At Canton, Hsü Nai-chao's inclusion of Ch'i's works in his 1849 *Min-kuo-chai* compendium was certainly aimed at remedying the military weakness exposed by British aggression. Perhaps the boldest plan was that of the Kiangsi writer Li Tsu-t'ao, a fervent Ch'i disciple, who in 1852 advocated building a provincial army on Ch'i's principles, to be under the command of regular provincial officials. With a somewhat different twist, this is what was actually done by Tseng Kuo-fan the following year in Hunan, though as we shall see in the next chapter the command structure was built outside regular provincial channels. Obviously, Ch'i's military writings were an important element in China's early attempts at military self-strengthening. Hu Lin-i (whose own interest in Ch'i can be dated at least as early as 1844/45) was to find them indispensable to his own efforts in Kweichow.[39]

---

38. Hu, *I-chi*, 52:2b; 56:20–21.

39. Tso, *Ch'üan-chi, shu-tu*, 1:10b. Li Tsu-t'ao, "Chih-yen i-tse," *Mai-t'ang wen-lüeh*, 3:25–27b. Li Tsu-t'ao, an aged *chü-jen* well known as a teacher, had turned

Hu's elite force was small, professional, and highly disciplined. Recruits were drawn partly from local t'uan-lien militia units and partly
from the cream of the local garrisons. The force was divided into
companies (*shao*) of 45 men, platoons (*tui*) of 15, and squads (*hang*)
of 7. Each company had about 30 firearms. "The platoons have flags
of different colors; each man has a yellow cloth attached to his
shoulders with the character *yung* (brave) printed on it, and wears
a printed waist-tag [indicating his name and unit]." This scheme of
organization was borrowed directly from Ch'i Chi-kuang's manual of
military organization and later was to make its appearance in Tseng
Kuo-fan's Hunan army. Hu took care to recruit sturdy, obedient peasant youths rather than vagabonds or city slickers, another Ch'i prescription. Discipline was harsh. Any soldier who retreated in battle was to
be beheaded, as was any caught stealing from the Miao (evidently a
common complaint) or molesting innocent civilians. The funds for
maintaining this force were raised by Hu himself and remained outside
the regular prefectural budget. This was not a simple case of personal
wealth being turned to public purposes. The same resources that
allowed many a local official to build a fortune in a few years were also
available for such projects as special military recruitment. Any official
whose duties placed him in the stream of tax transmission had access
to plenteous sources for either personal enrichment or more worthy
enterprises.[40]

By 1852 Hu's elite force had reached a size of only about 270 men,
which was approximately the number Hu led into Weng-an district
to quell a tax-resistance rebellion in 1853. The Weng-an case will serve
to illustrate how Hu used his highly militarized professional unit in
combination with his methods of local control. In Weng-an, a largely
Miao district some 70 miles northwest of Li-p'ing, local administration
had so far broken down by the late Tao-kuang period that villagers
took the problem of security into their own hands by organizing a
congeries of multiplex associations called the *"lang* league" (*lang-
yueh*).[41] The league executed bandits by drowning, with no reference

---

in his later years from literary studies to the study of political and military
affairs. *Ch'ing-shih lieh-chuan,* 73:19. Shang-kao 1870, 8:40a-b.

40. Hu, *I-chi,* 52:25b–26b; 53:4–5b, 12; 57:12b–13. Ch'i Chi-kuang, *Chi-hsiao
hsin-shu,* 1:8–17. Lo Erh-kang, *Hsiang-chün hsin-chih,* 89.

41. The origin and significance of *"lang"* are obscure; inasmuch as the
graph *lang* is similar in all but one element to the graph *hsiang* (a rural subdivision), it is conceivable that the *lang-yueh* developed out of a *hsiang-yueh* local
indoctrination system. It is also possible that the term was derived from the Miao

to the judicial powers of the magistrate. In every few villages was set up a "public office" where general meetings were held at harvest time or on other occasions of public concern. The leaders, called *lang-shou,* were mostly commoners, though some lower gentry belonged to the league. Because Weng-an was a Miao border area, much of the league's membership (though evidently not all of it) must be assumed to have been ethnically Miao. The association covered only a small section of the district, and accordingly a succession of inept magistrates raised no objections to it.

It even appears that officials accepted the *lang-yueh* as a pao-chia system. There is no evidence that magistrates selected or examined local headmen, nor that there was a decimal registration system of any sort. Nevertheless, to consider the *lang* headmen as pao-chia headmen was definitely in the magistrate's interest, because his ability to control the district was thereby less likely to be called into question. It was later charged that the *lang* league had been "falsely using the name of pao-chia,"[42] and it must be admitted that it lacked entirely an essential bureaucratic component of the pao-chia system: possession by the magistrate of effective judicial authority and the power to appoint and dismiss local headmen. It provides another example of the tendency of natural units (in this case the multiplex village associations) to take over the functions of bureaucratic units at the corresponding scale of organization.

An economic catastrophe in the early Hsien-feng reign brought about a basic change in the role of the league. During the prolonged drought in Hunan in the late 1840's, food shortages were relieved by shipments from Kweichow, with the result that rice prices in Kweichow were uncommonly high. Officials, including those in Weng-an, turned the occasion to profit by squeezing extra money from the peasantry, who were able to meet the high demands only because they were receiving a higher price for their rice. Around 1851 the Hunan harvests improved, and grain prices in Kweichow fell precipitously. The extraordinary surtaxes, however, were not reduced, and because the peasants now had no way to meet their payments, tension between the district yamen and the populace grew acute.

---

language. This last possibility is suggested by one of Hu's references to *lang,* in which the term seems to designate a customary rural subdivision in Miao areas. *I-chi,* 58:33. Sources for the Weng-an episode are Weng-an 1915, 3:2b–5b; 4:2b–20. Hu Lin-i, *I-chi,* 56:22–26; 57:6b. Weng-an 1915 draws partly from Hu and partly from local sources.

42. Hu, *I-chi,* 57:6b.

Under these intolerable conditions the *lang* league assumed a new and rebellious role. Throughout the district it became the leader of resistance to taxes, and its influence spread accordingly. In May and June of 1852 the league leaders began to extend their authority by selecting headmen ("disorderly ruffians" as Hu Lin-i called them) in villages hitherto outside the league. Each had a specified area of control, which might comprise anywhere from several tens to several thousands of households, depending on the number of villages involved. The league leaders now assumed in addition to full judicial powers the sole authority to collect and transmit taxes. This was in effect a variant of *pao-lan* and another illustration of how this "abuse" could serve as a community response to exorbitant taxation. By standing forth as a buffer between taxpayers and bureaucracy, the league became the only effective governing power in the countryside. It was able to be so partly because the taxpayers (particularly the small peasant proprietors) needed its protection, and partly because it exercised strict discipline over dissenters. Any who refused to join up and submit to its authority was liable to have his property confiscated. Hu Lin-i estimated in 1853 that from 80 to 90 percent of the populace was under its control.[43]

That the leaders of the league had no desire to press the issue to open revolt can be seen from the fact that taxes were actually offered to the officials in amounts corresponding to the lawful quotas. Yet the league's control over legal cases and taxes gave it a double stranglehold over officialdom. Further, the leadership had taken the precaution of collecting arms and forming a militia based on the multiplex village associations. The peasants were to provide fowling pieces and wooden cannon. A complicating factor was that by 1852, if not earlier, the leadership of the league had been infiltrated by a secret society, evidently of White Lotus affiliation. By public subscription were constructed a number of community temples, each of which housed a copy of the Lotus Sutra, to serve as centers of both spiritual and temporal affairs. These temples replaced the earlier "public offices" (*kung-so*) and served as the headquarters of the local associations. This heterodox orientation made it all the less likely that the league could continue to coexist with local officials. Finally, provincial authorities had to take a hand. They ordered Hu Lin-i to proceed to Weng-an with his force of picked fighters.

---

43. Hu, *I-chi*, 57:6.

With 320 men, Hu arrived in Weng-an on October 2, 1853, and set up camp in a field outside the city walls, where he gathered gentry from both city and countryside and began negotiations. Though rural gentry had been involved in the *lang* league (some were still hiding in the hills) Hu found it necessary to use them as intermediaries with the villagers. He had a low opinion of the Weng-an gentry, and found "not one of any talent," but was compelled to work with them "so that upper and lower can be in contact, and the feelings of officials and people can be harmonized." To the gentry he explained that he would "offer amnesty to anyone who had been compelled to join" and was only interested in capturing the leaders.[44]

From the first, the *lang* leadership had shown themselves amenable to neither negotiation nor surrender, and on October 7 converged on Hu's camp with a large force of armed peasants. When Hu sent two *sheng-yuan* with a batch of "pardon certificates" offering an opportunity to surrender, the leaders angrily denounced Hu's emissaries and smashed the certificates. They then cut the bridges leading to the city and attacked Hu's force from three directions. In the battle that followed, Hu's better-disciplined force was able to disperse the ill-organized peasant militia, in the process killing or capturing some 60 men.

Hu had now successfully intimidated the local populace by demonstrating the military impotence of the league, but there remained the task of establishing a local control system that would continue to operate after his troops had left the district. At this pivotal moment arose a controversy between Hu and acting magistrate Hsu Ho-ch'ing, a Hunan *chin-shih* whose views on local administration were at best only marginally Confucian. Hsu refused to view rebellion as a political problem; he considered that there was no segment of the populace with which the official could bargain, no real contradiction between leaders and followers that could be exploited by the astute administrator. Because there was an unbridgeable gulf between subjects and rulers, the magistrate of a rebellious area had no choice but to slaughter or be slaughtered.

Even before the battle of October 7, Hsu Ho-ch'ing had been skeptical of Hu's policy of capturing leaders and freeing followers. He did not believe the villagers would surrender or turn over the *lang* cadres, and the battle of October 7 convinced him. The rebel chiefs, he said,

---

44. Hu, *I-chi*, 57:5.

were well entrenched and could not easily be caught. Hu and his troops ought therefore to "burn the fortified villages one by one and kill the inhabitants." Hu refused, replying that the survivors, if any, would surely become roving bandits. Also, the victims of this kind of mopping-up campaign were never the hard-core rebels but invariably the old and weak, the women and children; the rebels always escaped in time. Hsu Ho-ch'ing countered that, even if they escaped, they would be helpless after their villages were destroyed. But Hu would not countenance a wholesale slaughter; quite apart from the moral problem, "the head rebels and their unwilling followers are still not united in purpose," and an oppressive policy would drive them together. Once one or two fortified villages were burned, the surrounding areas would grow more intractable than ever.[45]

Hu had both the rank and the troops, and his views therefore prevailed. He then announced that village representatives were to come to the city, surrender arms, and receive "pardon certificates." These certificates were to be filled in village by village, and household by household, with the names of all inhabitants, which were then to be copied into local pao-chia registers. Some villages were ordered to turn over "notorious local bandits" (presumably the *lang* cadres) before pardon would be granted. Within a fortnight more than 100 fortified villages had complied, and the process continued. Hu made much of the fact that the keystone of his policy was local initiative. "Not a single yamen runner was sent into the countryside." This was "using local people to catch local bandits."[46] The surrender of arms was likewise given a voluntaristic flavor: each of the six taxing subdivisions (*li*) of the district was to delegate two men to receive these arms in a central bureau in the city. Actually, the surrender of arms and the compiling of registers were not exactly voluntary, but were occasioned by a shift in the balance of military power: the fact that the *lang* league was no longer able to dominate the populace or control communication routes leading into the city. Under the duress of Hu's presence with his *ch'in-ping*, a quasi-political decision was made by most of the fortified villages to join the new order.

But the problem of long-term local control remained. Once the *lang* league was suppressed, its leaders scattered or killed, Hu adopted what at first glance seems a remarkable policy: he used the old multiplex local associations as the administrative units of his "pao-chia and

45. Hu, *I-chi*, 56:24b–25; 57:1b.
46. Hu, *I-chi*, 57:3b.

t'uan-lien" system. In place of the *lang* leaders, Hu chose "men of talent, character, and substance" as pao-chia officials. "The *lang* rebels used the league to deceive the officials and kill the people. Now that the system is supervised by officials, the six reins are in our hands." As might be expected, Hsu Ho-ch'ing objected that "the rebels falsely used the name pao-chia while openly resisting the officials. Now, if we undertook pao-chia without first killing a great many people in order to establish our authority, would we not simply be inheriting the system that the rebels have built up?" Hu replied that the purposes to which the multiplex associations were turned depended entirely on who controlled them. With "talented men of good character and respectable family" in charge there was no reason to fear that the associations would again become the instrument of rebellion.[47]

What proportion of these "talented men" were actually degree-holding gentry and what proportion influential commoners, the evidence does not reveal. What is clear, however, is that Hu was relying on the natural units of local coordination (the existing multiplex associations and the fortified villages of which they were formed) and that the headship of these natural units was to be in the hands of orthodox and influential community figures. In view of Hu's preference for literati (*tu-shu-jen*) as local headmen, we can assume that such men were chosen wherever they were available.[48]

The system as it took shape in practice was actually called *t'uan-chia*: the multiplex units (called *t'uan,* rather than *pao*) were agencies of both local defense and police registration; each fortified village was taken to be a *chia* unit. Such a substitution of terms at the multiplex scale of organization was not an uncommon event in nineteenth-century China, and we find a number of other instances in which a *t'uan-chia* system of local control was a natural outgrowth of the mid-century crisis. This substitution indicates unmistakably a devolution of pao-chia responsibilities into the hands of those in rural society who were most capable of carrying them out: the orthodox local elite who were active in local defense.[49]

47. Hu, *I-chi*, 57:3b, 6b.
48. Hu, *I-chi*, 54:10.
49. The Weng-an gazetteer prints an undated chart of the *t'uan-chia* system, which was clearly an outgrowth of Hu Lin-i's reorganization of the district's local control system in 1853. There were in all 133 *t'uan* in the district, each of which governed anywhere from two to thirty-five fortified villages. Here we are obviously dealing with a congeries of multiplex *t'uan* organized along customary lines of

Thus was brought under control a district in which broad masses of the population—including portions of the gentry—had been implicated in rebellion. Hu's strategy rested on the presupposition that local leaders would naturally prefer to enter the orthodox power structure if given a chance to do so, not unreasonable in the light of Chinese historical experience. It depended also on an assumption that military operations are, in their root nature, a component of politics. This assumes, in turn, that there is no gap between ruler and ruled that cannot somehow be bridged by negotiation. Confucianism at its most effective lacked the institutionalized paranoia that underlies pure despotism; it took for granted that, save for the most perverted of renegades, one's domestic opponent inhabited the same moral and political world as oneself. Hsu Ho-ch'ing "hated the evil-doers with a vengeance and had his mind set on extermination."[50] Hu's nature was more patient: he was ready to undertake the tedious process of accepting the surrender of the district, village by village and household by household. "To put in order a disorderly country is like untangling a tangled string," wrote Hu, meaning that it was intricate and slow, and that peace and prosperity were not to be achieved by speed and violence. It was best to achieve a quasi-political settlement where possible by coming to terms with the natural units of rural society.[51]

For all his labors in local administration, Hu had been of course vitally concerned with the Taiping Rebellion from the days of its earliest outbreak in Kwangsi. Not content to trust to the highly misleading official reports of Ch'ing commanders on the scene, Hu had sent his own agents into Kwangsi and Hunan to keep watch on the rebellion's progress.[52] For a time in 1852 it was unclear whether the Taipings would proceed northeastward into Hunan or northwestward into Kweichow, and Hu had a number of forts built at strategic points in the strategic border areas. His military thinking at this point was primarily defensive; he was most reluctant to intervene in affairs across the border or allow his lieutenant Han Ch'ao to do so, on the grounds

---

intervillage cooperation and headed by those in possession of natural local power and influence. Weng-an 1915, 4:2b–20.

T'uan-lien as a local defense organ seems not to have been conspicuously successful in Weng-an during the remainder of the Hsien-feng and T'ung-chih periods. Ling T'i-an, *Hsien-t'ung Kuei-chou chün-shih shih*, 1:36.

50. Hu, *I-chi*, 56:25.
51. Hu, *I-chi*, 57:4b.
52. Hu, *I-chi*, 54:2b; 55:11b.

that his local responsibilities were of the first importance and that his troop strength and financial resources should be husbanded against future emergencies.[53]

It was the safety of his home province, Hunan, that caused Hu the keenest anxiety. In the spring of 1852, when the Taipings were still in Kwangsi, Hu began a correspondence with Ch'eng Yü-ts'ai, governor-general of Hunan and Hupeh. Even if the Taipings were beaten in Kwangsi, wrote Hu, this did not mean that Hunan was safe from rebellion. The safety of Hunan depended ultimately on local conditions: the effectiveness and honesty of its officials and the community efforts of its elite. The key to avoiding local disturbances was to place local control and defense under the command of reliable gentry. If pao-chia and t'uan-lien under gentry management had been effective in Kweichow, how much more effective it would be in richer Hunan, where able gentry were more numerous. Hu was anxious to cement relations between gentry and provincial officials in Hunan and recommended to Ch'eng a number of gentrymen in whom high trust might be placed. The best was Tso Tsung-t'ang, from the district of Hsiang-yin, whom Hu had previously recommended to Lin Tse-hsü, and who, he hoped, might be invited to a staff position. Getting no result from Ch'eng, in late June he wrote Chang Liang-chi, the governor of Hunan, again recommending Tso as an exceptionally promising staff man, and Chang subsequently invited Tso to his headquarters.[54]

To Chang Liang-chi Hu confided his own longing to cast off his administrative duties and join the battle in his native Hunan, but lamented that Li-p'ing was still so unsettled that he could not in good conscience leave it. By autumn, however, the Taiping armies had invaded the heart of Hunan and were besieging Changsha, the provincial capital. Chang Liang-chi now made strenuous efforts to have Hu transferred to the front. There seems little doubt that Hu would have gone to Hunan at this point, save for his special relationship to the

53. Hu, I-chi, 53:3–4; 54:9a-b. The previous year Tso Tsung-t'ang had written to Hu urging extensive use of fortifications to supplement local control systems like t'uan-lien and pao-chia. Tso's military thinking was essentially defensive, with enclaves valued over mobility. The trouble with Ch'ing strategy in Kwangsi, he thought, was that "the rebels are always the host, while we are always the guest," meaning that the rebels paid greater attention to their base area defenses and local organization, while the imperial forces labored vainly in mobile operations. Hu Lin-i's approach to Kweichow's military problems was probably influenced by Tso at this point. Tso, Tso Wen-hsiang-kung ch'üan-chi, shu-tu, 2:2–5.

54. Hu, I-chi, 53:12–15b; 54:1–2. Tso and Hu were close friends, related by marriage.

governor-general of Yunnan and Kweichow, Wu Wen-jung, wh
obtained his *chin-shih* degree in 1819, the same year as Hu's
Hu Ta-yuan (d. 1841). Wu was thus in a quasi-parental relationship to
Hu Lin-i, and when he asked that Hu be retained for a time in
Kweichow, Hu stayed on. It was not until a year later, after Wu had
himself been transferred to the Hunan–Hupeh governor-generalship,
that Hu was able to enter the battle.

During the early months of 1854 the Taipings' westward campaign
was in full swing, and Wu Wen-jung's capital, the strategic city of
Wuchang, was in constant danger. Wu Wen-jung found his own forces
too weak to take the field and summoned help from two men who owed
him a special debt of loyalty: his classmate's son, Hu Lin-i, and the
former metropolitan official Tseng Kuo-fan, a Hunanese *chin-shih* who
was marshalling land and water forces in central Hunan. Tseng had
been Wu Wen-jung's examinee in the metropolitan examination of
1838 and thus bore to him the responsibilities of a student toward his
teacher. Hu Lin-i immediately readied his personal force of Kweichow
fighters, which had by now been expanded to some 700 men, and
marched toward the front. Hu himself had been promoted to Taotai of
the Kuei-tung circuit, which gave him easier access to provincial funds
for troop support. Tseng, who had resisted earlier appeals from the
court to move into Hupeh, now prepared to move up with a fleet of
gunboats. But before either force arrived, Wu was humiliatingly defeated in a bungled attempt to recover the prefectural city of Huang-
chou and drowned himself rather than face capture (February 12,
1854).[55] It was not long thereafter that Hu put himself and his forces
at the disposal of Tseng Kuo-fan, who was emerging as the leader of
the anti-Taiping struggle.

C. Tseng Kuo-fan and the Hunan Army

The leader of the elite's opposition to the Taipings was the Hunanese scholar-official Tseng Kuo-fan (1811–1872). He was born to a landlord family that was not of gentry rank but was doggedly pressing
upward in the social scale.[56] His father presented himself no fewer
than seventeen times for the local examinations, finally gaining the

---

55. Hu, *I-chi, hsing-chuang,* 54:1; 3b–4. *Ch'ing-shih,* 4666–4667; *Tseng Wen-
cheng-kung ch'üan-chi, nien-p'u,* 1:6; Chien Yu-wen, *Ch'üan-shih,* 1028–1029.

56. Teng Ssu-yü's assertion that Tseng came from a "poor peasant family"
(Hummel, *Eminent Chinese,* 751) is not consistent with other sources.

sheng-yuan degree in 1832.[57] Against this background of persistent effort but modest success, Tseng's own rise is striking. After gaining the *chin-shih* degree in 1838, he embarked on a career in the metropolitan bureaucracy. Hanlin academician, junior vice-president of several boards, and finally acting senior vice-president of the Board of Civil Office, by the time of the Taiping Rebellion he was solidly in the upper stratum of the metropolitan elite.[58] His high academic and political rank and the network of personal connections that grew out of it were essential to his leadership in the decades that followed.

Early Militarization in Hsiang-hsiang

During his long service in Peking, Tseng of course remained closely in touch with events at home, events that were cause for increasing worry. The floods and droughts of 1849 that had scourged Chiang Chung-yuan's district affected also central Hunan and in Hsiang-hsiang brought about the first stages of militarization. When famine victims in the southern part of the district rioted and took food from the rich, a *sheng-yuan* named Wang Chen left a teaching post to mobilize and train a militia of several hundred men around his home area. After the rioters had been dispersed by troops from the local garrison, Wang disbanded his own force and petitioned the magistrate to issue relief grain promptly.

Wang Chen was a man of boundless energy and imposing personality who came from a family on the margins of the lower gentry; his great-grandfather and grandfather had been lower degree holders, but his father had not. Wang himself associated with some of the best-known gentry of the vicinity—particularly Lo Tse-nan (whose student he was) and Liu Jung, a close friend of Tseng Kuo-fan.[59] Though without eminent scholarly rank, Wang was unusually active and influential in local affairs. In 1845, at the age of 20, he had organized a multiplex association in his home area of Chu-chin-ch'ü in the form of a "local covenant" (*hsiang-yueh*), a voluntary enterprise to promote morality, encourage agriculture, aid the indigent, and secure local

---

57. Lo Erh-kang, *Hsiang-chün hsin-chih*, 46.

58. On Tseng's Peking career and the development of his thought during this period, see Han-yin Chen Shen, "Tseng Kuo-fan in Peking, 1840–1852: His Ideas on Statecraft and Reform," *Journal of Asian Studies* 27.1:61–80 (November 1967).

59. Lo Cheng-chün, *Wang Chuang-wu-kung nien-p'u* in *Wang Chuang-wu-kung i-chi*, (mimeographed reprint of a Kuang-hsu ed., Yangchow, n.d.) *shang*:1–12.

order. There is some evidence that this group, led by gentry, assumed pao-chia type functions in investigating and reporting heterodox behavior. It was almost certainly this multiplex grouping that served as the organizational nucleus for Wang's militia organization four years later.[60]

The rising social unrest that prompted Wang's *hsiang-yueh* enterprise was driven to dangerous heights by the natural disasters of 1849. Wang took the lead in organizing famine relief, and it is in this context that he sparked the early stages of militarization in Hsiang-hsiang. The reason famine inevitably stirred up riots was of course that shortages were never evenly borne. There were those who had stocks of grain and were hoarding it against a price rise or selling it elsewhere. These hoarders were already the targets for mobs of desperate people who attacked their homes and took their grain. If the established order were to survive a famine, it was necessary not only that the elite intervene to provide relief and coax grain out of the rich but also that there be a center of organization alternative to that of the elite's local rivals, the Triads: some extraordinary effort to secure the men of military age for the orthodox order by feeding them and organizing them. One expedient was public works: dredging and diking the silt-clogged rivers, expenses to be paid by the rich households. Another expedient was militia. There is evidence that Wang's militia enterprise of 1849 was intended not only to protect his home area but also to provide a nucleus of organization and support for the young men of stricken peasant families.[61]

Disaster relief by itself, however, was not enough. Shortly after the violence in the famine area, Wang joined other gentry in a complaint to provincial authorities about the corruption and viciousness of the district administration and the highly inflated tax levies which, along with natural disasters, were driving the peasantry to rebellion. Obtaining no redress, the local elite deputed Wang to journey to Peking to make the district's problems known on higher levels of government. Apparently Wang's intended contact in Peking was the best known *chin-shih* of the district, Tseng Kuo-fan. Wang set forth in early au-

60. Wang, *Nien-p'u, shang*:6. *I-chi*, 24:12b–16b.

61. A suggestion that Wang's militia was closely connected with famine relief is contained in a letter written to Tseng Kuo-fan by his friend, Kuo Sung-tao, who had heard that disaster victims from a wide area were "flocking to Wang's leadership." Wang, *Nien-p'u, shang*:11b. See Wang's essay on famine relief in *I-chi*, 24:23–25b. For a more explicit connection between militia and famine relief, see Ch'i Piao-chia's formula in Chapter I.C above.

tumn, 1849. On his way through the district of Hsiang-yin, he paid a call on Tseng's close friend, the *chin-shih* Kuo Sung-tao, who was much impressed with Wang and sent with him an enthusiastic letter of introduction to Tseng, particularly calling Tseng's attention to Wang's successful organization of militia in Hsiang-hsiang. Wang then resumed his journey, but having reached the city of Wuchang he fell seriously ill, abandoned his mission, and returned to Hsiang-hsiang to recuperate.[62]

In 1850, a year ominous with threats of local disorder, occurred a decisive change of district administration. Chu Sun-i, a *chin-shih* from Kiangsi, arrived in Hsiang-hsiang to assume duties as acting magistrate. Whether Chu's appointment had been engineered by the Hunan group in Peking, we cannot determine, but Chu had certainly been briefed on local problems and personalities, for he immediately summoned Wang Chen (only a *sheng-yuan*) and sought his advice and aid. Wang petitioned him to end corrupt practices by allowing the local people to pay their taxes at the district seat in person, thus eliminating the predacious yamen underlings as intermediaries. Chu agreed, and promised that the old system would never be resumed. This promise was engraved on a stone tablet and erected at the city gate. In practice, the new system meant that assessment and accounting would be largely supervised by the local elite, a development that recalls the arrangement in Lin-hsiang and strengthened the elite's power to control local resources.[63]

By autumn of the next year, 1851, it was apparent to Wang that the campaign against the Taipings in Kwangsi was not going well and that the rebellion was likely to spread northward into Hunan. With Chu Sun-i's encouragement, Wang undertook to impress upon his fellow gentry the urgent necessity for local defense. "At that time," he later wrote, "the rebels were still in Kwangsi, and who knew what the words t'uan-lien meant? People who heard the idea invariably covered their ears and fled."[64] But now the militarization of Hsiang-hsiang began in earnest. By the time the Taipings crossed into Hunan in June 1852 Chu Sun-i had issued a set of t'uan-lien regulations in concert with local gentry. These envisaged a local defense system based almost entirely on natural local divisions. The lineage was the basic unit from

62. Wang, *Nien-p'u*, *shang*:11a-b.
63. Wang, *Nien-p'u*, *shang*:12b.
64. Wang, *Nien-p'u*, *shang*:13. See Wang's pronouncements t'uan-lien, one a remarkable *pai-hua* broadside aimed at the peasantry: *I-chi*, 24:16b–22b.

which militia were to be raised; lineages then were grouped into multiplex units (*t'uan*), according to pre-existing patterns of inter-community cooperation. Headmen were to be the natural leaders of each level of coordination, ranging from the head of a *fang* (a segment of a higher-order lineage), to the head of the multiplex *t'uan*. We must assume that this early militarization by the Hsiang-hsiang elite was quite uneven. Three years later, no more than 70 or 80 percent of Hsiang-hsiang's settlements were estimated to be carrying out t'uan-lien, and undoubtedly the proportion was much smaller in 1852. Probably the large, rich lineages were the first to raise militia, especially since the threat of rebellion was still seen as largely internal, and the leadership of the larger lineages had most to lose.[65]

The entry of the Taipings into Hunan meant that the defensive efforts of local lineages would probably not suffice to stem the tide of rebellion. Wang was beginning to envision his military responsibilities in larger terms, and sometime during the summer of 1852 wrote to Chu Sun-i asking permission to raise a force of "civilian soldiers" (*min-ping*) that could effectively defend the district borders. Chu concurred, and together with his friend K'ang Ching-hui and his teacher Lo Tse-nan Wang set about raising a more highly militarized force of fighters. Though most of his recruiting was done among men who had already been inscribed on local t'uan-lien rolls, his men had at first little understanding of military affairs. It is said that when Wang was handing out numbered tunics (by which the men were identified in ranks) the recruits were ashamed to wear them until Wang himself stepped forth and put on a tunic emblazoned with the number "one." This was an early indication of the resolution of the lower civil gentry, who were quite prepared to hazard their dignity along with their lives to defend their native districts and the prevailing social order.[66]

This new force grew to about 1,000 men, organized in three battalions (*ying*) commanded by Wang, Lo Tse-nan, and Lo's brother, Hsin-nan. Its financial base is somewhat obscure, though there is strong evidence that it received public monies through the patronage of Chu Sun-i.[67] During the siege of Changsha by the Taipings, from September

65. Hsiang-hsiang 1874, 5:5b–8.
66. Wang, *Nien-p'u, shang*:13b–14.
67. A letter from Liu Jung to Chu Sun-i, evidently written in the summer of 1852, mentions a proposal by Wang Chen and K'ang Ching-hui to raise a force of about a thousand men, which would be supported by "borrowing military funds" (*chieh chün-hsiang*), that is, funds normally appropriated for the support of regular military forces. Though we have no evidence that such funds were

through November 1852, the force was stationed so as to guard the Hsiang-hsiang district seat. Once the siege was lifted and the Taipings again set forth for destinations unknown, Wang petitioned to be allowed to lead his men outside the district in pursuit, thus frankly abandoning his defensive aims. In view of the uncertain military situation, his request was denied. But by January or early February of 1853, Hunan Governor Chang Liang-chi felt it desirable to have an additional force of *yung* at his disposal in the provincial capital (Chiang Chung-yuan's Ch'u-yung were already there) and asked Chu Sun-i to recommend likely leaders. Chu recommended Wang Chen, Lo Tse-nan, and their coadjutors, and thus it was that the three Hsiang-yung battalions left their native district and came to Changsha.

Though there is much convincing evidence in Wang Chen's chronological biography to the effect that Wang was the real initiator of militarization in Hsiang-hsiang, two other key figures must be mentioned: Chu Sun-i and Lo Tse-nan. Chu was an official as remarkable for his political prudence as for his energy and ability. He took pains in particular to cultivate the close friends of the influential Tseng Kuo-fan. Lo Tse-nan (related to Tseng through their children's engagement) he recommended for the honorary title "filial, honest, upright and orthodox" (*hsiao-lien fang-cheng*), which could qualify a man for official appointment. To Tseng's intimate companion and Lo's student, Liu Jung, he granted preferment in the district examination. He sought out, for counsel, Lo's other students Wang Chen and K'ang Ching-hui. All these men, though low in gentry rank, gained by reflection from Tseng a special luster that marked them out for unusual influence in their home district. It is beyond doubt that Chu's support, both moral and financial, was a decisive factor in the militarization of the Hsiang-hsiang elite.[68]

Lo Tse-nan's influence was of quite a different sort. Born in 1808, he was 17 years older than Wang Chen and by 1851 had long been revered as a teacher in Hsiang-hsiang. Deeply imbued with neo-Confucian philosophy, he had surmounted poverty and personal tragedies to become a character of extraordinary and widespread moral influence. Though originally drawn into militia work by the enthusiasm of his students, he found himself in a position of natural leadership there-

---

actually appropriated, Chu's enthusiastic patronage of this enterprise would likely have included some financial backing. Wang, *Nien-p'u, shang*:13b.

68. *Ch'ing-shih*, 4843, 4892. *Lo Chung-chieh-kung nien-p'u, shang*:11, in Lo Tse-nan, *Lo-shan i-chi* (1863), ts'e 8.

after and became a dominant figure in the command echelon of the Hsiang-yung after 1852.[69]

By correspondence with friends and family, Tseng was well aware of the increasing pace of local militarization when, in July of 1852, he requested leave to visit his home. He had just been appointed supervisor of the Kiangsi provincial examination and asked the throne for twenty days leave to permit him to return from this assignment via Hsiang-hsiang (only eight days travel from Nanchang). He cited the fact that his home lay athwart the probable northward path of the Taipings, that local society was increasingly fearful, and that his own family was becoming involved in "managing t'uan-lien." To request home leave (and to secure a convenient examination assignment) was a decision Tseng had made a year earlier, and the new danger to Hsiang-hsiang now made his return doubly urgent.[70] Tseng undoubtedly wanted to oversee the arrangements that were being made to defend Hsiang-hsiang and to confer with family and friends. The throne's permission secured, Tseng set out for Kiangsi on August 9. A month later, traveling through Anhwei, he learned that his mother had died; as the rules prescribed, he immediately resigned his official duties and returned home in mourning, arriving in Hsiang-hsiang the sixth of October.[71]

During the autumn that Tseng remained at home, the military fortunes of the dynasty continued their plunge. Though the siege of Changsha was broken, thanks largely to the efforts of Chiang Chung-yuan outside the walls, the Taiping host was now loose in the central waterways. Surging northwestward from Changsha they reached I-yang on the Tzu River, a major tributary of the Yangtze, where they commandeered many boats. Moving now northeastward, they crossed Tung-t'ing lake, conquered the strategic city of Yueh-chou at its mouth, and entered the great river itself. By late December they had seized Han-

69. Lo Erh-kang, *Hsiang-chun hsin-chih*, 68–70. During the crucial year of 1851 Lo was teaching in Changsha in the home of the late Ho Ch'ang-ling (leader of the "statecraft" school) and was therefore not directly involved in the early military initiatives of his students, Wang Chen and K'ang Ching-hui. In 1852, however, he did participate directly in troop training. Lo, *Nien-p'u, shang*:12; Wang, *Nien-p'u, shang*:14a-b. Among Lo's students were numbered many of the Hsiang-chün's original commanders and staff officers: Wang Chen, Liu Jung, K'ang Ching-hui, I Liang-kan, Lo Hsin-tung, Lo Chen-nan, Li Hsu-pin, Li Hsu-i, Yang Ch'ang-chün. Wang, *Nien-p'u, shang*:7b–9; Lo Erh-kang, *Hsiang-chün hsin-chih*, 55–62.

70. Tseng, *Tsou-kao*, 1:54; *Shu-cha*, 1:27a-b.

71. Tseng, *Nien-p'u*, 1:32b–33.

yang in Hupeh, just across the river from Wuchang, the provincial capital.[72] It was just after the fall of Han-yang that the court ordered Tseng Kuo-fan to cooperate with the Hunan governor, Chang Liang-chi, in managing t'uan-lien in Hunan.

The Policy Background of the "T'uan-lien Commissioners"

A distinct ambivalence was built into the official model of local militarization, an inclination to seek gentry initiative combined with a fear of its implications. This ambivalence continued as the mid-century rebellions gathered force. Since the rebellion of Lei Tsai-hao in 1847, the court had been edging toward a policy of encouraging t'uan-lien in the countryside. Invariably, though, it clung to the received wisdom of the White Lotus suppression, particularly close official supervision and a low level of militarization. T'uan-lien was most frequently mentioned in concert with pao-chia and *chien-pi ch'ing-yeh*, the foundations of local control policy in the Chia-ch'ing era: institutions that stressed police control more than military strength. The development of private irregular forces was definitely not what the court had in mind. Indeed, when in mid-1850 a memorialist called attention to the chaos in Kwangsi and noted that villages were raising their own *yung* to fight alongside the regular troops, the court reacted with alarm. An edict in reply ordered officials to get control of these local units to prevent their becoming agencies of disorder or rebellion.[73]

In the early years of the rebellion, at least through 1852, the court retained its faith in bureaucratically organized control systems. In October 1850 Hsu Kuang-chin, the Liang-kuang governor-general, was ordered to imitate the *chien-pi ch'ing-yeh* system of the early Chia-ch'ing period. T'uan-lien was to play a part by preventing the rebels from "hooking up" with the populace, clearly a form of police control.[74] In June 1851 Grand Secretary Cho Ping-t'ien commended to the throne Kung Ching-han's essays on rebel suppression, which the throne in turn commended to provincial officials. A year later, when the Taipings were about to break into central China, the court was still promoting the rebel-suppression techniques of the White Lotus period.[75]

72. Kuo T'ing-i, *Jih-chih*, 196–198.
73. *Ch'ing shih-lu*, Hsien-feng, 12:3b.
74. *Ch'ing shih-lu*, Hsien-feng, 17:10b.
75. *Chiao-p'ing Yüeh-fei fang-lueh* 13:27–28.

Besides *chien-pi ch'ing-yeh,* the standard nostrums inevitably included pao-chia. The court saw t'uan-lien and pao-chia as similar and complementary institutions, and accompanying the encouragement of t'uan-lien were orders to revive the pao-chia system throughout the empire. In response, a number of provincial officials duly reported to the throne the promulgation of new pao-chia regulations.[76]

The court's insistence on bureaucratic control of local militarization grew from an unshakeable mistrust of independent military activities by the elite, a mistrust that was in some measure a reflection of the attitude of provincial officials, to whom irregular military activity of any sort simply called attention to the rural anarchy that they preferred to ignore. Like the aging and incompetent governor of Kwangsi, Cheng Tsu-ch'en (cashiered in November 1850), many officials sought safety in ignorance.[77] They were not only unwilling to take action against rebels but also reluctant to allow local lineages to take matters into their own hands. The elite in Kwangsi had become so busy with militia work by the summer of 1851 that the provincial examinations were twice postponed. Yet many officials gave this kind of venture a lukewarm or hostile reception.[78]

As a result there developed a sharp cleavage of interest between local officials, fearful of trouble, and the orthodox elite, fearful for their lives and property. The remedy for local interests who wanted to promote militia work was to go over the heads of the provincial bureaucracy and reach the throne through the censorate or private connections in the capital. Tu Shou-t'ien, president of the Board of Punishments and confidant of the Hsien-feng Emperor, passed on to the throne reports from Kwangsi gentry that accused local magistrates of indifference to militia: when a certain gentryman in Hsiang-chou had defeated a band of rebels with his own local force, the magistrate failed to distribute rewards to the men, who then dispersed in a huff.[79] On another occasion it was charged that officials in Hunan either refused to accept reports of "sect rebels" in their districts or else passed such reports up the line with the word "bandit" (*tao*) changed to "petty thief" (*ch'ieh*).[80] Unable to get protection from local authorities, the gentry of several prefectures in Kwangsi sent a delegation to Peking in October

76. *Ch'ing shih-lu,* Hsien-feng, 17:10b; 29:1b; 33:29b; 34:16; 36:4b,9; 37:8b; 38: 11; 61:30b–31.

77. Wang K'un, *Tun-pi sui-wen-lu* in Hsiang Ta, *T'ai-p'ing t'ien-kuo,* IV, 354.

78. *Ch'ing shih-lu,* Hsien-feng, 35:15b; 39:10b.

79. *Ch'ing shih-lu,* Hsien-feng, 27:13a-b.

80. *Ch'ing shih-lu,* Hsien-feng, 38:13.

1850, headed by the *chü-jen* Li I-yung, to submit their accusations through the censorate. This episode followed the pattern of the T'ien Jun proposal (see Chapter II.B), which probably represented a gentry move through the censorate over the heads of local bureaucrats.[81]

Perhaps in response to gentry complaints of this kind, seconded by influential sympathizers within the Peking bureaucracy, the court began to show a limited tolerance for private anti-rebel initiative. On October 12, 1850, it authorized a certain degree of local self-help. Hsu Kuang-chin was to make it known that "if there are gentry or merchants who can undertake t'uan-lien on their own (*tzu-wei t'uan-lien*) and contribute funds for military expenses, so that they are able to defend themselves and their families, they are to be severally rewarded according to their merits."[82] This seems a clear summons to the wealthy to take arms in their own defense. Yet what is striking about the court's policy at this juncture is not a new faith in extra-official military units or a change in the official view of what t'uan-lien ought to be but rather the caution and tentativeness with which such an expedient was authorized. Possessed of patently unreliable information about events in the south, prodded by gentry complaints, and no doubt mindful of the gentry's abiding interest in the local (though not necessarily national) status quo, the court gingerly sought help where help seemed forthcoming; and was probably aware that it was sanctioning a process already well underway. But its mistrust of irregular military forces remained. Only three days after calling on gentry and merchants to organize t'uan-lien, the court reiterated a long-standing prohibition against private manufacture or ownership of firearms.[83]

It is with this background in mind that we must assess the meaning of Tseng Kuo-fan's appointment to manage t'uan-lien in Hunan. Tseng was one of a number of officials selected by the court around this time in various provinces. These supervisors of t'uan-lien, later to be known as t'uan-lien commissioners (*ta-ch'en*) were mostly former vice-presidents of boards, ex-provincial governors, treasurers, or judges, or of similarly high official backgrounds, who happened to be living in their home districts. Unlike regular official appointments, these were not limited by the rule of avoidance. Tseng's close ties with Hunan gentry were what the court desired particularly to exploit. Well aware that local militarization was accelerating in South and Central China, the

81. *Ch'ing shih-lu*, Hsien-feng, 16:15.
82. *Ch'ing shih-lu*, Hsien-feng, 17:12b.
83. *Ch'ing shih-lu*, Hsien-feng, 17:17b.

court now sought to control it by bringing the foremost of the local elite—the high-ranking official–gentry—into the network of local responsibility. This was the essence of Tseng's role as a semi-official coadjutor of the regular provincial authorities. In appointing the t'uan-lien commissioners, the court was seeking, not to promote new military enterprises, but to control a militarization process that was already well underway.[84]

The Formation of the Hunan Army

Tseng had his own definite views about local militarization and was quite out of sympathy with the way it was developing in the countryside. In particular the formation of armed units by the local elite—made possible by the local fund-raising powers the elite was now assuming—placed unbearable hardships on the peasantry. Here Tseng's view was even more conservative than the court's: t'uan-lien should be largely demilitarized and should function as a version of pao-chia entirely for purposes of internal security. Local defense would be in no need of special funds were it manned entirely by peasants armed with farm tools. Without need for funds, t'uan-lien could give the less scrupulous gentry no opportunity to "divide the fat" by extorting t'uan-lien expenses from the villagers. The formula by which Tseng's views became best known was "emphasize the *t'uan,* but not the *lien,*" that is, the grouping but not the drilling. *T'uan,* Tseng wrote, was really nothing more than pao-chia: the drawing up of registers, the ferreting out of the criminal or disloyal, tasks cheaply financed and swiftly accomplished. In this respect Tseng's views were close to those of Tso Tsung-t'ang, who considered t'uan-lien more useful for internal consolidation than for external defense.[85]

In the end, however, Tseng's own course of action was decided by a more radical conviction: that village militarization, however energetically pursued, was entirely insufficient to meet the military needs of the times. Like Chiang Chung-yuan and Hu Lin-i, Tseng understood that a more highly militarized force was needed if the orthodox elite were to stem the tide, to forestall the dynasty's downfall as well as their own.

To understand his subsequent role and the true character of the

84. Lo Erh-kang, *Hsiang-chün hsin-chih,* 22–24, gives a list of the t'uan-lien commissioners appointed in 1853.

85. Tseng, *Shu-cha,* 2:11. Tso, *Shu-tu,* 2:2b.

Hunan Army that he was now to found, we must remember that Tseng entered the process of militarization when that process was already well begun. Unlike Chiang Chung-yuan and Wang Chen, he never had to build a *yung* force de novo, but rather found himself in the position of bringing together forces already in existence. He was always in the position of recruiting commanders, rather than recruiting troops. He was, in other words, at a higher level of command from the beginning: a position he owed, partly to his high official rank, partly to his prominence and influence among the Hunan gentry, and partly to the strategic position in which fortune had placed him.

During the early months of 1853, Tseng began to put together a coalition of *yung* forces at Changsha. To the thousand or so men already mobilized by Lo Tse-nan and Wang Chen were added contingents of specially picked men from the *lü-ying*, headed by an able Manchu officer, T'a-ch'i-pu, and new battalions from Hsiang-hsiang, recruited by Tseng's younger brother, Kuo-pao, and other gentry. Magistrate Chu Sun-i himself was detached from his duties and called upon to raise a *yung* contingent. From Hsin-ning and Pao-ch'ing in the south came new groups of *yung*, recruited by Chiang Chung-yuang's younger relatives and by the military-minded prefect of Pao-ch'ing, K'uei-lien. Chiang Chung-yuan himself, now appointed provincial judge of Hupeh, had left much of his original Hsin-ning force in Changsha under the command of his brother, Chung-chi, and Liu Ch'ang-yu.[86]

Tseng was evidently not at all sure that the court would sanction new military enterprises of this scope and he therefore (being a t'uan-lien commissioner) reported that he was forming a "large *t'uan*." Whether or not the court was reassured by this standard terminology, Tseng shortly abandoned the fiction and did not again use t'uan-lien terms to describe his forces.[87]

Tseng's original plan was to build this coalition of *yung* forces into an army of perhaps 10,000 men, which he would then put under the command of his protégé, Chiang Chung-yuan, whom he considered a more suitable military leader than himself. But events of that summer revealed glaring weaknesses in the organization and discipline of Chiang's Hsin-ning force, and Tseng was forced to the conclusion that

86. Lo, *Hsiang-chün hsin-chih*, 30–33; Chien Yu-wen, *Ch'üan-shih*, 1053–1054; Tseng, *Nien-p'u*, 2:1–7b.
87. Tseng, *Tsou-kao*, 1:47.

the new army must be built under his own leadership and upon his own model.[88]

That model, as Lo Erh-kang has demonstrated, was borrowed largely from the techniques of Ch'i Chi-kuang, the Ming expert on military organization and training, techniques we have already seen borrowed for Hu Lin-i's *ch'in-ping*. When Tseng first arrived in Changsha he found Ch'i's recruiting and training formulae already being used by Lo Tse-nan and Wang Chen.[89] Without discussing here the specific training methods advocated in Ch'i's writings, it will be sufficient to point out those basic organizational features that were most significant for the structure of the Hunan Army: (1) emphasis on small-unit training and discipline and (2) reliance on a network of personal loyalties, extending upward from squad level to the very top of the command pyramid.[90] The key role of the small unit commander, along with the emphasis on personalism, were both reflected in a basic Ch'i Chi-kuang prescription: that each echelon of commanders recruit the echelon immediately below it, thus linking military command structure to pre-existing bonds of loyalty and obligation. This system stands in marked contrast to that of the regular Ch'ing armies, in which personal loyalties were kept rigidly in check and all parts of the organization were deemed interchangeable.

The recruitment and command structure of the Hunan Army was thus in important respects a reflection of certain governing principles of Chinese social structure in general. Embodied in Tseng's army were those inclinations toward subordination and patronage usually expressed in familistic and quasi-familistic relationships, particularly that between teacher and disciple. At the bottom of the military ladder, these relationships grew naturally out of lineage ties. Between commanders on the middle and upper levels they grew from teacher-disciple bonds (such as those between Wang Chen and Lo Tse-nan, between Chiang Chung-yuan and Tseng Kuo-fan) and from quasi-fraternal or classmate bonds (such as those between Tseng and Hu Lin-i, both in a filial relationship to Wu Wen-jung) or between Tseng

88. Wang K'ai-yun points out that, for all its high morale, Chiang's *yung* force never achieved a tight internal organization; even after it had entered the Yangtze campaigns and had greatly expanded in numbers, its command structure was little more sophisticated than that of the band of 300 with which Chiang had first entered the service of Wu-lan-t'ai. *Hsiang-chün chih* (1909) 15:1b.

89. Lo-Tse-nan, *Nien-p'u, shang*:13.

90. Lo Erh-kang, *Hsiang-chün hsin-chih*, 84–94.

and Liu Yü-hsun (see the next section). What Tseng was building was, in one sense, an officer corps; but in another sense it was a "family" (men-hu) of personal disciples.

Personal loyalties were particularly strong on the level of the ying or battalion of 500 men. So vital were these attachments that an individual battalion was often designated by its commander's personal name (for example, the T'ing battalion, from the courtesy name of its commander, Pao Ch'un-t'ing, usually known as Pao Ch'ao). A battalion whose commander either died or retired usually could not be placed under the command of a new leader but had to be disbanded and replaced by a newly recruited unit.[91]

In Tseng's hands, Ch'i Chi-kuang's organizational precepts thus became a means of reconciling central direction with multitudinous personal loyalties. Brought together in a coalition under Tseng Kuo-fan's direction, a multitude of yung units were raised to a new level of militarization, being now connected to larger strategic aims, linked to richer sources of financial support through Tseng's official connections, and enabled to campaign far beyond provincial boundaries.

That personal loyalties were not invariably of benefit to military organization is shown by the case of the original organizer of the Hsiang-yung, Wang Chen. The very qualities that put him in the forefront of local militarization—independence, ambition, and a certain fractiousness of spirit—led him to break with Tseng Kuo-fan in 1853. Wang was unwilling to place himself under Tseng's command, claiming that his loyalty extended exclusively and particularly to Lo Tse-nan. With the support of Hunan Governor Lo Ping-chang, he established his own yung organization, which thereafter remained in Hunan, becoming known as the "old Hsiang battalions," in distinction to Tseng's Hsiang-chün (Hunan Army).[92]

Local Control in Hsiang-hsiang after 1852

As Tseng Kuo-fan became increasingly involved in the broader campaign against the Taipings, events in his home district acquired a momentum of their own. In Hsiang-hsiang, as in other Hunan districts, the forms of local militarization and control varied widely from Tseng's original conceptions. Tseng, as we have seen, had hoped to keep t'uan-lien virtually demilitarized and to prevent the emergence of auton-

91. Lo Erh-kang, Hsiang-chun hsin-chih, 137–145.
92. Chien Yu-wen, Ch'üan-shih, 1060–1062.

omously financed military organizations in the countryside. Upon his return to Hsiang-hsiang in the autumn of 1852 he wrote that, though he was not yet acquainted with Chu Sun-i's regulations, it seemed to him quite unnecessary to found t'uan-lien bureaus anywhere but within the district city, where a force of perhaps 400 paid fighters might be maintained under direct official control.[93] Simple local control militia, needing no financing or training, would not require the facilities of a bureau.

But it was not long before Tseng had to come to grips with the rebellious temper of the Hunan peasantry. In 1853 he wrote a letter, in his capacity as provincial supervisor of t'uan-lien, to "upright gentry and elders" on the subject of local dissidence. The districts were infested with "secret-society outlaws, heterodox religious sects, bandits, and riffraff (*p'i-kun*)": to deal with these types was ultimately the task of the local elite. Tseng then declared open season on wandering deserters, upon those bands of riffraff who were beginning to undertake direct expropriation of hoarded grain (the practice known as *ch'ih p'ai-fan*), and upon those habitually unruly elements who spread malicious propaganda and shook public confidence. All these might be killed outright with the blessing of the authorities. This bloody directive reflected the emergence throughout rural Hunan of powerful local *t'uan* bureaus that were already taking the law into their own hands. Tseng himself, convinced that the existing order was threatened by mortal danger from within, did not shrink from measures of extreme cruelty: hundreds of ragged suspects, shipped off to Changsha by local magistrates, were beheaded by his orders.[94]

T'ang Feng-ch'en, who succeeded Chu Sun-i in the magistracy of Hsiang-hsiang, issued t'uan-lien regulations that were largely in accord with Tseng's stated preferences. T'uan-lien in the villages was to be closely tied to pao-chia. Registers were to be drawn up listing all males between 15 and 50; each household was to provide one man for militia service. These levies were to be strictly non-professional and to remain under the control of lower-level pao-chia headmen. But T'ang, like Tseng Kuo-fan, had to face the fact that the prevailing social turmoil could not be contained by standard bureaucratic control organs. The weight of evidence suggests that his effort to demilitarize and bureaucratize t'uan-lien was only minimally successful. First, the local defense associations that had begun under Chu Sun-i's magistracy, based on

93. Tseng, *Shu-cha*, 1:45b–46.
94. Tseng, *Shu-cha*, 2:4b; *Nien-p'u*, 2:2a-b. Hsiang-hsiang 1874, 5:9.

lineage and on natural multiplex divisions, remained largely untouched by the new regulations. T'ang was forced to accept the existence of autonomous lineage militia forces outside the format of his pao-chia based registration system.[95] Second, at a higher level of militarization emerged groups called "*yung* hundreds" (*pai-yung*): trained, professional contingents, whose commanders were the newly powerful gentry figures known as "ward commanders" (*tu-tsung*).

The emergence of these *tu-tsung* was the most significant development in the evolution of local control in Hsiang-hsiang during the years of the Taiping Rebellion. The *tu*, or wards, of which there were 47 in the district, were originally tax-collecting subdivisions that represented areas of equal tax quotas. Apparently these units served as part of the *li-chia* taxing system and were also used at one time as the upper echelons of pao-chia. In its pao-chia role, each ward had a chief functionary known as the ward headman (*tu-cheng*), a commoner responsible for registering the populace of the 30 or 40 communities (covering as much as 100 square miles) in his ward, and for reporting illegal behavior. The ward headman remained an important part of Chu Sun-i's local control system, as head of a pao-chia network that paralleled t'uan-lien. But after 1853 he was increasingly overshadowed by a new figure, the ward commander, who gathered to himself the police functions of the ward through his control of the ward security force. In addition to the part-time conscripted militia of the villages, over which he was given nominal authority, the ward commander controlled a unit of trained mercenaries (the *pai-yung*), which formed the real cutting edge of his police power. The professional character of the *pai-yung* is suggested by the ward commanders' increasing appetite for funds, which were raised by an assessment on land and managed by the training bureau (*lien-chü*) in each ward. Though the wards differed considerably in size, in their new role they were clearly organizations of the extended-multiplex scale, superimposed upon a congeries of multiplex *t'uan* and independent lineage units, and capable of extracting funds from a broad area for the support of the *pai-yung* security corps.[96]

The emergence of the *tu* as a key unit in the militarization of Hsiang-hsiang may have been due less to its importance in pao-chia than to its role in *li-chia*, the tax-collecting system. Chu Sun-i's decision to abandon the much abused procedure by which tax collection was

95. Hsiang-hsiang 1874, 5:16a-b.
96. Hsiang-hsiang 1874, chüan 1. Also 5:5b–22.

supervised by yamen underlings placed a degree of taxing authority in the hands of the elite, whose influence over local taxation now began to increase as a consequence of their role in militarization. This was a process similar to the one we have observed in nearby Lin-hsiang and elsewhere.

The Ladder of Militarization

I have been discussing the t'uan-lien system in Hsiang-hsiang in the context of local control, but it must also be seen alongside the Hunan Army as part of a single military system. Besides bolstering the stability of his home area, t'uan-lien in Hsiang-hsiang and other Hunan districts was a pool of manpower for Tseng's higher-level forces. Initially, when Tseng decided "to recruit able-bodied males from the *t'uan* (*t'uan-ting*) as official *yung*" he had available several *yung* detachments already formed: those of Wang Chen and Lo Tse-nan, whose men had already been detached from their communities. For new recruits and replacements, however, he had to draw continually from Hunan manpower. His commanders naturally sought men who had received some training, or at least had been registered. Units like the *yung* hundreds of the *tu-tsung* were an obvious source, and many men left them to enroll in the battalions of the Hunan Army. This situation generated some friction between Hunan Army commanders and local officials who were reluctant to see their district security forces depleted. But more plenteous sources of recruits were the local t'uan-lien associations, with their registers of able-bodied men, some of whom had received at least rudimentary training. As the military threat to Hunan diminished in the late 1850's the militia forces of the *t'uan* ceased to train regularly and soon lost whatever military character they had been able to muster. Nevertheless, the multiplex associations themselves continued to play an important role in recruitment for the Hunan Army, and the web of interpersonal connections that underlay them remained a crucial factor in drawing fresh manpower from rural Hunan. When Tseng Kuo-pao (Kuo-fan's brother) returned home in 1859 to raise a new battalion, it was to the heads of the local *t'uan* that he turned for help in recruitment.[97] With their lists of registered males, and their roles as centers of community organization, the *t'uan* bureaus were able

---

97. Hsiang-hsiang 1874, 5:11, 20b. Wu Hsiang-hsiang, ed., *Hsiang-hsiang Tseng-shih wen-hsien*, IX (Taipei, 1959), 5592 (letter from Tseng Kuo-pao to Tseng Kuo-fan, 1859).

to facilitate the orderly transition of men from civilian to military life, to guarantee their behavior while in service, and to oversee their demobilization. This last function was particularly important if the Hunan Army were ultimately to be disbanded without grievously disrupting civil society. It was in effect a safeguard against total militarization.

D. Liu Yü-hsun and the Defense of Nanchang

The building of the Hunan Army, as we have seen, depended on Tseng Kuo-fan's ability to weld together *yung* units through personal loyalties and thus create a mobile, centrally directed force that could campaign beyond its provincial base. But Tseng's ability to challenge the Taipings for regional hegemony depended also upon his ability to form alliances with the elite in other provinces in order to gain local support and security for his army. In Nanchang, the strategic capital of neighboring Kiangsi province, Tseng was able to ally with a multi-level military organization led by a local *chü-jen*, Liu Yü-hsun (1806–1876), an organization with which Liu effectively dominated his home district for fifteen years. Liu's power extended downward into a network of vigorous t'uan-lien associations, and upward to the Kiangsi Army (Chiang-chün), a new *yung* force founded under Tseng's patronage. Through Liu, Tseng made the elite of Nanchang a vital adjunct to his campaigns.

The Origins of T'uan-lien around Nanchang

In the autumn of 1852, Liu had already resigned a post as sub-prefect and returned to Nanchang to observe mourning for his dead mother, when the news arrived that the Taipings had laid siege to Changsha, capital of Hunan. This clear threat prompted him to open a recruiting bureau in Chung-chou (a customary sub-district division where his native village was located), where he began to assemble funds and manpower. Liu and his chief collaborator, the *chü-jen* Wan Ch'i-ying, headed two of the richest and largest lineages in the vicinity, which naturally formed the backbone of the new force. This unit, which seems at first to have contained but a few hundred troops, was on a full-time paid basis and was trained by hired cadres in the use of firearms, swords, and spears.[98]

In the winter of 1852–53, Liu led his *yung* force to the provincial capital to cooperate in what was called the gentry *t'uan* bureau, actually a recruiting office set up within the city under official sponsorship, which had mustered three *yung* "armies" totalling some 1,800 men. These armies, not well articulated, were but a loosely coordinated congeries of *yung* units, which retained much of their original autonomy. This grouping seems similar to the "large *t'uan*" that Tseng Kuo-fan formed at Changsha at about the same time, which later became the nucleus of the Hunan Army. As spring approached, and news reached Nanchang that the Taipings were headed downriver, Liu left the city and led his men back to Chung-chou. It is made to appear in official accounts that Liu was asked to do so by the governor, Chang Fei, to provide "external support" to the city in case of a siege. But it seems certain that Liu actually made the move on his own initiative. Rural Chung-chou was the source of both troops and supplies for Liu's force. Liu undoubtedly felt that his primary interests lay with his lineage in the countryside, where it had widespread land holdings, rather than in the administrative city of Nanchang.[99]

Liu's Chung-chou bureau now became the nucleus of an extended-multiplex association with ramifications throughout the district. The *chü-jen* Yen I, a close personal friend of Liu and Wan, hastened back from Peking, where he had been attending the metropolitan examination, and secured from the governor a commission "to manage jointly the tasks of training *yung*, raising funds, protecting the locality, aiding the defense of the provincial capital and keeping the villages under control." With this considerable mandate Yen set up a recruiting and fund-raising bureau in neighboring Nan-chou, in the market town of Shang-k'an-tien, in collaboration with the leaders of four local lineages. Almost immediately three more bureaus were set up under similar circumstances, making a total of five. The primacy of the

98. Nanchang 1870, 28:2. Nanchang militarization is well documented in chüan 28 of this gazetteer. Pages 1–13 contain a detailed account of the formation and personnel of t'uan-lien bureaus; pages 13–38b narrate the campaigns of the Kiangsi Army and include relevant memorials and essays; pages 39–50b contain a list of 267 Kiangsi Army officers who were rewarded with official rank. Biographies of Liu Yü-hsun are in Kiangsi 1881, 140:47b–48; also Liu Fu-ching, *Nan-feng Liu hsien-sheng wen-chi* (1919) 3:22–24b.

99. Nanchang 1870, 28:1b, 11b, 13b.

Chung-chou bureau as the "head bureau" was assured, not by its seniority, but by Liu's intimacy with provincial authorities in Nanchang. So close were Liu's direct ties to the provincial yamen that the authorities of Nanchang district itself proved of very little consequence in the development of Liu's military organization.[100]

The *yung* contingent maintained by this extended-multiplex t'uan-lien association, known locally as the "Five-Bureaus *yung*" (*wu-chü-yung*), assumed a dominant role in the defense and local control of the Nanchang area. During the Taiping siege of Nanchang, from June 24 until September 24, 1853, the "Five-Bureaus *yung*" were credited with keeping supply lines open to the south of the walled city. Even more significant was their role in the suppression of local revolt. The siege of Nanchang was the occasion for widespread peasant uprisings throughout the district. When the district authorities could not handle the problem, Liu and Wan appealed directly to the governor, who sent members of his staff to the Chung-chou bureau to cooperate with Liu's headquarters. In the end some two score local people were rounded up and beheaded. After this impressive beginning, the Chung-chou bureau quickly assumed a position as the de facto judicial authority of the district, and "suspicious characters" were regularly sent there to be dealt with.[101]

During the next two years, the militarization of Nanchang district grew more complex. Throughout the district arose new multiplex and extended-multiplex associations, most centered on market towns. The number of part-time militiamen in the district grew to several tens of thousands. On a higher level of militarization was formed the Kiangsi Army, a mobile professional force under the patronage of Tseng Kuo-fan. In both these developments Liu Yü-hsun played a central role. For new bureaus throughout the district Liu was able to furnish official connections and confer legitimacy. After the siege of Nanchang was lifted, Liu was granted the rank of prefect and named deputy commissioner of t'uan-lien for Kiangsi province. He thus became the key link between the rural gentry and the provincial bureaucracy. In 1857, for instance, Liu was instrumental in founding a new local defense association in the turbulent region bordering Chin-hsien district. After an appeal from gentry representatives, Liu "ordered the *sheng-yuan* Chiang Ying-men and the rich and upright *chien-sheng* Chiang Ying-chü to undertake t'uan-lien forthwith." These men then collaborated

100. Nanchang 1870, 28:2b–4.
101. Nanchang 1870, 28:4–6b.

with at least eight powerful lineages (four of them across the district border in Chin-hsien) to form an association embracing some 120 villages.[102]

The Formation of the Kiangsi Army

In the spring of 1855, Tseng Kuo-fan was camped at Nanchang, trying there to rebuild his battered naval forces after their defeat at the hands of Shih Ta-k'ai on February 11. The Taipings were then in a strong position throughout the waterways of central China, holding Kiukiang, at the mouth of Poyang Lake, and Anking, which commanded the western approach to the Heavenly Capital at Nanking. With their third conquest of Wuchang on April 3, they now controlled the three most strategic points on the Yangtze. Tseng was determined to move back into Poyang Lake and ultimately to break the bottleneck at Kiukiang and Hukow. With his characteristic concern to guard rear lines of communication, he decided to form an auxiliary force that could secure the southern entrances to the lake in the area of Nanchang. He and the Kiangsi governor, Ch'en Ch'i-mai, prevailed upon Liu Yü-hsun to undertake the task, which entailed building several dozen boats and recruiting *yung*. In asking Liu to form the Kiangsi Army, Tseng was drawing principally upon the capability of the Five-Bureaus *yung* for river and lake fighting; the Kiangsi Army was originally designed as a naval force, though it later acquired land auxiliaries. Having had Liu brought into the official hierarchy as deputy t'uan-lien commissioner, Tseng then had him recruit a force of five battalions (*ying*), evidently organized on the pattern of the Hunan Army. The original size of this unit was probably about 2,500– 3,000 men. Liu remained commander until his retirement in 1868.[103]

Tseng and Liu were quasi-classmates (*t'ung-nien*), as both had obtained the *chü-jen* degree in 1834. More important in Tseng's view of him, Liu had demonstrated that he had the support of the Kiangsi gentry and could be an effective troop commander. Liu now set up a shipyard at Shih-ch'a, south of Nanchang on the Kan River. This shipyard and its products were initially a center of controversy between Tseng and Ch'en Ch'i-mai, who wanted the ships allocated to one of his own protégés. But not long afterwards Tseng impeached Ch'en for incompetence and assorted misdemeanors, and Ch'en was shortly re-

---

102. Nanchang 1870, 28:8–9.
103. Tseng, *Tsou-kao*, 5:63b; Nanchang 1870, 28:14, 23–28.

lieved of his post. Thereafter Liu was clearly under Tseng's command and patronage.[104]

The Kiangsi Army was new in 1855, yet its foundations were being built as early as 1852, when Liu began his militia organizing in Chung-chou. Though it operated on a provincial level, it bore a close and continuing relationship to the Five Bureaus and other local defense associations in Nanchang. Many of the officers and *yung* of the new force were in fact recruited from the *t'uan* bureaus. This close relationship, however, raises certain questions: we may ask, for instance, whether entire militia units from the bureaus were incorporated into the Kiangsi Army under their own commanders, and if so, what happened to the local t'uan-lien associations themselves? Comparing a list of local t'uan-lien leaders with a list of 267 officers of the Kiangsi Army who were rewarded with official rank, we find that only 13 out of 140 *t'uan* leaders appear also as Kiangsi Army officers. This disparity suggests that Liu drew his officers, not from among the top leaders of local associations, but from among their subordinates and lesser colleagues. Organizationally, the line between the t'uan-lien bureaus and the Kiangsi Army remained distinct. The *t'uan* leaders, with 13 exceptions, remained at the head of their local bureaus, attending primarily to problems of local control. Their militia units were depleted by the recruitment of *yung* for the Kiangsi Army, but we may assume that the gaps were filled by replacements from the pool of registered men in the villages. This upward movement of personnel from the t'uan-lien associations, and particularly from the Five Bureaus, into the Kiangsi Army continued throughout the years of the rebellion.[105]

The Persistence of the T'uan-lien Associations. Despite the continuing demands of a higher-level unit, which drew resources away from the original Five Bureaus, the original bureaus continued to function. The Nan-chou bureau affords an example of this organizational persistence. Formed in 1853 by Yen I in cooperation with gentry from the Chao, Yao, Yü, and Huang lineages, it suffered successive crises of leadership, caused partly by the death of some of its founders and partly by the migration of gentry into the Kiangsi Army. In 1855, when the neighboring Chung-chou bureau was deprived of its top leaders (Wan Ch'i-ying died and Liu Yü-hsun became commander of

104. Tseng, *Tsou-kao*, 5:61 ff. Nanchang 1870, 28:24.
105. Nanchang 1870, 28:1–13, 15a-b, 29–50b.

the Kiangsi Army), Yen I assumed its leadership by virtue of his close personal ties to Liu. Yen thus became primarily a liaison officer between the local components of the Five Bureaus and officials on higher levels, dispatching and coordinating local *yung* as the needs of the larger campaign required. The Nan-chou bureau now found it necessary to coopt a new gentry manager, surnamed Fan, thus bringing in the personnel and resources of an additional lineage. During the next few years several of the bureau's top leaders died, yet lineage representation was maintained by the addition of gentry members from the dead leaders' families: Fan Jang-chieh was replaced by Fan Jang-ch'un, his brother or cousin; Huang Jung by his son, Huang Shih-fu; Chao Li-chieh by his grandson Chao I-ch'ien and several others from the Chao lineage; Yao Shao-lien by his son, Yao Wen-ming. Family continuity was undoubtedly the factor that enabled the Nan-chou militia to survive as a locally oriented unit despite the pressures of outside events.[106]

Lineage and Militarization

Indeed, the militarization of Nanchang as a whole can only be understood if it is related to the kinship structure that lay beneath it. The dominating position of Liu Yü-hsun in the military affairs of Nanchang can be attributed in part to the size and wealth of the Liu lineage in its native area of Chung-chou, a "vicinage" (to use Maurice Freedman's term) some 30 miles from the walled city. The Liu formed what Freedman would call a "higher-order lineage," a group of related local lineages spread over a number of settlements, owning some common property and participating in a commonly supported lineage corporation. In his pious essay on the charitable activities of his lineage organization, Liu Yü-hsun wrote (in the 1860's) that the more than ten charitable schools of the Liu lineage were supported by contributions from four branch lineages (*chih-tsu*) besides his own. This description of lineage cooperation for support of education is probably a fair analogy of cooperation for defense a decade earlier. Yü-hsun's own branch at Tzu-ch'i was the dominant one, and his own contributions (in the form of income-producing lands) the most substantial. Indeed, the local history refers to the entire multi-community organization as the "Liu lineage (*shih*) of Tzu-ch'i." A parallel

106. Nanchang 1870, 28:4–5.

example of this kind of powerful higher-order lineage were the Wan centered in the nearby village of Ho-ch'i, headed by Liu's friend and collaborator, Wan Ch'i-ying.[107]

The ability of a wealthy, landholding lineage such as the Liu of Tzu-ch'i to raise manpower and funds was evident on various levels of militarization. When Liu Yü-hsun was organizing the head t'uan-lien bureau at Chung-chou, he drew talent largely from among his own kinsmen. This in-group from Tzu-ch'i was also a key element in the formation of the Kiangsi Army: Tzu-ch'i Lius were the largest single lineage group in a list of Kiangsi Army men who received special civil and military honors from the government, a fact that points not only to their abundance in the army as a whole but also to their favored status in the army's command echelons.[108] The Taipings, who soon became aware of the central role played by the Tzu-ch'i lineage in the Kiangsi Army, made a particular effort to attack the Lius' home area, hoping thereby to destroy the local t'uan-lien associations, to which the army was intimately bound by kinship, and upon which it relied for funds and manpower. The close interaction between levels of militarization among their opponents was apparently well understood by the Taiping command; but their attack on Chung-chou was not successful.[109]

Looking beyond the preeminent Liu lineage at the composition of the Kiangsi Army as a whole, it becomes clear that the army's officer corps was in large measure an extension of the local *t'uan* bureaus. Out of a list of 22 bureaus in the district, the leaders of eight certainly had relatives who were Kiangsi Army officers (that is, brothers, or cousins in the same generation, whose personal names include a common character). Such an abundance of sibling and collateral relationships suggests that there must also have been many father-son links that we cannot discern from the lists.

It is important to remember that in Chinese rural society elitism was a factor not only within lineages, but also between them. The dominating position of certain lineages in local military affairs was

---

107. Freedman, *Chinese Lineage and Society*, 21–23. Liu Yü-hsun's "I-hsueh chi" was printed in Nanchang 1870, 36:4b–5b. The distribution of surnames and their village locations can be studied in the "Surnames and lineages" (*hsing-shih*) section of Nanchang 1870, chüan 35 and 36. On lineage school-lands and their donors, see Nanchang 1870, 36:5b–7.

108. The Liu lineage provided 33 out of 234 names; the Wan lineage of Ho-ch'i was also well represented. Nanchang 1870, 28:39–50.

109. Nanchang 1870, 20:89a-b.

undoubtedly a reflection of their dominating position in other spheres of local society. Looking at the composition of Nanchang *t'uan* bureaus, the unequal division of leadership posts is immediately apparent. Though our information does not allow us to identify *t'uan* leaders with particular lineages in all cases, we can get a bare suggestion of the narrowness of the leadership group from the fact that out of more than 200 surnames recorded in the district, only 31 were represented in the leadership of t'uan-lien bureaus. The actual lineage representation within these 31 surnames must have been even narrower.[110]

The place of kinship structure in Nanchang's militarization, however, cannot be studied apart from the economic relationships within lineages and between them. During the years of rebellion, the orthodox elite was threatened as much by class tension within their own lineages and communities as by the armies of the Taipings. A lineage such as the Liu of Tzu-ch'i, which was large and, from a corporate standpoint, wealthy, was also highly stratified. The ability of a man like Liu Yü-hsun to donate lavishly to the school lands of the lineage indicates not only his own wide landholdings, but also a high prevailing rate of tenancy. Much of the tenancy relationship existed within the framework of the kinship structure itself: Liu landlords controlling Liu tenants.[111] In this situation in which exploitation was built into the kinship structure and the maintenance of corporate income-producing lands depended upon a high rate of tenancy, there were obviously powerful forces tending to pull apart such large and landlord-ridden lineages as the Liu. Of the activities of the Triad society within Nanchang we have no direct evidence. But we do know that the presence of the Taipings in Kiangsi touched off a number of Triad revolts during the chaotic summer of 1853.[112] In Nanchang itself, uprisings exploded throughout the rural portions of the district while the walled city was under siege. It is likely that Triad organizers had

110. Compare the information in Nanchang 1870, chüan 28 with that in chüan 35–36. Some of these 200-odd surnames, it should be noted, were no longer extant and were included in the record for purely antiquarian interest. The exact number of extinct surnames is not ascertainable from the record, and therefore the proportions mentioned above are merely suggestive.

111. The tendency of this landlordism to remain within lineage boundaries is suggested by a case of 1860, in which the Liu lineage of Tzu-ch'i laid claim to a sizable parcel of land that had long been occupied by tenants of the Chia and T'ao lineages. The case was brought to court and decided in the Lius' favor, whereupon Chia and T'ao tenants were ousted and new tenants "invited," undoubtedly of the Liu surname. Nanchang 1870, 36:7a-b.

112. Kuo T'ing-i, *Jih-chih*, 265, 267.

been active among the tenants of the big lineages and perhaps also among poor lineages that were victims of the kind of inter-lineage "imperialism" I have referred to earlier. The kind of militarization undertaken by Liu Yü-hsun and his collaborators certainly took place in a context of increasing social polarization, in which the elite was in daily competition with heterodox groups for the allegiance of the peasantry.

There is convincing evidence that the t'uan-lien movement in Nanchang (like that in Hsiang-hsiang) was undertaken with the requirements of that competition clearly in mind: the need to provide centers of organization and economic relief that could serve as alternatives to those offered by Triad lodges. The preface to the t'uan-lien treatise in the Nanchang local history (compiled under Liu Yü-hsun's supervision) states unambiguously that the purpose of militarization was, above all, local control; and that local control was not primarily a question of police coercion, but rather of pre-empting the service and allegiance of village manpower. Every man who was mobilized to defend against external enemies was one less potential rebel and troublemaker. Military service, suitably rewarded, could "transform the evil designs" of the shifty and rancorous "small man." Added to its organizational and moral functions was militarization's crucial economic function: in a population wracked by high rents and usury, with thousands of families at the end of their economic rope, militarization functioned as a species of relief. "Gather the liquid assets of a rural area and use them to feed the hard-to-govern young men of that area. Thus can you avert unforeseen disaster." Organized along lineage lines, militarization in Nanchang was thus designed to tighten kinship bonds and dull the edge of class conflict. As for those smaller and poorer lineages not brought into the fold, or others who might be dissatisfied with things as they were, forceful treatment was ready to hand.[113]

Financial Administration: Likin and the Kiangsi Army

The close social links between the Kiangsi Army and the Nanchang t'uan-lien structure found striking practical expression in finance. Besides supplying the army with officers and men, local t'uan-lien bureaus served as the army's financial agents throughout

113. Nanchang 1870, 28:1a-b.

the district. A t'uan-lien bureau typically began its existence with a formal mandate from officialdom to raise funds in the surrounding community. Such a mandate generally included taxing authority of broad but unspecified scope, under the heading of raising supplies (*ch'ou-hsiang*) and urging contributions (*ch'üan-chüan*). This taxing authority was exercised partly through assessments on land rents, as we have seen in the case of Hsiang-hsiang; there may in addition have been arrangements made with officials whereby "contributions" would be rewarded with recommendation for official rank or promotion (*i-hsü*). The connection of local contributions with rank awards will be discussed in greater detail in Chapter V.A, below. But during the course of the rebellion emerged another source of funds, which gradually became the backbone of military finance and played a key role in the operation of the Kiangsi Army: the likin tax.[114]

Even before the Kiangsi likin system was formally introduced in 1855, local t'uan-lien bureaus were already well established as officially legitimized taxing and fund-raising centers. Hence it is not surprising that likin collection was simply taken on as another aspect of their activities in this field once the tax was officially sanctioned. The lack of a prescribed administrative format in the early days of likin made it inevitable that local gentry managers play a major role. Militia bureaus, after all, already had the administrative staff and the coercive authority necessary for a smoothly working tax system. The armed river patrol boats of Liu's local bureaus served handily for tax inspection and enforcement. The use of local militia facilities for collection seems to have been a general feature of likin in its early years.[115]

Although likin in Kiangsi was instituted officially in September 1855, not until December 1856–January 1857 was a provincial likin bureau formed to standardize regulations and supervise local stations. As an administrative organ superimposed upon a vigorous existing system of local initiative, the provincial likin bureau naturally had trouble getting local stations under control. Many stations were run by t'uan-lien bureaus under Liu Yü-hsun's patronage, and it proved virtually impossible to bring this tax network under provincial regulation. Beginning in early 1857, provincial authorities tried to simplify likin procedures and establish regular exemptions whereby goods in transit could be taxed only a limited number of times, with excise rates

114. Nanchang 1870, 28:4,6,7b.
115. Nanchang 1870, 28:13. For another reference see Yü-lin 1894, 18:33. On the early years of likin see Lo Yü-tung, *Chung-kuo li-chin shih,* 68.

lowered for each succeeding collection point. But Liu's taxing stations remained outside this schedule of exemptions, although Liu maintained formal relations with the provincial bureau by making monthly reports of revenue and expenditure and by turning over any "surplus" funds.[116]

In 1860, after Tseng Kuo-fan had become governor-general of Liangkiang, a further attempt was made to centralize the Kiangsi likin. Tseng's elevation to high provincial office at last made it possible for him to control provincial revenues directly and thereby to provide a secure financial base for his military campaigns. His new logistical plan was "to use Hunan and Hupeh as a source of troops, and Kiangsi as a source of funds."[117] To this end Tseng worked out an agreement with the Kiangsi governor that all revenue from tribute silver would be controlled by the governor and used to support provincial forces, including the regular army units and those *yung* forces assigned to provincial defense. Tseng would control all revenue from the likin and from the sale of brokerage commissions (*ya-shui*) for the support of "troops campaigning outside the province." Tseng's revenues would not pass through the office of the provincial treasurer. To gather his taxes, Tseng established a new bureau in Nanchang to govern both brokerage commissions and likin.

Liu's Kiangsi Army was ostensibly a provincial *yung* force and therefore might be supposed to come under the category of units financed by the regular provincial revenues; on the other hand, Liu was a protege of Tseng, and might thereby have fit into the regular likin-funding channel. But as it turned out, Liu's army fit into neither category. Through the local bureaus located at key communications centers in Nanchang district, Liu continued to operate his own separate likin network, complete with its own bookkeeping and enforcement systems.

The next several years saw an effort by provincial officials to get control of likin for provincial purposes. During the final Taiping offensive in 1864, Governor Shen Pao-chen was given permission to divert half the Kiangsi likin back into the provincial treasury; and later that year, the remainder of the likin officially reverted to the province. In 1866 ensued a major drive to centralize the Kiangsi likin; only the major taxing stations were to be retained and 31 lesser ones shut down. Even for the larger stations, certain categories of tax, such

116. Liu K'un-i, *Liu K'un-i i-chi* (Peking, 1959), 183–184. See also Beal, *Likin,* 42.
117. Tseng, *Tsou-kao,* 11:50.

as that on resident merchants, were to be stopped. There is no evidence that this meant a major reduction in total revenues. Rather it suggests an attempt to increase the proportion of likin coming into the provincial treasury and to reduce the proportion retained by local bureaus by forcing out of business those bureaus over which the provincial government had least control. Likin simplification, which inevitably meant its centralization by provincial authorities, seems to have been a major element in the growth of provincial power after the rebellion. We see a similar example in Kweichow, for instance, undertaken as early as 1859 by Han Ch'ao.[118]

The centralization of likin eventually proved ruinous for the financial independence of the Kiangsi Army. In 1868, someone in the provincial government impeached Liu Yü-hsun, alleging misappropriation of funds. Further, it was charged that Liu "personally managed the finance of the Kiangsi Army, and the provincial treasurer had no way of investigating the matter." In response the court ordered governor Liu K'un-i to seek detailed financial reports from Liu Yü-hsun and to report any unauthorized expenditures. The governor was also to memorialize as to whether the Kiangsi Army could not be disbanded, now that the rebellion was over, and whether the likin stations it controlled could not be abolished. If the army was still needed for patrolling the waterways, then the governor should appoint a regular official under his own command to take it over. Liu K'un-i replied that he had placed the expectant taotai Ho Ying-ch'i in charge of the Kiangsi Army's naval contingents, had abolished seven of its likin stations and had placed the rest under the control of the provincial likin bureau. Funds were now to be disbursed through regular provincial channels. Also, steps were being taken to disband the force by stages, beginning with the larger gunboats.[119]

Although Liu Yü-hsun was cleared of the personal charges against him, this affair forced him out of military command and brought about the dissolution of his army. His retirement may well have been the condition for his exoneration. Clearly his financial independence had become intolerable to certain elements in the provincial government. His personal military machine, built on close liaison with many local

118. Liu K'un-i, *I-chi,* 184–185; Tseng, *Tsou-kao,* 21:60; *Ch'ing-shih,* 4809. For a detailed discussion of the evolution of fiscal procedures during this period, see Lo Erh-kang, *Hsiang-chün hsin-chih,* 132–137. Provincial governors and governors-general were by this time gathering all revenues under their own control, successfully bypassing the regular agents of the Board of Revenue.

119. Liu, *I-chi,* 187; Nanchang 1870, 28:38b.

militia bureaus, could not survive the centralizing trends then operating in provincial finance.

The Kiangsi Army never outgrew its provincial matrix. Indeed, Liu Yü-hsun resisted all attempts to move either him or his forces outside Kiangsi. In 1857, though appointed military-affairs intendant for a circuit in Kansu, he managed to be kept in Kiangsi through the intercession of the governor. In 1860, when the Taipings under Li Hsiu-ch'eng were attacking the lower Yangtze cities, the governor-general of Chekiang and Fukien and the governor of Chekiang begged the court to order Liu, through Tseng Kuo-fan, to transfer the Kiangsi Army eastward to their relief. These pleas were resisted, first by the Kiangsi governor and ultimately by Tseng Kuo-fan, both of whom stressed the local ties of the Kiangsi Army and the impracticability of transferring it outside the province. Again in 1864, efforts were made to transfer Liu away from Kiangsi, this time without his army. The throne ordered Liu to proceed to Kansu as provincial judge and to aid in suppressing the Moslem rebellion. Shen Pao-chen, then governor of Kiangsi, memorialized on Liu's behalf to ask that he be kept in his home province to nurse a recurring respiratory ailment. The tenacity with which Liu held on to his provincial base suggests that the preoccupations of the Kiangsi Army were not much different from those of the local t'uan-lien associations from which it arose: the protection of local lineages and their property.[120]

120. Nanchang 1870, 28:16, 23–28, 32b; Tseng, *Tsou-kao,* 15:44.

V. PARALLEL HIERARCHIES
OF MILITARIZATION

A. Orthodox and Heterodox Hierarchies

Here let us consider as a hypothesis that differences in political and ideological orientation in traditional China did not necessarily involve differences in scales and modes of organization. The same kinds of linkages and the same levels of organization would then be visible within both the orthodox, gentry-dominated Confucian culture and the various heterodox, secret-society dominated sectarian subcultures. If this were so, it could be attributed either to the pervasive influence of the dominant cultural forms or else to a single set of organizational principles that were built into Chinese society. Our study so far has concerned militarization that grew from the resources and leadership of the orthodox Confucian elite. There is some evidence to suggest that certain organizational forms of this elite militarization were shared by groups with different social origins and political orientations, groups that had been placed, either by circumstance or ideology, in opposition to the Ch'ing establishment.

To illuminate the structural outlines of nineteenth-century militarization it may be useful to propose here a general typology of military forms that will embrace the various levels of militarization in both orthodox and heterodox camps. Similarities between comparable levels in orthodox and heterodox modes suggest unmistakably the concept of parallel military hierarchies (see Figure 8). First the orthodox hierarchy, the development of which we have already discussed, may be summarized briefly here.

Figure 8. Parallel military hierarchies in South and Central China, by descending order of level of militarization.

Orthodox	Heterodox
The regional army	The community in arms
Yung (mercenaries)	*Ku* (bandits)
T'uan-lien	*T'ang* (secret-society lodge)

The Orthodox Hierarchy

Level One: T'uan-lien. On the lowest level of militarization stood the t'uan-lien association, in simplex and higher scales of organization. Militia units raised by these associations typically retained close ties to village society. They achieved area security not by mobility and professionalism but by proliferating ties to other associations nearby.

Level Two: Yung. Frequently the bridge between level one and level two units was the head bureau of an extended-multiplex *t'uan,* which was able to draw sufficient wealth from the surrounding area to support a force of mercenaries on a more or less permanent basis. The *yung* forces hired by such bureaus were an important element in nineteenth-century elite militarization. Professional *yung* forces hired by gentry associations were increasingly in evidence as the rebellion proceeded. Many gentry apparently shared the conviction of Feng Kuei-fen, of Wu-hsien, Kiangsu, that genuine non-professional militia were too weak willed and too ill trained to be of any use whatever and that gentry and merchant wealth might better be spent on small mercenary forces.[1] There were in addition many other kinds of level two units. The term *yung,* denoting irregular loyalist forces in general, covered a broad range of types, all of which were distinguished from t'uan-lien militia by greater mobility and professionalism: (1) contingents of mercenaries such as the *yung* from Ch'ao-chou, recruited ad hoc by regular Ch'ing military commanders to supplement regular troops; (2) units raised by local bureaucrats, such as Hu Lin-i's personal force in Kweichow; (3) independent units raised by local elite, like Chiang Chung-yuan and Wang Chen. Though

1. Feng Kuei-fen, "Chüan-yung chu-chiao kung-tieh" in *Hsien-chih-t'ang chi* (1876), 9:14–15.

such local *yung* units were capable of extended service and wide mobility, they were not necessarily absorbed by higher level forces.

Level Three: the Regional Army. It was Tseng Kuo-fan's achievement to bring *yung* units together into a larger organization, give them unified strategic direction, and connect them to broader sources of financial support. His unique clarity of orientation, added to his high official connections, provided a standard around which could rally the ablest of the provincial elite. His deep-dyed neo-Confucianism, added to Ch'i Chi-kuang's canons of military organization, provided a framework within which personal loyalties could be reconciled with central command.

The Heterodox Hierarchy

Level One: The T'ang as a Base for Militarization. The high tide of rebellion in Kwangsi lasted only until 1852, when the Taipings migrated northward in a body (save for some remnants that were unable to join the main group) and thus left the Kwangsi environment. Thereafter the dominant rebel group in that province was the Triads, or Heaven and Earth Society (T'ien-ti hui), and the local history of the 1850's in both Kwangsi and Hunan was largely dominated by the spread of Triad influence. Various Triad groups had cooperated with the God-Worshiping Society in the years just preceding the Taiping uprising at Chin-t'ien, and certain Triad leaders, most notably the Kwangtung pirate leader Lo Ta-kang, joined their forces to the Taipings. But after the Taipings had departed, Triad organization evolved along lines peculiar to itself. In the early fifties, many Triad local chapters called themselves worshiping societies (*pai-hui*—actually *pai* was a term also used by Triads to denote their own ritual oath) and took on fragments of Taiping symbolism; this represented perhaps genuine inspiration from the Taipings, or else a device to draw in remnant Taiping sympathizers. But from 1856 onwards, the "worshiping societies" are less in evidence, and Triad organization becomes generally associated with the local group known as the *t'ang*.[2]

2. Among the literature on the Triads, consult Hirayama Amane (Shū), *Chung-kuo pi-mi she-hui shih* (Shanghai, 1934); John Ward and W. G. Stirling, *The*

With the standard explanation of Triad organization there can be no quarrel: the local Triad lodge was called *t'ang* (hall) or *shan-t'ang* (mountain hall), a designation borrowed from the great fictional tradition of Chinese outlawry, the *Shui-hu-chuan,* in which appears the Liang-shan chung-i-t'ang (The Loyal and Righteous Hall of Mount Liang). The names of Triad lodges were ordinarily based on this pattern (for example, Chung-hua-shan pao-kuo-t'ang—The Nation-Protecting Hall of Mount Chung-hua), though the mountain name bore no relation to the actual location of the lodge.[3]

It is worth suggesting, though, another aspect of the *t'ang,* which may illuminate its role as a community organization. In old China the word *t'ang* was used for voluntary associations of a broad range of types, established for various sorts of benevolent and mutual-aid activities. The *t'ang* was very much a part of orthodox Chinese culture. The term itself suggests respectability and elevated purposes and is connected with both ancestor worship and folk religion. Ancestral halls (*tz'u-t'ang*) and small community temples (for example, Kuan-yin *t'ang*) contributed to the pious overtones of the term, as did the vaguely religious coloration of certain charitable institutions called *t'ang.*[4] But despite these religious overtones, the charitable *t'ang* were entirely secular in their funding and management. The Chih-yuan-t'ang in Ch'uan-sha, Kiangsu, described by C. K. Yang, which engaged in "helping orphans, widows, and the aged and in giving free burial plots, medical aid, rice, and clothing to the needy," was endowed by 63 donors, all secular. Thus, although the *t'ang* may have been imbued with miscellaneous religious notions of charity,

---

Hung Society, or the Society of Heaven and Earth (London, 1925–1926); William Stanton, *The Triad Society, or Heaven and Earth Association* (Shanghai, 1900). On the growth of Triad influence in Kwangsi, see Hsieh Hsing-yao, *T'ai-p'ing t'ien-kuo ch'ien-hou Kuang-hsi ti fan-Ch'ing yun-tung* (Peking, 1950), 181–192. See also Chung Wen-tien, *T'ai-p'ing-chün tsai Yung-an* (Peking, 1962), 161–165.

3. Lo Erh-kang, *T'ai-p'ing t'ien-kuo-shih chi-tsai ting-miu chi* (Peking, 1955), 67–68. Lo points out the surprising extent to which Ch'ing officials were successfully misled by this naming system, gamely searching for Triad headquarters on the actual mountains appearing in the lodge name. See also Lo's general discussion of the *Shui-hu-chuan*'s influence on the Triads: *T'ien-ti-hui wen-hsien-lu* (1942), 77–85.

4. G. William Skinner describes the character and activities of the Pao-te shan-[benevolent] t'ang in Bangkok, which "was based on highly eclectic (Confucian, Buddhist, and Taoist) religious sanctions." *Chinese Society in Thailand: An Analytical History* (Ithaca, 1957), 257. It is not surprising to find organizations of this sort listed under "religious institutions" in local gazetteers (e.g. P'an-yü 1871, 15:18b).

it drew wholly from secular resources and was entirely compatible with the worldly, agnostic culture of the orthodox elite.[5]

The term *t'ang* was also closely connected with the family as an economic unit: a deed to property owned in common by a family was often made out in a hall (*t'ang*) name rather than in the name of an individual, to simplify and ensure the heritability of commonly owned property.[6] Contributions to community activities were frequently registered under such a family hall-name, and many *t'ang* of this sort are included in a list of contributors to the Sheng-p'ing association during the anti-British mobilization of 1841. Other entries in this list testify to the general utility of the *t'ang* designation in financial record keeping. Many contributing *t'ang* were listed without surnames, a clear indication that these were multi-lineage, mercantile, or other groups that had banded together to contribute one or more five-tael "shares" to the militia enterprise. Some multi-village leagues (*yueh*) also contributed under common *t'ang* designations. Finally, the seven-man committee at the Sheng-p'ing headquarters which managed the funds for the entire association was itself identified, as a fund collector and disburser, by a *t'ang* name.[7]

These roles of the *t'ang* in the orthodox culture—as a charitable or religious institution and as a handler of common property—should be kept in mind as we approach the considerable body of source material on the "*t'ang* bandits" (*t'ang-fei*) of the 1840's and 1850's.[8] The hundreds of *t'ang* that arose in South China during the mid-nineteenth century were indeed Triad lodges and thus may be assumed to have embodied common political orientations. But these *t'ang* were primarily local organizations, founded to meet local community needs. These needs were in the first instance economic. The key figure in a local *t'ang* was commonly termed "rice-host" (*mi-fan-*

---

5. C. K. Yang, *Religion in Chinese Society* (Berkeley, 1961), 336.

6. C. K. Yang, *A Chinese Village in Early Communist Transition*, (Cambridge, Mass., 1959), 91–92, describes the practice of using "hall-names" as it was observed in recent times.

7. *San-yuan-li shih-liao*, 141–151.

8. After the mid-century crisis had subsided, a group of scholars sifted the historical records of the Kwangsi rebellions. The results were published as supplements to the *Kuang-hsi t'ung-chih chi-yao* (1889) under the titles, *Kuang-hsi chao-chung-lu*, *P'ing-kuei chi-lueh*, *Ku-fei tsung-lu*, and *T'ang-fei tsung-lu*. In 1950 appeared two important monographs based partly on these materials: Hsieh Hsing-yao, *T'ai-p'ing t'ien-kuo ch'ien-hou Kuang-hsi ti fan-Ch'ing yun-tung* and Laai I-faai, "The Part Played by the Pirates of Kwangtung and Kwangsi Provinces in the Taiping Insurrection" (unpub. diss., University of California, 1950).

chu): a local leader who was able to secure the allegiance of the destitute of the community by providing them with grain. Such leaders were not ordinarily members of the gentry but rather their heterodox counterparts: Triad organizers. Their economic power arose either out of their own personal wealth or out of their ability to mobilize their adherents for outlawry. The spoils from robbery went into a common treasury; which, in addition to assuring *t'ang* members a fair allocation of goods, served also to bind them together in awareness of a common fate and to confirm the rice-host in his indispensable role as custodian of common wealth.

T'ang were also involved in the "tax resistance" (*k'ang-liang*) movement that played an increasingly prominent part in rural affairs during the mid-century decades. Official corruption and economic disasters frequently drove communities to organize themselves to resist tax collectors or, through the influence of the local elite, to force officials to moderate their demands. One form of this resistance was *pao-lan*, which we have observed in the case of Ch'ung-yang and Lin-hsiang districts, in which local leaders inserted themselves between the villages and the district yamen. But tax resistance often took the form of armed struggle, carried on by a multiplex village association, and involving a definitive break with the local bureaucracy. In this latter form of resistance, the *t'ang* of South China were inevitably involved. The concomitant to the common treasury of the *t'ang* was the gathering of community wealth for community purposes (including, of course, militarization) and the protection of that wealth from the demands of the bureaucracy and its agents. In certain prefectures of central and western Kwangsi, the cooperation of numerous *t'ang* in tax resistance resulted in cutting communications routes for an entire decade and the effective expulsion of officialdom—and its taxing agents—from the rural hinterland. The government's dogged opposition to *pao-lan* must be seen in the light of what *pao-lan* could ultimately lead to: the creation of a local, unofficial taxing authority which, relying on its economic power, could support the kind of local militarization that threatened the lifeline between the bureaucracy and the rural communities.[9]

9. See the fascinating, though theoretically overburdened article on tax resistance by Yokoyama Suguru, "Chūgoku ni okeru nōmin undō no ichi keitai: Taihei tengokuzen no 'kōryō' undō ni tsuite," *Hiroshima daigaku bungakubu kiyō*, no. 7:311–349 (1955). On the rice-host system, see Hsieh Hsing-yao, 32–35; Laai I-faai, 118.

Seen from the standpoint of local militarization, the character of the *t'ang* as a community organization is quite apparent. The kind of militarization that the *t'ang* undertook for illegal pursuits and community protection was militarization on the lowest level. Bands of armed men belonging to a *t'ang* remained tied to their local community and to the rice-host's treasury. The *t'ang* was thus in certain respects identical to the *t'uan*: its spatial dimension was enlarged not by military mobility but by forming alliances with similar organizations in nearby communities. Like the *t'uan*, the *t'ang* had a natural tendency to form multiplex associations. Though men from a number of communities could be mobilized in this way, they were not thereby separated from their local ties.[10]

T'ang was not the only name used for local secret society lodges; we also find the term *kuan* used to designate a branch office of a *t'ang*. Possibly the derivation of *kuan*, like that of *t'ang*, is the corresponding orthodox organization, in this case the *hui-kuan* (which Ho Ping-ti has called *Landsmannschaften*), a club set up away from home by gentry or merchants from a particular area. We find *kuan* being set up by the Triad conquerors of Kuei-hsien in 1854. Among overseas Chinese in the Straits Settlements the term *hui-kuan* was actually used to designate a Triad lodge; also used in that locality was the term *kung-ssu*, the normal term for a legitimate business association. The important fact about these terms is that they were all supposed to designate organizations that, while secret and illegitimate, were inseparable parts of ordinary, everyday society. They existed not as groups cut off from the normal order of life (like bandit gangs in the hills) but as functioning parts of local society. Triad membership offered protection and guidance amid the manifold difficulties and dangers of ninenteeth-century community life. Thus it is not surprising that the militarization of such groups remained on a low level, with members remaining within the local community until forced out of it by repression or economic disaster.[11]

Level Two: The Bandit Gang. The *t'ang's* low level of militarization is particularly striking when compared to that of the *ku*,

10. See the table of Kwangsi *t'ang* and their regional affiliations in Hsieh Hsing-yao, 38–47, based on material in the *T'ang-fei tsung-lu*.

11. On secret-society lodges see William Stanton, *The Triad Society*, 76–86. On the Kuei-hsien Triads, see Liang Lien-fu, "Ch'ien-chai chien-wen sui-pi" in *Chin-tai-shih tzu-liao*, no. 1:7 (1955). On *hui-kuan*, see Ho Ping-ti, *Chung-kuo hui-kuan shih-lun* (Taipei, 1966).

roughly translatable as "gang," a group of roving bandits. The years following the Opium War saw a marked proliferation of such bands throughout the south, but especially in Kwangtung and Kwangsi, the provinces most directly affected by the opium traffic and by the disruption of trade routes that followed the opening of Shanghai. With the shift of the tea trade to the new entrepot, the traffic of goods along Kwangtung's North River dwindled, throwing thousands out of work. Disturbances along the North River route also endangered the opium traffic, some of which was forced westward into the Kwangsi rivers along with its bands of outlaw transporters and protectors. The Kwangsi underworld was further swollen by seacoast pirates, who, having been the object of vigorous supression by the British during the late 1840's, were forced to migrate up the West River and seek new fortunes on the inland waterways. The newcomers were better armed than local bandits because of their former connection with the highly dangerous and competitive opium trade. To these outsiders were added many gangs of inland origin, composed of men who had been detached from their communities by the harshness of the times and the lure of plunder, and thousands of rootless mercenary troops who had been demobilized after the Opium War. Thus by 1850 the south was scourged by roving bands of armed men, who preyed upon the local populace but were tied to no local community and remained essentially outside local society.[12]

The most notorious of the river pirates, a man from Wu-hsuan named Ch'en Ya-kuei, headed a cutthroat band of several thousand, which arose in 1846 and coursed through the Kwangsi rivers, pillaging the towns on either bank. In 1849 they actually managed to conquer the district seats of Li-p'u and Hsiu-jen; they did not garrison them but fled with their spoils. So brutal were Ch'en's pirates that they were effectively alienated from public support; with the countryside in arms against them, they were hunted down and killed in 1850. The Triad pirates Chang Chao and T'ien Fang, who had migrated inland from the Pearl River delta, were similarly at war with local society but saw for themselves a political future: they considered linking their forces with the Taipings and actually joined their encampment at Chin-t'ien for a short time. Unable to stomach the Taipings' strict discipline and stern religion, they departed. In

12. Laai, "Pirates," 45, 62–66, 151.

1852 they sold their services to the Ch'ing side for a time but soon returned to outlawry and were killed in 1853.[13]

Ch'en Ya-kuei, Chang Chao, and T'ien Fang represent extreme cases in which armed bands were wholly separated from local society, with no local interests to protect, no restraints, no public support, and no future. Why militarization of this type was so widespread in the southern provinces is a subject that requires much more thorough research into the constitution of southern society than has yet been accomplished. In Kwangtung, a prime factor was undoubtedly lineage feuding and the creation thereby of a ready pool of young men skilled in fighting. To this might be added the custom in Hakka communities whereby much of the field work was done by women and the men were left comparatively idle. In any event, endemic social factors were added to the peculiarly disturbed condition of the southern provinces under the impact of the Canton trade to produce a type of militarized group that, in its separation from local society, must be clearly distinguished from village-based groups such as the *t'ang*.[14]

The *t'ang* and the *ku* bandits thus clearly represent two different levels of militarization. The preface to the *T'ang-fei tsung-lu* (A general account of *t'ang* bandits) points out the significant fact that "roving bandits" commonly allowed their hair to grow, whereas the "*t'ang* bandits" shaved their foreheads in the officially prescribed manner. Quite apart from its anti-Manchu symbolic function, the question of hair growth was of considerable importance to anyone involved in outlawry. A man without the standard shaved forehead could not quickly rejoin the surrounding community in a pinch. Like a man in uniform, his fortunes were tied to those of his military organization, of which he was necessarily a full-time member. Cohesiveness and separateness, leading to greater professionalism and mobility, were the characteristics of the *ku*. *Ku* were typically more ambitious than *t'ang* in their military enterprises and might attack and hold walled cities. Military organization was more complex and might include a rudimentary system of ranks.[15] There sometimes

13. Hsieh Hsing-yao, 5–10.

14. Yao Ying, *P'ing-tsei shih-i chuang, shang Sai chieh-hsiang* cited in Sanō Manabu, *Shin-chō shakai shi, nōmin bakudō*, pt. 3, p. 11.

15. *Ku-fei tsung-lu,* 1:8b. *T'ang-fei tsung-lu,* 1:1. See also Chien Yu-wen, *Ch'üan-shih,* 183–186.

arose a certain degree of confusion between *t'ang* and *ku* bandits, since various roving gangs found it convenient to assume *t'ang* names "to facilitate recruitment" from among local people. Yet the basic conceptual distinction between these two forms of heterodox militarization emerges unmistakably from the record.[16]

Level Three: The Community in Arms. The Society of God-worshipers represented in several respects a form of militarization quite distinct from both the professional bandit gangs and the Triad rebels. These differences were historically decisive ones, for they led to the formation, in 1850, of the Taiping Kingdom: a community in arms that presented a revolutionary challenge to the old order. Hung Hsiu-ch'üan and Feng Yun-shan, founders and propagators of the new pseudo-Christianity, converted dozens of communities during their missionary work in the years 1844–1850. These communities lay in a number of districts but principally in Kuei-hsien and Kuei-p'ing in southern Kwangsi. The success of these missionizing ventures was largely due to conflicts endemic to village society in these areas: the converts were for the most part Hakkas, members of a linguistically distinct group that had come to South China in several waves of migration over the course of centuries. These Hakka communities were embroiled in a form of conflict with their neighbors, the indigenous (*pen-ti*) population, that was in many respects indistinguishable from the interlineage vendettas we have observed to be a common feature of rural life in the south. Hung and Feng were themselves Hakkas; their missionizing efforts naturally proceeded along paths that were socially and linguistically most accessible to them. In the new creed the Hakka congregations found both a unifying force and a justifying faith. Thus by 1850 the Hakkas, though not the only group to have received Hung's revelation, were by far the most numerous and the best represented in the leadership elite.

It was in the summer of 1850 that the call went out to assemble the faithful at Chin-t'ien, a village in the district of Kuei-p'ing where the God-worshipers had established a base. Many of the more than 10,000 who responded were in fact already homeless people: whole communities forced from their homes by the vengeance of powerful enemies. Many of the others had found the pressures of economic and

16. *T'ang-fei tsung-lu,* 1:1. Hsieh Hsing-yao (p. 48) minimizes the distinction between *t'ang* and *ku* for this reason. Nevertheless, information in the *T'ang-fei tsung-tu* plainly indicates a basic difference in social and organizational character.

communal struggle so unbearable that they uprooted themselves—men, women, and children—with few regrets, burning their homes behind them. Added to these peasant families were groups of workmen from rural industries, miners and charcoal burners, who had already been separated from their homes and from the bonds of a settled society. All who came to Chin-t'ien gave into a common treasury whatever goods they had been able to salvage from their former lives and thus foreclosed the road of return.[17]

The crucial distinction to be drawn between the armed God-worshipers and other forms of local militarization is that the Hakkas were militarized as whole communities. This was not a matter of men being separated from their homes and attached to a military group, as seems to have been the case with bandit gangs, but of large numbers of family groups, including presumably whole lineages, pulling up stakes and forming a new social grouping, a grouping that was of necessity militarized because of its irreducible antagonism with its neighbors. This antagonism, which had begun in the embattled and socially isolated Hakka villages, now took the form of a general alienation from the values of the established order. That the Taiping creed developed theoretical provisions for a whole new social order was due in part to the manner in which the original contingents had been separated from their social matrix: as communities, with a vision of a new and purer community life and with the kind of concrete interest in a collective future that only a community—and not a band of detached armed men—is likely to develop. Like their orthodox counterpart, the regional army, the Taipings embodied a firmer political orientation and a more complex organization than level-two groups and were thereby enabled to sustain a more powerful military machine for a longer time over a larger area of operations.

B. Interaction and Integration

Having outlined in schematic form the parallel hierarchies of militarization that emerged during the decades of rebellion, we have now

17. Lo Erh-kang, "Heng-ting-tun lun K'o-chia jen yü T'ai-p'ing t'ien-kuo shih k'ao-shih" in Wu Hsiang-hsiang, *et al.*, eds., *Chung-kuo chin-tai-shih lun-ts'ung* (Taipei, 1959), 1st ser., IV, 156–160. *P'ing-Kuei chi-lueh*, 1:2. An extensive account of the early fortunes of the God-worshipers is found in Chien Yu-wen, *Ch'üan-shih*, I. In English, consult Franz Michael, *The Taiping Rebellion*, 21–50.

to consider two subsidiary problems: (1) similarities and interaction between orthodox and heterodox forms on analogous levels, and (2) modes of vertical integration among different levels within each mode or hierarchy.

T'uan and T'ang as Related, Alternative Forms of Local Organization

The basic structural similarities between *t'ang* and *t'uan*, and the dangers in differentiating too sharply between them on grounds of supposed ideological differences, can be illustrated by the case of the Cheng-i t'ang of Liu-yang, Hunan. A dozen miles from the district seat lived Chou Kuo-yü, a man of substance and ability, who had bought himself lower ninth brevet rank, a position on the margins of the local elite. Chou was also a member of the Triad society. In 1834/35 he founded the Cheng-i (summon the righteous) t'ang, a Triad local chapter. Within the leadership were three functional groups, known as "martial stalwarts," "dialecticians," and "scribes and accountants," suggesting the three tasks of military defense, proselytizing, and administration of common goods or relief donations.[18]

Chung Jen-chieh's rebellion of 1842 in neighboring Ch'ung-yang was the occasion for the Cheng-i t'ang to assume broader responsibilities for community defense. It will be remembered that Chung's uprising stimulated the elite of adjacent districts to take an active role in militarizing their communities, and thus it affected Liu-yang. The Cheng-i t'ang became the nucleus of a multiplex association that ultimately embraced perhaps 20,000 people and could mobilize a militia force of about 4,000 armed men.[19] Because local security remained a problem after Chung's rebellion was crushed, the Cheng-i t'ang and neighboring multiplex groups persisted into the late 1840's and early 1850's; and when the Taipings reached northern Hunan in the autumn of 1852, Liu-yang society remained divided into a multitude of local defense associations.

During their summer in southern Hunan the Taipings had been highly successful in recruiting local Triads to their cause, and naturally they continued to recruit during the siege of Changsha (October 13–November 30, 1852). Triad members among them were

18. Liu-yang 1873, 13:9.
19. Chiang Chung-yuan, *I-chi, hsing-chuang,* 13b. Hunan 1885, 79:55b. Tso Tsung-t'ang, *Ch'üan-chi, shu-tu,* 2:5–6b. *Ch'ing shih-lu,* Hsien-feng, 81:3–4b.

undoubtedly aware of Chou Kuo-yü's community power in neighboring Liu-yang, and the Taiping leaders duly sent a messenger to Chou with a letter asking him to mobilize his followers and join the rebellion. But before Chou could respond, a *sheng-yuan* named Wang Ying-p'in, a long-time enemy of Chou's and head of a rival defense organization, learned of the Taiping letter and denounced him to the authorities.

Chou was now horrified by the prospects before him. He had evidently decided that he had more to lose than to gain by uprooting himself and his militiamen to follow the Taipings on their uncertain path. Now compromised, he hastened to cement his relations with the old order. He sent his nephew with a contingent of 300 men into the district city ostensibly to guard the prison and the government granary but actually to preempt a position as a legitimate militia organization. But the situation was now slipping out of Chou's control. The Cheng-i t'ang, linking a number of lineages, had grown by that time to a size not easily manageable. Two of Chou's adherents, Tseng Shih-chen and Teng Wan-fa, mobilized armed men, burned the local academy that served as the headquarters of the Wang t'uan-lien organization, and killed Wang Ying-p'in himself. Afterwards the mob razed and pillaged nearby wealthy households.[20] The magistrate, kindly but ineffectual, besought gentry of neighboring rural areas to mediate between the feuding factions but was forced by Teng and Tseng to accept their offer of a force of one or two thousand militiamen to serve as an additional guard in the district seat, thus rendering the Cheng-i t'ang immune to punishment by higher officials and revenge by injured neighbors.

The safety of the Cheng-i t'ang now depended on the preoccupation of Ch'ing forces with the fight against the Taipings, but once the siege of Changsha was lifted and the Taipings had departed, the distressed gentry of Liu-yang sought and received outside aid. Tso Tsung-t'ang, now serving as an adviser on the staff of the Hunan Governor Chang Liang-chi, wrote Chiang Chung-yuan that to break the power of the Cheng-i t'ang, an amnesty should be offered to the rank and file. The organization was now quite large, containing perhaps 4,000 men under arms, of whom many were not genuinely committed to revolt. An indiscriminate attack on the Cheng-i t'ang as a whole was likely to drive leaders and followers closer together,

20. Tso, *Ch'üan-chi, shu-tu,* 2:5a-b. Liu-Yang 1873, 13:9.

when what was needed was to separate them. In the end, this policy prevailed. Chiang Chung-yuan, who had just succeeded in putting down a revolt in nearby Pa-ling, led his troops into the district. After announcing that only the leaders of the Cheng-i t'ang would be punished, he was able to defeat the hard-core rebels and disperse the rest to their homes with "pardon certificates." Chou Kuo-yü fled but was captured and executed the following year.[21]

The reason the Cheng-i t'ang is so difficult to classify is that it existed for nearly two decades within the accepted order, and since 1841 had actually been engaged in local militarization on a perfectly respectable basis. It was in fact not distinguishable from the numerous other multiplex associations in the vicinity. Its acceptance as a multiplex t'uan is attested to by several reliable sources: the Hunan gazetteer of 1885 recounts that it originated "as a t'uan"; a memorial from Hunan Governor Chang Liang-chi states that it had been founded for entirely legitimate purposes of community defense; and Tso Tsung-t'ang, in what was evidently a slip of the pen, referred to it as a t'uan even after the assault on Wang Ying-p'in's organization.[22]

It is important here not to be confused by purely formal distinctions. Here was a multiplex association embracing some dozens of villages, which was capable of mobilizing about 4,000 men on a low level of militarization and was obviously embroiled in vendettas with similar groups nearby. In northern Hunan the t'ang as a local defense group had evidently not yet acquired unambiguously heterodox connotations. What seems to have happened was that the crisis of 1841–42 led to the expansion of the t'ang's activities and to the formation of a large multiplex grouping, the majority of whose adherents were not secret-society members at all but had accepted the leadership of the Cheng-i t'ang in local defense. Chou's Triad affiliation was not the most important factor in his local militia leadership. More important was his community status as head of a multiplex association (indistinguishable in most respects from the t'uan of nearby areas), a status he was evidently reluctant to lose by casting his lot with the Taipings. But the internal ties of this multi-lineage grouping were loose. Chou was unable to control the leading groups of allied lineages and was in the end compromised by the mob

21. Tso Tsung-t'ang, Ch'üan-chi, shu-tu 2:5–9b. Hunan 1958, 1:35.
22. Hunan 1885, 79:55b; Ch'ing shih-lu, Hsien-feng, 81:3–4b; Tso, Ch'üan-chi, shu-tu, 2:6.

rampages led by the zealots Teng and Tseng against the rival Wang organization. Tso Tsung-t'ang was aware of Chou's secret-society connections but even suggested at one point that the magistrate work secretly with Chou in order to catch Teng, Tseng, and their followers (not more than a few hundred among the whole Cheng-i t'ang organization, thought Tso).[23]

Two conclusions arise from the Cheng-i t'ang case. A multiplex local defense association could run afoul of the established order because of its loose internal cohesion and lack of common political orientation. Second, the character of local militarization did not differ significantly between level-one orthodox and heterodox groups. The fact that a secret-society leader like Chou Kuo-yü was able to organize a multiplex defense association more or less indistinguishable from those of neighboring groups and thus blend into the local surroundings for more than a decade suggests that the terms *t'ang* and *t'uan* were at times really superficial distinctions applied to organizations that were structurally indistinguishable and politically indeterminate.

The record abounds in similar illustrations of the political indeterminacy of level-one groupings. The Nien Rebellion was based on multiplex associations (*t'uan*) that were infiltrated or suborned by secret-society leaders of White Lotus affiliation. But in their origins, these multiplex groupings seem to have been indistinguishable from *t'uan* of the orthodox variety: walled villages, linked (often under gentry leadership) for purposes of self-defense. Like the local defense associations of South China, the initial militarization of the Huai-pei Nien communities often began in intervillage vendettas. So closely were these rebel confederations associated with standard patterns of rural militarization that an account of military operations in Shantung during the Nien rebellion includes a treatise on "*t'uan*-rebels" (*t'uan-fei*).[24] In the south, the wavering loyalty of *t'uan*, and their close structural similarities with *t'ang*, were as perplexing to local administrators as they were later to official historians. "Ostensibly *t'uan*, secretly rebels," wrote one chronicler.[25] Some self-proclaimed *t'uan* had secret-society affiliations that made them

---

23. Tso, *Ch'üan-chi, shu-tu,* 2:7. Another source pictures Tso as less compromising: Wang Ting-an, *Hsiang-chün chi* (1889), 2:1b.

24. *Shan-tung chün-hsing chi-lueh,* (Shanghai, 1879), chüan 22. Chiang, *The Nien Rebellion,* 16.

25. *T'ang-fei tsung-lu,* 1:1.

indistinguishable from *t'ang*. Others changed from *t'uan* to *t'ang* as a result of conflicts with officialdom. One suspects that, conversely, many *t'ang* that reached an accommodation with officialdom were listed in the record as *t'uan*.[26]

On the second level of militarization, too, the character of particular groups was often mutable or indeterminate. Inasmuch as these groups were already detached from normal social and economic ties, opportunities of the moment could be decisive in determining their affiliations. Many a bandit leader was brought over to the loyalist side by the prospect of greater gain or brighter future. One of the most prominent Ch'ing commanders, Chang Kuo-liang (original name, Chia-hsiang) had begun as a small merchant in Kwangtung. Slandered and ruined by a rival, he went underground, migrated westward, and surfaced in Kwangsi as one of the most vicious of the roving Triad bandits. In 1849 a local Ch'ing commander bribed him and several hundred of his followers into the loyalist military system. His bravery and ruthlessness propelled him to high command, and he became one of the Taipings' most dogged antagonists. Cases like this one were complemented by numerous transitions in the opposite direction. Bands of *yung* recruited by local gentry or officials were always a latent menace; for if they had for any reason to be demobilized, they were likely to turn to banditry or rebellion out of necessity.[27] On the highest level of militarization, by contrast, crossing political lines was relatively rare. Though there were isolated cases of defection, the degree of commitment was apparently high enough at that level to keep political lines well defined.

Vertical Integration and the Role of the National Elite

Though we have used the term "parallel hierarchies" to describe the various levels of orthodox and heterodox militarization, it is quite apparent that vertical integration on the orthodox side was by far the more cohesive and sustained. Connections among the orthodox elite were successfully maintained from village and multi-village as-

26. Liang Lien-fu, "Ch'ien-chai chien-wen sui-pi" in *Chin-tai-shih tzu-liao* no. 1:17 (1955), the case of T'ang P'ing-san; *Ku-fei tsung-lu*, 1:8, the case of Li Chin-kuei.

27. Lo Erh-kang, "Chang Chia-hsiang k'ao" in *T'ai-p'ing t'ien-kuo shih chi-tsai ting-miu-chi*, 140–145; also *Ch'ing shih-lu*, Hsien-feng, 32:6; 35:2. Chou Ch'ang-sen, *Liu-ho chi-shih* (1886), reprinted in Hsiang Ta, *T'ai-p'ing t'ien-kuo*, V, 160.

sociations up to the level of the regional army. By contrast the opposition was far less successful in binding its corresponding elites into an effective hierarchy that could carry on the contest for empire on all levels of society. There will of course always remain a suspicion that apparent differences in this respect are magnified by differences in the type and amount of documentation. Among the many valuable resources controlled by the orthodox elite was the written language, and the record is dominated by accounts of the orthodox hierarchy. Further, because loyalty and unity, patronage and subordination were values to be promoted, these accounts inevitably brighten somewhat the picture we get of integration on the orthodox side. Yet even with this kind of distortion taken into account, there were important differences.

Considering first the difficulty of integrating different levels on the heterodox side, the key relationship was certainly that between the Taiping leadership and the leaders of the Triad Society, the dominant secret-society group in South and Central China, which we have seen as a dominating force on the lowest level of heterodox militarization. As a number of studies have demonstrated, the early collaboration between God-worshipers and Triads did not long survive the restructuring of the Taiping Kingdom at Yung-an, and from 1853 the Taiping leadership showed a much diminished interest in cooperating with secret societies. There were indeed a number of instances in which Triad uprisings were in some way coordinated with Taiping plans, through the mediation of the few Triad leaders such as Lo Ta-kang who held high rank in the Taiping Kingdom. Triad groups were excellent prospects for recruitment in the early years of the movement, and on occasion large contingents fled their home areas to join forces with the Taipings. Yet there is little evidence of sustained cooperation between Triad and Taiping leaderships. Particularly in Taiping occupied areas, where lower-level heterodox groups might have furnished local security and economic support, there is no indication that Taiping and secret-society leaders were able to come together in long-term patterns of cooperation. There were, indeed, efforts to bring the movements together on a symbolic plane, the leadership of each seeking legitimacy in terms of the symbols of the other. There are preserved remnants of Triad propaganda efforts to picture Taiping leaders as having been "invested" with their ranks by a legitimate Ming successor, as well as Taiping efforts to appeal to Triad loyalties by use of traditional

Triad titles in proclamations.[28] But there is little to suggest that such propaganda was in any significant degree a reflection of practical reality. Though the Taipings were sometimes able to form ad hoc alliances with local strongmen (t'u-hao) who had no secret-society affiliation,[29] their record with Triad groups is not impressive.

Indeed there were a number of reasons why Taipings and local heterodox groups could not join effectively in building a military hierarchy to rival that of the orthodox elite. One was the undiminished imperial pretension of the Triads: a covert, ceremonial usage in peaceful times, which flowered into a vigorous Ming restorationism during the nineteenth century, complete with Ming pretenders and Ming reign titles. Though the Taipings affected Ming habits and hair styles, their political thinking and their religious revelation had brought them far beyond visions of Ming restoration. Though united in their hatred of the Manchus, Taipings and Triads were not able to accommodate their respective views of the future. It may even be suggested that the Triads, so accustomed to survival in the existing ecology of rural Chinese society, had no convincing, well-articulated view of the future. Here, precisely, we can discern both the unique strength of the Taiping movement and its besetting weakness. The rebellion of the God-worshiping Society can in one sense be understood as one of the many ethno-linguistic revolts that marked the late period of Ch'ing rule. The Hakka-Punti conflicts in Kwangsi, like the Miao-Han conflicts in Kweichow, Hunan, and elsewhere, were inflamed by an economic crisis that drove a swelling population to compete for an inadequate acreage of arable land. Under stress, society tended to cleave along preexisting fault lines: the ethnic and linguistic divisions of South and Central China. The Hakkas, though ethnically Han, functioned as a discrete subculture because of linguistic distinctness and long-inbred awareness of their separate status. Their fate was to become bearers of a vision. Separateness and oppression were transformed into a chosen-people mythology and a militant messianism. Zeal was matched by intolerance, so that the social relations of the Taipings bore ever afterward the indelible

28. Chin Yü-fu et al., eds., *T'ai-p'ing T'ien-kuo shih-liao* (Peking, 1959), 264–266; Hsiao I-shan, *Fei-yü-kuan wen-ts'un*, (Peking, 1948), 7:20–24. Lo Erh-kang, *T'ai-p'ing t'ien-kuo shih pien-wei chi* (Shanghai, 1950), 231–238.

29. See the case of Ho Wen-ch'ing, of Chu-chi, Chekiang, an adventurer who brought his band of fighters over to the Taiping side in 1861. Ho had been a "t'uan-lien" leader under official patronage. Chu-chi 1908, 15:15b; Huang-yen 1877, 38:24.

stamp of their origins in rural Kwangsi. Though able to attract legions of the rootless and dispossessed, they were incapable even of the kind of tactical tolerance needed to form stable working relationships with local heterodox groups that were themselves embedded in the Chinese countryside. The same factors that produced their uncompromising political utopianism made it hard to find allies in the fight for empire.

The military hierarchy of the orthodox side was by no means dependent only on shared outlook and ideology but grew from an intricate network of personal relationships that stretched from village to imperial capital. These personal relationships were, in turn, tied to the institutions through which the elite exercised its dominance over Chinese society. The multiplex *t'uan,* as we have seen, grew out of customary patterns of elite interaction, and was in some cases simply one aspect of a generalized elite association at the multiplex scale of organization. The case of Liu Yü-hsun's Nanchang organization illustrates how such relationships could be used to form an interacting military system of first- and second-level military groups. When we come to the question of how these groups interacted with level-three groups such as the Hunan army, we are dealing with a set of personal associations that reached all the way to the summit of elite society, associations nurtured by the bureaucratic centralization of the Chinese empire, in which Peking, as the hub of the examination system, played a major role. The cosmopolitan character of the Chinese literati, which gave them an organizing capacity far superior to their heterodox rivals, is exemplified by the structure of the national elite's Hunan component.

The Hunan Army's command structure was dependent upon preexisting interpersonal relationships, relationships that had a significance far beyond the military sphere. As Figure 9 illustrates, the principal commanders of the Hunan Army were closely related through kinship, academic connections, and long-standing patterns of patronage and loyalty. The skein of interconnection could be traced much farther through the leadership group.

The close integration of the Hunan elite was a product of both the Ch'ing academic system and the network of patronage and loyalty that ran through the bureaucracy. An examination of elite interconnections reveals a complex interplay of these two factors. A number of prominent men were linked by their connections to two of the great scholar-officials of the preceding generation: T'ao Chu

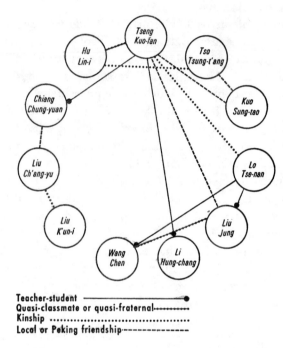

Figure 9. Pre-existing relations among commanders and staff officers of the Hunan Army.

Sources: Tseng, *Nien-p'u;* Hu, *I-chi;* Chiang, *Hsing-chuang;* Wang, *Nien-p'u;* Lo, *Nien-p'u;* Hummel, *Eminent Chinese.*

and Ho Ch'ang-ling. Tso Tsung-t'ang and Hu Lin-i were both related to T'ao Chu by marriage. Tso had been personally very close to T'ao and had been appointed tutor of T'ao's son. Tso had studied for a time at the Ch'eng-nan academy at Changsha, which was run by Ho Ch'ang-ling's brother, Hsi-ling. Through his connections with the Ho family, Tso undoubtedly was known to the scholar Wei Yuan, Ho Ch'ang-ling's trusted associate, and it may have been partly by Wei Yuan's suggestion (as well as Hu Lin-i's recommendation) that he was introduced to Wei's friend Lin Tse-hsü in about 1839. Lo Tse-nan was also tied to the Ho family, by close friendship with Ho Ch'ang-ling and as tutor of Ho's son. In the capital, a Hunan group centered upon Tseng Kuo-fan and also, apparently, upon Tso Tsung-t'ang's brother, Tsung-chih. To both these men Chiang Chung-yuan owed his successive advancements in the official hierarchy. Friendships formed in Hunan student circles at Peking—such as that between Chiang and Liu Ch'ang-yu—were at least as important as local ties in binding these men in quasi-fraternal relationships. To his own generation in Hunan, Tseng was linked by classmate bonds formed in the Yueh-lu academy at Changsha, by marriage ties to Lo Tse-nan, and to Hu Lin-i by their mutual loyalty to Wu Wen-jung.

The term "national" rather than "provincial" is applied to this elite group for two reasons: first, the group's internal connections were dependent upon the bureaucratic-academic system on the national level; and second, the group was able to reach beyond provincial boundaries to form associations with elites in other provinces. The quasi-fraternal bonds between Tseng Kuo-fan and Liu Yü-hsun are a case in point. Links between Hunan and Kiangsi were important to Tseng's military operations, particularly in view of Tseng's effort to draw Kiangsi financial resources into his coffers. The most striking example, of course, is the case of Li Hung-chang and the Anhwei elite, which became allied to the Hunan group through Li's early student relationship to Tseng in Peking. Peking was a place where intra-provincial ties were cultivated and strengthened, largely through the activities of the provincial *hui-kuan* (or *Landsmann-schaften,* to use Ho Ping-ti's translation). It was also a place for broadening one's acquaintance. Tseng was naturally very active in the management of *hui-kuan* affairs while in Peking, but his circle of friendships extended well beyond the Hunan group. Among his intimates were scholars from Kwangtung, Kwangsi, Chekiang, and elsewhere. Among his student-protégés (*men-sheng*) many were of course Hunanese. Yet he also had a fair number from Szechwan, where he had supervised a provincial examination and thus acquired protégés, and a scattering from other provinces, like Li Hung-chang. Had he actually conducted the Kiangsi examination in 1852 as planned, he would thereby have acquired a group of protégés from that province as well.[30]

To the question of why the Hunan elite was the first to form a successful hierarchy of militarization, only suggestions can be offered. Part of the answer must certainly lie in the distinctive ideological orientation of certain segments of the Hunan elite. In Hunan, the hegemony of the empirical research school of "Han scholarship" had never been as secure as in the lower Yangtze provinces. Accordingly the revival of interest in Sung moral philosophy was able to attain considerable momentum in Hunan by the early nineteenth century. This revival affected a long line of scholar-activists, from Yen Ju-i in the period of the White Lotus Rebellion, through Ho Ch'ang-ling and T'ao Chu, to Tseng Kuo-fan. Tseng and his circle were animated by a vigorous puritanism that stressed self-cultivation along with social activism. Nourished in the two great Changsha academies, Yueh-lu and Ch'eng-nan, this stern and practical philosophy played a major role in nineteenth-century history. There is little doubt that the ability of the national elite to crush the mid-century rebellions owed much to the intellectual resurgence of its Hunan component.[31]

Geographic and social factors must also be explored. It is apparent that Hunan possesses extensive mountainous border areas with a high degree of ethnic diversity and that it forms the drainage basin of several major rivers (the Hsiang, Tzu, Yuan, and Li) that put most areas in convenient communication with the Yangtze valley (see Figure 10). Thus Hunan in the nineteenth century partook of the self-reliant and martial character of the South China mountains, with their unceasing ethnic conflict and the resulting high degree of militarization, as well as of the cosmopolitan character and rich culture of the central Yangtze area. Unlike Kwangsi, also a diverse and highly militarized society, Hunan looked inward toward the major communication routes of central China, rather than outward toward Canton and the sea. Its river systems linked the elites of the border districts with

30. Tseng, *Chia-shu*, 77 (letter of June 27, 1844).
31. On Hunan Sung scholarship, see Ch'ien Mu, *Chung-kuo chin-san-pai-nien hsueh-shu shih* (Taipei, 1957), 569–595. On the Yueh-lu and Ch'eng-nan academies, see Shan-hua 1877, 11:40–70.

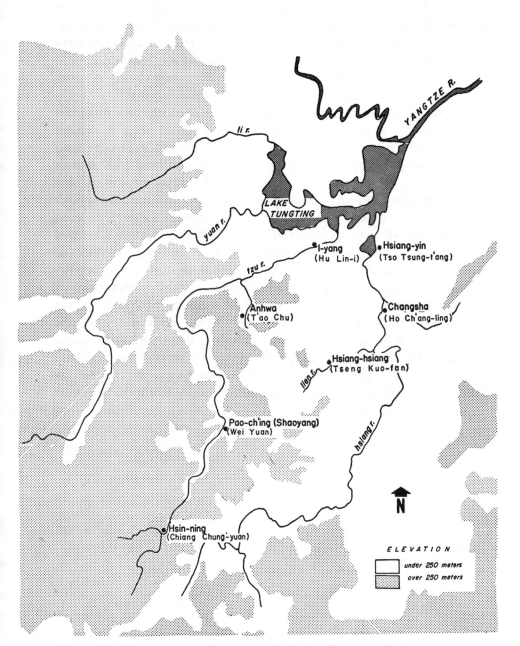

Figure 10. Hunan topography seen in relation to elite connections.

the elites of the plains. The military capacities of such border figures as Chiang Chung-yuan could thus be joined to the leadership and ramified official connections of the central Hunan gentry. Thereby the military initiative and close integration of the Hunan elite may perhaps be traced to that province's peculiar combination of socio-geographic diversity and intraprovincial communications.

Looking beyond Hunan to the general phenomenon of military hierarchies, it is apparent that the integration of elites on various levels was the central connective force. This stated, it becomes clear that the orthodox elite possessed communications facilities that their heterodox rivals could not match. Heterodoxy had its internal communications, of course. The strength of secret societies among river transport workers, for example, gave these societies access to communities all over Central China; the shared mythology of Triad groups made possible a certain degree of regional collaboration among them. Yet for communications linking village and market-town society to the apex of national politics nothing could match the traditional academic system and the manifold interpersonal links that it created and nourished. Faced with a common enemy, the multi-level orthodox elites were able to put their internal communications at the service of an integrated military system—from the local police and regimentation of village based t'uan-lien up to the massive striking force of the regional armies—which could contest for power on all levels of society.

VI. MILITIA, THE STATE, AND REVOLUTION

A. Socio-strategic Problems of the Taiping Rebellion

There would seem to be three requisites for a successful seizure of power by a rebellion in old China: (1) the rebel group must destroy or absorb the armed forces of the incumbent regime; (2) it must seize the administrative cities of the empire, from district up to imperial capital, thus appropriating the nodes of economics and communication and the symbols of political legitimacy; (3) it must establish control of rural areas, to secure their productivity and military manpower on a regular basis. It might be remarked that the second and third requisites are closely linked, because the successful operation of government requires a stable administrative relationship between city and countryside. Historical experience suggests that although the ultimate consolidation of a regime requires all three, yet the three need not proceed in any set order. It is not at all clear, for instance, that it is necessary first to eliminate the incumbent's armies on a national basis. The existence for some years of a well-defended and well-governed regional regime with a vigorous claim to legitimacy might generate enough support and attract enough defectors to turn the tide. Also, it is clear from experience that rural revolution may precede the capture of administrative centers. Thus the temporal sequence of these requisites is not fixed, though it would appear that the prolonged lack of one or more of them might dim the prospects of a rebel regime. From the outset the Taipings had a clear conception of these power requisites. Alongside the military struggle went an effort to achieve total control over China's population at all scales of organization.

The Taiping Attempt to Establish Local Government

The Taipings' most important normative document, the *Land Regulations of the Heavenly Dynasty (T'ien-ch'ao t'ien-mou chih-tu)*, issued in the winter of 1852–53, was based on the civil-military hierarchy of the *Rites of Chou*. It prescribed the basic unit of society as 25 families, under the control of a sergeant (*liang-ssu-ma*), who would oversee the total religious, economic, and military life of the group. Over the sergeant was a pyramidal hierarchy of officers, each of which (as in the *Rites of Chou*) was to control both the civil administrative unit at his level of command, as well as the military unit to be drawn from it. Superimposed on this pyramid were the traditional units of district and prefecture, the officers of which were responsible to the upper levels of the imperial hierarchy (see Figure 11).

The question of how and to what extent this ideal system was realized in practice has been much studied, but the fragmentary and contradictory character of the evidence has made the study difficult and in many respects inconclusive. One difficulty is that in the Taiping case the system must be studied on two levels, the military and the civilian. Though the ideal system from which it was drawn envisaged a hierarchy of officers combining civil and military roles, and a populace of farmer-soldiers, in practice the Taipings had to apply the system first to a wholly militarized organization (their army) and only later extend it to the civilian populace in conquered areas. Taiping army organization was minutely worked out, at least as early as 1852, when the organization manual *T'ai-p'ing chün-mu* was issued. Running through this work is a theme of joint civil-military administration: each unit bore a regional designation as part of its organizational title, for instance, "the front battalion of the front regiment of the yellow-banner [army] of Tao-chou, Hunan" (T'ai-p'ing Hu-nan Tao-chou huang-ch'i [chün] ch'ien-ying ch'ien-lü)," a designation that indicates not only the provenance of the men in the battalion, but also the future organization of local government in Tao-chou once hostilities were ended and the regime secure. Later, however, the Taipings abandoned hope of extending their military organization directly into civil society. This is suggested by the fact that after 1853, a Taiping army unit commonly included men from various regional backgrounds.[1]

---

1. *T'ai-p'ing chün-mu*, reprinted in Hsiang Ta, *T'ai-p'ing t'ien-kuo* I, 122. Also see Li Ch'un, *Tai-ping t'ien-kuo chih-tu ch'u-t'an* (Peking, 1963), 184.

Figure 11. Taiping local government organization.

Officer	Jurisdiction	Subordinates
Imperially appointed *administrators* (*shou-t'u-kuan*)		
Tsung-chih (prefect)	Prefecture	Varying number of *chien-chün*
Chien-chün (magistrate)	District	Varying number of *chün-shuai*
Locally selected *administrators* (*hsiang-kuan*)		
Chün-shuai (general)	12,500 households[a]	5 *shih-shuai*
Shih-shuai (colonel)	2500 households	5 *lü-shuai*
Lü-shuai (major)	500 households	5 *tsu-chang*
Tsu-chang (captain)	100 households	4 *liang-ssu-ma*
Liang-ssu-ma (sergeant)	25 households	5 *wu-chang*
Wu-chang (corporal)	5 households	–

Sources: Chien Yu-wen, *T'ai-p'ing t'ien-kuo tien-chih t'ung-k'ao* (Hong Kong, 1958), 377-381; Li Ch'un, *T'ai-p'ing t'ien-kuo chih-tu ch'u-t'an, tseng-ting-pen* (Peking, 1963), 286-288.

[a] For a discussion of varying numbers in different calculations see Li Ch'un, 287-288. The numbers above follow Li's figures.

The great difficulty in extending this system to a large rural population was of course in imposing a highly artificial set of standard-sized units upon the natural organizational forms of local society. The *Land Regulations* contains prescriptions for the sequential establishment of rural governing units. "In establishing an army (*chün*, the administration unit) first appoint an army commander (*chün-shuai*) for each 13,156 households. Next, appoint the five regimental commanders (*shih-shuai*) under him; next, appoint the five battalion commanders (*lü-shuai*) under each of those; next, . . . ," and so on.[2] The

2. *T'ien-ch'ao t'ien-mou chih-tu*, Hsiang Ta, *T'ai-p'ing t'ien-kuo*, I, 325. On the discrepancy between this figure and the 12,500 figure in Figure 11, see Li Ch'un, 287–288.

trouble with this plan is that it assumes the prior existence of accurate and complete population registers, presumably inherited from the old regime, which in many cases were not in fact available. The very process of registering the peasantry required the appointment of officers. Thus in those districts where the Taipings managed to form some semblance of local government, local officers (*hsiang-kuan*) were invariably instituted from the top down, in a very vague relationship to the size of the population to be governed (whereas adherence to the strict numerical pattern would require appointment from the bottom up). This method of appointment was necessitated by the pressing need to establish some kind of control over such districts and particularly to tax them for the immediate requirements of the Heavenly Court.[3] Under the chaotic conditions of the mid-nineteenth century, there was little chance that such an elaborate administrative system as that envisaged by the Taiping *Land Regulations* could ever be realized in practice or that the movement could establish the kind of tight discipline over the peasantry that such a system might make possible.

Taiping control over rural areas was further vitiated by the shortage of able cadres within the movement itself. The Taiping bureaucracy was in practice just as superficial as the old Ch'ing system. Local government was based on a fundamental division between the prefectural and district officials (*shou-t'u-kuan*), appointed usually from among old and reliable Taipings (*lao hsiung-ti*); and the lower administrators (*hsiang-kuan*), from the *chün-shuai* downward, who were to be selected from among indigenous people. The striking weakness of this system is apparent when one considers that the *liang-ssu-ma*, the sergeant in charge of 25 families, was supposed in theory to exercise sweeping powers over the community, including the supervision of the people's religious life. Obviously ideological and spiritual discipline of this sort could hardly be enforced by any but the most reliable and well-indoctrinated cadres, personnel that the Taiping apparatus could not provide in adequate numbers. This problem of rapidly extending revolutionary control over large masses of people was one the Communists faced in 1949. Their methods of meeting the problem cannot be discussed here in detail, but it is worth mentioning that they had at

---

3. The most detailed studies of this question are by Kawabata Genji: "Taihei Tengoku ni okeru gōkan setchi no jittai," *Tōhōgaku ronshū* 1:167–179; and "Taihei Tengoku ni okeru gōkan sōchi to sono haikei," *Shigaku zasshi,* 63.6:34–50, both of which appeared in 1954. Both rely largely on material from local gazetteers.

their disposal a large pool of young intellectuals, of whom few needed to be taught to despise the old regime and of whom some had already absorbed a modicum of vulgar Marxism. Many of these people were trained rapidly in special indoctrination centers to fill the suddenly expanded need for local activists. A century earlier, such human resources were unavailable.[4]

The "selection" (*chü*) of local people to fill jobs in the Taiping administrative hierarchy was certainly no different from the selection (*chü*) of local headmen in the t'uan-lien system: these posts were either filled or controlled by the indigenous community power structure. Though "selected" by the community, they were in no way democratically chosen but rather fit the old pattern in which the strong governed the weak in the Chinese countryside with only occasional interference by regular officialdom.[5] One study of local appointments in the T'ai lake region of Kiangsu and Chekiang reveals that *hsiang-kuan* were drawn from a wide range of local types, including lower gentry, former yamen clerks, constables (*ti-pao*), heads of rich households, and local strongmen (*t'u-hao*). These functionaries were not firmly under the control of regular Taiping civil administrators, because they owed their appointments and their powers to nearby military commanders. More important, they were almost invariably holdovers from the old regime.[6]

Nor is it surprising to discover that in many cases the administrative areas governed by Taiping rural functionaries were the preexisting local divisions inherited from the old order, particularly the units of the *li-chia* tax registration system. In the T'ai-hu area the colonel (*shih-shuai*) governed an area that was identical with the standard *tu;* under him, the next rank of official seems to have been in charge of a single *t'u;* the old *hsiang* division, where it existed, was often put under a *chün-shuai*. The all-important post of *liang-ssu-ma* seems generally not to have been filled at all. In instances where such lower-level officials existed, they seem to have functioned merely as tax-collection aides, and there is no evidence that they controlled the prescribed number of households.[7] We are immediately reminded of the fact that the t'uan-lien system of the orthodox elite also found the *li-chia* ap-

---

4. In the later years of the Taipings, the personnel problem grew so acute that in some cases even the district magistrates were chosen from among local people. For examples see Li Ch'un, *Ch'u-t'an*, 292–293.

5. See for instance, Hsiang-hsiang 1874, 5:17; Hua-jung 1882, 6:9b.

6. Kawabata in *Tōhōgaku ronshū*, 177–178.

7. Kawabata in *Tōhōgaku ronshū*, 171–176.

paratus a convenient organizational format, and there is ample reason to suppose that the reasons in the two cases were the same: to facilitate grain requisitions from the peasantry. A local taxing apparatus that could serve the Ch'ing government could be turned to the purposes of local power holders in either camp. With the character of Taiping local administration so generally determined by the function of grain requisition, the *chün*, or army, the top unit of the local administrative hierarchy, served principally as a unit for assessment and collection of taxes.[8] There is no evidence that it served as an administration unit for military conscription, nor that it exercised the kind of pervasive control over local society envisaged by the early Taiping leadership.

A general survey reveals a wide variation between districts in which Taiping local government was relatively effective and districts in which it was exceedingly superficial. Areas conquered in the Taiping western expedition of 1853–54, particularly those near Anking in Anhwei province, remained under Taiping control for many years and exhibited a fairly complete range of administrative functions, including the holding of civil service examinations. Other areas, such as those upriver in Hupeh, seem to have remained under only tenuous control. But even in the most successfully governed districts, Taiping administration suffered from grievous defects. The pattern of taxation, for instance, seems to have given rise to the same type of local conflict as existed under the old regime: excessive and irregular levies, including armed expropriation, incited armed resistance among the people. The result was little different from the tax resistance (*k'ang-liang*) movements that characterized many districts under Ch'ing control and gave rise to the same type of local militarization.[9]

The Taipings' reliance on indigenous leadership to staff their sub-district administration was an entirely understandable development. It fit the old pattern of Chinese rebellion, in which utopian leadership must in the end face up to concrete problems of local administration. The alternative, after all, was beyond Taiping resources: a thorough-going social revolution in the countryside, village by village, in which

8. Kawabata in *Tōhōgaku ronshū*, 171–173.

9. The fascinating account of conditions in Ch'ien-shan, Anhwei, reveals difficulties of local government in a district under prolonged Taiping control. See Ch'u Chih-fu's *Wan-ch'iao chi-shih*, extracts from which are printed in Chien Yu-wen, *T'ung-k'ao*, 397–400. On local resistance in Ch'ien-shan, see Hu Lin-i, *I-chi*, 39:19b–21b.

the old elite would be replaced by a new elite whose interests and loyalties were closely bound into the Taiping system. For such a task, the Taipings had neither the personnel nor the methodology. It is entirely possible, too, that the virulent Han ethnism of the Taipings blinded them, in certain respects, to the social question. At any rate, the establishment of Taiping rule in many districts (especially in the latter years of the movement) was simply a matter of investing existing local leaders with Taiping titles. This meant not only that the status quo was largely undisturbed but that the Taipings faced continued resistance and obstruction from among their new allies. In various districts in the lower Yangtze area, for instance, t'uan-lien leaders accommodated themselves to the Taiping occupation of the administrative cities but continued at the same time to husband their own power and preserve their ties to the old order. Near Soochow a strongman named Hsu P'ei-yuan (evidently a commoner of the *t'u-hao* type) had for years dominated his area by virtue of his wealth and his leadership of a multiplex t'uan-lien association. With this considerable figure (and with others nearby) the Taipings had to come to terms. An agreement was worked out whereby Hsu was given a Taiping rank and left in charge of his old multiplex association. A Taiping chief in the city of Soochow, himself a former Ch'ing official, gave him complete charge of household registration and grain collection and conceded that nobody in his area would be compelled to grow hair in the Taiping fashion. Hsu secretly maintained contact with Ch'ing officialdom and with the gentry refugee community in Shanghai, from which he solicited "expenses" for his clandestine anti-Taiping activities.[10]

These opportunistic policies of the Taipings in the administration of the lower Yangtze area must be seen alongside parallel Taiping efforts to normalize the peasant economy by encouraging the return of refugees, including landlords, and leaving undisturbed the indigenous social structure.[11]

In many areas nominally conquered by the Taipings, however, the situation was more desperate. Often there was neither a rigorous application of Taiping administrative codes nor an effective accommodation with existing elites but rather a state of continuous guerilla

10. Hua I-lun, *Hsi-Chin t'uan-lien shih-mo chi* in *T'ai-p'ing t'ien-kuo tzu-liao*, (Peking, 1959), 121–131. Li Ch'un, *Ch'u-t'an*, 298–301.

11. For a general treatment of this subject see Ihara Hirosuke, "Taihei tengoku no gōson tōji," *Shigaku kenkyū* 86:42–56 (September 1962).

warfare in which Taiping control scarcely spread beyond the walls of the administrative city.[12] In many such districts the Taipings had succeeded in ousting the Ch'ing administrators from the walled city but not in destroying the local t'uan-lien groups of the rural elite, which continued to contest the countryside under official patronage. The following examples are but two of the many instances in which the Taipings remained, in effect, besieged in the cities, while the orthodox elite controlled the countryside.

Local Militarization in Huang-kang. During their sweep through Hupeh on their way downriver in early 1853, the Taipings evidently made no concerted attempt to institute local government in captured districts. Gathering hordes of recruits and vast stores of wealth from Wuchang and nearby river towns such as Huang-chou, they abandoned the fallen cities and pressed on toward Nanking. But later in the year they mounted a major westward expedition, forged up the Yangtze again, and turned their attention to holding and governing the strategic towns that dominated the supply route to the Heavenly Capital.

The district of Huang-kang, whose seat was in the walled prefectural city of Huang-chou, lies on the Yangtze about 20 miles east of Wuchang. In this district, to all appearances under firm Taiping occupation, the establishment of local government was a slow and difficult undertaking. Shortly after taking the prefectural city in late 1853, the conquerors appointed their own prefect and magistrate and set about expanding their area of control. In the major sub-district administrative centers (*chen*) such as T'uan-feng, Yang-lo and Ts'ang-fu (which were also key economic centers) the Taipings stationed local officials and ordered that tax registers be compiled. Exactly how far down the scale such officials were appointed is open to question. In T'uan-feng, for example, was appointed a *chün-shuai*. The area surrounding this town was named a *hsiang*, for purposes of local administration. No such *hsiang* had existed under the old system, and we may suppose that it represented the natural market area of T'uan-feng. One organizational chart suggests that within this *hsiang* were established local officers down to the level of *liang-ssu-ma*.[13] This is doubtful,

---

12. The phrase "guerilla warfare" is used by Kawabata in *Shigaku zasshi*, p. 39; one may discount the technical accuracy of the term, yet it seems appropriate to draw the analogy with rural warfare of the present era.

13. Chang Te-chien, ed., *Tsei-ch'ing hui-tsuan* (originally compiled in 1854–55),

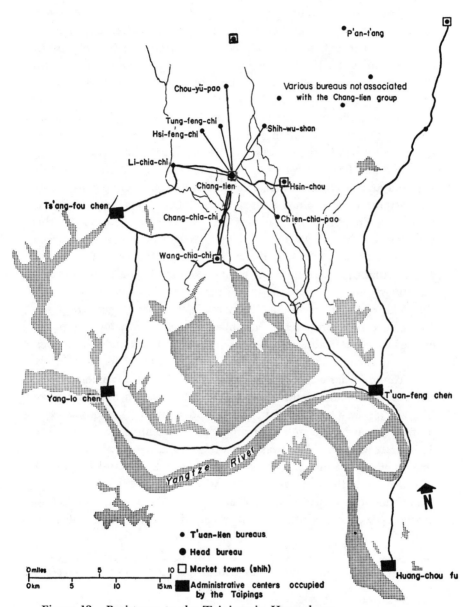

Figure 12.   Resistance to the Taipings in Huang-kang.

however, because during the early months of 1854 the Taipings were still demanding "tribute offerings" (chin-kung), a form of crude extortion that clearly implies the absence of regular tax registers.[14]

The effort to extend civil rule downward from the big sub-district centers had a predictably disruptive effect upon local society and gave rise to the first organized resistance. An incident of February–March 1854 set the pattern for a long series of clashes between the Taipings and the Huang-kang lineages. During a foray into the countryside, evidently to obtain grain, a band of Taipings sacked the market town of Chang-tien and killed some of its inhabitants. Possibly the town had been slow in responding to Taiping orders to compile registers and establish responsible officers. As an example to future recalcitrants the Taipings hung a severed head in a nearby village, which was inhabited by the Hsu and Pa lineages. Furious at this brutal intimidation, the Hsu and Pa seized farm tools and attacked the Taipings, killing 23 of them and routing the rest. The record suggests that this was a spontaneous mob action. As late as the previous year there had been virtually no militia organization in Huang-kang. But once a commitment had been made, military organization followed. In concert with gentry at Ch'ien-chia-pao (probably a standard market town), the elite of Chang-tien formed an extended-multiplex t'uan-lien association that soon linked up t'uan-lien bureaus in six more communities and mustered more than 10,000 militiamen. Of the bureaus that made up this confederation, one was in a market town (shih) of at least intermediate status, and a number of others were probably in at least standard or minor market centers (see Figure 12). This confederation, which was called the Liu-ho banner,[15] was able to amass sufficient resources to keep its militia at a high state of readiness and to provide the men with rations while in service.

The character of the elite leadership of the Chang-tien organization is worth discussing briefly, for it exemplifies the considerable role

---

reprinted in Hsiang Ta, T'ai-p'ing T'ien-kuo, III, 25–347. For Taiping administration in Huang-kang, see p. 94 of this edition. Also see Kawabata in Tōhōgaku ronshū, 173.

14. Huang-kang 1882, 24:26b.

15. Huang-kang 1882, 24:26b–28. Liu-ho means "Heaven, Earth, and the Four Directions." The banner was apparently a customary term for multiplex units in use north of the Yangtze; it was a common Nien designation, for instance, and can thus be regarded as a regionalism common to both heterodox and orthodox organizations. On the Nien banners see Chiang Siang-tse, The Nien Rebellion, 23–28.

Figure 13. Officially recognized t'uan-heads in the Chang-tien militia association, 1854.

T'uan head	Number
Civil *chü-jen*	2
Military *chü-jen*	1
Civil *sheng-yuan*	9
Military *sheng-yuan*	4
Chien-sheng	7
Purchased titles	7
Wen-t'ung	1
Commoners	9

Source: Huang-kang 1882, 24:28.

played by men who held no formal gentry status (see Figure 13). An officially recognized list of *t'uan-chang* (*t'uan*-heads) dating from 1854 contains only three members of the upper gentry. Of the holders of purchased titles or *chien-sheng* degrees, many might already have been *sheng-yuan*. But nearly a quarter of those listed had neither regular nor purchased status; these must be assumed to have been either merchants, or landowners of the *t'u-hao* (local strongman) variety, whose wealth and influence made them key allies of the Ch'ing establishment and whose community importance made them functionally indistinguishable from gentry as far as local militarization was concerned. Awarding such men the title *t'uan-chang,* on the same basis as regular gentry, had an important role in securing their loyalty and making collaboration with the invaders less attractive to them.

The experience of the communities in the Chang-tien area was shared by a number of other places in the district as the Taipings sought to extend their control into the countryside. The magistrate of Huang-kang, Weng Ju-ying (1807–1855), who had fled his yamen, was himself busy organizing resistance in the northeast region of the district. Rather than incur official disgrace, he had stayed within his jurisdiction and had set up something of a yamen-in-exile in the countryside, where he remained as a guest of the lineages of P'an-t'ang, a town some fifteen miles northeast of Chang-tien. This situation was not uncommon in areas affected by rebellion.[16] The relationship between the magistrate and the local militia organizations can be seen as a symbiosis, in which the *t'uan* bureaus received the stamp of

16. For other examples see Kuei-hsien 1894, 6:22; Lin-hsiang 1872, 8:8b; Hu Lin-i, *I-chi,* 39:19b.

legitimacy by the patronage of officialdom; the magistrate received, besides refuge, at least the semblance of authority. Weng's presence was therefore valuable and much in demand. By July 1854 it was apparent that the Chang-tien banner association was becoming the most powerful center of orthodox resistance in the district. Through the intermediacy of a *chü-jen* in the leadership group, Weng was persuaded to leave P'an-t'ang and establish his headquarters within the Chang-tien area. The force of P'an-t'ang militiamen he brought with him were shortly sent back home, and Weng remained "to deploy forces and issue edicts." In this way the Chang-tien confederation gained paramount influence over the magistrate and obtained his official blessings. His presence in the Huang-kang countryside thus enabled elements who opposed the Taipings to militarize with all the trappings of official approval. Multiplex associations that were organized, financed, and commanded by the local elite became, by virtue of Weng's presence, official *t'uan*. The title *t'uan-chang* was awarded to numerous local leaders after Weng became a functioning part of the system, and many of these men were recommended for brevet official ranks after the recapture of the walled city in October 1854.

The pattern of confrontation between the Taipings and local interests can be seen (Figure 12) as a rather thin beach-head of rebel control, based on the big communications centers, facing a well-organized resistance in the hinterland. Balked in their attempt to administer the countryside, the Taipings unleashed terror on the villages. A punitive expedition led by the Taiping General Wei Cheng in the early autumn of 1854 burned down more than 600 dwellings but accomplished little more. A large body of *yung* from the Chang-tien confederation stood and gave battle, and the invaders were forced to withdraw. Despite their internal rivalries, orthodox rural interests preserved a surprisingly tough core of social and military control that the Taipings proved unable to penetrate.[17]

The Siege of Yuan-chou. The prefectural city of Yuan-chou (the present I-ch'un) in Kiangsi dominates the road that runs westward from Nanchang, through the strategic Wukung and Yun-hsia mountains, to Changsha and the river towns of eastern Hunan. Yuan-chou had weathered the first onslaught of the Taipings. In 1853 gentry founded a bureau within the walls, raised several tens of thousands

17. Huang-kang 1882, 24:26b–27.

of taels, and hired 500 *yung* for defense. The city's defenses were evidently sufficient to ward off Taiping remnants fleeing from the battle of Hsiang-t'an in late April 1854. Early in 1855 the Yuan-chou gentry weathered a graver threat: a local rebellion, assisted by elements of the city population. The hired *yung* force countered with a cruel slaughter inside the city, and outside, t'uan-lien militia of a certain Liu lineage killed and captured many.[18]

Retribution came in early 1856, when the Taipings attacked in force. Late in the preceding year, Shih Ta-k'ai and Wei Chün had launched a two-pronged thrust at Hunan, hoping thereby to subdue Tseng Kuo-fan's home base. Wei's army was checked at Lin-hsiang, and Shih, rather than advance on Hunan alone, turned his forces toward Kiangsi. By February of 1856 eight key prefectural cities had fallen to him, and two thirds of Kiangsi was under his sway. Now his forces were swelled by several tens of thousands of Kwangtung Triads who had fled from the wreckage of the Red Turban Revolt to join forces with the Taipings.[19] The attack on Yuan-chou came on January 8; panic had swept ahead of Shih's army, and by the time the Taipings arrived the *yung*, along with the city's civil and military officials, had fled.

Once in possession of the walled city the Taipings immediately undertook to reestablish civil government. The first step was to substitute officials of their own, at prefectural and district levels, for the departed officials of the Ch'ing. Despite the radical Taiping prescriptions for reorganizing local society, there was no attempt to alter the existing bureaucratic divisions of district and prefecture, levels of administration so ingrained in Chinese bureaucracy that they were able to survive even a social and administrative program as iconoclastic as that of the Taipings. Both the Taiping prefect (*tsung-chih*) and magistrate of the concentric district of I-ch'un (*chien-chün*), however, were supervised by Li Neng-t'ung, an official specially deputed by the Heavenly Court with the high rank of guard-in-waiting (*shih-wei*).

More problematic was the Taiping campaign to establish local administration in the countryside, which was undertaken in earnest during the early spring of 1856. At first there were edicts posted "insulting the rural gentry and coercing the people" as the loyalist chronicler put it—a widespread propaganda effort proclaiming the

18. This account is based primarily on I-ch'un 1870, 5:22–31, and Yüan-chou 1874, 5:21–27.

19. Chien Yu-wen, *Ch'üan-shih*, 1342. On the Red Turban Revolt see Wakeman, *Strangers at the Gate*, 139–156.

new order. All the rural *hsiang* were ordered to compile household registers and collect taxes. At the same time, the Taipings recognized the precarious character of their control and set about strengthening the city's defenses. Using forced labor they built towers, blockhouses, and stone ramparts and dug a deep moat around the walls. Just outside the city gate was stationed a battalion of tough Kwangtung Triads. At the same time as they were reaching outward to control the hinterland, the Taipings were drawing inward and establishing an essentially defensive position within the city.

By May 1856 the Taiping hegemony of the district was already being challenged, albeit not very impressively: a force of some 100 freebooting "soldiers and *yung*," of origins unknown, entered the district calling itself an "official army." It established control over a group of villages, drafting manpower and extorting "contributions." The Taipings quickly sent an expeditionary force from the city. The "official army" fled, abandoning its local draftees, many of whom were killed. A much more serious challenge appeared almost immediately, however, in the form of a large force of Hunan *yung* under Liu Ch'ang-yu, Chiang Chung-yuan's old associate and now one of Tseng Kuo-fan's generals, which encamped in the district and forced the Taipings to draw within the walled city.

With Liu's force as a screen, the rural elite immediately began to mobilize their resources. During August and September gentry set up 30 t'uan-lien bureaus, each of which mobilized a thousand or more part-time militiamen from local lineages. Liu Ch'ang-yu called upon these bureaus to raise funds for the support of his own troops, and some 100,000 taels were garnered during the autumn months. The speed and size of this gentry effort suggest plainly that the structure of rural society, and particularly the influence and resources of the important lineages, had barely been penetrated by the city-based Taipings. The arrival of Liu's Hunan Army battalions was enough to set off a vigorous local control effort by the indigenous elite.

Now the Taipings within the walls were in real danger. After a relief column failed to reach the city, Li Neng-t'ung, the highest-ranking Taiping official at Yuan-chou, sent word that he was prepared to defect. In mid-December 1856 he slipped out of the city, and Liu Ch'ang-yu launched a full-scale attack on the west gate. By prearrangement, 1,000 of Li's men laid down their arms; the Kwangtung Triads fled, and the city was soon taken with great slaughter among the civilian residents. Liu now clamped his own control over the district's t'uan-lien apparatus, milking the local bureaus for funds and recruits during the next few years.[20]

Though the strategic pattern suggested by the above instances was by no means universal, it was a very common one. As the rebellion was fought out in scores of rural districts, the Taipings all too frequently found themselves, in effect, besieged within city walls, surrounded by a violent and unstable hinterland, in which the old order was still powerful.[21] These local patterns lent a general pattern to the Taiping Rebellion, a pattern suggested obliquely by the nineteenth-century historian who wrote that "the White Lotus pillaged the countryside but did not attack cities . . . whereas the Taipings attacked cities but did not pillage the countryside."[22] This generalization, though too sweeping, embodies a central strategic truth: that the Taiping Rebellion revolved around a contest for the possession of walled cities and for the control of communications routes between them. The importance of the walled city stemmed partly, of course, from the existing state of military technology. We may speculate further, however, that the importance of city walls to the Taipings stemmed also from the movement's political pretensions and psychological foundations. A dynasty with a claim to universal dominion, the Taiping Kingdom required the physical appurtenances of legitimacy. The empire could hardly be ruled from a village hut. The immediate targets of the Taipings were therefore the yamens, garrisons, and temples of the Ch'ing establishment, all of which they sought to replace with counterparts of their own. Thus the great walled cities were natural targets. But the city wall was more than a symbol of legitimate government. It was a symbol also of the alienation of the Taipings from their social environment. The rebels were outsiders from the first. Their violent pilgrimage began with their expulsion from their homes and ended with their establishment of new homes in strange territories. The Hakka leadership of this wandering tribe, accustomed to linguistic

20. See the supplement on t'uan-lien in I-ch'un 1870, 5:28b–31.

21. Many examples could be adduced. For instance, in Fen-i district, Kiangsi (near Yuan-chou), the rural gentry, along with their wealth and their t'uan-lien associations, weathered the Taiping occupation of the city; immediately upon recapture of the district, bureaus were set up for supplying funds to the Hunan army. Fen-i 1871, 5:12b–16; in T'ai-ho, Kiangsi, brisk resistance in the countryside continued during rebel occupation of the walled city. T'ai-ho 1878, 9:19; in Chu-chi, Chekiang, a lineage militia led by a local soothsayer, Pao Li-shen, set up an effective center of resistance, so that the Taipings "dared not send a company out of the city." Chu-chi 1909, 15:17b–19.

22. Hunan 1885, 79:55.

distinctness and social separateness, found the walled city an enclave within which this distinctness and separateness, now reinforced by religion, could be promoted and protected. The defensive mentality of the Taipings, so closely allied to their aggressiveness and messianism, was not generally understood by contemporary observers.

The difficulty the Taipings experienced in bridging the gap between city and countryside was due also to the objective conditions that confronted them, namely, the capacity of the old order for survival and particularly its mechanisms of local militarization. Here the t'uan-lien system and the military hierarchy into which it was integrated played a key role. It is certainly not true to say that the Taipings were always unsuccessful in securing at least the limited collaboration of local gentry. Some, as we have seen, served the Taipings as local administrators (hsiang-kuan); others, in long occupied areas, attended Taiping civil-service examinations; still others were so deeply implicated in collaboration that they had to buy off Ch'ing officials when their districts were retaken.[23] Nevertheless, the t'uan-lien system seems generally to have served as an effective alternative to collaboration. It was able to do so for two main reasons.

First, it was a mechanism for drawing local leadership into the Ch'ing system through the award of official ranks and titles, and through the increase of local school quotas (hsueh-o)—the gateway to lower gentry status—in districts noted for their loyalty. Such rewards proved an important channel of social mobility on the local level. They might consist of brevet ranks on the lower orders of the scale, or (less frequently) of actual official appointments. Taking a single, well-defined instance, a total of 54 individuals in P'ing-chiang were rewarded for local defense during the rebellion of Chung Jen-chieh; most were already either holders of brevet rank or office, or regular degree holders, and were rewarded by additional rank (see Figure 14). Those not granted rank were given official placards which cited them for "righteous defense of the community."[24] There is no doubt that rewards of this sort for military merit (chün-kung), ever more lavishly distributed as the rebellion wore on, meant significant advances in status for many thousands of people in affected districts. For men on the bottom

23. Civil service examinations were held—and well attended—in the Anking area. See Ch'u Chih-fu, Wan-ch'iao chi-shih in Chien Yu-wen, T'ung-kao, 398. On gentry collaboration also see the case of Hsing-kuo department in Hu Lin-i, I-chi, 84:2a-b.

24. P'ing-chiang 1875, 37:6. For a summary of the official rank system, see Hsieh Pao-chao, The Government of China, 1644–1911 (Baltimore, 1925), 125.

Figure 14. Rewards of rank for defenders of P'ing-chiang, 1842.

Original status	Number of persons	Reward
Chü-jen[a]	3	Raise 1 grade
Sub-director of schools	1	Raise 1 grade
First class assistant department magistrate	1	Raise 1 grade
Military *chü-jen*[a]	2	Raise 1 grade
Ling-sheng	1	Sixth brevet rank
Commoner	1	Sixth brevet rank
Ling-sheng	1	Ninth brevet rank
Sheng-yuan	2	Ninth brevet rank
Military *sheng-yuan*	4	Ninth brevet rank
Chien-sheng	4	Ninth brevet rank
T'ung-sheng	3	Ninth brevet rank
Unknown	1	Raise 1 grade
First class assistant department magistrate	2	Raise 2 merits
Lower ninth rank	1	Eighth brevet rank
T'ung-sheng	2	Eighth brevet rank

Source: P'ing-chiang 1875, 37:6.

[a] Presumably already held substantive or brevet rank, though listed by academic degree.

fringes of the elite, such status might mean early entry into officialdom; a *sheng-yuan* of Nanchang, for instance, who was cited for effective management of a t'uan-lien bureau, was granted the title of sub-director of studies (*hsün-tao*) with priority for immediate appointment to a substantive post. For commoners, rewards of brevet rank and military decorations meant considerable distinction in local society.[25]

Even more important was the fact that, by the early T'ung-chih period, the t'uan-lien system had become an adjunct to the system of rank purchase. Funds contributed to local defense associations counted alongside actual military merit in the award of brevet ranks and the expansion of school quotas. Rewards for such contributions appear to have fallen within the categories of recommendation (*pao-chü*) and evaluation (*i-hsu*), the system whereby a man might be promoted in rank for special merit, and cannot be considered rank-sale in the strict sense. Nevertheless, the effect was much the same. It appears that in

25. Nanchang 1870, 28:7b; Hu Lin-i, *I-chi*, 13:4b–5.

some areas rewards to *t'uan-lien* contributors far overshadowed those dispensed through the regular rank-sale (*ch'ou-hsiang*) offices. In Fen-i, Kiangsi, for example, gentry petitioned the magistrate to have local t'uan-lien contributions (some of which seem to have been made during the period of Taiping occupation) counted toward rank awards. This request was passed up to Tseng Kuo-fan, who obtained the court's approval. The records of rank-purchase and t'uan-lien contributions were kept in separate registers (see Figure 15).[26] Thus t'uan-lien be-

Figure 15. Rewards for t'uan-lien and rank-purchase contributions, Fen-i district.

Category	Amount	Rewards
T'uan-lien contributions (up to 1865)	62,160[a]	271 rank certificates + Permanent school quotas raised 7 slots each, civil and military (9 percent increase)
Rank-purchase (*ch'ou-hsiang*) (1856–1863)	45,218[a]	129 rank certificates

Source: Fen-i 1871, 5:14b-16b.

[a] Figure for t'uan-lien in ounces of silver; figure for rank-purchase in strings of 1,000 copper cash. Exchange rates varied widely with time and place, but an official proclamation of 1853 equated one ounce (tael) of silver to 2,000 copper cash. Lien-sheng Yang, *Money and Credit in China: A Short History* (Cambridge, Mass., 1952), 68.

came a mechanism whereby purely local militarization could be rewarded, in very concrete form, by the state.

A second aspect of the t'uan-lien system made it particularly effective as a bond between local elite and officialdom: its theoretical status as an element of the state system. Here let us recall the development

26. On the rank-sale system, see Hsu Ta-ling, *Ch'ing-tai chüan-na chih-tu* (Peking, 1950). Though the figures for Fen-i, as shown in Figure 15, are not precisely comparable, they serve to suggest the relative importance, to the district elite, of the rank-sale and t'uan-lien categories in local social mobility. Some administrative awkwardness was caused by the fact that multiplex t'uan-lien associations led by Fen-i gentry often comprised some settlements outside the district borders, and roughly one eighth of the amounts reported came from such extra-district sources. In the end, however, rewards were distributed in accord with the standard district boundaries. For another illustration of the distribution of rank and degree certificates in return for purely local fund raising, see Hsiang-hsiang 1874, 5:24b, particularly the case of the Hsieh lineage of Po-shih.

of t'uan-lien during the White Lotus period, and farther back, the larger subject of government-sponsored militia discussed in Chapter I. The officials of the Chia-ch'ing period had drawn upon a tradition of government militia institutions, along with elements of utopian social theory, to construct a model of local militarization that was compatible with the requirements of the bureaucratic state. Within this model local militarization could be absorbed into the official system and legitimized before it became a threat to the state's military monopoly. The local elite, which played such a central role in militarization, could be linked to the official system by considering *t'uan-chang* and *t'uan-tsung* to be a species of state functionaries.

Much of the effectiveness of such a system depended on purely verbal legitimation, and legitimation was the next best thing to actual control. Much of the militarization of the Taiping years and afterwards did not fit the official model at all. Bureaucratic control was often weak or purely nominal, as powerful members of the upper gentry, such as Liu Yü-hsun, assumed de facto command of their native districts. The low level of militarization prescribed by the official model was frequently exceeded, as local resources were mobilized to support professional fighting units. Nevertheless, continual reference to t'uan-lien and the use of t'uan-lien titles and terminology capitalized on the natural reluctance of local leaders to pose the issue of ultimate authority.

Indeed, the years of the rebellion saw a considerable stretching of the meaning of t'uan-lien. The 1885 edition of the Hunan local history points out that fighting alongside government troops were many irregular units that "gave rations to their troops, established a battalion system, . . . received public monies before local contributions were exhausted, and still used gentry as commanders. This is what is called 'recruiting *yung*' and should not be included under the heading 't'uan-lien'." But some of the units this writer allows to remain in the category t'uan-lien (including the Hsiang-yung and the Ch'u-yung) ought, by his own criteria, to be excluded. Another local history compounds the confusion by reporting that "t'uan-lien was of two types," the first of which included forces like the Hsiang-yung and Ch'u-yung, and the second, nonprofessional village-based militia.[27]

This uncertainty about what the category t'uan-lien included was a sign of the times. After 1850 many irregular units that, by virtue of their professionalism and mobility, belong on the second level of

27. Hunan 1885, 79:56; P'ing-chiang 1875, 36:6b.

militarization, were in fact referred to as t'uan-lien and were recruited and financed by local associations that called themselves t'uan-lien bureaus. Their gentry commanders commonly bore standard t'uan-lien titles. Yet their men were full-time fighters and their spheres of operation went well beyond the confines of the multiplex or extended multiplex associations that sponsored them. Save for the name, there is little to link such *yung* forces to the official version of t'uan-lien as a village-based defense and control system. Liu Yü-hsun's "Five-bureaus *yung*" in Nanchang was a force of this type. Another example is that of Ta Hsi, a rich pawnshop operator in Kiangsu, who hired a band of fighters to protect his businesses and later, under the patronage of the Ch'ing commander, Hsiang Jung, became a considerable military figure with the title *t'uan-tsung*.[28] When Tseng Kuo-fan first proposed recruiting fighters at Changsha, he referred to his headquarters as a "large *t'uan*."[29] A military organization of this sort clearly bore little relation to a multiplex local defense association. As a final example of the broadening meaning of t'uan-lien in this period, official documents of 1850 state that the rebel Li Yuan-fa was caught by *hsiang-yung* or *shen-yung* (gentry braves), but the *P'ing Kuei chi-lueh*, a history published in the early Kuang-hsu reign, reports that he was captured by "t'uan-lien." Both sources appear to refer to the *yung* units founded by Chiang Chung-yuan and the lineages allied to him.[30]

The reason t'uan-lien terminology was often applied to professional, mobile forces was not that the official meaning had been forgotten. On the contrary, it was precisely the established theoretical status of t'uan-lien as a state institution that made its verbal trappings attractive. Using t'uan-lien terms and titles was a way for *yung* units to regularize their relations with the bureaucracy. The borrowed terminology enabled them to operate within the limits of the Ch'ing order and made the breach of the state's military monopoly symbolically innocuous. It should be noted that it was this calculated terminological inexactitude that gave rise to the idea (still current) that t'uan-lien or *t'uan* meant a kind of military unit. This meaning was only valid for level-two military forces, and only after about 1850. In its historical origins t'uan-lien was clearly a local control apparatus as much as a militia system; and, as applied to level-one village units, *t'uan* meant the association that sponsored the militia, and not the militia itself.

28. Chü-jung 1904, 9:3b–4b and 19B:3a-b.
29. Tseng, *Tsou-kao*, 1:47.
30. *Ch'ing shih-lu*, Hsien-feng, 3:14b, 9:16b–17; *P'ing-Kuei chi-lueh*, 1:2.

Even within the orthodox camp, t'uan-lien as a form of local militarization was by no means universally admired, and there is ample
evidence that it contributed in many ways to chaos and exploitation,
particularly as formal bureaucratic restraints upon it grew weaker. By
the 1860's Tseng Kuo-fan and other officials were actually prepared to suggest that it be entirely proscribed.[31] Tseng, it will be
recalled, already had substantial doubts about lower-level gentry
militarization; and (as we have seen in the case of Liu Yü-hsun) the
consolidation of provincial power in the 1860's brought provincial
bureaucracies into conflict with semi-autonomous t'uan-lien systems.
Chu Sun-i, original promoter of the Hsiang-yung and a fervent advocate of t'uan-lien, gave a scathing indictment of t'uan-lien in Kwangsi
in 1858. Not only was it a way for local notables to make big profits
by extorting funds from their communities, it was also a weapon with
which to intimidate and control local officials.[32] And as we have seen,
the line dividing t'uan-lien from local heterodox groups was often a
thin one.

Some modern writers have seen t'uan-lien as primarily an instrument
of class power in the hands of the propertied elite.[33] Evidence such as
Chu Sun-i's apparently first-hand account leaves no doubt that it did in
fact often serve the class interests and augment the wealth of its sponsors. Quite apart from outlawry and extortion, the official record
abounds in examples of its being used to deal with "bandits" who were
unmistakably the poor and dispossessed of the local community rising
in desperation against grain hoarders or usurers.[34] But evidence of this
sort has to be balanced against cases in which it was primarily a means
of defense against intruders from other areas, in which community and
lineage interests were compelling enough to offset intracommunity
struggles.

To avoid interpretations that do violence to a complex record,
t'uan-lien should be seen as a many-faceted institution that reflected

31. Tseng, *Nien-p'u*, 6:24; *Hu-nan wen-cheng, kuo-ch'ao wen*, 31:31b.
32. Chu Sun-i, "T'uan-lien shuo," *Huang-ch'ao ching-shih-wen hsu-pien* (Sheng
K'ang ed.), 81:13.
33. See, for instance. Imahori Seiji's argument that t'uan-lien became an instrument of class struggle in certain Pearl River delta communities and thus
played a role in the fragmentation or "modernization" of feudal social relations.
"Shin-tai ni okeru nōson kikō no kindaika ni tsuite," *Rekishigaku kenkū*, 191:3–17;
192:14–29 (1956); and Sasaki Masaya's convincing rebuttal: "Juntoku-ken kyōshin
to tōkai jūrokusa," *Kindai Chūgoku kenkyū*, no. 3:206 (1959).
34. Hsiang-hsiang 1874, 5:9.

the many-faceted social identity of its chief practitioner, the local gentryman. The characteristic flavor of gentry life resulted from the combination of roles in which the gentryman found himself. A degree holder, by virtue of his formal status, was a pillar of the imperial Confucian order, which embodied his personal career goals and enforced his legal privileges. But he had many roles besides his formal political-academic one. He was closely attached to his village or town, and in diminishing levels of affection, to his district, prefecture, and province. Historic, economic, and kinship associations infused a powerful localism into his self-image. The prosperity and security of his home district, along with less tangible local pride and affection, were the motive forces of his role as local man. On a smaller scale, but with stronger affect, was his role as a member of family and lineage. His lineage role was especially important if he was in a position of particular influence and responsibility within his lineage organization. Finally, the gentryman had a role as possessor, protector, or acquirer of wealth. Though it has often been pointed out that there was no necessary connection between wealth and gentry status, yet it remains true that the special powers, immunities, and connections of the gentry were helpful for getting rich and staying rich, especially on the upper levels of the gentry hierarchy. Thus, the gentryman often found himself the protector of local property relations and the social status quo.

T'uan-lien, with its respectable ideological overtones and political status, carefully constructed by its official sponsors, played an important part in the working-out of the gentryman's manifold social obligations and interests. Under the t'uan-lien rubric the gentry were able to exercise their role as protectors of the community and at the same time see to it that law and order (that is, the safety of the local establishment) were preserved. The integral connection between outer defense and inner control was invariably stressed by t'uan-lien theorists. The protection of property was thereby placed in a context of common concern. Wealth was being employed, not merely to protect itself, but to preserve the community. One's role as property owner was made meaningful and acceptable in terms of one's role as member of lineage and community. For the less socially responsible types, t'uan-lien was just another of the many local opportunities for profit that grew out of the special privileges and responsibilities of gentry status.

Just as class antagonisms were partly covered over by t'uan-lien, so were the dangerous implications of private military activity. It was in the nature of the imperial military monopoly that private, local military ventures could not long exist in a political and ideological limbo. The t'uan-lien system legitimized local military leadership that the bureaucracy did not initiate and could not effectively control. Next to control, legitimation was the next best thing; and t'uan-lien, with its theoretical status as an auxiliary arm of the state, was a medium through which local leaders could identify themselves with the imperial regime.

B. The Breakdown of the Traditional State

The Influence of Militarization on Local Government

Militarization left a strong imprint on Chinese administration in the decades following the suppression of the mid-century rebellions. Various aspects of this have been extensively studied—particularly the influence of the new armies on China's military system and the development of regionalism—and will not be treated here.[35] Little studied, however, is another side of this problem, one with implications for the vast unexplored subject of late nineteenth- and early twentieth-century social history. The local militarization of the Taiping years affected the character of Chinese administration on the district level and shaped the relationship between district administration and the local elite in ways that were to last through the Republican period. It is through the study of local militarization, among other things, that one may approach the problem of what happened to the rural elite during the tumultuous decades surrounding the 1911 Revolution, during which both the formal mechanisms and ideal foundations of the traditional state were destroyed. It is clear that this elite did not simply disappear as a result of the abolition of the examination system and the formal privileges accorded it by the old regime. In what ways it changed its character, and in what ways it sought to adapt itself to its changed environment, must form the central theme of future research into the social history of modern China. It is worth suggesting that one starting point for such research is the condition of the rural

---

35. Among the many monographs on this subject, see Lo Erh-kang, *Hsiang-chün hsin-chih*; also his "Ch'ing-chi ping-wei chiang-yu ti ch'i-yuan," *Chung-kuo she-hui ching-chi shih chi-k'an* 5.2:235–250 (1937); Hatano Yoshihiro, "Hokuyō gum-batsu no seiritsu katei," *Nagoya daigaku bungakubu kenkyū ronshū,* 5:211–262 (1953); Wang Erh-min, *Huai-chün chih* (Taipei, 1967). In English see Ralph Powell, *The Rise of Chinese Military Power, 1895–1912* (Princeton, 1955) and Stanley Spector, *Li Hung-chang and the Huai Army* (Seattle, 1964).

elite in the decades immediately following the Taiping Rebellion, and the role of local militarization in shaping that condition.

The rise of the t'uan-lien system in south and central China during the late 1840's and early 1850's was a response to conditions that survived the rebellion's defeat. Local banditry, peasant unrest, weak and corrupt bureaucracy, were all persisting features of the nineteenth-century rural landscape. Hence the multiplex and extended-multiplex *t'uan* remained important elements of local organization. Most important, however, was a process by which the *t'uan*, with its gentry leadership, was brought into the formal structure of local government. The records of the post-Taiping years contain considerable evidence that the *t'uan* now began to function as an official sub-district administrative organ assuming functions of the pao-chia, and in some cases of the *li-chia*. With respect to *li-chia*, we have already observed how and why the *t'uan* invaded the realm of tax collection in Lin-hsiang and other districts. In some areas this situation seems to have perpetuated itself. A good illustration is the district of Hsin-hua in Hunan, where in 1862 sixteen extended-multiplex *t'uan* became formal components of the hierarchy of tax-collection units. In Hua-yang, Szechwan, the *t'uan* had become solidified by the early Republican period into an omnibus unit with functions embracing tax collection, local police, and militia conscription.[36]

With respect to pao-chia, it was even easier to fit gentry-led t'uan-lien associations into the system. We have already called attention to the bias of the official t'uan-lien model, as reflected in the *Hsiang-shou chi-yao*, for keeping local militarization strictly within existing lines of bureaucratic control. This bias was mirrored in the thinking of many district-level officials, some of whom made valiant efforts to retain effective control over t'uan-lien within their jurisdictions. One way of doing so was to use t'uan-lien as a militarized version of pao-chia, as a means of reviving police registration and control. The common feature of such attempts was the relegation of t'uan-lien to primarily nonmilitary uses and the recruiting of smaller, professional forces to do the serious fighting. This had been the essence of Fang Chi's system in the White Lotus period. An outstanding example in the Taiping years was that of Wen Shao-yuan, magistrate of Liu-ho district, Kiangsu. Wen was advised by the historian Hsü Tzu, who drew up a set of t'uan-lien regulations that were almost certainly based on material in Hsu

36. Hsin-hua 1882, 2:16–22; Hua-yang 1934, 4:1–7.

Nai-chao's *Hsiang-shou chi-yao*. There emerged in Liu-ho a *t'uan-chia* system, in which pao-chia and t'uan-lien had merged, the *t'uan* replacing the *pao* as the upper unit of regimentation. Militia were conscripted on the basis of registration and their function was largely restricted to local control. On a higher level, Wen Shao-yuan commanded an effective force of mercenaries. Though Liu-ho lay on the left bank of the Yangtze directly opposite the Taiping capital, Wen and Hsu managed to keep the Taipings at bay until 1858, in which year the district was overrun and Wen was killed.[37]

The other side of this coin was the need to entrust police responsibilities to those elements in rural society best fitted to carry them out: the gentry managers of the t'uan-lien associations. Consequently the gravitation of pao-chia into the hands of local gentry was a common feature in rural China of the Hsien-feng reign and after. It will be recalled that Hu Lin-i in Kweichow had been a forerunner in the trend toward entrusting the elite with formal powers, a trend he continued to promote during his governorship of Hupeh. The conventional pao-chia system was not even mentioned in t'uan-lien regulations drawn up by him shortly before his death in 1861, and the local supremacy of "gentry managers" (*shen-tung*) was to be the cornerstone of local order.[38] That these gentry managers and their militia retained decisive local power in that area is suggested by an official effort to reinstate the pao-chia system around Wuchang during the 1880's, in which all formal responsibilities were unambiguously placed under the control of the gentry. This system, devised by Wuchang Prefect Li Yu-fen, relied on commoners only for the two lowest levels of pao-chia (the *p'ai* and the *chia*), both of which were to be overseen by "the gentry of the *li* (*li-shen*)," and over them, by a high-ranking gentryman (*tsung-shen*) in each *hsiang*.[39]

It must be understood that the entrusting of formal administrative

37. Material on the Liu-ho defense system is in Liu-ho 1884, chüan 8; Liu-ho 1920, 9:10–14; Chou Ch'ang-sen, *Liu-ho chi-shih;* Hsu Tzu, *Wei-hui-chai wen-chi* (1861), chüan 7. Hsu, appropriately enough, was a specialist in the history of Ming loyalism and claimed that he inspired the defenders of Liu-ho with tales of last-ditch Ming resistance against the Manchus. See the preface to his *Hsiao-t'ien chi-nien fu-k'ao* (completed 1861; reprint, 2 vols., Peking, 1957). Hsu, a Liu-ho *chin-shih*, had served on the Historiographical Board in Peking. See Hummel, *Eminent Chinese*, 324–326.

For another example of t'uan-lien-pao-chia merging, dating as early as the Tao-kuang period, see Ch'en Chin, ed., *Nan-shan pao-chia shu* (1845), 34–35.

38. Lu Tao-ch'ang, *Wei-hsiang yao-lueh* (1885), 2:1–4b.

39. Li Yu-fen, *Wu-chün pao-chia shih-i che-yao* (1887), 3:1–2b.

powers to gentry *t'uan* managers was seen by late Ch'ing officials as a reform measure. It was part and parcel of the attempt to revive effectiveness and integrity at all levels of government, an attempt pressed most vigorously during the "restoration" of the T'ung-chih period (1862–1874) but one that really originated with the great administrators of the "statecraft school" (*ching-shih-p'ai*) of the early nineteenth century. During the years of rebellion, local reform at the district level became a necessity if the loyalty and active assistance of the elite were to be secured. One of the most pressing problems was that bane of late Ch'ing society, corruption. To the rural inhabitants, the refined and decorous corruption of a magistrate was somewhat more remote from their daily lives than the naked extortion of the clerks and yamen runners, who were the nearest and most visible predators. Hence it was often possible to mollify the local elite by stripping from clerks and runners those formal tasks of government through which their rackets operated—particularly tax collection and police powers—and entrusting those tasks to the gentry themselves. Hu Lin-i, for example, commented in 1854 (with reference to t'uan-lien management) that the evils of clerks and runners were deeply ingrained in rural society and could not be erased overnight but that as far as possible the magistrate should "use upright gentry as his ears and eyes, heart and liver," and stop relying on clerks and runners to manage affairs at the local level.[40] It was considerations of this sort that had led Chu Sun-i in Hsiang-hsiang to take tax collection out of the hands of yamen underlings at the insistence of Wang Chen and other gentry. Thus the entrusting of formal powers to the elite was less a devolution of power out of the magistrate's hands than a shifting of power from a relatively uncontrollable and dangerous group (the clerks and runners) to a relatively sympathetic and predictable group (the gentry), or so it could be rationalized.

One of the restoration's leading theorists, Feng Kuei-fen, considered the gentry's takeover of local administration an inevitable answer to the breakdown of local control machinery. This was not a problem of the T'ung-chih period alone, he thought, but dated from early Ch'ing times. The great seventeenth-century scholar Ku Yen-wu had called attention to it and had suggested reviving the rural administrative divisions of Han times. But Feng objected that neither the Han

---

40. Hu Lin-i, *I-chi*, 84:1b. On the ideology and program of the T'ung-chih Restoration, see Mary Wright, *The Last Stand of Chinese Conservatism: The T'ung-Chih Restoration, 1862–1874* (Stanford, 1957).

system nor the prescriptions of the *Rites of Chou* was applicable to the huge population of Ch'ing times (he calculated that the latter system, if applied, would require more than 25,000 functionaries in an average district). But clearly the Ch'ing system was unworkable, for pao-chia had proved a wholly ineffective answer to local chaos. Pao-chia functionaries were too lowly either to exercise influence or to impose sanctions. Since the rise of rebellion, however, there had grown up the t'uan-lien system, from which had emerged the gentry managers of the multiplex and extended-multiplex associations (*t'u-tung* and *tsung-tung*—Feng was evidently describing the system in his own district of Wu-hsien, where t'uan-lien associations had been based on the units of the *li-chia* system). The old pao-chia headmen had been helpless because they possessed neither official status nor influence. But the gentry managers, though not officials, were "near to officialdom" and were therefore successful in ruling the countryside.[41] Feng's analysis suggests that the new role of the gentry in local administration was an answer, not only to the problems of the late nineteenth century but to a persisting problem of the late imperial age: the inadequacy of the traditional bureaucratic system to govern a rural population that was growing alarmingly in density and a social system increasingly unbalanced by economic competition.

Gentry Power and "Local Self-government"

It appears, then, that growing out of the turmoil of civil war was enhanced power for the local elite, often exercised within the formal apparatus of sub-district government. The importance of this development cannot be overemphasized, for the power of the elite in the old system had been exercised primarily through informal channels. Informal power had indeed been the elite's own preference, because petty local administrative tasks were hardly consistent with the dignity of gentry status. But now the gentry often found it necessary to oversee local administration in its own interest, a role to which they had become habituated by the growing importance of local defense associa-

41. Feng was not satisfied with the gentry manager system, however, and proposed substituting a new system in which commoner-managers, elected by the populace and appointed by the magistrate, would be given quasi-official status (they would be entertained as if gentry, and the magistrate would communicate with them by means of notes (*chao-hui*), not official edicts; they would be punishable, however, as regular commoners). Feng Kuei-fen, "Fu hsiang-chih i" in *Chiao-pin-lu k'ang-i* (1897), 10–12b.

tions during the years of crisis. At least one of the roots of the old order—the power of the traditional elite in rural China—seems thus to have survived the Taiping holocaust in surprisingly vigorous condition.

Looking ahead into the period when the structure of the imperial state collapsed, the question now arises as to how the local power of the elite was affected by the major institutional changes that surrounded the birth of the Republic. Here we are entering one of the great uncharted areas of modern history. So little has the social development of late nineteenth- and early twentieth-century China been studied that here we can offer only the most tentative suggestions as to the direction research might take. One promising point of entry is the so-called local self-government (ti-fang tzu-chih) movement, which began in the last years of the Ch'ing and persisted through the Republican period, a movement sponsored by the dying imperial regime as the initial step towards adopting a constitution. This belated effort of the dynasty to modernize its administration relied in many respects upon the example of Japan, which had undertaken the task a generation earlier, and there is little doubt that "local self-government" was initially borrowed from the Japanese system of the same name. In Japan this innovation was begun during the early Meiji period, under the direction of Yamagata Aritomo and others, and was based partly on models supplied by the German adviser, Mosse. It involved a sweeping reorganization of Japan's local government and the substitution of a uniform, simplified administrative system for the diverse, complex traditional one. The aim was not to lay the groundwork for a system of representative government or local autonomy but to create a modern, centralized and rationalized form of local administration that could strengthen Japan's case for abolition of the unequal treaties.[42]

The term tzu-chih, as understood by its Ch'ing sponsors, meant neither representative government nor local autonomy. It was but a complement to kuan-chih or "rule by [centrally appointed] officials." Surely, wrote the court, local self-government was the foundation of a constitutional system, but it certainly involved no sort of "independence," or "departure from official rule." It was to exist "within the sphere of official rule" and was merely to fulfill those tasks that official rule was not able to perform. Naturally the court's purpose was to delineate the balance of power between the regular bureau-

---

42. Tōkyō shisei chōsakai, ed., Jichi gojūnen shi: Seido hen (Tokyo, 1940), 1–14.

cracy and local interests, retaining for the former the control of all substantive functions and leaving the latter only residual service duties. To set in motion the machinery for local self-rule, officials were to "select orthodox gentry" (a time-honored phrase) to implement a detailed set of regulations sent down from Peking, which involved establishing deliberative assemblies and administrative committees on district and provincial levels.[43] Under this system it was proposed that local elite would perform administrative tasks relating to education, public health, charitable relief, public works, and a vague residual category including miscellaneous tasks relegated by custom to gentry management, all under the supervision of regular appointed officials. Here was no departure in principle from the traditional practice of relying on the gentry for routine administration at the local level.

Though the provincial assembly movement in the years just before the revolution did provide a format for enlarged gentry and merchant participation in government and indeed set off an explosion of political interest among the moneyed and literate elite in the provincial capitals,[44] yet data from the local level suggest that the principal effect of local self-government was simply to legitimize the customary powers of the rural elite in their home communities. Here emerges the paradoxical character of the local self-government movement as it developed in the early decades of the Republic. On the one hand, it formed part of a growing body of political doctrine that envisaged the re-

---

43. *Ch'ing shih-lu,* Hsuan-t'ung, 5:35–36. In the large body of literature that may be consulted on the *tzu-chih* movement are Ch'ien Tuan-sheng, *Min-kuo cheng-chih shih* (Changsha, 1939), esp. vol. II; Li Tsung-huang, *Chung-kuo ti-fang tzu-chih tsung-lun* (Taipei, 1954); Wada Sei, *Shina chihō jichi seido hattatsu shi* (Tokyo, 1939).

44. See the fascinating study by John Fincher, "Political Provincialism and the National Revolution," in Mary Clabaugh Wright, ed., *China in Revolution: The First Phase, 1900–1913* (New Haven, 1968), 185–226. This book has raised to a wholly new level our understanding of the pre-revolutionary decade. It appeared too recently for its findings to have been adequately absorbed into the present study, but is causing me to rethink my own work rather thoroughly. For the present, my views seem closest to those of Ichiko Chūzō, whose contribution to this volume, "The Role of the Gentry: An Hypothesis" (297–317) supports the thesis that "local self-government" was an opportunity for the conservative local elite to expand their influence. It does seem clear, at least, that our attempts to resolve this problem must take account of the differing orientations of elites on the national, provincial, and local levels. My own hypothesis that modernization produced, or widened, cleavages within the elite as a whole might make it possible to narrow the cleavage between Professors Wright and Ichiko on this question. It does, I believe, complicate the issue to consider "the gentry" in this matter as an undifferentiated category.

building of the Chinese state along modern lines by integrating local communities and the central government through a system of representation. This body of doctrine was fed copiously by American progressive thought, imported by such indefatigable modernizers as Tung Hsiu-chia, an expert in municipal administration, and of course Sun Yat-sen. Despite its many ambiguities, Sun's thought was fairly clear in its insistence that modernity—particularly widespread political participation—could not be imposed from the top down but had to be generated by local communities and gradually extended to the national level. For Sun, local self-rule was to bring about not the dispersion of authority but national political integration. On the other hand, the specifically modernizing aims of the more progressive exponents of local self-government were more than offset by the forces of tradition, for which the self-government movement simply justified and perpetuated the local governing powers assumed by the rural gentry of the late Ch'ing period.

The way in which local self-government was integrated with existing gentry powers is suggested by the evolution of the sub-district administrative division known as the *tzu-chih ch'ü* (self-government area), which came commonly to be called simply *ch'ü*. This division, which came into widespread use after the Revolution of 1911, assumed a formal existence in the local self-government codes promulgated during the last few years of the imperial regime. Its intended functions seem to have been mainly those of police control and registration. After the revolution the *ch'ü* was distinguished by being the only administrative division permitted by President Yuan Shih-k'ai to operate a representative assembly. From the early years of the republic until the establishment of the Nationalist government in 1928, the *ch'ü* was recognized in administrative codes as the smallest effective governing unit. Its headman, the *ch'ü-chang* or *ch'ü-tung*, was invested with the responsibilities of local registration and police, as well as education, sanitation, local public works, and all those customary local service functions traditionally performed by the gentry. As in the old system, the district magistrate was to exercise ultimate control. A modern touch, however, was the provision for nomination of candidates for *ch'ü-chang* by ballot (by an electorate restricted by property and literacy qualifications) and the appointment of the *ch'ü-chang* by the magistrate from among those nominated.[45]

45. On the administrative history of the *ch'ü*, consult *Cheng-chih kuan-pao*, no. 445:2 (January 1909); *Nei wu fa-ling li-kuei chi-lan* (Peking, n.d.) 11th cat-

If we look beneath the normative provisions of the administrative codes, there is convincing evidence that the *ch'ü* in actual practice was very little influenced by the quasi-modernism of *tzu-chih*, but was really a gentry organization that evolved from the multiplex and extended-multiplex associations formed during the mid- and late nineteenth century. The *chü's* real origins are made plain by cases like that of Shun-te district near Canton. There the basic structure of the *ch'ü* divisions emerged in 1884 during the Sino-French war. "During the French invasion of Vietnam," reads the gazetteer, "the district formed *t'uan* for defense. It was decided to divide the district into 10 [extended-multiplex] *t'uan*, to hire *yung* and train them regularly. Though the *yung* were disbanded after the war, the system itself was retained. In the latter years of the Kuang-hsu reign, the district was divided into self-government *ch'ü*, and thus the [present] system of 10 *ch'ü* was established. The villages that formerly were controlled by the 40 *pao* [a pao-chia division] mostly came under the control of the *ch'ü*."[46]

In other instances the *ch'ü* emerged directly from a standard administrative division that had come under gentry management. In Hsiangch'eng, near Soochow, around 1910, the *tu* of the *li-chia* system were simply renamed *ch'ü*, and their gentry headmen began to busy themselves with the prescribed rituals of establishing local self-government. These gentry were already involved in practically every matter of importance in local government, including tax collection and militia, and were also substantial landowners. The social significance of local self-government is suggested by a 1910 case in which a mob of angry peasants burned the "local self-government preparation bureau" after its gentry managers had begun a registration drive and had added local self-government "expenses" to their ordinary rent requisitions. To their tenants, local self-government was simply an extension of the tax collection, rent collection, militia, and police authority the gentry already possessed.[47]

The importance of the *tu* as an instrument of gentry authority in

---

egory, 1–21); *Fa-ling ch'üan-shu* (Peking, 1916) 1914, no. 4, 7th category, vol. 39:5–12, also 9th category, vol. 31:17; *Fa-ling chi-lan,* (Peking, 1917) 6th category, 109–116; Ch'ien Tuan-sheng, *Min-kuo cheng-chih shih,* 545, 659–675; Li Tsunghuang, *Chung-kuo ti-fang tzu-chih tsung-lun* (Taipei, 1954), 113–114.

46. Shun-te 1929, 1:1.

47. Kojima Yoshio, "Shin-matsu no gōson tōji ni tsuite: Soshūfu no ku, to tō o chūshin ni," *Shichō,* 88:16–30 (1964). This is an important pioneer study of late Ch'ing social history.

the last years of the Ch'ing recalls the case of Hsiang-hsiang, in which the emergence of the ward commanders (*tu-tsung*) after 1853 was the most significant aspect of the elite's response to rebellion. As a matter of fact, the survival of these Hunan *tu* organizations into the Republican period is verified by that remarkable document of rural research, Mao Tse-tung's 1927 *Report on the Hunan Peasant Movement*. The *tu* and the *t'uan*, he reported, had taken on the local self-government appellations then current, respectively *ch'ü* and *hsiang*. The *tu* was an extended-multiplex association embracing from 10,000 to 60,000 people, with its own armed force, taxing power, and judicial authority. The *t'uan*, which seems to have grown out of the old lineage-dominated multiplex associations, was a lesser power but one still to be reckoned with. The *tu* and *t'uan* heads were "kings of the countryside" and the effective arbiters of all local affairs. A Kuomintang report of the early thirties confirms the fact that these local associations were virtually autonomous satrapies.[48]

Throughout the Republican period, government authorities on both provincial and national levels attempted fitfully to rationalize local administration by bringing such satrapies under bureaucratic control. Nevertheless, the *ch'ü* remained stubbornly attached to indigenous rural forms. A 1917 edict, for instance, notes that in the case of Shantung "the titles of the *ch'ü*-heads in the various districts are not uniform. Some are called *she-chang*, some *li-chang*, some *pao-chang*, some *t'uan-chang*." This persistence of old realities under supposedly new administrative rubrics was quite typical of the chaos of the Republican period and is but one instance of the superficiality of modernization efforts in a social context that was changing only at a painfully slow pace.[49]

One of the characteristic difficulties in interpreting local data from the Republican period is the definition of what the elite really consisted of. The end of the examination system, brought about during the Manchu reform movement just prior to the 1911 Revolution, meant that the formal distinctions by which the gentry had been defined were no longer applicable. What is clear at least is that the gentry's position was too firmly embedded in rural China to be swept away peremptorily by an edict from Peking. The difficult question that our research must contend with is that of the relative proportions

48. Mao Tse-tung, *Mao Tse-tung hsuan-chi* (Peking, 1951), 1:30; Hunan cheng-fu, *Hu-nan-sheng hsien-cheng pao-kao* (Changsha, 1931), 42.

49. *Fa-ling chi-lan hsü-pien* (Peking, 1920), 8th category, p. 7.

of continuity and change: How much of the old gentry managed, by adapting themselves to changed conditions, to survive into the new era? How much did the very process of adaptation affect the character of the class? And to what extent was the composition of the rural elite altered by the influx of new men and new money? Studies of this subject are sparse. So far none has succeeded in providing a coherent and systematic picture of how the rural elite of the twentieth century was really constituted and how it emerged from that of the nineteenth.[50] Here we can offer only some hypotheses based on a very tentative exploration. If nothing else, we can show the importance of starting such an investigation from the historical standpoint.

Nobody who has read even desultorily in twentieth-century sources will have missed the frequent mention of traditional social appellations meaning gentry: the terms *shen* and *shen-shih* occur regularly in accounts of rural conditions and quite plainly refer to a class whose style of life, social status, and political pretensions were not notably different from those of the old degree-holding elite.[51] Twentieth-century investigators thought they were observing a group of people whose characteristics (save for formal degree status) placed them within the generally understood class of gentry. One may argue that such observers were insufficiently precise in their scheme of social classification. Though this is undoubtedly true, yet the fuzzy definitions in the work of a trained anthropologist like Fei Hsiao-t'ung are not due to a lack of concern with methodological questions but rather to a search for functional description instead of formal classification. What Fei means when he includes "educated landowners" within the gentry category for the twentieth century is that such men enjoyed prestige and exercised powers like those of the group known historically as *shen-shih*. Fei assumes, no doubt, that under the traditional system it was precisely such men that might qualify themselves for formal gentry status by taking and passing government examinations or by purchasing degrees and titles. Though by the 1930's it is questionable what percentage of these *shen-shih* actually had held formal gentry status under the old

50. In Yung-teh Chow's interesting study of the twentieth-century gentry, *Social Mobility in China: Status Careers Among the Gentry in a Chinese Community* (New York, 1966), the question of how that class was related historically to the gentry of traditional China is unfortunately largely neglected.

51. For examples of such terminology dating from the 1920's and 1930's see Li Wen-chih, ed., *Chung-kuo chin-tai nung-yeh shih tzu-liao*, III (Peking, 1957), 382–384; Mao Tse-tung, *Hsüan-chi*, I, 30; Feng Ho-fa, *Chung-kuo nung-ts'un ching-chi tzu-liao* (Shanghai, 1935), 880–881.

regime, it would be unreasonable to rule out a certain degree of social continuity.[52] It seems fair to assume that much of the social history of rural China in the modern period consists of the efforts of the old elite to adapt itself to a changing environment.

One salient aspect of that environment was the abolition of the old formal distinctions by which the gentry's relation to the state had been defined. The end of the examination system did mean the end of certain definite perquisites and opportunities, for which alternatives had now to be found. Though a gentry family's local position rested upon many factors that were not mere products of formal degree status (the elitist structure of the kinship system, the prestige of learning and leisure, and frequently the ownership of land), formal degree status had in certain ways been indispensable to the survival of the gentry as a class. First, the social eminence attached to higher degree status gave the upper gentry personal access to local officials, a privilege that could be translated into favorable tax assessments and legal judgments as well as immunity from the ubiquitous predation of corrupt yamen underlings. Second, formal gentry status meant statutory exemption from labor service or the money tax into which it had been commuted. Third, and most important, formal gentry status was a means of income. Office holding was a well-traveled road to fortune. On the local level, there were various fees obtainable through customary gentry services, such as managing dike repair or local defense. Clearly, if the rural gentry were to survive, it now had to forge new links to the formal structure of state power.

The local self-government system was naturally a ready expedient. Many local accounts bear witness to the efforts of the rural elite to maintain their community dominance by taking control of the self-government apparatus, a process that we have traced to the t'uan-lien system in late Ch'ing times and one that continued well into the period of the Nationalist government of the 1930's and 1940's. In Shensi, a

52. Fei Hsiao-t'ung, *China's Gentry: Essays in Rural-Urban Relations* (Chicago, 1953), 32.

There were of course certain unusual economic forces operating upon the rural elite during the late nineteenth and early twentieth century. The extent to which the class was being altered by basic changes in economic patterns (such as the increasing monetization of rents, the replacement of share-rents by fixed rents, and the increase in absentee landlordism) still awaits systematic study.

The material in volume I of Li Wen-chih, *Tzu-liao,* is organized with precisely these questions in mind. How much the selection of materials was influenced by the theoretical requirements of the current periodization scheme remains to be determined.

notable strengthening of elite control was achieved through the local self-government organs. An account of 1931 pictures gentry (*shen*) obtaining posts as *ch'ü-chang* and other local positions through bribery; in these positions they proceeded to extort huge sums through forced contributions (*p'ai-chüan*). Another reporter writes of powerful gentry (*hao-shen*) governing all local affairs through the Ch'ü Self-government Office; this account notes particularly that the rather dispersed and informal power of the gentry in former times was newly concentrated and legitimized by control of the self-government apparatus. In Kwei-chow (according to a report of 1938) the *pao* of the old pao-chia system had become, under the self-government system, largely autonomous units headed by local strongmen (*t'u-hao*), all of whom were big land-lords. Such men were called commanders (*ssu-ling*) or *t'uan*-heads (*t'uan-chang*), another suggestion of the origins of their power in the local militarization of the late Ch'ing. The general picture of the 1930's and 1940's shows a process in which local landlords (most having a specifically gentry life-style) strengthened their hold over the local self-government system.[53]

The Disintegration of the Traditional Elite

Our evidence thus suggests strongly that China's rural elite survived into the twentieth century and indeed in some respects solidified its position in local society. Nevertheless, though much of the old order in rural districts remained intact as the nineteenth century drew to a close and indeed persisted into the Republican period, there were obviously new forces at work that prevented the reconstruction of the Chinese polity along traditional lines. What was it that so affected the structure of the Chinese elite as a national body, that it was rendered unable to reestablish a unified and effective government in China after 1911?

Here let us look beyond the actual content of modernization—the particular values and techniques involved in the confrontation of cultures—and consider the gross structural effects of the process upon the Chinese elite. Early modernization was mainly a phenomenon of the cities, especially the treaty ports, and left rural China relatively untouched. Centered as it was upon the cities, the modernizing process

53. Li Wen-chih, *Tzu-liao*, III, 382–384. See also Hsing-cheng-yuan nung-ts'un fu-hsing wei-yuan-hui, comps., *Shan-hsi-sheng nung-ts'un tiao-ch'a* (Shanghai, 1934), 148–149.

began to produce a new urban elite that found it increasingly hard to identify itself with the problems of rural China. The gap between modernizing and pre-modern cultures thus tended to become coterminous with the gap between city and countryside. Despite its notable attainments in the modern sectors of industry, politics, journalism, and scholarship, the new urban elite was less and less capable of playing a role in the central task of Chinese government: the administration of a predominantly rural society from an urban administrative base.

What Fei Hsiao-t'ung has called the "social erosion" of rural society was exacerbated by the process of modernization.[54] As the cities entered further into the new culture, they stimulated the flow of talent out of the villages and towns of the interior, and this traffic was increasingly one-way. Those of the elite who entered careers in the modernizing sectors of urban life found it hard to retain their ties with the pre-modern culture of market town and district seat. This was even more the case with those who went abroad for study. Even the most politically radical among the young urban elite had little to offer toward solving the problems of rural China. The divisive effects of modernization upon the elite drew warning cries from radical rural reconstructionists such as Liang Sou-ming and T'ao Hsing-chih, both of whom sought to reidentify young, progressive urbanites with the problems of the countryside. It appears that the ability of the late Ch'ing literati to hold the old order together under the stress of internal rebellion stemmed partly from the ability of high-ranking bureaucrats like Tseng Kuo-fan to participate to some extent in both urban and rural cultures, to bind their elite strata with a chain of common values. But in the twentieth century, the drastically widened cultural gap between city and countryside precluded the emergence of such figures. The integration of elites on various levels of society—a key element in the Ch'ing establishment's triumph over its internal enemies—could not be sustained in a context of modernization. It is not surprising that the reintegration of the national polity, when finally it came in 1949, should have been accompanied by efforts to produce a new elite with cultural roots in both modern and pre-modern sectors of Chinese life.

The Kuomintang and the Nanking government were in many respects outgrowths of the modernizing urban culture. Despite political rhetoric to the effect that its natural allies were the rich and powerful

54. Fei, *China's Gentry*, 127–142.

in rural society, there is some evidence in the administrative history of
the 1930's that the semi-modernized Nanking government often proved
an intrusive and unwelcome competitor of the rural elite. By the mid-
thirties, the Nationalist authorities were in fact trying to weaken the
influence of the petty rural satraps, to strip from them their local police
power, and to bring local security within the purview of a regular
government police apparatus and an all-pervasive pao-chia system.[55]
The difficulties that the Nanking government experienced in building
an effective pattern of local control were inherited by the Japanese
invaders, who found themselves essentially no better off than the indigenous governments through which they attempted to govern. Indeed, their difficulties in controlling rural areas from urban bases recall
the difficulties of the Taipings a century earlier.

By contrast, the structure of local militarization that developed in
North China under Communist auspices during the anti-Japanese war
bears certain striking resemblances to the orthodox structure we have
observed in the mid-nineteenth century. Its mutually supporting levels
of militarization ranged from the part-time militia to the full-time
guerrilla, to the fully professional army. Its elites on various levels were
bound together by new techniques of organization and a new set of
common orientations.[56] It should be instructive to study the organization and strategic context of this and similar revolutionary military
systems in the light of traditional patterns of local militarization. Such
multi-level hierarchies have been able to offer a formidable challenge
to city elites that are socially and politically alienated from their rural
surroundings: whether, as in the Taiping case, they are alienated by
extraprovincial origins and esoteric ideology; or, as in the case of the
urban elite of China before 1949, because of their cultural ties to the
Western world.

55. Su Sung-fen, ed., *Hsien-hsing ti-fang tzu-chih fa-ling chieh-shih hui-pien*
(Shanghai, 1934), 147–153. Li Tsung-huang, *Chung-kuo ti-fang tzu-chih kai-lun*
(Taipei, 1949), 66–67. *Hu-nan-sheng hsien-cheng pao-kao*, 2, 42.
56. Li Chan, *Chan-tou-chung ti chieh-fang-ch'ü min-ping* (Hong Kong, 1947),
22–32. Gaimushō chōsakyoku, comps., *Chūkyō gairon* (Tokyo, 1949), 58-72.

BIBLIOGRAPHY

Sources Cited in the Notes

Balazs, Étienne. *Le Traité économique du "Souei-Chou."* Leiden, 1953.

Beal, Edwin George, Jr. *The Origin of Likin, 1853–1864.* Cambridge, Mass.: East Asian Research Center, Harvard University, 1958.

Chang Chung-li. *The Chinese Gentry: Studies on their Role in Nineteenth-Century Chinese Society.* Seattle: University of Washington Press, 1958.

———— *The Income of the Chinese Gentry.* Seattle: University of Washington Press, 1962.

Chang Te-chien 張德堅. *Tse-ch'ing hui-tsuan* 賊情彙纂 (Intelligence handbook on the Taipings). 1854–1855. Reprinted in vol. 3 of Hsiang Ta, ed., *T'ai-p'ing t'ien-kuo,* 25–347.

Changsha hsien-chih 長沙縣志. (Gazetteer of Changsha district, Hunan). 1871.

Ch'en Chin 陳僅, ed. *Nan-shan pao-chia shu* 南山保甲書 (Pao-chia manual for the Nan-shan [Ch'in-ling, Shensi] area). 1845.

Ch'en Yin-k'o 陳寅恪. *Sui-T'ang chih-tu yuan-yuan lueh-lun kao* 隋唐制度淵源略論稿 (Preliminary exploration of the sources of Sui and T'ang institutions). Peking, 1954.

Cheng-chih kuan-pao 政治官報 (Official government gazette). Peking, c. 1908–1911.

Ch'i Chi-kuang 戚繼光. *Chi-hsiao hsin-shu* 紀效新書 (New manual of effectiveness). Reprinted and annotated in Hsu Nai-chao, *Min-kuo-chai ch'i-chung,* ts'e 11–15.

———— *Lien-ping shih-chi* 練兵實紀 (True record of troop training). Reprinted and annotated in Hsu Nai-chao, *Min-kuo-chai ch'i-chung,* ts'e 16–20.

Ch'i Piao-chia 祁彪佳. *Ch'i Piao-chia chi* 祁彪佳集 (Works of Ch'i Piao-chia). Peking, 1960.

Ch'i Tso-kuo 戚祚國. *Ch'i shao-pao nien-p'u* 戚少保年譜 (Chronological biography of Ch'i Chi-kuang). Kuang-hsu (?) reprint of an 1847 edition.

Chiang Chung-yuan 江忠源. *Chiang Chung-lieh-kung i-chi* 江忠烈公遺集 (Works of Chiang Chung-yuan, posthumously collected). 1864. With supplement: *Hsing-chuang* 行狀 (Record of official career).

Chiang Siang-tse. *The Nien Rebellion.* Seattle: University of Washington Press, 1954.

Chiang Shih-yen 江世焱, ed. "Ya-p'ien chan-cheng ch'ien-hou Hsin-ning, Wu-kang nung-min ch'i-i ti pu-fen tzu-liao" 鴉片戰爭前後新寧武岡農民起義的部分資料 (Partial source materials on peasant uprisings in Hsin-ning and Wu-kang before and after the Opium War) in *Hunan li-shih tzu-liao* 湖南歷史資料 (Materials on Hunanese history), no. 1: 49–65, (1958).

Chiao Hsun 焦循. *Meng-tzu cheng-i* 孟子正義 (The *Mencius*, with commentaries). Peking, 1958.

Chiao-p'ing Yueh-fei fang-lueh 剿平粵匪方略 (Documentary history of the anti-Taiping campaigns). 1872.

Chien-ch'ang hsien-chih 建昌縣志 (Gazetteer of Chien-ch'ang district, Kiangsi). 1871.

Chien Yu-wen 簡又文. *T'ai-p'ing t'ien-kuo tien-chih t'ung-k'ao* 太平天國典制通考 (Encyclopedic study of Taiping institutions). Hong Kong, 1958.

—— *T'ai-p'ing t'ien-kuo ch'üan-shih* 太平天國全史 (Complete history of the Taiping Rebellion). Hong Kong, 1962.

Ch'ien I-chi 錢儀吉. ed. *Pei-chuan chi* 碑傳集 (Collection of memorial biographies). 1893.

Ch'ien Mu 錢穆. *Chung-kuo chin-san-pai-nien hsueh-shu shih* 中國近三百年學術史 (A history of Chinese scholarship during the past three hundred years). Taipei, 1957.

Ch'ien Tuan-sheng 錢端升. *Min-kuo cheng-chih shih* 民國政制史 (History of governmental institutions in the Republican period). Changsha, 1939.

Chin-shu 晉書 (History of the Chin dynasty). K'ai-ming ed., Shanghai, 1935.

Chin Yü-fu 金毓黻, et al., eds. *T'ai-p'ing t'ien-kuo shih-liao* 太平天國史料 (Historical sources on the Taiping Rebellion). Peking, 1959.

Ch'ing-shih 清史 (History of the Ch'ing dynasty). Taipei, 1961.

Ch'ing-shih lieh-chuan 清史列傳 (Collected biographies of the Ch'ing period). Taipei, 1962.

Ch'ing shih-lu, see *Ta-ch'ing li-ch'ao shih-lu*.

Chou Ch'ang-sen 周長森. *Liu-ho chi-shih* 六合紀事 (Account of events at Liu-ho), 1886. Reprinted in vol. 5 of Hsiang Ta, ed., *T'ai-p'ing t'ien-kuo*, 149–170.

Chou-li 周禮 (Rites of Chou). *Ssu-pu ts'ung-k'an* ed.

Ch'ou-pan i-wu shih-mo 籌辦夷務始末 (Complete record of management of barbarian affairs). Peking, 1930.

Chow Yung-teh. *Social Mobility in China: Status Careers among the Gentry in a Chinese Community*. New York: Atherton Press, 1966.

Chu-chi hsien-chih 諸暨縣志 (Gazetteer of Chu-chi district, Chekiang). 1909.

Chu K'ung-chang 朱孔彰, ed. *Chung-hsing chiang-shuai pieh-chuan* 中興將帥別傳 (Unofficial biographies of military commanders of the Restoration period). 1897.

Chu Sun-i 朱孫詒. "T'uan-lien shuo" 團練說 (On t'uan-lien) in Sheng K'ang, ed., *Huang-ch'ao ching-shih-wen hsu-pien*, 1897. 81: 13.

Ch'u Chih-fu 儲枝芙. *Wan-ch'iao chi-shih* 皖樵紀實 (Ch'u Chih-fu's true record). From a manuscript copy owned by Lo Erh-kang, written some time after 1860, parts printed in Chien Yu-wen, *T'ai-p'ing t'ien-kuo tien-chih t'ung-k'ao*, pp. 397–400.

Chü-jung hsien-chih 句容縣志 (Gazetteer of Chü-jung district, Kiangsu). 1904.

Ch'ü T'ung-tsu. *Local Government in China under the Ch'ing*. Cambridge, Mass.: Harvard University Press, 1962.

"Chung Jen-chieh k'ou-shu" 鍾人杰口述 (Chung Jen-chieh's oral confession) in *Chin-tai-shih tzu-liao;* 近代史資料 (Materials on modern history). 1963. 1: 2–4.

Chung-kuo k'o-hsueh-yuan, chin-tai shih tzu-liao pien-chi tsu 中國科學院近代史資料編輯組 (Chinese Academy of Sciences, modern history sources editorial group), ed. *T'ai-p'ing t'ien-kuo tzu-liao* 太平天國資料 (Sources on the Taiping Rebellion). Peking, 1959.

Chung Wen-tien 鍾文典. *T'ai-p'ing-chün tsai Yung-an* 太平軍在永安 (The Taiping army at Yung-an). Peking, 1962.

Eberhard, Wolfram. *Conquerors and Rulers: Social Forces in Medieval China*. Leiden: E. J. Brill, 1952.

d'Encausse, Hélène Carrère, and Stuart Schram. *Le Marxisme et l'Asie, 1853–1964*. Paris, 1965.

Fa-ling chi-lan 法令輯覽 (Compendium of laws and ordinances). Peking, 1917.

Fa-ling chi-lan hsü-pien 法令輯覽續編 (Compendium of laws and ordinances, continued). Peking, 1920.

Fa-ling ch'üan-shu 法令全書 (Complete digest of laws and ordinances). Peking, 1912 and 1916.

Fei Hsiao-t'ung. *China's Gentry: Essays in Rural-Urban Relations*. Chicago: University of Chicago Press, 1953.

Fen-i hsien-chih 分宜縣志 (Gazetteer of Fen-i district, Kiangsi). 1871.

Feng Ho-fa 馮和法, ed. *Chung-kuo nung-ts'un ching-chi tzu-liao* 中國農村經濟資料 (Materials on Chinese village economy). Shanghai, 1935.

Feng Kuei-fen 馮桂芬. "Chüan-yung chu-chiao kung-tieh" 捐勇助剿公牒 (Gentry petition on using mercenaries to aid in suppressing the rebellion) in *Hsien-chih-t'ang chi* 顯志堂集 (Collected essays from the Hsien-chih hall). 1876. 9: 14–15.

———— "Fu hsiang-chih i" 復鄉職議 (Proposal for reinstituting a system of local headmen) in *Chiao-pin-lu k'ang-i* 校邠廬抗議 (Essays of protest from the studio of Feng Kuei-fen). 1897. 1: 10–12b.

Fincher, John. "Political Provincialism and the National Revolution" in Mary Wright, ed., *China in Revolution: the First Phase, 1900–1913*. New Haven: Yale University Press, 1968. 185–226.

Freedman, Maurice. *Lineage Organization in Southeastern China*. London: London School of Economics, Monographs on Social Anthropology, no. 18. 1958.

———— *Chinese Lineage and Society*. London: Athlone Press, 1966.

Gaimushō chōsakyoku 外務省調査局 (Japanese Foreign Office, Investigation Bureau), comps. *Chūkyō gairon* 中共概論 (A general study of the Chinese Communists). Tokyo, 1949.

Hangchow fu-chih 抗州府志 (Gazetteer of Hangchow prefecture, Chekiang). 1898.

Hatada Takashi 旗田巍. "Chūgoku ni okeru senseishugi to 'sonraku kyōdōtai riron' " 中國における專政主義と村落共同體理論 (Despotism in China and the theory of village *gemeinschaft*), in *Chūgoku kenkyū* 中國研究 (Researches on China), 13: 2–12 (1950).

Hatano Yoshihiro 波多野善大. "Hokuyō gumbatsu no seiritsu katei" 北洋軍閥の成立過程 (Development of the Peiyang warlords) in *Nagoya daigaku bungakubu kenkyū ronshū* 名古屋大學文學部研究論集 (Collected studies from the faculty of letters of Nagoya University), no. 5: 211–262 (1953).

Hibino Takeo 日比野丈夫. "Gōson bōei to kempeki shōya" 鄉村防衞と堅壁清野 (Village defense and wall-strengthening/field-clearing) in *Tōhō gakuhō* 東方學報 (Review of Asian studies), no. 22: 141–155 (Kyoto, 1953).

Hirayama Amane (Shū) 平山周. *Chung-kuo pi-mi she-hui shih* 中國祕密社會史 (History of Chinese secret societies). Shanghai, 1934. Chinese trans. of a Japanese ed.

Ho Ch'ang-ling 賀長齡. "Chin-sheng hsia-yu ko-ying chuan-she pu-tao ping-ting i" 黔省下游各營專設捕盜兵丁議 (Proposal for establishing bandit-catching troops in all the battalions in lower Kweichow) in Lo Ju-huai 羅汝懷, ed. *Hu-nan wen-cheng* 湖南文徵 (Collection of essays by Hunanese authors), 14: 8–11 (1871).

——— ed. *Huang-ch'ao ching-shih wen-pien* 皇朝經世文編 (Collected essays on statecraft from the period of the reigning dynasty), 1886 ed.

Ho I-k'un 何貽焜. *Tseng Kuo-fan p'ing-chuan* 曾國藩評傳 (Critical biography of Tseng Kuo-fan). Taipei, 1964. Photographic reprint of the 1937 ed.

Ho Ping-ti 何炳棣. *Studies on the Population of China, 1368–1953*. Cambridge, Mass.: Harvard University Press, 1959.

——— *The Ladder of Success in Imperial China: Aspects of Social Mobility, 1368–1911*. New York: Columbia University Press, 1962.

——— *Chung-kuo hui-kuan shih-lun* 中國會舘史論 (On the history of *Landsmann-schaften* in China). Taipei, 1966.

Hsiang-hsiang hsien-chih 湘鄉縣志 (Gazetteer of Hsiang-hsiang district, Hunan). 1874.

Hsiang Ta 向達 et al., eds. *T'ai-p'ing t'ien-kuo* 太平天國 (The Taiping Rebellion). Peking, 1952.

Hsiao I-shan, *Fei-yü-kuan wen-ts'un* 非宇館文存 (Collected essays of Hsiao I-shan). Peking, 1948.

Hsiao Kung-ch'üan. *Rural China: Imperial Control in the Nineteenth Century*. Seattle: University of Washington Press, 1960.

Hsieh Hsing-yao 謝興堯. *T'ai-p'ing t'ien-kuo ch'ien-hou Kuang-hsi ti fan-Ch'ing yun-tung* 太平天國前後廣西的反清運動 (The anti-Ch'ing movement in Kwangsi before and after the Taiping Rebellion). Peking, 1950.

Hsieh Pao-chao. *The Government of China, 1644–1911*. Baltimore: Johns Hopkins Press, 1925.

Hsin-ning hsien-chih 新寧縣志 (Gazetteer of Hsin-ning district, Hunan). 1893.

Hsing-cheng-yuan, nung-ts'un fu-hsing wei-yuan-hui 行政院農村復興委員會 (Executive yuan, rural reconstruction committee), ed. *Shan-hsi-sheng nung-ts'un tiao-ch'a* 陝西省農村調查 (Investigation of villages in Shensi). Shanghai, 1934.

Hsu Nai-chao 許乃釗. *Hsiang-shou chi-yao* 鄉守輯要 (Essentials of rural defense) in *Min-kuo-chai ch'i-chung*, ts'e 3–5.

——— *Min-kuo-chai ch'i-chung* 敏果齋七種 (Seven titles from the Min-kuo studio). 1849.

Ch'eng-shou chi-yao 城守輯要 (Essentials of city defense) ts'e 1–2.

Hsiang-shou chi-yao 鄉守輯要 ts'e 3–5.

Chi-hsiao hsin-shu 紀效新書 ts'e 11–15. (Ch'i Chi-kuang)

Lien-ping shih-chi 練兵實紀 ts'e 16–20. (Ch'i Chi-kuang)

Hsu Ta-ling 許大齡. *Ch'ing-tai chüan-na chih-tu* 淸代捐納制度 (The rank-sale system in the Ch'ing dynasty). Peking, 1950.

Hsu Tung 徐棟, ed. *Pao-chia shu* 保甲書 (Manual of *pao-chia*). 1848.

Hsu Tzu 徐鼐 *Wei-hui-chai wen-chi* 未灰齋文集 (Collected essays from the Wei-hui studio). 1861.

———— *Hsiao-t'ien chi-nien fu-k'ao* 小腆紀年附考 (Supplementary chronicle of the Ming loyalist regime). Completed 1861. Peking reprint, 1957.

Hsueh Ch'uan-yuan 薛傳源. *Fang-hai pei-lan* 防海備覽 (Manual on coastal defense). 1810.

Hu Lin-i 胡林翼. *Hu Wen-chung-kung i-chi* 胡文忠公遺集 (Works of Hu Lin-i, posthumously collected). 1875.

Hua I-lun 華翼綸. *Hsi-chin t'uan-lien shih-mo chi* 錫金團練始末記 (Complete account of t'uan-lien in Wu-hsi and Chin-kuei), n.d., in Chung-kuo k'o-hsueh-yuan, ed., *T'ai-p'ing t'ien-kuo tzu-liao*, 121–131.

Hua-jung hsien-chih 華容縣志 (Gazetteer of Hua-jung district, Hunan). 1882.

Hua-sha-na 花沙納. *Te Chuang-kuo-kung nien-p'u* 德壯果公年譜 (Chronological biography of Te-leng-t'ai). 1857.

Huang-ch'ao cheng-tien lei-tsuan 皇朝政典類纂 (Sources on governmental institutions of the reigning dynasty, arranged by category). 1903.

Huang-ch'ao ching-shih wen-pien, see Ho Ch'ang-ling.

Huang-chou fu-chih 黃州府志 (Gazetteer of Huang-chou prefecture, Hupeh). 1884.

Huang En-t'ung 黃恩彤, et al., eds. *Yueh-tung sheng-li hsin-tsuan* 粵東省例新纂 (Precedents for the governance of Kwangtung province, newly compiled). 1846.

Huang-kang hsien-chih 黃岡縣志 (Gazetteer of Huang-kang district, Hupeh). 1882.

Huang Liu-hung 黃六鴻. *Fu-hui ch'üan-shu* 福惠全書 (Complete manual for securing felicity and benefits). 1694.

Huang P'eng-nien 黃彭年. "*Chiang Chung-lieh-kung mu-piao*" 江忠烈公墓表 (Funerary eulogy of Chiang Chung-yuan). Printed as a supplement to Chiang Chung-yuan, *Chiang Chung-lieh-kung i-chi*.

Huang-yen hsien-chih 黃巖縣志 (Gazetteer of Huang-yen district, Chekiang). 1877.

Hucker, Charles. "The Governmental Organization of the Ming Dynasty," *Harvard Journal of Asiatic Studies*, 21: 1–66 (1958).

Hummel, Arthur W., ed. *Eminent Chinese of the Ch'ing Period*. Washington, D.C.: United States Government Printing Office, 1943–44.

Hunan cheng-fu 湖南政府 (Hunan provincial government), ed. *Hu-nan-sheng hsien-cheng pao-kao* 湖南省縣政報告 (Report on district government in Hunan province). Changsha, 1931.

Hunan sheng-chih 湖南省志 (Gazetteer of Hunan province). 1958. Daian photographic reprint, n.d.

Hunan t'ung-chih 湖南通志 (Gazetteer of Hunan province). 1885.

I-ch'un hsien-chih 宜春縣志 (Gazetteer of I-ch'un district, Kiangsi). 1870.

I-yang hsien-chih 益陽縣志 (Gazetteer of I-yang district, Hunan). 1874.

Ihara Hirosuke 伊原弘介. "Taihei tengoku no gōson tōji: Kōso, Setsukō chihō o chūshin ni" 太平天國の鄉村統治：江蘇，浙江を中心に (Taiping village control: A study centering on areas in Kiangsu and Chekiang) in *Shigaku kenkyū* 史學研究 (Historical research), 86: 42–56 (1962).

Ikeda Makoto 池田誠. "Hokōhō no seiritsu to sono tenkai" 保甲法の成立とその展開 (The establishment and development of the *pao-chia* system) in *Tōyōshi kenkyū* 東洋史研究 (Researches in East Asian history), 12.6: 1–32 (1954).

Imahori Seiji 今堀誠二. "Shin-tai ni okeru nōson kikō no kindaika ni tsuite: Kantō-shō Kōsan-ken chihō ni okeru 'kyōdōtai' no suiten katei ni tsuite" 清代における農村機構の近代化について：廣東省香山縣地方における共同體の推轉過程について (The modernization of village structure in the Ch'ing period: the process by which *gemeinschaft* was transformed in Hsiang-shan district, Kwangtung) in *Rekishigaku kenkyū* 歷史學研究 (Historical researches), 191: 3–17; 192: 14–29 (1956).

Kawabata Genji 河鰭原治. "Taihei tengoku ni okeru gōkan setchi no jittai" 太平天國における郷官設置の實態 (The actual realities of the establishment of local officials in the Taiping Rebellion) in *Tōhōgaku ronshū* 東方學論集 (Collected studies on East Asia), 1: 167–179 (1954).

——— "Taihei tengoku ni okeru gōkan sōchi to sono haikei" 太平天國における郷官創置とその背景 (The establishment of local officials in the Taiping Rebellion and its background) in *Shigaku zasshi* 史學雜誌, 63.6: 34–50 (1954).

Kiangsi t'ung-chih 江西通志 (Gazetteer of Kiangsi province). 1881.

Kitamura Hirotada 北村敬直. "Shin-dai no jidaiteki ichi: Chūgoku kindaishi e no tembō" 清代の時代的位置：中國近代史への展望 (The historical position of the Ch'ing era, a perspective on Chinese modern history) in *Shisō* 思想 (Thought), no. 292: 47–57 (1948).

Kiukiang fu-chih 九江府志 (Gazetteer of Kiukiang prefecture, Kiangsi). 1874.

Ko Shih-chün 葛士濬 ed. *Huang-ch'ao ching-shih-wen hsu-pien* 皇朝經世文續編 (Collected essays on statecraft from the reigning dynasty, continued). Shanghai, 1898 ed.

Kojima Yoshio 小島淑男. "Shin-matsu no gōson tōji ni tsuite: Soshūfu no ku, to tō o chūshin ni" 清末の郷村統治について：蘇州府の區，圖董を中心に (Village rule in the late Ch'ing: Based on a study of *ch'ü* and *t'u* heads in Soochow prefecture) in *Shichō* 史潮 (Historical tide), no. 88: 16–30 (1964).

Ku Chi-kuang 谷霽光. *Fu-ping chih-tu k'ao-shih* 府兵制度考釋 (An investigation into the *fu-ping* system). Shanghai, 1962.

Ku-fei tsung-lu, see *Kwangsi t'ung-chih chi-yao*.

Ku Yen-wu 顧炎武. *T'ien-hsia chün-kuo li-ping shu* 天下郡國利病書 (Institutional geography of various jurisdictions in the empire) in *Ssu-k'u shan-pen ts'ung-shu, ch'u-pien* 四庫善本叢書初編 (Collection of rare books in the four treasuries, first series). Taipei, 1959–1963, t'ao 19–23.

Kuan-tzu 管子. Wan-yu wen-k'u ed.

Kuan-tzu chi-chiao 管子集校 (Collected critical materials on the *Kuan-tzu*). Kuo Mo-jo 郭沫若 et al., eds. Peking, 1956.

Kuang-tung sheng, wen-shih yen-chiu-kuan 廣東省文史研究館 (Research institute for the literature and history of Kwangtung province), ed. *San-yuan-li jen-min k'ang-Ying tou-cheng shih-liao* 三元里人民抗英鬥爭史料 (Historical materials on the anti-British struggles of the people of San-yuan-li). 1964 Daian reprint of the 1959 Canton ed.

Kuei-hsien chih 貴縣志 (Gazetteer of Kuei district, Kwangsi). 1894.

K'uei-lien 魁聯. "Yü t'uan-lien shih" 諭團練示 (Proclamation ordering t'uan-lien) in Ko Shih-chün, ed., *Huang-ch'ao ching-shih-wen hsu-pien*, 81: 8.

Kung Ching-han 龔景瀚. *Tan-ching-chai ch'üan-chi* 澹靜齋全集 (Complete works from the Tan-ching studio). 1826.

Kung Tzu-chen 龔自珍. "Pao-chia cheng-ming" 保甲正名 (On rectifying the name of *pao-chia*), in *Kung Tzu-chen ch'üan-chi* 龔自珍全集 (Complete works of Kung Tzu-chen). Shanghai, 1959, I, 96–97.

Kuo T'ing-i 郭廷以. *T'ai-p'ing t'ien-kuo shih-shih jih-chih* 太平天國史事日誌 (Day-by-day chronicle of the Taiping Rebellion). Taipei, 1963.

Kwangsi t'ung-chih chi-yao 廣西通志輯要 (Essential portions of the Kwangsi provincial gazetteer). 1881.

Supplements:

    Kwangsi chao-chung lu 廣西昭忠錄 (Kwangsi martyrology)

    P'ing Kuei chi-lueh 平桂紀略 (Record of the pacification of Kwangsi)

    Ku-fei tsung-lu 股匪總錄 (General account of *ku* bandits)

    T'ang-fei tsung-lu 堂匪總錄 (General account of *t'ang* bandits).

Laai I-faai. "The Part Played by the Pirates of Kwangtung and Kwangsi Provinces in the Taiping Insurrection." Unpub. diss. University of California, 1950.

Legge, James. *The Chinese Classics*. 3rd ed. Hong Kong, 1960.

Lei Hai-tsung 雷海宗. *Chung-kuo wen-hua yü Chung-kuo ti ping* 中國文化與中國的兵 (Chinese culture and the Chinese military). Changsha, 1940.

Li Chan 力斬. *Chan-tou-chung ti chieh-fang-ch'ü min-ping* 戰鬥中的解放區民兵 (The militia in the liberated areas during the war). Hong Kong, 1947.

Li Ch'un 酈純. *T'ai-p'ing t'ien-kuo chih-tu ch'u-t'an* 太平天國制度初探 (Preliminary study of Taiping institutions). Rev. ed., Peking, 1963.

Li Huan 李桓, ed. *Kuo-ch'ao ch'i-hsien lei-cheng, ch'u-pien* 國朝耆獻類徵初編 (Collected biographies of the Ch'ing period, categorically arranged, first series). N.d.

Li Ju-chao 李汝昭. *Ching-shan yeh-shih* 鏡山野史 (Unofficial history from Ching-shan). Printed in Hsiang Ta, *T'ai-p'ing t'ien-kuo*, III, 3–21, from an unpub. ms. about 1864.

Li-p'ing fu-chih 黎平府志 (Gazetteer of Li-p'ing prefecture, Kweichow). 1892.

Li Tao 李燾, ed. *Hsu tzu-chih t'ung-chien ch'ang-pien* 續資治通鑑長編 (Collection of materials for an annalistic history of the Northern Sung). Taipei, Shih-chieh shu-chü reprint, 1961.

Li Tsu-t'ao 李祖陶. "Tu Ch'i Wu-i *Chi-hsiao hsin-shu Lien-ping shih-chi* yu shu" 讀戚武毅紀效新書練兵實紀有述 (On reading Ch'i Chi-kuang's *New Manual of Effectiveness* and *True Record of Troop Training*) in *Mai-t'ang wen-lueh* 邁堂文略 (Collected essays of Li Tsu-t'ao). 1865. 3: 1–24b.

Li Tsung-huang 李宗黃. *Chung-kuo ti-fang tzu-chih tsung-lun* 中國地方自治總論 (A complete account of local self-government in China). Taipei, 1954.

Li Wen-chih 李文治, ed. *Chung-kuo chin-tai nung-yeh shih tzu-liao* 中國近代農業史資料 (Materials on the history of Chinese agriculture in the modern period). Peking, 1957.

Li Yu-fen 李有棻. *Wu-chün pao-chia shih-i che-yao* 武郡保甲事宜摘要 (An outline of pao-chia administration in Wuchang prefecture). 1887.

Liang Fang-chung 梁方仲. "Ming-tai ti min-ping" 明代的民兵 (The militia of the Ming period) in *Chung-kuo she-hui ching-chi-shih chi-k'an* 中國社會經濟史集刊 (Chinese social and economic history review), 5.2: 201–234 (1937).

Liang Lien-fu 梁廉夫. "Ch'ien-chai chien-wen sui-pi" 潛齋見聞隨筆 (Notes on events seen and heard of from the Ch'ien Studio) in *Chin-tai-shih tzu-liao* 近代史資料 (Materials on modern history), no. 1: 1–20 (1955).

Liang-shan hsien-chih 梁山縣志 (Gazetteer of Liang-shan district, Szechwan). 1867.

Lin-hsiang hsien-chih 臨湘縣志 (Gazetteer of Lin-hsiang district, Hunan). 1872.

Lin Tse-hsu 林則徐. *Lin Wen-chung-kung ch'üan-chi* 林文忠公全集 (Complete works of Lin Tse-hsu). Taipei reprint, 1963.

Lin-t'ung-hsien hsu-chih 臨潼縣續志 (Gazetteer of Lin-t'ung district, Shensi, continued). 1890.

Ling T'i-an 凌惕安. *Hsien-T'ung Kuei-chou chün-shih shih* 咸同貴州軍事史 (History of military affairs in Kweichow during the Hsien-feng and T'ung-chih periods). 1932.

Liu Chin-tsao 劉錦藻, ed. *Ch'ing-ch'ao hsu wen-hsien t'ung-k'ao* 清朝續文獻通考 (Encyclopedia of source materials for the Ch'ing dynasty). Shanghai: Commercial Press, 1936.

Liu Fu-ching 劉孚京. *Nan-feng Liu hsien-sheng wen-chi* 南豐劉先生文集 (Collected essays of Mr. Liu of Nan-feng). 1919.

Liu-ho hsien-chih 六合縣志 (Gazetteer of Liu-ho district, Kiangsu). 1884.

Liu-ho-hsien hsu-chih kao 六合縣續志稿 (Draft continuation of the gazetteer of Liu-ho district, Kiangsu). 1920.

Liu K'un-i 劉坤一. *Liu K'un-i i-chi* 劉坤一遺集 (Works of Liu K'un-i, posthumously collected). Peking, 1959.

Liu-yang hsien-chih 瀏陽縣志 (Gazetteer of Liu-yang district, Hunan). 1873.

Liu Yü-hsun 劉于潯. "I-hsueh chi" 義學紀 (Account of charitable schools) in Nanchang 1870, 36: 4b–5b.

Lo Cheng-chün 羅正鈞. *Wang Chuang-wu-kung nien-p'u* 王壯武公年譜 (Chronological biography of Wang Chen) in Wang Chen, *Wang Chuang-wu-kung i-chi*, ts'e 1–2.

Lo Chung-chieh-kung nien-p'u 羅忠節公年譜 (Chronological biography of Lo Tse-nan) in Lo Tse-nan, *Lo-shan i-chi*, ts'e 8.

Lo Erh-kang 羅爾綱. "Ch'ing-chi ping wei chiang-yu ti ch'i-yuan" 清季兵爲將有的起源 (The origin of personal armies in the late Ch'ing period) in *Chung-kuo she-hui ching-chi shih chi-k'an* (Journal of Chinese social and economic history), 5.2: 235–250 (1937).

———— *Hsiang-chün hsin-chih* 湘軍新志 (A new treatise on the Hunan Army). Changsha, 1939.

———— *T'ien-ti-hui wen-hsien lu* 天地會文獻錄 (Bibliographic studies of sources relating to the Heaven and Earth Society). Hong Kong reprint, n.d. Preface dated 1942.

———— *Lü-ying ping-chih* 綠營兵志 (A treatise on the Army of the Green Standard). Chungking, 1945.

———— "Chang Chia-hsiang k'ao" 張嘉祥考 (A study of Chang Chia-hsiang) in Lo Erh-kang, *T'ai-p'ing t'ien-kuo shih chi-tsai ting-miu chi*, pp. 140–145.

—————— *T'ai-p'ing t'ien-kuo shih pien-wei chi* 太平天國史辨偽集 (Refutation of untruths in the historiography and source materials on the Taiping Rebellion). Shanghai, 1950.

—————— *T'ai-p'ing t'ien-kuo shih chi-tsai ting-miu chi* 太平天國史記載訂謬集 (Collected critical essays on historical accounts of the Taiping Rebellion). Peking, 1955.

—————— *T'ai-p'ing t'ien-kuo shih-kao* 太平天國史稿 (Draft history of the Taiping Rebellion). Peking, 1955.

—————— "Heng-ting-tun lun K'o-chia-jen yü T'ai-p'ing t'ien-kuo shih k'ao-shih" 亨丁頓論客家人與太平天國事考釋 (An investigation and explanation of Huntington's study of the connection between the Hakkas and the Taipings) in Wu Hsiang-hsiang 吳相湘 et al., eds. *Chung-kuo chin-tai-shih lun-ts'ung* 中國近代史論叢 (Collected studies on modern Chinese history). Taipei, 1959. 1st ser. IV, 156–160.

Lo Ju-huai 羅汝懷, ed. *Hu-nan wen-cheng* 湖南文徵 (Essays from Hunan). 1871.

Lo Tse-nan 羅澤南. *Lo-shan i-chi* 羅山遺集 (Works of Lo Tse-nan, posthumously collected). 1863.

Lo Yü-tung 羅玉東. *Chung-kuo li-chin shih* 中國釐金史 (History of likin). Shanghai, 1936.

Lu Hsiang-sheng 廬象昇. *Lu Chung-su-kung chi* 廬忠肅公集 (Collected works of Lu Hsiang-sheng). 1875.

Lu Tao-ch'ang 盧道昌. *Wei-hsiang yao-lueh* 衛鄉要略 (Essentials of local defense). 1885.

Ma Shao-ch'iao 馬少僑. *Ch'ing-tai Miao-min ch'i-i* 清代苗民起義 (Miao revolts in the Ch'ing period). Wuhan, 1956.

Mao Tse-tung 毛澤東. *Mao Tse-tung hsuan-chi* 毛澤東選集 (Selected works of Mao Tse-tung). Peking, 1951.

Ma Tuan-lin, 馬端臨, ed. *Wen-hsien t'ung-k'ao* 文獻通考 (Encyclopedia of source materials). Shanghai: Commercial Press, 1935.

Miao-chiang t'un-fang shih-lu 苗疆屯防實錄 (Veritable record of military agricultural colonies on the Miao borders). Mimeographed ed. Yangchow, 1961.

Michael, Franz. "Military Organization and Power Structure of China during the Taiping Rebellion," *Pacific Historical Review*, 18.4: 469–483 (1949).

—————— *The Taiping Rebellion: History and Documents*, Vol. I: *History*. Seattle: University of Washington Press, 1966.

Na-yen-ch'eng 那彥成. *Na Wen-i-kung tsou-i* 那文毅公奏議 (Memorials of Na-yen-ch'eng). 1834.

Nagano Akira 長野朗. *Shina-hei, tohi, kōsōkai* 支那兵, 土匪, 紅槍會 (China's soldiers, local bandits, and Red Spears Society). Tokyo, 1938.

Nanchang hsien-chih 南昌縣志 (Gazetteer of Nanchang district, Kiangsi). 1849.

Nanchang hsien-chih (Gazetteer of Nanchang district, Kiangsi). 1870.

Nan-k'ai ta-hsueh li-shih-hsi 南開大學歷史系 (Nankai University, Department of History), ed. *Ch'ing shih-lu ching-chi tzu-liao chi-yao* 清實錄經濟資料輯要 (Selected economic materials from the *Ch'ing shih-lu*). Peking, 1959.

Nei-wu fa-ling li-kuei chi-lan 內務法令規例規輯覽 (Digest of laws, ordinances and regulations concerning internal affairs). Peking, n.d., but probably 1918.

Ning-hsiang hsien-chih 寧鄉縣志 (Gazetteer of Ning-hsiang district, Hunan). 1867.

Ogasawara Seiji 小笠原正治. "Sō-dai kyūsenshū no seikaku to kōzō" 宋代弓箭手の性格と構造 (The nature and structure of the archery militia of the Sung period) in Tōkyō Kyōiku Daigaku 東京教育大學 (Tokyo Education University), ed. *Tōyōshigaku ronshū* 東洋史學論集 (Collected studies on East Asian history), 3: 81–94 (1954).

Ou-yang Hsiu 歐陽修. *Hsin T'ang-shu* 新唐書 (New history of the T'ang dynasty). K'ai-ming ed.

Pa-ling hsien-chih 巴陵縣志 (Gazetteer of Pa-ling district, Hunan). 1891.

P'an-yü hsien-chih 番禺縣志 (Gazetteer of P'an-yü district, Kwangtung). 1871.

Peck, Graham. *Two Kinds of Time*. Boston: Houghton Mifflin, 1950.

P'ing-chiang hsien-chih 平江縣志 (Gazetteer of P'ing-chiang district, Hunan). 1875.

P'ing Kuei chi-lueh, see *Kwangsi t'ung-chih chi-yao*.

Po-po hsien-chih 博白縣志 (Gazetteer of Po-po district, Kwangsi). 1832.

Powell, Ralph. *The Rise of Chinese Military Power, 1895–1912*. Princeton: Princeton University Press, 1955.

Pulleyblank, Edwin G. *The Background of the Rebellion of An Lu-shan*. London, 1955.

Rinji Taiwan Kyūkan Chōsakai 臨時臺灣舊慣調查會 (Temporary commission of the Taiwan Government-general for the study of old Chinese customs), ed. *Shinkoku gyōsei hō* 清國行政法 (Administrative laws of the Ch'ing dynasty). Tokyo and Kobe, 1910–14.

des Rotours, Robert. *Traité des fonctionnaires et traité de l'armée, traduits de la nouvelle histoire des T'ang*. Leyden, 1948.

San-yuan-li shih-liao, see Kuang-tung sheng wen-shih yen-chiu kuan.

Sano Manabu 佐野學. *Shin-chō shakai shi* 清朝社會史 (Social history of the Ch'ing dynasty). Tokyo, 1947.

Sasaki Masaya 佐佐木正哉. "Juntoku-ken kyōshin to tōkai jūrokusa" 順德縣鄉紳と東海十六沙 (The gentry of Shun-te district and the sixteen delta areas of Tung-hai) in *Kindai Chūgoku kenkyū* 近代中國研究, 3: 163–232 (1959).

———, ed. *Shin-matsu no himitsu kessha: shiryō hen* 清末の祕密結社, 資料篇 (Secret societies in the late Ch'ing period: Source materials). Tokyo, 1967.

Shan-hua hsien-chih 善化縣志 (Gazetteer of Shan-hua district, Hunan). 1877.

Shan-tung chün-hsing chi-lueh 山東軍興紀略 (A brief account of military operations in Shantung). Anonymous, Shanghai ed. of the Kuang-hsu period.

Shen, Han-yin Chen. "Tseng Kuo-fan in Peking, 1840–1852: His Ideas on Statecraft and Reform." *Journal of Asian Studies*, 27.1: 61–80 (November 1967).

Shen Pao-chen 沈葆楨. "Tsou-ch'ing pien-ping fen-li chün-hsien che" 奏請弁兵分隷郡縣摺 (Memorial asking that troops be attached to prefectures and districts). Copy of an unpub. draft of 1854, in possession of Mr. David Pong.

Sheng K'ang 盛康, ed. *Huang-ch'ao ching-shih-wen hsu-pien* 皇朝經世文續編 (Collected essays on statecraft from the reigning dynasty, continued). 1897.

Shun-te hsien-chih 順德縣志 (Gazetteer of Shun-te district, Kwangtung). 1929.

Skinner, G. William. *Chinese Society in Thailand: An Analytic History*. Ithaca: Cornell University Press, 1957.

——— *Leadership and Power in the Chinese Community of Thailand*. Ithaca: Cornell University Press, 1958.

———— "Marketing and Social Structure in Rural China." *Journal of Asian Studies*, 24: 3–43, 195–228, 363–399 (1964–1965).

Spector, Stanley. *Li Hung-chang and the Huai Army*. Seattle: University of Washington Press, 1964.

Stanton, William. *The Triad Society, or Heaven and Earth Association*. Shanghai, 1900.

Su Sung-fen 蘇松芬, ed. *Hsien-hsing ti-fang tzu-chih fa-ling chieh-shih hui-pien* 現行地方自治法令解釋彙編 (A case-book of interpretations of current ordinances on local self-government). Shanghai, 1934.

Suemitsu Takayoshi 末光高義. *Shina no himitsu kessha to jizen kessha* 支那の祕密結社と慈善結社 (China's secret societies and benevolent societies). Dairen, 1939.

Sun Chin-ming 孫金銘. *Chung-kuo ping-chih shih* 中國兵制史 (History of Chinese military systems). Hong Kong, 1959.

Sun I-jang 孫詒讓. *Chou-li cheng-i* 周禮正義 (Commentary on the *Rites of Chou*). *Ssu-pu pei-yao* ed.

Suzuki Chūsei 鈴木中正. *Shin-chō chūkishi kenkyū* 清朝中期史研究 (History of the mid-Ch'ing period). Tokyo, 1952.

———— "Shimmatsu jōgai undō no kigen" 清末攘外運動の起源 (The origin of the antiforeign movement in the late Ch'ing) in *Shigaku zasshi*, 62.10: 1–28 (1953).

———— *Chibetto o meguru Chū-In kankeishi* チベットをめぐる中印關係史 (History of Sino-Indian relations with respect to Tibet). Tokyo, 1962.

Szechwan t'ung-chih 四川通志 (Gazetteer of Szechwan province). 1816.

Ta-Ch'ing hui-tien shih-li 大清會典事例 (Statutes and precedents of the Ch'ing dynasty). Kuang-hsu ed.

Ta-Ch'ing li-ch'ao shih-lu 大清歷朝實錄 (Veritable records of successive reigns of the Ch'ing dynasty). Mukden, 1937.

T'ai-ho hsien-chih 泰和縣志 (Gazetteer of T'ai-ho district, Kiangsi). 1878.

T'ai-p'ing chün-mu 太平軍目 (Taiping military organization). 1852. Reprinted in Hsiang Ta, *T'ai-p'ing t'ien-kuo*, I, 119–152.

T'ang Ch'ang-ju 唐長孺. *Wei-Chin Nan-pei-ch'ao shih lun-ts'ung* 魏晉南北朝史論叢 (Essays on the history of the Wei, Chin, and Northern and Southern dynasties). Peking, 1955.

T'ang-fei tsung-lu, see *Kwangsi t'ung-chih chi-yao*.

Teng Ssu-yü. *The Historiography of the Taiping Rebellion*. Cambridge, Mass.: East Asian Research Center, Harvard University, 1962.

T'ien-ch'ao t'ien-mou chih-tu 天朝田畝制度 (Land regulations of the Heavenly dynasty). 1852. Reprinted in vol. 1 of Hsiang Ta, *T'ai-p'ing t'ien-kuo*, 319–326.

Tōkyō shisei chōsakai 東京市政調査會 (Tokyo municipal government study association), ed. *Jichi gojūnen shi: Seido hen* 自治五十年史: 制度編 (Fifty years of self-government: Institutional section). Tokyo, 1940.

Torr, Dona, ed. *Marx on China, 1853–1860: Articles from the New York Daily Tribune*. Bombay, 1952.

Ts'en Chung-mien 岑仲勉. *Fu-ping chih-tu yen-chiu* 府兵制度研究 (A study of the *fu-ping* system). Shanghai, 1957.

Tseng Kuo-fan 曾國藩. *Tseng Wen-cheng-kung ch'üan-chi* ("Complete" works of Tseng Kuo-fan). 1876.

Tsou-kao 奏稿 (Memorials)

Nien-p'u 年譜 (Chronological biography)

Shu-cha 書札 (Letters)

P'i-tu 批牘 (Official endorsements and memoranda)

—— *Tseng Wen-cheng-kung chia-shu* 曾文正公家書 (Tseng Kuo-fan's letters to his family). Taipei, 1957.

Tso Tsung-t'ang 左宗堂. *Tso Wen-hsiang-kung Ch'üan-chi* 左文襄公全集 (Complete works of Tso Tsung-t'ang). Reprint of the 1892 ed., Taipei, 1964.

Shu-tu 書牘 (Letters)

Tu Yu 杜佑, ed. *T'ung-tien* 通典 (Encyclopedia of political and social institutions). Shanghai: Commercial Press ed.

Wada Sei 和田清. *Shina chihō jichi hattatsushi* 支那地方自治發達史 (History of the development of local self-government in China). Tokyo, 1939.

Wakeman, Frederic Jr. *Strangers at the Gate: Social Disorder in South China, 1839–1861*. Berkeley: University of California Press, 1966.

Wang Chen 王鑫 *Wang Chuang-wu-kung i-chi* 王壯武公遺集 (Works of Wang Chen, posthumously collected). Mimeo. reprint of a Kuang-hsu ed. Yangchow, n.d., but probably 1958 or after.

Wang Chih 王植. *Ch'ung-te-t'ang kao* 崇德堂稿 (Notes from the Ch'ung-te hall). Preface 1759.

Wang Erh-min 王爾敏. *Huai-chün chih* 淮軍志 (Treatise on the Anhwei Army). Taipei, 1967.

Wang K'ai-yün 王凱運. *Hsiang-chün chih* 湘軍志 (Treatise on the Hunan Army). 1909.

Wang K'un 汪堃 *Tun-pi sui-wen-lu* 盾鼻隨聞錄 (Notes taken while on military service [against the Taipings]) in vol. 4 of Hsiang Ta, *T'ai-p'ing t'ien-kuo*, 351–430.

Wang Ting-an 王定安. *Hsiang-chün chi* 湘軍紀 (Chronicle of the Hunan Army). 1889.

Wang Ying-fu 王應孚. "T'uan-lien lun, shang" 團練論, 上 (On t'uan-lien, part 1) in Sheng K'ang, ed. *Huang-ch'ao ching-shih-wen hsu-pien*, 81: 7–8 (1897).

Wang Ying-lin 王應麟, ed., *Yü-hai* 玉海 (General encyclopedia), 1806 ed.

Wang Yü-ch'üan 王毓銓. *Ming-tai ti chün-t'un* 明代的軍屯 (Military agricultural colonies of the Ming period). Peking, 1965.

Ward, John, and W. G. Stirling. *The Hung Society, or the Society of Heaven and Earth*. London, 1925–26.

Wei Yuan 魏源. *Sheng-wu chi* 聖武記 (Chronicle of imperial military campaigns). Ku-wei-t'ang ed. 1842.

—— *Ku-wei-t'ang wai-chi* 古微堂外集 (Second collection of Wei Yuan's works). 1878.

Wen Chün-t'ien 聞鈞天. *Chung-kuo pao-chia chih-tu* 中國保甲制度 (China's pao-chia system). Shanghai, 1936.

Weng-an hsien-chih 甕安縣志 (Gazetteer of Weng-an district, Kweichow). 1915.

Wilbur, C. Martin, and Julie Lien-ying How, eds. *Documents on Communism, Nationalism, and Soviet Advisers in China, 1918–1927*. New York: Columbia University Press, 1956.

Wittfogel, Karl A. *Oriental Despotism: A Comparative Study of Total Power*. New Haven: Yale University Press, 1957.

Wright, Mary Clabaugh. *The Last Stand of Chinese Conservatism: The T'ung-Chih Restoration, 1862–1874*. Palo Alto: Stanford University Press, 1957.

―――― ed. *China in Revolution: The First Phase, 1900–1913*. New Haven: Yale University Press, 1968.

Wu Han 吳晗. *Chu Yuan-chang chuan* 朱元璋傳 (Biography of Chu Yuan-chang). Peking, 1949.

Wu-hsi Chin-kuei hsien-chih 無錫金匱縣志 (Gazetteer of Wu-hsi and Chin-kuei districts, Kiangsu). 1813.

Wu-hsi hsien-chih 無錫縣志 (Gazetteer of Wu-hsi district, Kiangsu). 1574.

Wu Hsiang-hsiang 吳相湘, ed. *Hsiang-hsiang Tseng-shih wen-hsien* 湘鄉曾氏文獻 (Documents of the Tseng family of Hsiang-hsiang). Taipei, 1959.

Wu-ling hsien-chih 武陵縣志 (Gazetteer of Wu-ling district, Hunan). 1863.

Wu-Yang t'uan-lien chi-shih 武陽團練紀實 (Account of t'uan-lien in Wu-chin and Yang-hu), in *Wu-Yang chih-yü* 武陽志餘 (Gazetteer of Wu-chin 武進 and Yang-hu 陽湖 districts, Kiangsu, supplement). 1888. Ts'e 16.

Yang, C.K. *A Chinese Village in Early Communist Transition*. Cambridge, Mass.: M.I.T. Press, 1959.

―――― *Religion in Chinese Society*. Berkeley: University of California Press, 1961.

Yang Lien-sheng. "Notes on the Economic History of the Chin dynasty," *Studies in Chinese Institutional History*. Cambridge, Mass.: Harvard University Press, 1961.

Yeh P'ei-sun 葉佩蓀. "Ch'ih-hsing pao-chia" 飭行保甲 (Order to implement pao-chia) in Hsu Tung, ed. *Pao-chia shu*, 2: 1–8.

Yen Ju-i 嚴如熤. *San-sheng pien-fang pei-lan* 三省邊防備覽 (Guide to the defense of the three-province border). 1830.

―――― *Lo-yuan wen-ch'ao* 樂園文鈔 (Essays of Yen Ju-i). Preface, 1844.

―――― "Yen-hai t'uan-lien shuo" 沿海團練說 (On t'uan-lien along the seacoast) in *Huang-ch'ao ching-shih wen-pien*. 1886 ed. 83: 31–33.

Yokoyama Suguru 橫山英. "Chūgoku ni okeru nōmin undō no ichi keitai: Taihei tengokuzen no 'kōryō' undō ni tsuite" 中國における農民運動の一形態: 太平天國前の抗料運動について (One form of the peasant movement in China: The "tax resistance" movement before the Taiping Rebellion) in *Hiroshima daigaku bungakubu kiyō* 廣島大學文學部紀要 (Proceedings of the Faculty of Letters, Hiroshima University). 7: 311–349 (1955).

Yu-hsien chih 攸縣志 (Gazetteer of Yu district, Hunan). 1871.

Yü-lin chih-li-chou chih 鬱林直隸州志 (Gazetteer of Yü-lin independent department, Kwangsi). 1894.

Yuan-chou fu-chih 袁州府志 (Gazetteer of Yuan-chou prefecture, Kiangsi). 1874.

GLOSSARY

An-shun 安順
Anking 安慶

Cha-pu 渣埠
chai 寨
Chang Chao 張釗
Chang-chia-wei 張家圍
Chang Fei 張芾
Chang Kuo-liang (Chia-hsiang) 張國
　樑（嘉祥）
Chang Liang-chi 張亮基
Changsha 長沙
Chang-tien 張店
Chang Yueh-ling 張岳齡
Ch'ang-an 長安
Ch'ang-p'ing 常平
Chao 趙
Chao Ch'ung-kuo 趙充國
chao-hui 照會
Chao I-ch'ien 趙以鈴
Chao Li-ts'an 趙立燦
Ch'ao-an 潮安
Ch'ao-chou 潮州
Ch'ao Ts'o 晁錯
Ch'ao-yung 潮勇
che-ch'ung-fu 折衝府
che-ch'ung tu-wei 折衝都尉
chen 鎮
Chen-yuan 鎮遠
Ch'en Ch'i-mai 陳啓邁
Ch'en-shan 臣山
Ch'en Ya-kuei 陳亞貴

Cheng-i-t'ang 徵義堂
Cheng Tsu-ch'en 鄭祖琛
ch'eng 城
Ch'eng Ch'i-i 程起義
Ch'eng-nan 城南
Ch'eng-shao-tu 程梢渡
Ch'eng Yü-ts'ai 程裔采
Chi-lung-shan 基隆山
Ch'i 齊
Ch'i Chi-kuang 戚繼光
Ch'i-chia-chün 戚家軍
Ch'i Chün-tsao 祁寯藻
Ch'i-kung 祁塤
Ch'i Piao-chia 祁彪佳
Ch'i-ying 耆英
Chia 價
Chia-ch'ing 嘉慶
chia-ping 家兵
Chia-ying 嘉應
Chiang Chün 江軍
Chiang Chung-chi 江忠濟
Chiang Chung-shu 江忠淑
Chiang Chung-yuan 江忠源
Chiang-ts'un 江村
Chiang Ying-chü 姜應菊
Chiang Ying-men 姜應門
chieh chün-hsiang 借軍餉
ch'ieh 竊
Chien-ch'ang 建昌
chien-chün 監軍
chien-pi ch'ing-yeh 堅壁清野
Ch'ien-chia-pao 錢家堡

Ch'ien-lung 乾隆
Ch'ien-shan 潛山
chih-chün 制軍
chih-tsu 支族
ch'ih-p'ai-fan 吃排飯
Chin (dynasty) 金
Chin (dynasty) 晉
chin-hsien 進賢
chin-kung 進貢
Chin-t'ien 金田
Ch'in 秦
ch'in-ping 親兵
ching-shih-p'ai 經世派
Ch'ing-lien-chiao 青蓮教
ch'ing-yeh 清野
Cho Ping-t'ien 卓秉恬
ch'o-chi 戲記
chou 州
Chou (dynasty) 周
Chou Kuo-yü 周國虞
Chou T'ien-chueh 周天爵
ch'ou-hsiang 籌餉
chu 主
Chu-chin-ch'ü 朱津區
chu-kuo 柱國
Chu Sun-i 朱孫詒
Chu Yuan-chang 朱元璋
Ch'u-yung 楚勇
chuang-ting 壯丁
Chung-chou 中州
Chung-hua-shan pao-kuo-t'ang 中華山
保國堂
Chung Jen-chieh 鍾人杰
chü 舉
ch'ü-chang 區長
ch'ü-tung 區董
Ch'üan-chou 全州
ch'üan-chüan 勸捐
Ch'üan-hsien 全縣
chün-fang 軍坊
chün-hu 軍戶
chün-shuai 軍帥
chün-t'uan 軍團

Fan Jang-chieh 范讓杰
Fan Jang-ch'un 范讓椿
fang 房

fang 坊
Fang Chi 方積
Fei (river) 淝
Fei Hsiao-t'ung 費孝通
Fen-i 分宜
Feng Kuei-fen 馮桂芬
Feng Yun-shan 馮雲山
fu-hu 府戶
Fu Nai 傅鼐
Fu Pi 富弼
fu-ping 府兵

Han 漢
Han Ch'ao 韓超
Han Chung 漢中
Han Shih-chung 韓世忠
Han-yang 漢陽
hang 行
hao-shen 豪紳
Ho Ch'ang-ling 賀長齡
Ho-ch'i 合燸
Ho-ch'un 和春
Ho-hsien 賀縣
Ho Wen-ch'ing 何文慶
Ho Ying-ch'i 何應祺
Hsia (dynasty) 夏
hsiang 鄉
Hsiang (river) 湘
Hsiang-ch'eng 湘城
Hsiang-chün 湘軍
Hsiang-hsiang 湘鄉
Hsiang Jung 向榮
hsiang-kuan 鄉官
hsiang-pao 相保
hsiang-ping 鄉兵
Hsiang-t'an 湘潭
hsiang-t'uan 鄉團
Hsiang-yang 襄陽
Hsiang-yin 湘陰
hsiang-yueh 鄉約
hsiang-yung 鄉勇
hsiao-lien fang-cheng 孝廉方正
hsiao-t'uan 小團
Hsieh 謝
hsieh-tou 械鬥
Hsien-pi 鮮卑
Hsin-hua 新化

Hsin-ning 新寧
Hsing-kuo 興國
hsing-shih 姓氏
Hsiu-jen 修仁
Hsu Ho-ch'ing 徐河清
Hsu Kuang-chin 徐廣縉
Hsu K'uei 許逵
Hsu Nai-chi 許乃濟
Hsu Nai-p'u 許乃普
Hsu P'ei-yuan 徐佩瑗
Hsu Tzu 徐鼎
hsueh-o 學額
Hu Lin-i 胡林翼
Hu Ta-yüan 胡達源
Hua-yang 華陽
Huai-yuan 懷遠
Huang 黃
Huang-chou 黃州
Huang Jung 黃榮
Huang-kang 黃岡
Huang Liu-hung 黃六鴻
Huang-pei-t'ung 黃背峒
Huang Shih-fu 黃仕福
hui-kuan 會館
Hukow 湖口
Hung-ch'iang-hui 紅槍會

I-ch'un 宜春
I-hsin-t'uan 一心團
i-hsu 議敘
i-ku 義穀
I Liang-kan 易良幹
i-ts'ang 義倉
I-yang 益陽

Kan (river) 贛
K'ang Ching-hui 康景暉
k'ang-liang 抗糧
Kiukiang 九江
ku 股
Ku Yen-wu 顧炎武
kuan-chih 官治
Kuan Chung 管仲
kuan-tu shang-pan 官督商辦
Kuan-tzu 管子
Kuei-hsien 貴縣
Kuei-p'ing 桂平

Kuei-tung 貴東
K'uei-lien 魁聯
Kung Ching-han 龔景瀚
kung-so 公所
kung-ssu 公司
Kung Tzu-chen 龔自珍
Kuo 郭
kuo-lu 啯嚕
Kuo Sung-t'ao 郭嵩燾
Kweilin 桂林

Lai Han-ying 賴漢英
Lan Cheng-tsun 藍正樽
Lang-ping 狼兵
lang-shou 榔首
Lang-yueh 榔約
Lao-yang-jen 老洋人
Lei Hai-tsung 雷海宗
Lei Tsai-hao 雷再浩
Li (river) 澧
li-chia 里甲
Li Chin-kuei 李錦貴
Li Fang 李芳
Li Hsiang-fen 李湘棻
Li Hsiu-ch'eng 李秀成
Li Hsu-i 李續宜
Li Hsu-pin 李續賓
Li I-yung 李宜用
li-ku 釐穀
Li Neng-t'ung 李能通
Li-p'ing 黎平
Li Po 李博
Li-p'u 荔浦
li-shen 里紳
Li Shih-te 李世德
Li Tsu-t'ao 李祖陶
Li Yu-fen 李有棻
Li Yuan-fa 李沅發
Liang Hsien-lin 梁獻林
Liang-shan 梁山
Liang-shan chung-i-t'ang 梁山忠義堂
Liang Sou-ming 梁漱冥
liang-ssu-ma 兩司馬
Liang T'ing-tung 梁廷棟
Liang Yu-ku 梁友穀
Liao (dynasty) 遼
lien-chang 練長

lien-chü 練局
lien tsung-chü 聯總局
Lin Fu-hsiang 林福祥
Lin-hsiang 臨湘
Lin Tse-hsu 林則徐
Ling Shih-pa 凌十八
Liu 劉
Liu Ch'ang-yu 劉長佑
Liu-ho 六合
Liu Jung 劉蓉
Liu K'un-i 劉坤一
Liu-yang 劉陽
Liu Yü-hsun 劉于潯
Lo Chen-nan 羅鎮南
Lo Ch'ing-chang 羅慶章
Lo Hsin-tung 羅信東
Lo-kang 羅岡
Lo Ssu-chü 羅思舉
Lo Ta-kang 羅大綱
Lo Tse-nan 羅澤南
Lu Hsiang-sheng 盧象昇
Lü K'un 呂坤
lü-shuai 旅帥
lü-ying 綠營
Lung-chüan-hsu 龍泉墟

Ma-t'ou 馬頭
Mao Tse-tung 毛澤東
Mei-hsien 梅縣
men-sheng 門生
Meng-shan 蒙山
mi-fan-chu 米飯主
Mi-le 彌勒
Miao 苗
min-chuang 民壯
min-ping 民兵
Ming (dynasty) 明
Ming-chiao 明教
Ming-liang 明亮

Na-yen-ch'eng 那彥成
Nan-chou 南州
Nan-ch'ung 南充
Nan-hai 南海
Nan-hsiung 南雄
Nanchang 南昌
Ni Ch'ang-kao 倪長誥

Nien 捻
Niu-t'ou-chai 牛頭寨

Pa-ling 巴陵
pai-hui 拜會
Pai-shang-ti-hui 拜上帝會
pai-yung 百勇
p'ai 牌
p'ai-chüan 派捐
P'an-yü 番禺
Pang-pang-hui 棒棒會
pao 堡
Pao Ch'ao (Ch'un-t'ing) 鮑超 (春霆)
pao-cheng 保正
pao-chia 保甲
Pao-ch'ing 寶慶
pao-chü 保舉
pao-lan 包攬
Pao Li-shen 包立身
Pao-te-shan-t'ang 寶德善堂
pei-wei-chün 背嵬軍
pen-ti 本地
p'i-kun 痞棍
P'ing-chiang 平江
Po-shih 白石
Poyang 鄱陽
pu-ch'ü 部曲

Sai-shang-a 賽尙阿
San-chiang 三江
San-yuan-li 三元里
Shan-t'ang 山堂
Shang (dynasty) 商
Shang-k'an-tien 上諶店
Shang Yang 商鞅
shao 哨
she 社
she-chang 社長
shen 紳
shen-chü 紳局
Shen Pao-chen 沈葆楨
shen-shih 紳士
shen-tung 紳董
Sheng-p'ing she-hsueh 昇平社學
sheng-shih lien-lo 聲勢聯絡
shih 氏
shih 市

Shih-ch'a 市汉
Shih-ching 石井
shih-shuai 師帥
Shih Ta-k'ai 石達開
shih-wei 侍衞
shou-t'u-kuan 守土官
shou-wang hsiang-chu 守望相助
Shuai-i-tu 蓑衣渡
Shui-hu-chuan 水滸傳
Shun-te 順德
Soochow 蘇州
ssu 司
ssu-ling 司令
Sui (dynasty) 隋

ta-ch'en 大臣
Ta Hsi 笪熙
Ta-lang-hsiang 大朗鄉
ta-pao 大保
ta-shen 大紳
ta-t'iao 大挑
ta-t'uan 大團
T'a-ch'i-pu 塔齊布
T'ai-hu 太湖
T'ai-p'ing chün-mu 太平軍目
T'ai-p'ing Hu-nan Tao-chou huang-
  ch'i [chün] ch'ien-ying ch'ien-lü 太
  平湖南道州黃旗 [軍] 前營前旅
t'ang 堂
t'ang-fei 堂匪
T'ang Feng-ch'en 唐逢辰
T'ang P'ing-san 唐聘三
tao 盜
T'ao 陶
T'ao Chu 陶澍
T'ao Hsing-chih 陶行知
Te-leng-t'ai 德楞泰
Teng Hsin-k'o 鄧新科
Teng Shu-k'un 鄧樹堃
Teng Wan-fa 鄧萬發
ti-fang tzu-chih 地方自治
ti-pao 地保
ti-t'uan 地團
t'i-tu 提督
t'ieh-pan 鐵板
T'ien-ch'ao t'ien-mou chih-tu 天朝田
  畝制度

T'ien Fang 田芳
T'ien Jun 田潤
T'ien-ti-hui 天地會
T'o-pa 拓跋
Ts'ai Yun-sheng 蔡運升
Ts'ang-pu 倉埠
Tseng Kuo-pao 曾國葆
Tseng Shih-chen 曾世珍
Tseng Tzu-po 曾自柏
tso-tsa 佐雜
Tso Tsung-chih 左宗植
tsu 祖
tsu-chang 卒長
ts'un 村
tsung-chih 總制
tsung-chü 總局
tsung-shen 總紳
tu-cheng 都正
tu-pao 都保
Tu Shou-t'ien 杜受田
tu-shu-jen 讀書人
tu-tsung 都總
t'u 圖
t'u-hao 土豪
t'uan 團
t'uan-chang 團長
t'uan-chia 團甲
t'uan-chieh fang-hu chih fa 團結防護
  之法
t'uan-fei 團匪
T'uan-feng 團風
t'uan-lien 團練
t'uan-pao 團保
t'uan-tsung 團總
t'uan-wei pao-chia 團爲保甲
tui 隊
t'un-t'ien 屯田
Tung Hsiu-chia 董修甲
Tung-p'ing 東平
Tung-t'ing 洞庭
t'ung-nien 同年
t'ung-sheng 童生
Tzu (river) 資
Tzu-ch'i 梓溪
tzu-chih ch'ü 自治區
tzu-wei t'uan-lien 自爲團練
tz'u-t'ang 祠堂

Wan Ch'i-ying 萬啓英
Wan Ting-en 萬鼎恩
Wang An-shih 王安石
Wang Chen 王鑫
Wang Ying-p'in 王應蘋
wei 圍
Wei (dynasty) 魏
Wei Cheng 韋正
Wei Chün 韋俊
wei-so 衞所
Wei Yuan 魏源
Wen Shao-yuan 温紹原
Weng-an 甕安
Weng Ju-ying 翁汝瀛
wu 塢
wu-chang 伍長
Wu Chih-chün 吳治均
wu-chü 五局
wu-chü-yung 五局勇
Wu-hsi 無錫
Wu-hsuan 武宣
Wu-kang 武岡
Wu-lan-t'ai 烏蘭泰
Wu Wen-jung 吳文鎔
Wuchang 武昌

ya-shui 牙稅
Yang Ch'ang-chün 楊昌濬
Yang-lo 陽邏
Yao 猺
Yao Shao-lien 姚紹濂
Yao Wen-ming 姚文明
Yao Ying 姚瑩
Yen I 燕毅
Yen Ju-i 嚴如熤
yu-min 莠民
Yü 余
Yü 喻
Yü-lin 鬱林
yü-ping yü-nung (min) 寓兵於農 (民)
Yü-wen T'ai 宇文泰
Yuan (river) 沅
Yuan-chou 袁州
yueh 約
Yueh Fei 岳飛
Yueh lu 嶽麓
yung 勇
Yung-an 永安
Yung-cheng 雍正
Yung-hsiu 永修

INDEX

Aborigines, *see* Miao; Yao
Administration units: distinction from tactical units, 19–20, 23, 24; in Ming-Ch'ing military systems, 24; in *Rites of Chou*, 26; as *pao*, 27
An-shun fu, 118
Anking, 194, 204
Archery militia, 21n
Army of the Green Standard, 10, 38

Bandit gangs (*ku*), 171–174
Banditry, 51, 52, 75, 103, 107
Banner, as local military form, 198
Barbarians, and Chinese militia policy, 53–57
Black Lotus Society (Ch'ing-lien chiao), 106
Border regions: militarization in, 117, 186; and White Lotus Rebellion, 39, 41, 47n; seacoast, 48; and Miao Rebellion, 53; Kwangsi, ethnic, 42n; Kweichow-Hunan-Kwangsi, 106, 111, 117, 118
Braves, *see* Yung
Bureaucratic control: over local militarization, 49, 142–145, 212–213; and t'uan-lien system, 58–59, 62, 89–90; weaknesses, 61–62, 101–102; efforts to strengthen, 92; over "local self-government," 216–217
Bureaucratic divisions: relation to natural forms, 64, 94–102; absorbed by Taiping system, 193. *See also* Li-chia system; Pao-chia system

Canton, British entry question, 57
Censorate, 144
Chai (stronghold), 42–43
Chang Chao, 172–173
Chang Kuo-liang, 180
Chang Liang-chi, 90, 134, 140, 142
Chang-tien, 198
Chao Ch'ung-kuo, 21
Ch'ao-chou, *see* Ch'ao-yung

Ch'ao Ts'o, 21
Ch'ao-yung (Ch'ao-chou *yung*), 78, 166
Che-ch'ung-fu, 18
Che-ch'ung tu-wei, 18
Chen-yuan fu, 118, 124
Ch'en Ch'i-mai, 155
Ch'en Ya-kuei, 172–173
Cheng-i t'ang, 176–179
Cheng Tsu-ch'en, 143
Ch'eng (walled stronghold), 17
Ch'eng-nan Academy, 185
Ch'eng-shao-tu, 45
Ch'eng Yü-ts'ai, 134
Ch'i Chi-kuang, 124–126, 147
Ch'i Chün-tsao, 113
Ch'i Piao-chia, 33, 137n
Ch'i-ying, 55, 57, 59
Chia-ping (military retainers), 15
Chiang Chung-chi, 110, 111, 146
Chiang Chung-yuan: early career, 108; and Lei Tsai-hao Rebellion, 108–109; as magistrate, 112; and Taiping Rebellion, 113–117; determinants of career, 116–117; at Changsha, 140, 141; as provincial judge, 146; suppresses Cheng-i t'ang, 177. *See also* Hunan elite; Tseng Kuo-fan
Chiang-ts'un, 73
Chien-pi ch'ing-yeh (strengthening the walls and clearing the countryside): Lu Hsiang-sheng's system, 41–42; history of term, 42n; promoted by Fang Chi, Tseng Tzu-po, Ming-liang, and Te-leng-t'ai, 43–44; endorsed by court, 45; in Yü-lin, *1840's*, 75; and Taiping Rebellion, 142. *See also* T'uan-lien system
Ch'ien-shan hsien, 194
Ch'ih p'ai-fan (grain expropriation), 149
Chin-t'ien, 113
Cho Ping-t'ien, 142
Chou Kuo-yü, 176–179
Chou T'ien-chueh, 91n
Chu-chi hsien, 203n

Chu Sun-i: t'uan-lien regulations of, 138; and Hsiang-yung, 139–140; raises *yung*, 146; criticizes t'uan-lien, 209

Chu Yuan-chang, 38

Ch'u-yung (Hsin-ning mercenaries), 114–116, 146

Ch'ü (local self-government area), 218–220

Ch'ü T'ung-tsu, 4

Chün-t'uan (tactical militia unit), 19, 20n

Chung Jen-chieh Rebellion, 98–99, 204. See also *Pao-lan*

Ch'ung-yang hsien, 98–99

Ch'üan-chou, 115

Civil-military roles: separation after Ch'in period, 11; and militarization, 12–14; separation under Ming and Ch'ing, 23; supposed nexus in Chou times, 24, 26, 27, 29; in Taiping system, 190

Civilian stalwarts (*min-chuang*): organization in Ming, 22–23, 96, 123; promoted by Yen Ju-i, 48

Class conflict: neutralized by militia systems, 33, 60–61; in Hsiang-hsiang, 137; grain expropriation, 149; within lineage, 159–160; and t'uan-lien, 209. See also Stratification

Commoners, as members of local elite, 4, 199

Communist Party: and Red Spears Society, 34–35; local activists, 192–193; military system, 225

Corruption, 89, 107, 108, 137; in tax collection, 98, 99; and local rebellion, 119–120; reform efforts, 214

Crop-watching corps, 33–34

Cudgel Society (Pang-pang hui), 107–109

District government: and White Lotus Society, 40; of Taipings, 192, 196, 201; after Taiping Rebellion, 211–215. See also Bureaucratic control; *Li-chia* system; Magistrate; Pao-chia system

Dynastic cycle, 3, 6

Dynastic decline: and civilizational decline, 1–3; and White Lotus Rebellion, 49; and Ch'ing military system, 126

Economy: inflation, eighteenth century, 6; monetization of, 6; link to military systems, 18–19, 22; and rebel-suppression, 47; conditions in late Ch'ing, 51; crisis in rural areas, 99

Eight Banners, 10

Elite: and institutional continuity, 3, 5; use of term "gentry," 4–5; national, provincial, and local elites, definition, 4; functional definition, 4, 67n; relationship to state, 5, 8–9; identification with Manchu interest, 7; formal privileges, 8, 222; role in t'uan-lien and pao-chia, 61–62; dominance of lineages, 79n; and market towns, 83; localist outlook, 116–117, 134, 153, 164; and irregular taxes, 90, 91; and likin, 91; and empirical scholarship, 93–94; natural forms of coordination, 104; in Hunan, 113, 183–188; conflict with local officials, 143–144; abolition of formal status, 222; disintegration in twentieth century, 223–225. See also Stratification; T'uan-lien system

Elite, local: and commoners, 4, 67n; combat White Lotus, 44–45; and tax-resistance, 98, 99, 100; role in local control, 120–122; and pao-chia system, 121–122, 132, 213; and tax collection, 99–100, 138, 151; appeal to throne, 143–144; in Taiping system, 193; survival in Taiping areas, 198–202; collaboration with Taipings, 199, 204; social roles, 210; abolition of formal privileges, 211; and "local self-government," 215, 218–223; character in Republican period, 220–222

Elite, national: role in militarization, 180–188

Engrossment, *see Pao-lan*

Entrusting military functions to peasants, see *Yü-ping yü-nung*

Equal field system, 21n

Ethnic conflict, 9, 105–107, 117, 182. See also Hakkas; Miao

Examination system, 8–9; and elite integration, 183, 186; under Taipings, 194

Extended-multiplex *t'uan*, see *T'uan*, extended-multiplex scale

Famine, 33, 137

Fang (walled stronghold), 17

Fang Chi: local control system of, 42–44, 102, 212; influence on official militia policy, 50, 59, 64

Fei Hsiao-t'ung, 221, 224

Fen-i hsien, 203n, 206

Feng Kuei-fen, 166, 214–215

Feng Yun-shan, 115, 174

Feuds, *see* Vendettas

Finance, of local militarization: in *chien-pi ch'ing-yeh*, 46; in extended-multiplex *t'uan*, 69; in lineage militia, 77–78, 89; and *t'uan* leadership, 85;

various methods, 87–92; of Hu Lin-i's force, 127; in Hsiang-hsiang, 139; of Kiangsi Army, 160–164
Finance, provincial, 162–163
Five-Bureaus *yung*, 152–154, 208
Freedman, Maurice, 77, 80
Fu: original meaning of, 15; under Sui and T'ang, 17–18
Fu Nai, 47
Fu Pi, 120
Fu-ping militia system: origins in Northern Wei, 15–16; under Yü-wen T'ai, 16–17; structure in Sui and T'ang, 18–20; theoretical significance, 19; and *yü-ping yü-nung*, 31n; utopian symbolism, 32

Gentry, *see* Elite
God-worshiping Society (Pai Shang-ti hui): besiege Yü-lin, 75, 103; and Li Yuan-fa, 110n; Hu Lin-i on, 119; and Triads, 167; militarization of, 174. *See also* Hung Hsiu-ch'üan; Taiping Rebellion
Guerrilla warfare, 40, 118–119, 196

Hair growth, 173, 195
Hakkas, 6, 173, 174, 203. *See also* God-worshiping Society; Hung Hsiu-ch'üan; Taiping Rebellion
Hall-names, *see* T'ang
Han Ch'ao, 90, 124, 163
Han Shih-chung, 122
Head bureau, *see* Tsung-chü
Hereditary soldiery: post-Han, 15; in Hsien-pi tradition, 15–16; under Ming and Ch'ing, 21, 23–24; Yung-cheng emperor on, 24
Heterodox mode of organization: Red Spears Society, 34–36; and social crisis, 51; historical documentation of, 64–65; and militarization, 105, 167–176; basic forms, 167–180
Ho Ch'ang-ling, 51–52, 185
Ho-ch'un, 115
Ho-hsien, 100
Hsiang (village or village cluster), 67, 95
Hsiang-hsiang hsien: militarization, 80, 136–142; local control, 148–151; in Republican period, 220. *See also* Chu Sun-i; Hunan Army; Lo Tse-nan; Tseng Kuo-fan; Tseng Kuo-pao; Wang Chen
Hsiang Jung, 112, 113, 114
Hsiang-kuan (Taiping local officials) 192
Hsiang-ping (military retainers in Western Wei), 17

Hsiang-shou chi-yao (Essentials of rural defense), 58–63, 213
Hsiang-t'uan (rural military communities in Sui), 17
Hsiang-yung, see *Yung*
Hsiang-yueh (local covenant), 136–137
Hsiao Kung-ch'üan, 94
Hsieh-tou, see Vendettas
Hsien-pi, 15–16, 29
Hsin-hua hsien, 212
Hsin-ning hsien, 106–112
Hsu Ho-ch'ing, 130–132
Hsu Kuang-chin, 57, 142, 144
Hsu K'uei, 121
Hsu Nai-chao, 58–63, 126
Hsu P'ei-yuan, 195
Hsu Tzu, 212–213
Hu-chüan (household tax), 90
Hu Lin-i: opposes irregular taxes, 91; early career, 118; analysis of local rebellion, 119–120; and Weng-an rebellion, 129–133; local control methods, 131–133, 213; and Taiping Rebellion, 133–135; and Wu Wen-jung, 135, 147; and T'ao Chu, 185; on local reform, 214. *See also* Hunan elite
Hua-yang hsien, 212
Huang-chou fu, 88n
Huang-kang hsien, 196–200
Huang Liu-hung, 27–28, 96
Hui-kuan (Landsmannschaften), 171, 185
Hunan Army: origins, 139–142, 145–147; organization, 147–148; social basis, 183–185. *See also* Ch'i Chi-kuang; Tseng Kuo-fan
Hunan elite, 113, 183–188; ideology, 186; social geography, 186–188. *See also* Hsiang-hsiang hsien; Hunan Army; Tseng Kuo-fan
Hung Hsiu-ch'üan, 6, 110, 174
Hung Liang-chi, 51

I-hsin *t'uan*, 75
I-ku (irregular tax) 90
Ichiko Chūzō, 217n
Integration of elites, 117, 147, 155, 180–188, 224
Interlineage imperialism, 79

Japanese sinology, 35

Kiangsi Army: origins, 154, 155–156; financial base, 160–164; demobilization, 163
Ku (bandit gangs), 166, 171–174
Ku Yen-wu, 214
Kuan-tzu, 30–31, 123

Kuei-hsien, 88n, 174
Kuei-p'ing hsien, 174
K'uei-lien, 102, 146
Kung Ching-han: promotes *chien-pi ch'ing-yeh*, 45-47; distaste for mercenaries, 50; influence on administrative theory, 62, 64; influence on Hu Lin-i, 119; views commended by Hsien-feng emperor, 142
Kung Tzu-chen, views on pao-chia, 26, 27
Kuo-lu bandits, 40
Kuo Sung-tao, 137n, 138
Kuomintang, 224–225
Kweichow: administrative problems, 52, 117; irregular tax systems, 90
Kweilin, 114, 115

Lai Han-ying, 79n
Lan Cheng-tsun Rebellion, 106
Lang league, 127–133
Lang-ping, 42n
Leadership: of *t'uan*, 66–67, 68, 71, 156–157; of lineage and village, 77; in Nanchang militarization, 80; financial commitment, 87; in Hsin-ning militarization, 111; of lineage militia, 116; of orthodox elite, 136; of Hunan Army, 147–148; continuity of, in t'uan-lien bureaus, 156–157; of Taipings, 174; in Huang-kang militarization, 198–199
Legitimation, 104, 200, 207–211
Lei Hai-tsung, 11–13
Lei Tsai-hao Rebellion, 109, 116, 119, 142. *See also* Chiang Chung-yuan
Level of militarization: definition, 14; in *chien-pi ch'ing-yeh* system, 46; of anti–White Lotus *yung*, 49–50; in official t'uan-lien model, 59, 62; in extended-multiplex *t'uan*, 69; schematic summary, 165–166; of *t'ang*, 171; changing terminology of, 207–208. *See also* Militarization; *T'uan*
Li-chia system: and t'uan-lien, 97–100, 215; and wards (*tu*), 150; and Taiping local government, 193; and "local self-government," 219. *See also* Bureaucratic divisions
Li Fang, 71
Li Hsiang-fen, 55
Li Hung-chang, 185, 186
Li I-yung, 144
Li-ku (supplementary tax), 90
Li Neng-t'ung, 201
Li-p'ing fu, 118, 134
Li Po, 107, 109, 110
Li Shih-te, 107, 108

Li Tsu-t'ao, 126
Li Yu-fen, 213
Li Yuan-fa Rebellion: general account, 109–112; influence on Hsin-ning militarization, 116; Hu Lin-i's analysis, 119; in official historiography, 208
Liang Hsien-lin, 103
Liang-shan hsien, 42–44
Liang Sou-ming, 224
Liang T'ing-tung, 71n
Liang Yu-ku, 45
Likin tax, 90–92, 161–163
Lin Fu-hsiang, 71n
Lin-hsiang hsien: patterns of militarization, 83–86, 88n; administrative reorganization, 97–100
Lin Tse-hsu, 134, 185
Lineage: and settlement patterns, 67n, 77, 80–82; and vendettas, 77–79; and simplex *t'uan*, 77–80; stratification among, 79, 158–159; elite dominance of, 79n; and multiplex *t'uan*, 80–82; higher-order, 80–82, 139, 157–158; and markets, 86–87; land income, 89; and Hsin-ning *t'uan*, 109; stratification within, 116, 159; and Hsiang-hsiang *t'uan*, 138–139, 149–150; leadership continuity, 156–157; and Nanchang *t'uan*, 157–160; and Kiangsi Army, 158
Ling Shih-pa, 75, 103
Liu Ch'ang-yu: and Li Yuan-fa Rebellion, 110, 111, 112, 116; and Ch'u-yung, 114, 146; at Yuan-chou, 202–203
Liu-ho hsien, 212–213
Liu Jung, 136, 139n
Liu K'un-i, 110, 116
Liu-yang hsien, 99, 176–179
Liu Yü-hsun: early militia work, 76, 152–154; and bureaucratic authority, 154, 207; forms Kiangsi Army, 155–156; and Tseng Kuo-fan, 155–156, 185; as lineage leader, 157–158; and Kiangsi likin, 161–163; retirement, 163
Lo Hsin-nan, 139
Lo-kang, 95
Lo Ping-chang, 148
Lo Ssu-chü, 50
Lo Ta-kang, 79n, 167
Lo Tse-nan: and Wang Chen, 136; character and influence, 140–141; and Hsiang-yung, 146; and Tseng Kuo-fan, 184, 185
Local control: and military agricultural colonies, 21: and pao-chia, 24–26; in White Lotus Rebellion, 41–48; and local defense, 60; in Kweichow, 118; Hu Lin-i's methods, 120; court policy, 142; in Hsiang-hsiang, 148–151; Feng

Kuei-fen's proposals, 214–215. *See also* Pao-chia system
Local rebellion, *see* Rebellion
"Local self-government" *(ti-fang tzu-chih)*, 215–223
Localism: in militarization, 86; in finance, 90; of elite outlook, 116–117, 134, 153, 164
Lu Hsiang-sheng, 41–42, 64, 102
Lü-ying, see Army of the Green Standard
Lung-ch'üan-hsu, 104

Magistrate: as head of t'uan-lien, 58–59; in Taiping-occupied areas, 199–200; and military affairs, 123
Maitreya (Mi-le-fo), 38
Manichaeism *(ming-chiao)*, 38
Mao Tse-tung, 220
Market structure, and natural scales of coordination, 76
Market towns: in multiplex militarization, 68, 71, 72, 76, 82–87, 104, 154; social functions, 83; and Taiping occupation, 196, 198
Marx, Karl, 1–2
Mencius, 30
Mercenaries, *see Yung*
Merchants, 88, 144, 199
Miao, 47, 53, 127
Migration, inter-provincial, 39
Militarization: spread of, 9; definition, 13–15; economic and social factors, 14; and nomadism, 29; non-official forms, 32–36; and famine relief, 33, 160; in White Lotus area, 44–45; of general populace, 48; during Opium War, 54; official model *(1849)*, 57–63; based on pao-chia, 62, 96–97; of local elite, 64; and market towns, 82–87; financial basis, 87–92; variant administrative bases, 102; and social organization, 106; and lineage, 109; on Hunan borders, 117, 186; of civil authority, 122–127; court policy on, 142–145; efforts to control, 144–145; ascent of manpower, 151–152, 156; role of extended-multiplex bureau, 166; of heterodox groups, 167–176; and t'ang, 167–171; of whole communities, 175; and social mobility, 204–206; influence on local government, 211–223
Military agricultural colonies *(t'un-t'ien)*: under Former Han, 21; under Ming, 21–22; under Ch'ing, 22, 42n; and alien ruling groups, 29; used against Miao, 47; influence on Yen Ju-i, 47, 48

Military systems: Ch'in, 12; nomadic, 14; Northern Wei, 15; Western Wei, 16–17; Northern Chou, 17; Sui and T'ang, 18–20, 42n; Ming, 21–22, 23–24, 125; Taiping, 190; Chinese Communist, 225. *See also* Militia
Military systems, Ch'ing: Army of the Green Standard, 10, 38; decline, 37–38; temporary revival, 49; after White Lotus Rebellion, 50; Ho Ch'ang-ling's views, 51–52; inadequacy for internal control, 52, 119; Tso Tsung-t'ang's views, 53; composition of armies, 106; role of civil officials, 122–124; modes of command, 125, 147; rigidity of organization, 125–126; Hu Lin-i's force, 127; Hunan Army, 147–148
Militia: definition, 13–14; and labor service, 22; remnants in Ming-Ch'ing military systems, 23; and local control, 24–28; based on pao-chia, 27–28, 80; Huang Liu-hung's system, 27–28, 96, 97; ideal components of, 28–32; natural forms of, 32–36; and famine relief, 33–34, 137; in *chien-pi ch'ing-yeh* system, 46; and community harmony, 61; historical tradition, 62; mechanics of concentration, 68–69; based on *hsiang-yueh*, 137. *See also* Elite; Leadership; Lineage; Militarization; Military systems; T'uan-lien system
Min-chuang, see Civilian stalwarts
Ming-liang, 44
Minorities, 107n. *See also* Miao; Yao
Modernization: of local government, 218; effect on elite, 223–225
Multiplex *t'uan,* see *T'uan*: multiplex scale

Na-yen-ch'eng, 48
Natural forms of coordination: and bureaucratic institutions, 32, 35–36, 64, 93–104, 128, 132; and local militarization, 32–35, 65, 97; in *she* (associations), 71–73; equivalent scales of organization, 76–77
Ni Ch'ang-kao, 111, 112
Nien Rebellion, 7; local structure, 179; and banners, 198n
Nomadism, 14, 29
Official rank: as reward, 45, 109, 200, 204–206; as badge of local leadership, 46, 47, 62, 121; purchase system, 67, 88, 89, 205–206
Opium War: and periodization, 1, 2; and China's military system, 53; and local militarization, 54–56, 71–73, 103;

rebellion during, 98; social aftermath, 172
Oriental Society theory, 35–36, 65

Pa-ling hsien, 178
Pai-yung (yung hundreds), 150
Pao Ch'ao, 148
Pao-chia system: functions in Northern Sung, 24–25; origins, 24–25, 33, 93; and local control, 25–26, 46, 48, 142, 145; Kung Tzu-chen's views on, 26; military elements, 26–27; as base for militarization, 27–28, 62, 80, 96–97; limitations in White Lotus areas, 39; as base for t'uan-lien, 43–44, 59; and natural units of organization, 44, 94–97, 128; distinguished from t'uan-lien, 59–61; exclusion of gentry, 61; inherent weakness, 61–62; decline, 100; and tax collection, 100n; and local elite, 121–122, 213; and *hsiang-yueh*, 137; orders to revive, 143; under Kuomintang, 225. *See also* Bureaucratic divisions; T'uan-lien system
Pao-lan (engrossment), 91, 97–100, 129, 170
Pao Li-shen, 203n
Peking, and national elite, 185
Personal loyalties, 147–148
Pi Yuan, 41
P'ing-chiang hsien, 92, 99, 104, 204
Pirates, 48
Population rise, eighteenth century, 6
Provincial assembly movement, 217
Provincial power, 163
Pu-ch'ü (military retainers), 15, 17

Rank, *see* Official rank
Rebellion: and regular military, 45–46; Miao (*1795*), 47, 53; in Ch'ung-yang, 98–99; Red Turban, 104, 201; of Lan Cheng-tsun, 106–107; of Lei Tsai-hao, 107–109; of Li Yuan-fa, 109–112; local, social mechanisms, 119; in Weng-an, 127–133; in Hunan, 149; in Nanchang, 154; in Pa-ling, 178; and national power, 189. *See also* Heterodox mode of organization; Nien Rebellion; Taiping Rebellion; White Lotus Rebellion
Red Spears Society (Hung-ch'iang hui), 34–36
Red Turban Rebellion, 104, 201
Rice-host (*mi-fan-chu*), 169–170
Regional army, 166, 167
Rites of Chou (Chou-li): security and conscription systems, 26; influence, 27; and Taipings, 190

Rural-urban links, *see* Urban-rural links

Sai-shang-a, 113
San-yuan-li incident, 54, 63, 71, 72
Scales of organization, 96
School quotas, 204
Self-strengthening, 53
She (association), 71, 95, 103. *See also* Sheng-p'ing association; *T'uan*
She-hsueh (association schools), 71–73, 95, 103
Shen Pao-chen, 124, 162, 164
Sheng-p'ing association, 69–73, 103, 169. See also *She-hsueh; T'uan*
Shih-ching, 73
Shih Ta-k'ai, 201
Shou-wang hsiang-chu (mutual defense). 30, 33
Shuai-i-tu, 115, 117
Shun-te hsien, 219
Simplex t'uan, See *T'uan:* simplex scale
Six marches (*liu-chen*), 15–16
Skinner, G. William, 76, 82
Social mobility, 93, 204–206
Soochow, 195, 219
Statecraft school, 47, 51, 214
Strategic hamlets, 42, 43
Stratification, 60. *See also* Class conflict; Lineage
Strengthening the walls and clearing the countryside, *see* Chien-pi ch'ing-yeh
Sun Yat-sen, views on local self-government, 218

Ta Hsi, 208
T'a-ch'i-pu, 146
Taiping Rebellion, 6–7; origins, 113, 174–175; early campaigns, 114–116, 138–142; and pirates, 172; and Triad Society, 167, 176–177, 181–183; social bases of ideology, 175, 182–183; *Land regulations*, 190, 191, 192; local government, 190–196, 201–202; local resistance to, 198–200; psychological foundations, 203; examination system of, 204. *See also* God-worshiping Society
T'ai-ho hsien, 203n
T'ang (hall, or lodge): level of militarization, 166, 171; significance of term, 168; as community organization, 168–169, 171; economic function, 169–171; and *t'uan*, 176–180
T'ang Feng-ch'en, 149–150
Tao-chou, 117
T'ao Chu, 52, 184, 185
T'ao Hsing-chih, 224

Tax-resistance *(k'ang-liang)*, 100, 129, 170, 194

Taxes: local, irregular, 89–91; and local elite, 97, 99–100, 138; and t'uan-lien bureaus, 161; under Taipings, 194. *See also* Finance; *Li-chia* system; Tax-resistance

Te-leng-t'ai, 44

Tenancy, 89, 159. *See also* Stratification

Teng Hsin-k'o, 111

Teng Shu-k'un, 110, 111, 112, 116

Ti-fang tzu-chih ("local self-government"), 215–223

Ti-t'uan (administration unit for militia), 19–20

T'ien Fang, 172–173

T'ien Jun, 56, 144

T'o-pa, *see* Hsien-pi

Triad Society: and White Lotus Society, 107, 108n; and Li Yuan-fa Rebellion, 109; revolts in Kiangsi, 159–160; and Taipings, 167, 181–183, 201; forms of local organization, 167–170; and Cheng-i t'ang, 176–179; socio-political outlook, 182

Ts'ai Yun-sheng, 45, 49

Tseng Kuo-fan: influenced by Fu Nai, 47n; and Chiang Chung-yuan, 112, 113, 147; and Hu Lin-i, 118, 135, 147; early career, 135–136; and Wang Chen, 137–138; return to Hsiang-hsiang *(1852)*, 141; on t'uan-lien, 145, 148–149, 209; leadership role, 145–146; and Liu Yü-hsun, 155–156, 164, 185; as Liang-kiang governor-general, 162; and regional army, 167; and Hunan elite, 185; interprovincial ties, 185–186; social role, 224

Tseng Kuo-pao, 146, 151

Tseng Tzu-po, 44n

Tso Tsung-chih, 113, 185

Tso Tsung-t'ang: on Ch'ing military system, 53; on Ch'i Chi-kuang, 126; recommended by Hu Lin-i, 134; early military thought, 134n; on t'uan-lien, 145; and Cheng-i t'ang, 177; and Ho Ch'ang-ling, 185; and T'ao Chu, 185

Tsung-chü (head bureau), 68, 86–87

Tu-shan chou, 124

Tu Shou-t'ien, 143

Tu-tsung (ward commanders), 150, 219–220

T'u-hao (local strongmen), 182, 193, 195, 199, 223

T'uan (local defense association): in late Ming, 41; based on *pao*, 43; used against White Lotus Rebellion, 43–44; meaning, in official model, 59; referring to multiplex scale only, 68; sizes, 76; non-bureaucratic factors, 93; as taxing subdivision, 97, 99–100, 212; basic nature, 102–104; as multipurpose unit, 103–104, 212; analogous to *t'ang*, 176–180; in Nien Rebellion, 179; and "local self-government," 220. See also *Fu-ping* militia system; *Li-chia* system; Natural forms of coordination; Pao-chia system; T'uan-lien system

T'uan, extended-multiplex scale: definition, 69; specific cases, 69, 83, 87, 153–155, 198; functions of bureau, 73, 166; as ward *(tu)*, 150; role in militarization, 166

T'uan, multiplex scale: definition, 67–69; leadership, 68; size, 68; as *she*, 71–73, 103; based on lineage, 80–82; in Lin-hsiang, 83; internal variations in wealth, 92; in Weng-an, 127; as *hsiang-yueh*, 136–137; and pao-chia, 131–132; as multi-lineage grouping, 139; and Hunan Army recruitment, 151–152; political indeterminacy, 178–180

T'uan, simplex scale, 66–67

T'uan-chia system, 132, 213. *See also* *T'uan-pao* system

T'uan-lien system: social-political functions, 35–36; historical background, 41–42; under Fang Chi, 43–44; based on pao-chia, 43–44, 48, 55, 145, 149, 213; under Tseng Tzu-po, 44n; under Yen Ju-i, 48–49; official view of, 49; T'ien Jun's advocacy of, 56; provincial officials' fear of, 55–56; distinguished from pao-chia, 59–61; character by mid-nineteenth century, 64; financial basis, 87–92; and *Li-chia* system, 97–100, 215; Hu Lin-i's system, 121–122; Chu Sun-i's system, 138–139; court policy on, 142–145; T'ang Feng-ch'en's system, 149–150; organizational stability, 156–157; and tax collection, 161; level of militarization, 166; in Taiping areas, 195, 196, 198–200; and rank-purchase, 205–206; changing use of term, 207–208; abuses, 209; and social roles of gentry, 209–210; and formal organization of local government, 212–215. *See also* Likin; Militarization; Militia; *T'uan*

T'uan-lien commissioners *(t'uan-lien ta-ch'en)*, 142–145

T'uan-pao system, 96. *See also* *T'uan-chia* system

T'un-t'ien, see Military agricultural colonies

Tung Hsiu-chia, 218

Tung-p'ing association, 74–75
T'ung-ch'eng hsien, 98
T'ung-chih Restoration, 214
Tzu-chih, 215–223

Urban-rural links, 45–46, 223–225
Utopianism, 29–32, 61–62, 183

Vendettas: and lineage militarization, 77–79; and Taiping leadership, 78–79; and Hakkas, 174; and Nien Rebellion, 179
Village, 65–67, 95

Wakeman, Frederic, 79n
Walls: and *chien-pi ch'ing-yeh*, 41–47; materials, 66; in village defense, 66, 75; terminology, 66n; and Taipings, 203
Wan Ch'i-ying, 152, 153, 156, 158
Wan Ting-en, 109
Wang An-shih, 24, 27
Wang Chen: early career, 136–140; and Hsiang-hsiang militarization, 138–140, 146; and Tseng Kuo-fan, 148
Wang Ying-p'in, 177
Ward commanders (*tu-tsung*), 150, 219–220
Wei Chün, 201
Wei Yuan, 99, 185
Well-field system, 30
Wen Shao-yuan, 212–213
Weng-an hsien, rebellion in, 127–133
White Lotus Rebellion: origins and character, 38–41; effect on Ch'ing dynasty, 49; defeat, 49; influence on administrative theory, 62. See also White Lotus Society
White Lotus Society: and Red Spears Society, 34; history and doctrine, 38; and Lan Cheng-tsun Rebellion, 106; and Triad Society, 107, 108n; in Kweichow, 117; in Weng-an, 129

Worshiping societies (*pai-hui*), 167
Wright, Mary C., 217n
Wu (stronghold), 42
Wu-hsi hsien, 96–97
Wu-kang chou, 106, 107
Wu-lan-t'ai, 113, 114, 115
Wu Wen-jung: and Chiang Chung-yuan, 112; and Hu Lin-i, 135, 147; and Tseng Kuo-fan, 147; and Hunan elite, 185

Yang Hsi-fu, 42n
Yao, 106, 107
Yen I, 153, 157
Yen Ju-i: and local defense systems, 47–49; distaste for mercenaries, 50; and t'uan-lien, 59, 64, 102; influence on administrative theory, 62
Yuan-chou fu, 200–203
Yueh (intervillage league), 95, 169
Yueh Fei, 122
Yüeh-lu Academy, 185
Yung (mercenaries): under Fang Chi, 43; used against White Lotus, 45, 49–50; official views on, 46–47, 62; mutinies, 50; hired by local elite, 90, 139–140; types, 105–106, 166–167; used against Taipings, 113; hired by local officials, 124; of extended-multiplex *t'uan*, 152–154; level of militarization, 166–167; and banditry, 172; legitimation of, 208. See also Ch'ao-yung; Ch'u-yung; *Yung* hundreds
Yung-an, 113, 114
Yung-cheng emperor, views on militia, 24
Yung hundreds (*pai-yung*), 150
Yü-lin independent chou, 75, 103, 104
Yü-ping yü-nung (*min*) (entrusting military functions to the peasants), 31–32, 48, 60
Yü-wen T'ai, 16–17, 32